ROMANCING THE FOLK

Romancing the

FO

*Public
Memory
&
American
Roots Music*

Benjamin Filene

The University of North Carolina Press

Chapel Hill & London

© 2000
The University of North Carolina Press
All rights reserved
Designed by Richard Hendel
Set in Monotype Garamond and Smokler types
by Keystone Typesetting, Inc.
Manufactured in the United States of America
The paper in this book meets the guidelines for
permanence and durability of the Committee on
Production Guidelines for Book Longevity of the
Council on Library Resources.
Library of Congress Cataloging-in-Publication Data
Filene, Benjamin.
Romancing the folk: public memory and American
roots music / Benjamin Filene.
     p.   cm.—(Cultural studies of the United States)
Includes bibliographical references, discography,
and index.
ISBN 0-8078-2550-6 (cloth: alk. paper)—
ISBN 0-8078-4862-x (pbk.: alk. paper)
1. Folk music—United States—History and criticism.
2. Popular music—United States—History and criticism.
I. Title. II. Series.
ML3551.F55   2000
781.62'13'00904—dc21   99-054367

04   03   02   01   00   5   4   3   2   1

To my parents and to Rachel, Eliza, & Hazel

CONTENTS

ILLUSTRATIONS

ACKNOWLEDGMENTS

This book could not have come about without the help of a number of institutions and people. A Jacob Javits Fellowship and a Whiting Fellowship in the Humanities helped subsidize my graduate work at Yale University. A John F. Enders Fellowship funded summer research, as did a Smithsonian Graduate Student Fellowship. The final draft of this book simply would not have been completed without the generous support of a National Endowment for the Humanities Fellowship for Independent Scholars.

Several archival collections were central to this work, and I am indebted to the people who made them accessible: Joe Hickerson, Judith Gray, Peter Bartis, and the rest of the staff of the Archive of Folk Culture at the Library of Congress; Jeff Place, Lori Elaine Taylor, and Tony Seeger at the Smithsonian's Center for Folklife Programs and Cultural Studies in Washington; and John Wheat and Linda Peterson at the Center for American History at the University of Texas at Austin. Yale University's marvelous library system was an invaluable asset. While there, I leaned heavily on Paul Constantine and Anne Ferguson at the Sterling Memorial Library; Ken Krilley and Helen Bartlett at the music library; and Karl Schrom at the record library. The interlibrary loan office, meanwhile, handled an ever mounting pile of requests.

Other people interacted with me only momentarily but left their mark on this study. John Cohen provided encouragement at the outset of this project. Ralph Rinzler, Bess Lomax Hawes, and Harold Courlander graciously consented to interviews at a very early stage in the work, while Alan Jabbour, Richard Kurin, Dan Sheehy, Peter Bartis, and Tony Seeger did so near its conclusion. Charles Shindo and Cheryl Brauner Laberge readily sent their theses, and Robert Cantwell generously shared his work on the 1960s folk revival while it was still in manuscript form. Bob Briar at Cutler's Records in New Haven was an ever cheerful help in tracking down recordings. Gary Kulik and the staff at *American Quarterly* helped tighten an earlier version of my chapter on the Lomaxes and Lead Belly. In the final stages, the book benefited immensely from the attention of the editorial staff at the University of North Carolina Press, in particular Pamela Upton and Grace Buonocore, and from David Perry's unwavering commitment to the project.

After I left Yale in pursuit of a career in public history, I was fortunate enough to arrive at an institution imbued with a strong sense of what makes history important and what makes it fun. The staff of the Outagamie County Historical Society (in Appleton, Wisconsin) brought passion, intelligence, and a can-do attitude to the pursuit of public history that continues to inspire me. The exhibits department of the Minnesota Historical Society in St. Paul, where I now work, generously allowed me to accept the NEH fellowship to complete this book. I am grateful to my colleagues at the society for their supportiveness during my leave of absence and for the lively and creative environment they provide me every day on the job.

At the deepest level, this book comes out of the dedication of a series of passionate teachers who, over the years, played major roles in my life. Marjorie Lancaster, Lawrence Bosc, John L. Thomas, William G. McLoughlin, James T. Patterson, and Michael Denning provided lessons and inspiration that I draw on every day. Michael Denning had the most direct contact with this work, and I am especially grateful to him for his encouragement, tough standards, and all-embracing creative vision. Jean-Christophe Agnew, James Fisher, and John Szwed offered key advice along the way as well. I have also benefited greatly from the searching insights and friendly criticism of a group of peers at Yale that met to discuss how to incorporate music into cultural history. The shifting membership of this gang of ¼ included Carlo Rotella, Suzanne Smith, David Stowe, Margaret McFadden, and David Phillips. I thank them for all their ideas and support. I also want to thank David Waldstreicher, who brought his keen intellect and generous instincts to bear on this work over more hamburgers and calzones than I, and probably he, care to remember.

As I was researching and writing this work, a group of friends brightened the scene immeasurably and broke down the isolation inherent in such a project. I am forever grateful to Jill Lepore, Jane Levey, Michael Weiss, Drew Caputo, and Holly Allen for the stability and joy they brought to my life. To my family I have the sort of debts one can never begin to repay and cannot hope to express adequately. I must give special acknowledgment to Peter Filene, historian-educator extraordinaire and reliable late-night conversationalist; to Jeanette Falk, who serves as a steadying influence and my internal voice of reason; to David Falk, who I like to think would have appreciated this work's ambition even if he never heard of Bob Dylan, much less Alan Lomax; and to Hilda Strasser, who is a model of how to live life with curiosity and zest.

Finally, in the years spent on this project, another relationship has grown, one that flowered much more naturally and easily than this work. From the beginning of this project to now, Rachel Filene Seidman has played all the roles acknowledged above: colleague, critic, teacher, friend, confidante, and, for the last eight years, family. I can't imagine it any other way. This relationship in turn has brought me another source of daily warmth and laughter. Eliza and Hazel Filene may wish for more pictures in this book, but I hope they'll enjoy hefting their copy and knowing that it is meant for them as well.

ROMANCING THE FOLK

INTRODUCTION

began this book because I stumbled across a great story. In the summer of 1933 John Lomax, an Old South patrician in a bowler hat, welded a 350-pound "portable" recording machine into the back of his Ford and took his starry-eyed seventeen-year-old son Alan on a driving trip through the South, stopping at all-black maximum security prisons to ask hardened convicts if they knew any good songs. At each prison they set up their equipment and recorded the convicts' singing on twelve-inch aluminum discs, which they later deposited at the Library of Congress in Washington. This story struck me as so strange and improbable that I wanted to tell it.

So, sixty years after the Lomaxes' expedition, I strapped my laptop computer into my Nissan and drove to the Library of Congress. I began to go through all the information I could find about the Lomaxes' trip, studying the letters they wrote to raise funds, listening to the recordings they made, and reading the correspondence they sent home from the road. I began to learn about the Library of Congress's Archive of American Folk-Song, where they worked, and about the network of scholars and folk music enthusiasts with whom they corresponded. I started to piece together the biographies of some of the singers the Lomaxes recorded on their expedition and to consider other singers from the period who likely served, explicitly or implicitly, as frames of reference to which the Lomaxes compared the musicians they encountered. The more I read, listened, and considered, the more I realized that the story of the Lomaxes' ride of '33 was remarkable not for its bizarre singularity but, rather, for its rich multiplicity. On the most literal level, for example, the Lomaxes' expedition to gather folk songs was not at all an isolated incident: it came out of the work of a generation of previous folklorists and, most dramatically, spawned dozens upon dozens of other field trips over succeeding decades, many of them led by the Lomaxes themselves. At a broader historical level, the Lomax trip pointed to an array of other stories that, combined, offered a way of piecing together a wide-ranging historical narrative of prime importance to twentieth-century American cultural history—the story of the emergence of the notion of American "roots" music and the concurrent formation (and continual reformation) of a canon of roots musicians. This narrative in turn enabled a multilayered exploration of some of the richest and most embedded questions facing contemporary cultural historians. How has race been constructed and how has it infused American popular culture? How have antimodernism and political radicalism operated in relation to the modern state? How have cultural workers defined America's cultural "margins" and "mainstream," how have they represented "the Other," and how, in the process, have they operated against or within the so-called culture industry? Finally, and in many ways overarching all of these questions, how has Americans' collective memory (or, really, memories) of their cultural heritage been shaped and transmitted?

The seemingly neatly packaged story of the Lomaxes in their Ford had opened up to reveal a myriad of historical and theoretical resonances. Indeed, it pointed to a larger story that proved to be multifarious in almost every respect except for one—having been told. This book sets out to do the telling.

As I have been suggesting, the Lomax story led me down a road that seemed to fork at every turn. Some of the directions I chose, it quickly became apparent, were desperately wrong turns, and I hastily beat my way back; others led me into rich territory that I did my best to investigate. Inevitably, of course, as I explored certain territories, I passed others by. As a result, those of you acquainted with the terrain I'm covering here will find that some high points familiar to you do not receive the lavish attention that another investigation might give them, while other features that you might not recognize are designated here with landmark status. Throughout, I have tried to chart my course with an eye toward plotting connections and suggesting new avenues for inquiry, rather than with a concern for coverage.

As a result, certain stars of the folk music firmament don't receive sustained attention here. I discuss Lead Belly extensively but mention Josh White and Aunt Molly Jackson only in passing. I consider Pete Seeger in some detail but treat Woody Guthrie mainly in relation to the influence he had on revivalists of the late fifties and sixties, long after he was an active performer. Bob Dylan plays a key role here, but Peter, Paul, and Mary, Phil Ochs, and Joan Baez only make cameos.[1] As these choices suggest, I have not set out to write a conventional history of twentieth-century folk music: I am looking to tell illustrative stories more than informational ones.

In addition to excluding some old favorites, therefore, I include certain other musicians who might raise the hackles of folk purists—figures like Muddy Waters and Chicago's urban bluesmen, or Dylan in the decades *after* he broke with the 1960s folk revival by going electric. These performers interest me precisely because they straddle the boundaries between "folk" and "commercial," "old-fashioned" and "modern." In doing so they highlight both the existence and the arbitrariness of such divisions and enable me to break out of—and, in fact, to call into question—rigid definitions of "pure" folk music. The notion held by early folklorists (such as Francis James Child and Cecil Sharp) of an unself-conscious, unmediated, and wholly uncommercial mode of musical expression strikes me as fundamentally flawed: almost all musicians, after all, are influenced by others and make use of their talent in social settings. Given the explosion of mass media, rigid definitions of folk music become especially illusory when applied to the twentieth century. Since the turn of the century, even seemingly isolated musicians have spent their afternoons listening to phonographs and dreaming of recording contracts. What makes the formation of America's folk canon so fascinating, though, is that just as isolated cultures became harder to define and locate in industrialized America, the notions of musical purity and primitivism took on enhanced value, even in avowedly commercial music. Twentieth-century Americans have been consistently searching for the latest incarnation of "old-time" and "authentic" music. Such terms may have lost their referents, but their cultural power has remained undiminished.

One might therefore imagine terms like "folk" and "pure" as ciphers waiting to be filled: people imbue them with meanings that have cultural relevance and power to them. My study is based on the idea that examining people's efforts to create meaning of this sort can offer insight into their values and their worldview. Instead of engaging in the debate over "pure" versus "impure" and "authentic" versus "inauthentic," therefore, this book explores how these dichotomies have been constructed and how they have shaped the way American music has been understood.

For me, then, "folk music" ceases to have much use as a descriptive term, since what I am trying to understand is the contradictory meanings

Americans have given it over the years. In its place, I have substituted two other terms. The first is "vernacular music." Following music historians H. Wiley Hitchcock and John Rockwell, I find this designation useful as a way to avoid setting up rigid criteria to distinguish "folk music" from "non-folk music."[2] "Vernacular music," I hope, serves as an overarching designation that can sit above the squabbling over what constitutes "true" folk music and can encompass most of the options. Appropriate to its usage in linguistics, I use "vernacular" to suggest songs employing a musical language that is current, familiar, and manipulable by ordinary people. In contrast to fine art or classical music, vernacular music demands only minimal formal training and material resources to produce it (although extensive formal training and mind-numbing resources certainly *can* be applied to it).

Under this definition, "vernacular" includes not only Appalachian mountain music or blues but also "pop" music, another tricky term that means different things to different people even within this study. Most directly, I use "pop" (and "popular") to refer to the Tin Pan Alley song tradition that is generally thought to have held sway from roughly the 1890s into the 1950s—music produced by song publishers and large recording companies that was written for and distributed to nationwide audiences.[3] More broadly, I use "pop" as well to identify the successors to the Tin Pan Alley tradition—commercial music written, produced, and promoted in efforts to reach large contemporary markets.

Under these definitions, such recent popular genres as hip-hop, grunge, and techno are vernacular. I hope introducing a term that appears in my subtitle, though, will make clear why I have excluded these styles from my discussion: within the domain of vernacular I am mainly interested in "roots" music. I use "roots" (a designation that comes out of rock criticism) to identify musical genres that, whether themselves commercial or not, have been glorified as the "pure" sources out of which the twentieth century's commercial popular music was created. Blues, for example, has drawn legions of fans who see it as rock's more emotional and rough-edged ancestor. In recent years, even some contemporary pop stars (Little Richard or Aretha Franklin, for instance) have come to be treated as roots musicians because of their pioneering influence on subsequent generations. "Roots," therefore, is a retrospective term. It shifts the focus of my study away from stylistic debates (which performers belonged to which musical traditions?) to questions of perceptions (who was *thought of* as exemplifying which traditions?).

My focus on perceptions accounts for the function that the term "folk music" does serve in the chapters that follow. Although I reject its *descriptive* validity, the phrase stands as shorthand for people's conceptions of "pure" vernacular music. "Folk music" may not refer to anything concrete, but many certainly have thought it did, so I use the term to imply the collection of assumptions and criteria people have ascribed to it.

The question of perceptions also connects to the key term in my subtitle, "public memory." Above all, this book seeks to understand how Americans have remembered their country's musical past, how these memories have been transmitted, and how these conceptions have both reflected and shaped Americans' cultural outlook. By "public memory," then, I mean the vague and often conflicting assumptions about the past that Americans carry with them and draw on, usually unconsciously, in their daily actions and reactions. In using the phrase, I do not at all intend to suggest that one can imagine a single, unified American "public" and certainly not that all the members of a given public could share identical sets of memories. On the contrary, as a cultural historian I am especially interested in how different public memories have competed and exerted cross-influences on American life.

My efforts to understand how Americans' musical memories have been formed have led me to put at the center of my story characters whose powerful role in American culture has long been overlooked by historians—cultural "middlemen" who move between folk and popular culture. These folklorists, record company executives, producers, radio programmers, and publicists "discovered" folk musicians, recorded them, arranged concert dates for them, and, usually, promoted them as the exemplars of America's musical roots. In doing so, they did more than deliver "pure" music: they made judgments about what constituted America's true musical traditions, helped shape what "mainstream" audiences recognized as authentic, and, inevitably, transformed the music that the folk performers offered. As my title indicates, they "romanced" the folk, in the sense both of wooing them as intimates and of sentimentalizing them as Other.

In exploring these issues, my focus is on illuminating the cultural matrix within which these figures operated, not on exposing their wrongdoings. I do not delve extensively into the financial exploitation, racial prejudice, and political corruption that surfaced in the brokers' relationships with folk performers. The music business as a whole is so rife with such misdeeds that, in and of themselves, they are not especially revealing to historians. I cite such stories, therefore, only when they help explain the motivations and worldview of the small group of cultural brokers who shaped our nation's sense of its musical heritage. I am more interested in understanding their intentions and in tracing their influence than in judging their ethics.

As for my periodic use of the term "middlemen," its gender specificity is partly a linguistic convenience—an attempt to avoid the ungainly "middleperson"—and to some extent an accurate statement about the brokers who shaped the folk music canon. Certainly some women were involved in folk entrepreneurship—I touch on the work of Josephine McGill, Loraine Wyman, Olive Dame Campbell, Margaret Mead, Ruth Crawford Seeger, and Bess Lomax Hawes—and of course there have been countless female folk singers. Nonetheless, historically the vast majority of folk canonizers have been male. Above all, though, I chose the main protagonists in my chapters (all men) to serve as case studies representing different approaches to roots music. Their stories are intended to illuminate the work of other brokers, both male and female, who are not directly represented.[4]

Most important, I want to call attention to these brokers as active agents. They have remained largely unrecognized, partly because of historians' inattention and partly because they themselves strove to cloak their power. Eager to promote the authenticity of the performers they worked with, the middlemen depicted themselves simply as cultural funnels channeling the musicians' raw, elemental power to popular audiences. Historians today, though, are well aware of the extent to which all cultural communication is mediated. I am attempting here to explore the work of a heretofore unrecognized group of cultural mediators and to place the assumptions that guided their work into a cultural-historical context.

I trace the efforts to preserve and popularize roots music over five chapters. Chapter 1 focuses on the years between roughly 1900 and 1930 and charts the emergence of the notion of a distinctly American, as opposed to European, folk tradition. It focuses on the motley assortment of hobbyists, professors, reformers, and commercial talent scouts who first worked to preserve American vernacular music. Subsequent chapters are organized thematically rather than chronologically, each centering on a particular type of folk music broker and on a corresponding strategy that characterized that intermediary's efforts to define America's musical heritage. I look at three such strategies and trace how each of them played out from roughly 1930 to the present. I have chosen to travel this broad expanse of time repeatedly, rather than taking a decade-by-decade approach, because it seems to me more analogous to how memory making really happens: memory is not built incrementally but is continually crafted and recrafted as material from the past is reencountered and reinterpreted. With a thematic organization, I can plot lines of influence across decades and show how the present assembles a patchwork culture out of the past.

Chapters 2 and 3, then, look at figures whom I call "folk promoters," middlemen such as the Lomaxes and Willie Dixon who communicated their musical visions by promoting certain musicians as archetypes of an "authentic" folk tradition. Chapter 2 looks in some detail at how such efforts shaped the career of one artist, Lead Belly, and Chapter 3 focuses on their impact on Muddy Waters. Chapter 4 considers advocates such as Alan Lomax and Richard Dorson who tried to use the federal government and the American university system as institutional outposts from which to enhance the status of folk culture. Finally, Chapter 5 introduces a substantially different set of brokers—people like Pete Seeger and Bob Dylan who came to the music as outsiders but themselves became performers and expositors of traditional music.

As Alan Lomax's appearance in several chapters illustrates, these categories frequently overlap. A middleman can appear in many different guises in his or her career and can employ several of these strategies at once: a "folk promoter," for instance, might use the government to popularize "authentic" music. These chapter divisions are somewhat artificial, then, but they are useful fictions in that they enable me to isolate important elements in the development of America's folk memory and to track their resonances more freely than a simple chronological approach would allow.

Although the chapters do not trace a linear narrative, they do speak to one another. Together, they chart the often tortuous paths by which performers have entered the "roots" canon. Certainly the variety of routes taken warns against a single paradigm for the process of canonization. Roots musicians might begin as downhome songsters, itinerant showmen, or urban pop singers; and they might be recorded first by antiquarians, folklorists, or commercial record producers. Most, but again not all, of the performers have a stage in their careers when they enlist producers and promoters to help them reach wider audiences; and some, such as Muddy Waters in the early 1950s, even achieve measurable commercial success. Generally, though, these artists achieve only limited and fleeting fame in the commercial realm. By itself, it seems, commercial success does not cement an artist's position in the nation's musical pantheon.

Rather, entry into the public memory depends on the efforts of the cultural workers who occupy the center of this study—the middlemen between folk and popular culture who *re*discover performers, *re*interpret their early recordings in relation to subsequent musical trends, and *re*-define the artists as folk forefathers and foremothers. Appropriately, then, public memory is formed by a recursive process, one that involves revisiting and reevaluating the culture of the past in the light of the present. Understanding the assumptions behind these valuations and the ways in which they are transmitted illuminates how American culture gets created and, just as important, how we come to recognize it as our own.

SETTING THE STAGE
IDENTIFYING AN
AMERICAN FOLK MUSIC
HERITAGE, 1900-1930

As late as 1910, most Americans would have been surprised to hear that America *had* any folk music. Of course rural whites and African Americans had been playing their traditional music since long before the 1900s, but they had done so, for the most part, out of the view of the middle and upper classes: outsiders had showed little interest in their culture, and, correspondingly, the rural musicians had had no reason yet to think of themselves as "the folk" or of their music as "folk" music. In the late 1800s, though, traces began to emerge of what would eventually become almost a national obsession with America's folk heritage.

The roots of this phenomenon stretched back to Europe. In the late eighteenth and early nineteenth centuries, European intellectuals turned their attention as never before to the vernacular culture of their countries' peasants, farmers, and craftspeople, launching what historian Peter Burke has called "the discovery of the people." Once scorned as ignorant and illiterate, ordinary people began to be glorified as the creators of cultural expression with a richness and depth lacking in elite creations. German philosopher Johann Gottfried von Herder (1744–1803), the most influential proponent of the new cultural outlook, contrasted the *Kultur des Volkes* ("culture of the people") with *Kultur der Gelehrten* ("learned culture") and made clear which of the two he favored: "Unless our literature is founded on our *Volk*, we [writers] shall write eternally for closet sages and disgusting critics out of whose mouths and stomachs we shall get back what we have given." To Herder, folk culture offered a way to escape the Enlightenment's stifling emphasis on reason, planning, and universalism in cultural expression. Folk forms could cleanse culture of the artificiality that, he felt, was poisoning modern life.[1]

Herder's ideas inspired a generation of intellectuals that came of age in the late eighteenth and early nineteenth centuries, initiating a flurry of efforts to identify and understand folk cultures. In 1778 Herder himself published a collection of song lyrics he had gathered and transcribed in the German border region of Riga (present-day Latvia). In titling the work, Herder used a newly emerging word, *Volkslieder*—folk song.[2]

Herder was certainly not the first to collect traditional music. In seventeenth-century England, old ballads were published in numerous collections, tapping into a fad among both the middle class and aristocratic for things "country."[3] Scholars believe that the first explicitly historical collection was *A Collection of Old Ballads*, published in 1723. The collection's anonymous editor directly stressed its antiquarian nature, emphasizing in the work's subtitle that the ballads were *Corrected from the best and most Ancient Copies Extant*. A second volume of the collection, issued later in 1723, accentuated the point further, advertising *Songs, more Antique, and upon far older Subjects* than those in the previous volume. These collections had astonishing popular appeal, becoming among the most popular books of the 1720s. Eventually three volumes of *Collections* were published, all appearing in multiple editions. Moreover, individual songs from the collections were reprinted as broadsides and sold from printers' stalls on the streets for largely lowbrow audiences. Historian Dianne Dugaw notes that to emphasize the songs' antiquity, publishers printed the broadsides "on heavy, old-fashioned folio paper decorated with woodcuts . . . of old-fashioned dress, weaponry, ship design, castles, and so on."[4]

Such antiquarian interest in songs laid the groundwork for a landmark ballad collection, *Reliques of English Poetry*, published in 1765 by English clergyman Thomas Percy. Percy's collection was based initially on an old manuscript he had rescued, he claimed, from a friend's maids, who were using it to light a fire, but *Reliques* also drew considerably on printed broadsides and on the popular *Collection of Old Ballads*.[5] Ignoring these low- and middlebrow antecedents, though, Percy depicted his ballads as works of high culture. He attributed the songs to early medieval minstrels who, he insisted, had been respected artists in medieval courts.[6]

Most contemporary readers, however, drew different lessons from *Reliques*. To an emerging generation of romantic poets and philosophers, including William Wordsworth, Samuel Taylor Coleridge, and Herder, the ballads in *Reliques* were popular poetry, evidence of the tremendous creative power of the untutored folk. Increasingly, intellectuals felt that for a country to have a distinctively national cultural voice, it must understand its folk culture.[7] In Britain and across the Continent, there was a surge of interest in documenting the range of folk cultural expression. Jakob and Wilhelm Grimm published their first collection of children's folk tales in 1812. Other enthusiasts issued books depicting the drama and rituals of popular festivals in Venice, England, and Russia. In 1819 the Austrian government ordered local authorities to collect folk songs.[8]

Even in this period, more than a century before folk revivalism truly took hold in America, the pursuit of folk culture involved a complex series of ideological decisions. First of all, not just anyone counted as "folk." Herder distinguished between the true *Volk* (primarily rural peasants) and the urban "rabble in the streets," who "never sing or rhyme but scream and mutilate." To Herder and other early collectors, true peasants were pure and artless and, usually, exotic. "The more wild and freely acting a people is," wrote Herder, "the more wild, that is, the more lively, free, sensuous and lyrically acting its songs must be!" Cultural treasure seekers visited remote villages and shepherd's huts, seeking, as Dr. Samuel Johnson put it in 1775, "primitive customs." Historian Burke recounts a scene of cultural encounter that would be reenacted countless hundreds of times over the next two centuries: "Craftsmen and peasants were no doubt surprised to find their homes invaded by men and women with middle-class clothes and accents who insisted they sing traditional songs or tell traditional stories."[9]

As Burke's description suggests, not all the songs and stories "the folk" knew made the grade as "folk song" or "folk tale" in the eyes of the early enthusiasts. Collectors feared that pure native cultures were being corrupted as transportation improved and literacy spread. Sir Walter Scott wrote that he gathered Scottish ballads fearing that the "peculiar features of [Scotland's] manners and character are daily melting and dissolving into [England's]." He described one singer as "probably the very last instance of the proper minstrel craft." Fired by this sense of being on a last-ditch rescue mission, collectors felt authorized to take drastic steps to reclaim the "original" essences of the cultural products they sought.

Thomas Percy admitted to making "corrections and additions" to the ballads he found. Elias Lönnrot gathered Finnish songs to the point that he felt no "singer could any longer compare with me in his knowledge of songs"; then he began freely arranging and rearranging songs as he saw fit, eventually assembling the Finnish national epic *Kalevala*, published in 1835.[10] Such editorial liberties increasingly provoked expressions of outrage among eighteenth- and early-nineteenth-century collectors, but the practice continued largely unabated well into the nineteenth century.[11]

From the start, then, "discovering" folk cultures involved reimagining them. Herder, the Grimms, and their followers romanticized and transformed the cultures they sought out. *Because* of these transformations, as much as in spite of them, their vision of the folk had extraordinary reach, extending well beyond their borders and exerting influence long after their deaths. The work of these early philosophers and collectors showed that the idea of "folk culture" had both power and plasticity. Scholars and intellectuals, artists, entrepreneurs, and "the folk" themselves have been shaping and reshaping the idea ever since.

The process by which American folk music eventually became defined as such and started moving into popular culture began with academics and antiquarian collectors. The progenitor of the American folk song movement was Harvard professor Francis James Child. Child seems an unlikely person to have sparked interest in American vernacular music. Born in 1825, he was a Shakespeare scholar and professor of rhetoric, known for his rigorous academic standards, his impatience with those who did not meet these standards, and his obsession with his meticulously cultivated rose garden.[12]

Child's other passion, however, was British ballads, a subject he pursued with the persistence of a bloodhound and the precision of a detective. Like Thomas Percy and the Grimm brothers before him, Child was very much a literary folklorist, one who treated folk song as popular poetry and analyzed songs as series of texts largely divorced from their tunes.[13] Also like the European folklorists, Child confined his interest to the ballad, which he defined as a "narrative song, a short tale in lyric verse." By no means, however, were all narrative songs anointed by Child as true ballads. Like many of his predecessors, Child felt that although in premodern times the ballad had been "a common treasure" passed on orally and enjoyed by all, it was now a long-dead art. The "sources of English and Scotch ballads," he lamented "may be regarded as sealed or dried up for ever."[14] The culprits in this story were commercial ballads and printed music, which together, Child believed, had polluted the oral tradition.

This narrative contained considerable class bias. Ballads had once been enjoyed by all, Child felt, but they had become tainted when educated classes had turned their attention to fine-art music, leaving the ballad form to "the ignorant and unschooled mass." Ballads printed for popular audiences as broadsides, which Child noted had been a thriving business from the sixteenth century onward, were "a different genus" from the ballads he treasured: "They are products of a low kind of *art*, and most of them are, from a literary point of view, thoroughly despicable and worthless." To ensure the purity of his collection, Child concentrated on songs that predated the printing press, which had come to Britain in 1475.[15]

Child's standards for the ballad's purity profoundly affected his methods of gathering songs. If no new folk songs of merit had been created in the last four centuries or so, Child saw little point in making contact with current folk communities and trying to dredge up songs from their collective memory. Certainly America, with its relatively recent traditions, held only limited interest for him. Although Child was known to encourage his students to collect (especially in European countries other than England, where "some utterly 'uneducated' poor old woman" might yet remember a delightful ballad), for the most part Child preferred archival sources as the most direct means of retrieving the songs of yesteryear.[16] The material that could "at this late day" be obtained from contemporary sources, Child stated, was "meagre, and generally of indifferent quality." With an air of finality Child dismissed living informants, proclaiming, "The material is not at hand." Child's ideal sources, summarizes historian Jo McMurtry, were "old manuscript collections which had been written down by private antiquarian hobbyists, straight from the singers' mouths, at some point in time before the tide of cheap printing had begun to alter the songs' traditional forms."[17]

If in his value system Child resembled the literary folklorists who had preceded him, he distinguished himself by the rigor with which he pursued his goals. Child's motto was "Do it so it shall never have to be done again," and to a great extent he achieved this goal in the course of his forty years of ballad scholarship.[18] Despite working in Massachusetts, thousands of miles away from his source materials, Child combed the British holdings of ballads with unprecedented thoroughness. Some collections he examined on his rare trips abroad, but mostly he relied on a network of overseas friends and helpers. Following Child's written instructions, they tracked down and transcribed material for him from archives and private collections across England and Scotland. After his friend James Russell Lowell was named American ambassador to London, Lowell coordinated some of these collecting efforts, occasionally rushing prize findings to Child via diplomatic pouch.[19]

Out of these efforts, Child published the most thoroughgoing works of ballad scholarship ever seen. First, between 1857 and 1858, he issued an eight-volume collection entitled *English and Scottish Ballads*. This work, based on previously printed sources, listed the words to hundreds of traditional British ballads. In later years, though, Child scorned it as hastily compiled and superficial in comparison with the magnum opus that followed.[20] In 1882 Child published the first volume of his masterwork, *The English and Scottish Popular Ballads*. The decision to add a "the" to the title of Child's 1857–58 book was significant, for in this series Child aimed for complete coverage of the Anglo ballad field. In a preface to the first volume, Child wrote, "It was not my wish to begin to print The English and Scottish Ballads until this unrestricted title should be justified by my having at command every valuable copy and every known ballad." Issued in ten parts between 1882 and 1898, *The English and Scottish Popular Ballads* numbered 305 different titles.[21]

This number alone, though, hardly conveys the extent of Child's obsession or the immensity of his achievement. Influenced by his days as a graduate student in Germany (ever after he kept a picture of the Grimms on the mantelpiece in his study), Child approached ballads with the mind-set of a scientist. His student (and eventual successor at Harvard) George Lyman Kittredge remembered, "As an investigator, Professor Child was at once the inspiration and the despair of his disciples. Nothing could surpass the scientific exactness of his methods and the unwearied diligence with which he conducted his researches." For each song in *The English and Scottish Popular Ballads*, Child printed every known variant (thirteen hundred in all), and he provided voluminous annotations explicating the songs' historical origins, the subjects to which they alluded, and the alterations they had suffered.[22]

Along with this effort to be definitive, Child brought to his ballad scholarship more rigid standards of editing than his predecessors. Although he drew extensively on previous collectors, Child was unsparing in his criticism of their penchant for doctoring texts. He criticized Thomas Percy, for example, for including verses that were "undoubtedly spurious" and pointedly attributed to him numerous "alterations and additions." At times, Child dubbed the work of other respected collectors "modernized," "twaddling," and "entirely worthless" because of impurities they had introduced.[23] Child outlined his own editing practices in the 1860 edition of his *English and Scottish Ballads*: "For the texts, the rule has been to select the most authentic copies, and to reprint them as they stand in the collections, restoring readings that had been changed without grounds, and noting all deviations from the originals . . . in the margin. Interpolations acknowledged by the editors have generally been dropped."[24]

For all his high-minded precision, of course, Child was by no means an unbiased analyst, even within the narrow segment of folk song that he admitted into view. In the same 1860 edition of *English and Scottish Ballads*, Child acknowledged that in two instances he had "greatly improved" the original texts. Child was also known at times to omit stanzas he found "tasteless." Child disciple Francis B. Gummere recalled Child's consternation when he encountered off-color material—ballads, Gummere noted, that "the Scotch call 'high-kilted' songs." "Yes, he had to print them," wrote Gummere, "but it was a poor business." He abhorred "the wanton and outrageous," and he "frowned on stories, phrases, allusions, which make deliberate sport of man's best impulses." One such offensive passage Child characterized as "brutal and shameless."[25] Child seems to have felt obliged to print some percentage of such material that he encountered, but he did not seek it out, and bawdy material certainly is underrepresented in *The English and Scottish Popular Ballads*. The loftiness with which Child treated his subject sometimes butted up against his drive to document the British ballad tradition in its entirety.

Nonetheless, the thoroughness of Child's exploration of British ballads and the sober air of scientism it projected carried immense power. His slice of folk song came to be seen as the touchstone against which all folk songs were judged. Although Child was in many ways a man born outside the time and, indeed, the country that held his heart, his influence extended long after his death and far beyond his Cambridge rose garden. At the turn of the twentieth century, when American scholars began to become interested in the songs *Americans* sang, their frame of reference was almost completely determined by the canon Child had established.

Concentrated interest in America's folk song tradition began among scholars and antiquarians who became fascinated with the culture of the Appalachian Mountains. The northern middle-class reading public had had some awareness of the Appalachian folk since the 1870s when local-color fiction writers had written stories based on "folk" characters and traditions.[26] Into the early 1900s, however, interest in mountain folk music was largely confined to a small group of enthusiasts who collected songs with an eye to printing them in academic journals. The first published collection of songs from the southern mountains consisted of one ballad and two songs that Lila W. Edmonds had collected in North Carolina's Roan Mountains. The *Journal of American Folklore* (which, along with the American Folklore Society, had been founded in 1888) printed it in 1893. A number of articles followed suit over the next two decades, mostly appearing in the *JAF*.[27]

These early collectors, although drawing on the Appalachians, were very much in the Child tradition of British song scholarship. They overwhelmingly focused on collecting ballads and were especially thrilled when they found a mountaineer who sang one of the songs Child had anointed as a true British folk ballad. It became habitual to note parenthetically where such finds belonged in Child's canon of 305 ballads—as in "'Lord Thomas and Fair Annet' (Child, No. 73)."[28] To these collectors, Child's work provided a frame of reference, a set of goals, and scholarly legitimation for the songs they were gathering. Following Child's example, the collectors published the texts but not the tunes of the songs they unearthed. Usually they made no effort to contextualize a song, to explain its importance in mountain culture, or to comment on the mountaineer who sang it. In the words of George Lyman Kittredge, "The text is the thing."[29] Most of the early collectors traveled the mountains as much to document Child's canon as to learn about Appalachian culture.

Although articles documenting folk songs were published steadily in the fifteen years or so after Lila Edmonds's 1893 collection, scholars and collectors did not become fully aware of the abundance of southern mountain songs until after 1910. First to spread the word of musical riches in the South were mountain settlement schools, such as the Hindman Settlement School in Knott County, Kentucky, which had been founded in 1902; the Log Cabin Settlement in Asheville, North Carolina (founded before 1895); Berea College (1869); and the Pine Mountain Settlement (1913).[30] Working to preserve what they saw as the mountaineers' traditional culture, these schools usually included folk song programs. Scholars and collectors who visited the schools heard the students sing and returned home talking about the musical mountaineers. In December 1908, Olive Dame Campbell visited the Hindman School and heard the children sing ballad tunes "as old as the hills—the real old plaintive folk tunes handed from mother to daughter." Inspired, Campbell began one of the most far-ranging collections up to that time, covering counties in Kentucky, Georgia, and Tennessee by early 1910.[31]

In 1911, Transylvania University professor Hubert G. Shearin published an article in the *Sewanee Review*, entitled "British Ballads in the Cumberland Mountains," that both signaled and helped further the growing interest in mountain songs. Shearin revealed that his collecting work had convinced him that the Appalachian region contained a vast trove of old-time British songs. "Like the belated April snows upon their shady slopes," he writes, "the folk-lore of the British Isles yet lingers here untouched and unchanged." Shearin goes on to list by number the nineteen Child ballads he unearthed and to make an emotional plea for collectors to hurry and track down other British ballads "before they have faded into the shadows of the past." "In another generation or two," Shearin warns, the ballads will be "but a memory" in the mountains: "The clank of the colliery, the rattle of the locomotive, the roar of the blast-furnace, the shriek of the factory whistle, and, alas, even the music of the school-bell, are already overwhelming the thin tones of the dulcimore [*sic*] and the quavering voice of the Last Minstrel of the Cumberlands, who can find scant heart to sing again the lays of olden years across the seas."[32]

Shearin's call to pursue the rich song heritage in the Appalachians marked the beginning of a great expansion of collecting efforts in the region. Ballad enthusiasts followed Shearin and Campbell to the mountains and issued numerous collections of their own.[33] Most important, folk song collectors began professionalizing after 1910. State folklore societies were organized in North Carolina and Kentucky in 1912, in Virginia in 1913, and in West Virginia in 1915. These societies were founded mostly by area English professors eager to systematize collecting work that hitherto had been done in a makeshift way by them and students in their classes.[34] In 1913 the head of the Virginia Folk-Lore Society, C. Alphonso Smith, tried to elevate ballad collecting into a national campaign. He enlisted the United States commissioner of education to issue a circular urging Americans to preserve the country's "ballad resources" before it was too late. The circular included an essay by Smith entitled "A Great Movement in Which Everyone Can Help," an alphabetical listing of Child ballads, and statements on the social necessity of ballad collecting. Smith quoted poet Sidney Lanier, who intoned, "I know that he who works in the way these . . . ballads point will be manful in necessary fight, fair in trade, loyal in love, generous to the poor, tender in the household, prudent in living, plain in speech, merry upon occasion, simple in behavior, and honest in all things."[35]

Smith wanted to galvanize ballad collectors to document the remnants of the Child canon before the songs inevitably disappeared from America. Shortly after Smith issued his circular, though, collectors began to emerge who saw no reason for the ballads to fade into "the shadows of the past." Josephine McGill, Loraine Wyman, and Howard Brockway shared Smith's and Shearin's fascination with surviving Child ballads, but rather than preserve them in destined-to-be-dusty tomes, they worked to popularize the tunes they collected.[36]

McGill, Wyman, and Brockway could embrace a less esoteric purpose for their work largely because they were not academics but private collectors and enthusiasts. McGill was a ballad lover from New York whose interest in the Appalachians had been piqued by local-color writer Lucy Furman's short stories and novels about the Hindman Settlement School. In 1914, using Hindman as her base, she spent the summer collecting ballads in the Kentucky mountains. Two years later, Wyman and Brockway, both classical musicians from New York, embarked on a somewhat more extensive trip that covered three hundred miles in seven Kentucky counties, including both the Hindman and Pine Mountain settlement schools.[37]

McGill's, Wyman's, and Brockway's interest in popularizing the music they collected shows through in the very form of the songbooks they published after their expeditions. McGill's *Folk Songs of the Kentucky Mountains: Twenty Traditional Ballads and Other English Folk-Songs* (1917) and the two books jointly edited by Wyman and Brockway, *Lonesome Tunes: Folk Songs from the Kentucky Mountains* (1916) and *Twenty Kentucky Mountain Songs* (1920), plainly aspire to different goals than the more academic collections. A comparison with Child's multivolume *The English and Scottish Popular Ballads* illustrates the differences. Child's tomes, chock-full of footnotes and cross-references and, in many cases, with lyrics written in Old English dialect, were meant to occupy a place of honor in a scholar's library. McGill's and Wyman and Brockway's books, in contrast, suggest that their publishers intended them to be used not by scholars but by families eager to make music at home. In a striking departure from previous folklorists' work, these three books feature not just a song's text but also its tune. Most significant, the tunes are scored with a simple piano accompaniment beneath the melody line. The song's words are written between the melody and accompaniment so that pianist and singers can easily sing along together.

In keeping with the emphasis on popularization, all three authors strove for conciseness and simplicity. None of these books aspires to Child-like completeness: they give no introductory material about individual songs, provide not a single footnote, and do not bother to specify the folk sources who sang each song to the collectors (they are thanked in prefaces). For convenience and price considerations, moreover, two

Folk songs for the middle-class parlor: left, *front cover of* Folk Songs of the Kentucky Mountains, *1917;* right, *front cover of* Twenty Kentucky Mountain Songs, *1920.*

of the three books came in paperback editions, and all are slim volumes.[38] Each contains between twenty and twenty-five songs and is roughly one hundred pages. Keeping the books short in part prevented them from looking too academic and intimidating; but doing so also allowed them to be thin, which, along with their unusually tall height, enabled them to fit easily on a piano's music stand.

A final indication that these books were made for a piano is that none of them has a title on its spine; instead they have elaborate and colorful covers, designs meant to face forward and be seen as a part of a parlor's decor. All three feature floral patterns, and, perhaps most significant, both McGill's book and Wyman and Brockway's feature images of the home. McGill's cover shows a quaint log cabin–like house in a tidy clearing by a mountain stream. The cabin has an open back porch, partly drawn curtains, and a red brick chimney from which smoke rises. Wyman and Brockway's *Twenty Kentucky Mountain Songs* shows a barefoot dulcimer-playing mother and five happy barefoot children sitting on a back porch overlooking verdant hills.

This move to link mountain music to the feminized realm of the home has significance on several levels. Most directly, it suggests that publishers were trying to appeal to women as consumers of songbooks.

Traditionally, middle-class women controlled cultural activities within the home, overseeing family reading, music making, and playacting; in middle- and upper-class families, at least, the parlor or piano room was decidedly in the woman's sphere. At another level, to depict a singing woman on the cover of Wyman's book says something accurate about the actual sources of the songs in the books: the strong majority of the songs Wyman, Brockway, and McGill collected came from women. Likewise, the more extensive mountain collection that Cecil Sharp and Olive Dame Campbell published in 1917 draws on vastly more women than men.[39] The preponderance of women in these collections may indicate that they felt more comfortable than men singing for collectors or that the collectors themselves felt more comfortable with female informants. Certainly countless Appalachian men did sing folk songs, but women may have been more likely to preserve the sorts of songs in which collectors were most interested. Scholars have noted that in American folk-singing traditions, men have tended to do more "public" singing—that is, in social gatherings involving people outside the family—while women have been more likely to sing in the "private" realm of the home, often while completing their domestic work. Folklorist Edward D. Ives speculates that the "domestic tradition" is more static and contains more old-fashioned songs, including more Child ballads.[40]

A final element in the gendered aspects of early folk song collecting is that many of the collectors themselves were women. Aside from McGill and Wyman, Lila W. Edmonds, Katherine Pettit, Olive Dame Campbell, Maud Karpeles, Louise Pound, Louise Rand Bascam, and Dorothy Scarborough all made pioneering contributions to song collecting before the mid-1920s. Pound and Scarborough operated in the more scholarly camp of the early folk song movement, but it is perhaps significant that the first collectors to try to extend the songs they found into middle-class women's parlor (Wyman and McGill) were women themselves.

Wyman's and McGill's parlor books represented the first efforts to popularize British ballads, but not until Englishman Cecil Sharp arrived in the Appalachians did Americans begin to appreciate the extent of the folk song heritage in the Appalachians. In some ways Sharp was a latecomer to the mountains. He did not make his first trip there until 1916, when he and his assistant, Maud Karpeles, accepted Olive Dame Campbell's invitation to visit and collect in western North Carolina. By this point, the *Journal of American Folklore* alone had published more than a dozen articles about mountain folk song; McGill, Wyman, and Brockway had completed the expeditions that would lead to their books; and Campbell's own collecting in the area had yielded seventy or eighty tunes.[41] Sharp's renown as a collector, though, rests not so much on his being the first to show any interest in mountain song but rather on his ability to crystallize and extend trends that had been emerging over the previous two decades.

Sharp used his status as an authority on British folk song to add weight to the notion that the mountains were rich in Child ballads. He bolstered this claim in part through the sheer numbers of traditional British songs he collected. In close to twelve months of collecting in Appalachia (spread over three expeditions between 1916 and 1918), Sharp collected more than 1,600 versions of 500 songs from 281 singers, almost all British-derived material.[42] Like his American predecessors, Sharp most eagerly sought Child ballads. In the book he published from his first expedition, *English Folk Songs from the Southern Appalachians*, thirty-seven of the fifty-five ballads he selected belonged to Child's canon. He privileged these thirty-seven by listing them first in the volume, adopting what folklore historian D. K. Wilgus refers to as the "Child-and-Other" organization so prevalent at the time.[43]

In other ways, too, Sharp's *English Folk Songs from the Southern Appalachians* reinforced trends that had been emerging in folk song scholarship since the late nineteenth century. To a great extent, it is an academic book in the Child tradition. It includes several variants of every song published, and in each case Sharp carefully notes the singer who sang the variant to him and when and where he collected it. Further, Sharp indicates for every song which mode or scale governs the tune, referring to an involved chart he gives in his introduction. For example, Variant C of "The Cruel Ship's Carpenter" is "Hexatonic. Mode 4, b (with sharpened 7th)."[44]

For all these academicisms, though, *English Folk Songs* reveals Sharp to be much more in sympathy with parlor-book popularizers like McGill and Wyman than Child would have been. The book treats folk songs not just as literature but as pieces to be sung. It includes the tunes as well as the songs' texts. Although in keeping with academic practice Sharp does not harmonize the tunes in *English Folk Songs*, he advocates harmonizing in the volume's introduction, saying that adding accompaniment would give the songs "a wider and more popular appeal."[45] He did add harmonic accompaniments to other of his folk song books. Sharp, then, was at the forefront of a slowly emerging group of collectors who refused, in Karpeles's words, to see folk songs as "precious objects [that] must be protected from common usage for fear of their vulgarization."[46] Sharp wanted to reintegrate folk songs into people's everyday lives.

As he worked to reinvigorate folk song traditions, Sharp's ultimate goal was to forge a national British culture. Folk songs, he felt, would help a young Englishman "know and understand his country and his countrymen far better than he does at present; and knowing and understanding them he will love them the more, realize that he is united to them by the subtle bond of blood and kinship, and become, in the highest sense of the word, a better citizen, and a truer patriot."[47] On the face of it, this vision of national culture was an extremely populist one. Sharp proposed uniting society around the songs (and dances) created by those whom he called "the common people."[48] Public-school education was the centerpiece of this plan. In *English Folk Songs from the Southern Appalachians*, Sharp wrote that "the value of such songs as these as material for the general education of the young cannot be overestimated." He felt folk songs were "the ideal musical food for very young children," provided the songs were English—"English folk songs for English children, . . . [not] German, French or even Scottish or Irish." With confidence, Sharp envisioned that when "every English child is, as a matter of course, made acquainted with the folk-songs of his country, then, from whatever class the musician of the future may spring, he will speak in the national musical idiom."[49]

This reference to the "musician of the future" suggests a more elitist side to Sharp's populism. Despite his respect for the songs of the "common people," Sharp did not believe that the commoners themselves were up to the task of creating the national music. Rather, they were to be commended for having preserved the raw materials out of which trained composers would create new music. In his introduction to *English Folk Songs* Sharp encourages high-art composers to assimilate the tunes into their work, saying that if composers were to "master the contents of this book" they would gain training "far better suited to [their] requirements than [they] would from the ordinary conservatoire."[50] Classical composers who used folk sources, such as Ralph Vaughan Williams, Percy Grainger, and Béla Bartók, were the true heirs of Sharp's brand of nationalism.

Along with this preference for trained composers, Sharp had a strong antipathy to the music to which the "common people" of his day actually listened. In trying to establish an English folk song tradition, Sharp explicitly hoped to undermine the popular music of the day. He proposed to "flood the streets . . . with folk-tunes, and those who vulgarize themselves and others by singing coarse music-hall songs will soon drop them in favour of the equally attractive but far better tunes of the folk. This will make the streets a pleasanter place for those who have sensitive ears, and will do incalculable good in civilizing the masses." Such hostility to contemporary popular culture was very much in step with a nostalgic reformist impulse that cut across the ideological spectrum in Britain in the early part of the century. As historian Georgina Boyes notes, "Culture had developed in ways which were widely perceived as 'unnatural.' Commercialism, progress, irreligion, science, capitalism or greed were variously proposed as fuelling a perverted descent into industrialisation, mass culture and urbanisation."[51] To Sharp and the revivalists, folk culture offered a way to knit society back together and return it to a simpler era—a peaceful time in which community bonds were held securely in place by class deference.

Like Child before him, Sharp felt that the England he cherished had disappeared several hundred years ago, leaving only fragments behind. Unlike Child, though, Sharp found a way to revisit the British past he had never known: he created it in America. The key to Sharp's attraction to the Appalachian mountaineers' culture was that they fit (or could be constructed to fit) his conception of old-time England. In his depictions of the mountain people he encountered, Sharp reinforced myths about the Britishness of America's folk song heritage.

From his earliest moments in the Appalachians, Sharp linked the mountaineers he saw to his idealized image of the English folk. Sharp had done extensive song collecting in Britain, but whereas in his home country he always was grasping at fragments, in America he felt he was seeing English peasant culture in full operation. In 1916 Sharp wrote that his work among the mountaineers had convinced him that the Appalachian singers were "just English peasants in appearance, speech, and manner"; or rather, "I should say that they are just exactly what the English peasant was *one hundred or more years ago*."[52] In his introduction to *English Folk Songs*, Sharp confidently asserted that the mountaineers' speech was "English not American," although he offered no evidence to explain or bolster this claim. As Sharp's companion, Karpeles, noted, Sharp had discovered the "England of his dreams in the United States of America."[53]

Sharp justified equating the mountaineers with old England by citing evidence to show that the mountaineers lived in a time warp—in a society still dominated by the barter system, still "talking the language of a past day" (Old English), and still beholden to the Bible and an "unrelenting" and "austere creed, charged with Calvinism." Sharp attributed this antiquated lifestyle to geographic isolation, depicting inhabitants of "sequestered mountain valleys" who "have for a hundred years or more been completely isolated and cut off from all traffic with the rest of the world."[54] Sharp saw the mountaineers' supposed insularity as a chance to escape his era and return to a culture he had given up for dead.

Closely linked to his penchant for locating the mountaineers in the past, Sharp idealized Appalachian culture as refreshingly natural and pure. In his writings he extrapolated from the supposedly clean and unadulterated folk songs he heard to imagine that the singers had wholesome and simple lifestyles as well. He praised the mountaineers for their "elemental wisdom, abundant knowledge, and intuitive understanding which those only who live in constant touch with Nature and face-to-face with reality seem to be able to acquire." Sharp contrasted this harmonious existence with what he saw as the spiritually empty routine of contemporary industrial life. The mountaineers, he felt, were "immune from that continuous, grinding, mental pressure due to the attempt to 'make a living,' from which all of us in the modern world suffer." Ignoring the moonshining and feuds that so preoccupied local-color writers, Sharp continued, "Here no one is 'on the make'; commercial competition and social rivalries are unknown. In this respect, at any rate, they have the advantage over those who spend the greater part of every day in preparing to live, in acquiring the technique of life, rather than its enjoyment." At times Sharp made the mountaineers' closeness to nature sound less like subsistence poverty than like an ascetic philosophy. He surmised that many people "set the standard of bodily and material comfort perilously low, in order, presumably, that they may have the more leisure and so extract the maximum enjoyment out of life."[55] In his excitement at having discovered Old England reincarnate, Sharp projected his antimodern bent onto the mountaineers.

Sharp's vision of mountain culture may seem romanticized, but his views were very much in tune with the conception of mountain culture that had been forming among early folk song collectors since the turn of the century. The early collectors depicted the mountaineers as still living in a rosy distant past in which plain-speaking farmers with upstanding values occupied quaint log cabins, worked in harmony with nature to feed their families, and entertained themselves by dancing old-time steps to old-time ballads. These collectors, then, much like the contemporary Arts and Crafts and New Country Life movements, located authenticity in a rural past. Idealizing mountain culture enabled them to challenge or at least sidestep the contemporary trends toward an urban, machine-driven industrial economy and a mass commercial culture. Whereas critics said the mountains existed in a state of "arrested development," Sharp spoke for most collectors by the 1910s when he replied, "I should prefer to call it a case of arrested degeneration."[56]

Underlying the early collectors' defense of old-time culture lay fear of another kind of degeneration as well: racial degeneration. Sharp's pursuit of pure English culture had a racial component that translated powerfully in the American setting. In trying to isolate the source of the cultural richness in the mountain communities, Sharp settled on race as the deciding factor. He wrote, "The reason, I take it, why these mountain people, albeit unlettered, have acquired so many of the essentials of culture is partly to be attributed to the large amount of leisure they enjoy . . . , but chiefly to the fact that they have one and all entered at birth into the full enjoyment of their racial heritage." In Sharp's view, racial inheritance in large part determines a culture's value. He observes that the mountaineers' "language, wisdom, manners, and the many graces of life that are theirs, are merely racial attributes which have been gradually handed down generation by generation." Sharp meant that the mountaineers were part of the *English* race, but his attitudes extended easily into the black-white dichotomy familiar to Americans. In 1918 he described Winston-Salem, North Carolina, as "a noisy place and the air impregnated with tobacco, molasses and nigger!" He told his diary that when his liberal hosts challenged his "dubbing the negroes as of a lower race," he attributed their objections to "a mere lack of education etc!"[57]

Sharp's emphasis on racial determinism adds a twist to the early ballad enthusiasts' insistence that the mountaineers were 100 percent British. Mostly white Anglo-Saxon Protestants, the song collectors asserted that mountain culture was America's authentic folk inheritance and at the same time stressed that the mountaineers were British. In effect, therefore, the collectors established *their* heritage as the true American culture. This racial message also gives another perspective on the educational efforts of early popularizers such as Sharp and the mountain settlement schools. In Sharp's view, "the primary purpose of education is to place the direction of the present generation in possession of the cultural achievements of the past so that they may as quickly as possible enter into their racial inheritance." He goes on to ask rhetorically, "What better form of music or of literature can we give them than the folksongs and folk-ballads of the race to which they belong, or of the nation whose language they speak? To deny them these is to cut them off from the past and to rob them of that which is theirs by right of birth."[58] Education here begins to sound like race indoctrination.

In the late 1910s, collectors of mountain songs were working in a time in which racial boundaries in America were being tested. Eastern European immigrants had flowed into the country in overwhelming numbers, prompting growing campaigns to Americanize the newcomers and to block further immigration; jazz was taking off in popularity in the nation's cities, signaling, as historian Kathy J. Ogren writes, that "black culture, like black people, could not be kept on the margins of American society" and sparking intense debate among white critics; and African American artists and intellectuals were creating a black culture of new vibrancy and openness in what would become known as the Harlem Renaissance.[59] In this context, the calls to use folk song education to pass on WASPS' "racial inheritance" sounds like a bid to preserve the centrality of Anglo-Saxon culture against outside challenges.

The point is not that, in an age of nativism, Jim Crow, and lynching, Cecil Sharp and his fellow folk song enthusiasts were strikingly or unusually racist. More significant, rather, is that there was a racial undertone beneath the earliest self-conscious efforts to define America's folk song heritage. This racial aspect was but one part, though, of a multifaceted mythology about the "true" folk that by the late 1910s was percolating slowly into American culture. This myth defined a folk song as an extremely old song, usually a ballad, that had originated from Great Britain and was currently sung by rural, isolated mountain people who were white, Anglo-Saxon Protestants.

To label these criteria a myth is not to dismiss them as baseless. Certainly Appalachian mountaineers sang a striking number of old British ballads; but in the early 1900s they also played fiddle tunes, sang hymns, and crooned sentimental pop songs.[60] For every ballad Sharp collected, he ignored countless other songs offered by the mountaineers. Similarly, most mountaineers did live in relatively rural settings, and some truly were isolated from modern roads and conveniences. Many parts of the mountains, though, were rapidly modernizing, and the region as a whole was in the midst of jolting economic upheaval. The more Sharp traveled, the more this reality confronted his romantic conceptions. In a 1917 letter, Sharp recounted his disappointment in arriving to collect in a small North Carolina town. To his regret the folk seemed to have been tainted by living too close to Waynesville, a more modernized town of two thousand.[61] "The log-cabins are primitive enough," wrote Sharp, "but their owners are clean, neat, and tidy, looking rather like maidservants in respectable suburban families. It is sad that cleanliness and good music, or good taste in music, rarely go together. Dirt and good music are the usual bed-fellows, or cleanliness and rag-time! So we move further on tomorrow." The following year Sharp arrived with high hopes in a small Virginia town "twenty-five miles from the [nearest] station." But he found the local residents "dressed in fashionable garments, low-necked dresses, high-heels and well-powdered faces. . . . The fact is the price of whisky has so gone up that 'moon-shining' has been exceedingly profitable and they are rolling in money. Songs were, of course, out of the question, and we retired [the] next day somewhat crestfallen." Finally, to some degree the racial component of the mountain myth was based on reality. Most of the mountain residents were white; but by no means all were. Even though Sharp and the early collectors documented only whites' songs, the 1910 census showed that 13.4 percent of the Appalachian population was black.[62]

To suggest inaccuracies in the early collectors' conception of the folk only confirms that they were telling a story about America's folk roots that, to them, was true and useful. The picture of the mountains that the early folklorists meticulously documented and enthusiastically propounded represented a choice on their part, whether conscious or not, to define America's folk music tradition in a certain way. Whatever inconsistencies the myth may have enveloped, in its time it had coherence and, for several decades, power.

The most significant effect of the myth of the white ballad singer was to help block African American folk music from gaining a central place in the canon of America's musical heritage. In the late nineteenth and early twentieth centuries, African American song enjoyed quite a widespread popularity, but the myths about the "true" American folk, coupled with raw prejudice, kept it from being anointed as America's folk music.

Interest in African American song actually predated interest in Appalachian mountain music. It was probably the first American music to be popular in communities outside of those in which it had originated. Nonblack audiences initially became interested in black song via the minstrel shows that drew enthusiastic audiences across the North in the middle decades of the nineteenth century. These shows' popularity depended on their claim that their dances, humor, and music authentically represented slave life. But since almost all the early minstrel performers were northern whites in blackface (African Americans did not begin to perform in blackface until after the Civil War), they had only very limited knowledge of actual African American traditions. Mostly, they overlaid spurious caricatures of blacks onto Anglo-American cultural forms. In fact, the melodies for two of the most popular early minstrel songs, "Jim Crow" and "Zip Coon," derived from English and Irish sources.[63]

In the 1870s, though, northerners became fascinated by African American spirituals as sung by African Americans themselves. This surge of interest in spirituals originated with the Fisk University Jubilee Singers. The Jubilee Singers were organized by George L. White, a white northerner who worked for the Freedmen's Bureau and was both a music teacher and the treasurer at Fisk. Founded in 1866 in Nashville, Tennessee, as a school for African Americans, Fisk was on the verge of bankruptcy by 1870. Desperate, White proposed a fund-raising concert tour. His proposal met with opposition from within the university community, but in October 1871 he and his group of nine singers, eight of whom were former slaves, headed north. After initial hardship, the group made contact with the Reverend Henry Ward Beecher of New York. He sponsored an appearance at his Plymouth Church that launched the Fisk singers on an immensely successful series of concerts. Less than seven months after they had set out from Nashville, they had earned twenty thousand dollars to meet the school's expenses. In June 1872 they sang at the World's Peace Jubilee in the Boston Coliseum, and in 1873 they made the first of a series of triumphant European tours, including a performance before Queen Victoria.[64]

The Fisk singers' concerts triggered a wave of faddish popularity. President Grant interrupted preparations for a cabinet meeting to receive the singers at the White House, and, it was reported, he "shook them affectionately by the hand, assured them he was informed of their enterprise and in full sympathy with it, and listened attentively as they sang 'Go down, Moses, way down in Egypt land / tell ole Pharaoh let my people go.'"[65] In the 1870s, publishers began issuing books that gave piano arrangements of the most popular "Jubilee Songs" and chronicled the singers' rise to success.[66] Other black schools, meanwhile, followed Fisk's lead and sent choirs of their own on tours to raise money. Most successful were the Hampton Institute's singers, who began their years of touring in 1873. By 1909, their songbook had been through five editions. Indeed, the popularity of spirituals continued to spread during the nineteenth century. In 1899 song collector William E. Barton noted that songs introduced by the Fisk singers appeared "at all manner of occasions from funerals to yachting parties" and that they had been republished in a range of books, "from collections of Sunday school melodies to books of college songs."[67]

The popularity of black songs, though, did not easily translate into acceptance of the singers. The Fisk and Hampton groups, for example, projected dignified images, dressing demurely and singing precise, formal arrangements of the spirituals. But northerners persistently identified them with minstrelsy. A Cincinnati paper advertised the Fisk singers by announcing, "A band of negro minstrels will sing in the Vine Street Congregational Church this morning. They are genuine negroes, and call themselves 'Colored Christian singers.'" Some of the imitators of the

Fisk group did not try to skirt the association with minstrelsy but rather capitalized on it. Historian Robert C. Toll notes that groups billed themselves as "genuine slave bands" and promised to appear in "full plantation costumes" and to sing the "quaint and weird" slave songs on "crude instruments of the south."[68]

A few people, though, began to see spirituals not as quaint tunes in a songbook or as exotic showstoppers but as important parts of America's heritage that needed to be preserved. Probably the first person to give African American songs serious consideration as folk music was Thomas Wentworth Higginson, a white colonel in the Union army who became fascinated with the spirituals his black troops sang. In 1867 he published the texts of several of these songs in the *Atlantic Monthly* and urged that they be preserved as part of America's cultural legacy: "History," he wrote, "cannot afford to lose this portion of its record."[69] Also in 1867, William Francis Allen, Charles Pickard Ware, and Lucy McKim Garrison published the first full-length treatment of African American song, *Slave Songs of the United States* (1867). The book was the product of abolitionist zeal. Allen and Ware, both Harvard educated, had taught during the war in freedmen's schools in the South. Garrison, the daughter-in-law of abolitionist William Lloyd Garrison and sister of architect Charles McKim, had at age nineteen transcribed black songs after the Carolina Sea Islands had fallen to Union forces. The young reformers were convinced of the significance of their finds. Wrote Allen, "These relics of a state of society that has passed away should be preserved while it is still possible." Subsequent advocates of spirituals struck a similar tone. In his introduction to Marshall W. Taylor's *Collection of Revival Hymns and Plantation Melodies* (1883), F. S. Hoyt described the black spiritual as "an important . . . contribution to the history of mankind," while the preface to the 1891 Hampton Institute songbook quoted Edward Everett Hale's assertion that spirituals were "the only American music."[70]

Almost half a century, then, before Cecil Sharp began exploring America's British-ballad heritage, collectors identified an American vernacular-music tradition centered on an African American form. Enthusiasts worked to preserve the spiritual as part of America's folk heritage, and efforts to popularize the form achieved considerable success in the late nineteenth century. The Fisk singers were far better known than their contemporary Francis J. Child, and the spiritual had a currency in nineteenth-century popular culture that no American roots music had ever before enjoyed. How can one account for the respect and popularity enjoyed by the music of a race so widely abused and ridiculed in nineteenth-century society?

Part of the answer lies in the spiritual as a form. In terms of cultural politics, the spiritual was a safe type of African American expression for early folk song collectors to canonize. It was, after all, a relic of slave days. Although many African Americans sang spirituals long after slavery, overall the songs went into steep and continuous decline among freedpeople after the Civil War. Former slaves quite consciously rejected the form. In 1874, in the preface to *Cabin and Plantation Songs As Sung by the Hampton Students*, Thomas P. Fenner, who had trained the first Hampton singers, highlighted the need to preserve spirituals by noting that the music was "rapidly slipping away. . . . The freedmen have an unfortunate inclination to despise it as a vestige of slavery; those who learned it in the old time when it was the natural outpouring of their sorrows and longing, are dying off."[71] Even the Fisk singers did not immediately embrace the spiritual. Although spirituals were sung in the school's chapel, none appeared on their first program in 1871. Only when their first tour seemed on the verge of failing did two spirituals get added. Since audiences responded strongly to these examples, the group began to focus exclusively on religious songs.[72] In struggling to preserve spirituals, then, nineteenth-century collectors identified African Americans with a form from which most African Americans wanted to distance themselves.

The content of spirituals also helps account for their appeal to nineteenth-century whites. On the surface at least, spirituals imply acceptance rather than direct, physical challenge to slavery. The songs suggest a decidedly otherworldly orientation, promising redemption not in the present but in the glorious world after death. "Go in the Wilderness," to take just one example, says,

I wait upon de Lord,
I wait upon de Lord,
I wait upon de Lord, my God,
who take away de sin of the world.[73]

Spirituals tend to describe the hardships of this life in terms of sorrow more than anger or defiance. In part, therefore, the spiritual may have appealed to whites because it told newly free but still dominated blacks not to redress current wrongs. Even as the popularity of black spirituals among whites suggested an embrace of African American culture, it also represented an effort to keep it at arm's length.

This ambivalence about black culture infused the language even of the pioneering collectors who strove to preserve the spiritual for posterity. They do not seem to have been entirely comfortable with the songs they heard and certainly not with the culture that produced them. F. S. Hoyt heard "weird but charming melodies." William E. Barton referred to the Fisk singers' "quaint, weird songs," while Robert Moton prefaced the fifth edition of the Hampton songbook with a reference to the songs' "rude words, wild strains and curious though beautiful harmonies." Thomas Higginson made hunting for spirituals sound like a botanist's search for a specimen. Traveling to the South, he wrote, gave him the chance to "gather on their own soil these strange plants, which I had before seen as in museums only." When he came across a promising song, he "carried it to [his] tent, like some captured bird or insect, and then, after examination, put it by."[74] Even though these nineteenth-century collectors worked to preserve the African American spiritual as an important part of America's heritage, they tended to depict black singers as exotic beings on the margins of society.

Black vernacular music became even more marginalized in the early twentieth century as the myth of the British ballad asserted itself. As the influence of Child's canon spread, few folklorists and ballad enthusiasts paid sustained attention to African American music. The main collector to study African American songs in the early 1900s, Howard Odum, depicted them as the manifestations of a bizarre alien culture. With doctorates in both sociology and psychology, Odum gathered songs less to preserve an American heritage than to discover what made those strange Negroes tick. In "Religious Folk-Songs of the Southern Negroes" (1909), he wrote that "the songs of the most characteristic type are far from elegant. Nor are they dignified in theme or expression. They will appear to the cultured reader a bit repulsive, to say the least. They go beyond the interesting point to the trite and repulsive themes. Nor can a great many of the common songs that are too inelegant to include [in the printed collection] be given at all." As with his nineteenth-century predecessors, Odum's encounter with African American music did not open him up to black society: "Little need be said," he stated, "concerning social and political equality. There is no absolute race equality in any sense of the word. Those who would assist the Negro should remember this and not exact too much of him, either in demanding his results or offering him the complete ideal of the whites."[75]

Early collectors exoticized African Americans in part to keep them at a distance and in part because black culture truly did differ markedly from the white middle-class life to which most collectors were accustomed. Even those early collectors who, unlike Odum, did not resort to outright racism to explain these differences could not completely recon-

cile themselves to what, from their points of view, were the more unusual aspects of African American culture. African American spirituals
achieved an astonishing degree of popularity in the nineteenth and early
twentieth centuries—up to a point, difference fascinated white Americans—but these songs could not break into the canon of America's folk
music. In the late nineteenth and early twentieth centuries, difference,
especially racial difference, precluded complete acceptance.[76] Negro
spirituals could be quaint, charming, even moving, but they could not
cross the barrier to become America's folk music.

Apart from the African American spiritual, the British-centered Child
canon received only one other significant challenge to its dominance
before the 1920s. In the 1870s and 1880s, a young boy named John
Lomax was captivated by the songs cowboys sang as they traveled past
his father's two-room house on the Chisholm Trail. His interest in the
music, though, lay largely dormant through years as an undergraduate at
the University of Texas, registrar at the university, and English professor
at Texas A&M. In 1906 Lomax, age thirty-nine, went to Harvard to do a
year of graduate work. There the successors to Francis J. Child, Professors Barrett Wendell and George Lyman Kittredge, responded enthusiastically when Lomax mentioned his love of cowboy song. They
helped him prepare a form letter to be sent to western newspaper editors
requesting "native ballads and songs of the West" and arranged for Harvard Press to print one thousand copies, which Lomax laboriously addressed and mailed. After Lomax returned to Texas, Wendell and Kittredge helped him win a prestigious postgraduate fellowship, newly
endowed at Harvard. Lomax became "Sheldon Fellow for the investigation of American ballads," an appellation that over the next three years
brought him five hundred dollars each summer to finance research and
song-collecting expeditions among the cowboys.[77]

   In 1910, Lomax published *Cowboy Songs and Other Frontier Ballads*, a
collection of more than a hundred songs, mostly drawn from scrap-
books, newspapers, and the responses he had received from the thousand circulars he had mailed. Ranging from a little-known tune called
"Home on the Range" to "Root Hog or Die," this material marked a
significant departure from the "Lord Randal" and "Sweet William" ballads of the Child tradition.[78] In canonizing cowboy songs instead of
ancient ballads, Lomax changed the face of the folk, replacing the sturdy
British peasant with the mythical western cowboy who "lived hard, shot
quick and true, and died with his face to his foe."[79] He also revised
Child's and Sharp's assumptions about the age of folk songs. Whereas

Child preferred fourteenth-century ballads, cowboys did not even exist in significant numbers until after the Civil War. In contrast to Child and Sharp, then, Lomax pointed toward a recent, indigenously American vernacular-music tradition.

The relative newness of the cowboy songs led Lomax to collecting methods that differed from Child's. Lomax found that, although declining, the cowboy song was still very much alive. This realization led him, like Sharp, to seek out songs not only from printed sources but from living informants as well.[80] Also like Sharp, finding contemporary examples of the songs he treasured led Lomax to attempt not just to document a song tradition but to revitalize one. In Lomax's case, though, his emphasis on popularizing songs led him to dispense with academic standards to an extent that would have galled Child. In *Cowboy Songs* Lomax does not identify the sources from whom he collected songs, and he edits some of the songs without indicating that he did so. Unlike Child and Sharp, moreover, Lomax dispensed with printing song variants and instead combined different versions of songs without indicating which lines came from which source. Lomax openly admits, "I have violated the ethics of ballad-gatherers, in a few instances, by selecting and putting together what seemed to be the best lines from different versions, all telling the story. Frankly the volume is meant to be popular."[81]

Even though Lomax challenged the boundaries of Child's canon and disregarded his collecting methods, as a student of Wendell and Kittredge he still very much located his work within the Child tradition. In *Cowboy Songs*, for instance, he persistently identifies American cowboy culture with the British folk tradition. Lomax rhapsodizes, "Out in the wild, far-away place of the big and still unpeopled west . . . yet survives the Anglo-Saxon ballad spirit that was active in secluded districts in England and Scotland." He goes on to connect the cowboy to the resonant mythology surrounding medieval England: "Dauntless, reckless, without the unearthly purity of Sir Galahad though as gentle to a pure woman as King Arthur, he is truly a knight of the twentieth century." Lomax credits the rugged cowboy with "a spirit of hospitality as primitive and hearty as that found in the mead-halls of Beowulf."[82]

In addition to these rhetorical homages to old England, Lomax and Child actually shared strikingly similar conceptions of the folk. Lomax's cowboys sang in a different country and in a different era than Child's peasants, but like Child (and Sharp), Lomax stressed that the character of the cowboys' songs derived from their isolation from modern society: "Illiterate people, and people cut off from newspapers and books, isolated and lonely—thrown back on primal resources for entertainment and for the expression of emotion,—utter themselves through somewhat the same character of songs as did their forefathers perhaps a thousand years ago." Lomax also worked to preserve the aura of murky origins that helped make Child's ballads seem authentic. "In only a few instances," he wrote, "have I been able to discover the authorship of any [cowboy] songs. They seem to have sprung up quietly and mysteriously as does the grass on the plains."[83] Lomax set out to expand more than to destabilize the Child canon.

Even in this more modest goal, Lomax had only limited success. His cowboy songs attracted some attention, but not enough to keep him from essentially giving up collecting for the fifteen years after 1916. Most of those years he spent heading the University of Texas's alumni association (the Texas Exes) and selling bonds in a Dallas bank.[84] Cowboy music did not truly penetrate America's popular memory until the 1930s when "singing cowboys" became the rage in movies and a series of cowboy-styled songs became radio hits.[85] Lomax's work also failed to spur much activity on the part of folklorists and ballad enthusiasts.[86] Into the twenties, then, the folk song canon shaped by Child and Sharp held sway. Despite the alternatives posed by spirituals and cowboy songs, "true" American folk song was defined as British-derived.

The first real breakthroughs in generating popular interest in indigenous American vernacular music were spurred not by folklorists or ballad enthusiasts but by commercial entrepreneurs. Commercial record companies became involved in folk music almost by accident. In the spring of 1920, recording scout Fred Hagar and his assistant, Ralph Peer, recorded for Okeh Records a young African American vaudeville singer, Mamie Smith, as she sang "Crazy Blues." Historian Bill C. Malone notes that Smith was "neither a blues singer nor a southerner (she was from Ohio)." But sales of "Crazy Blues" unexpectedly soared, and record companies became interested in making records that targeted rural southern blacks and urban blacks who had recently migrated from the country. In the early 1920s Peer began the unprecedented practice of leading regular field trips to the South to make commercial recordings of local singers.[87] As he accumulated recordings by African Americans, Peer labeled them "race records" and promoted them heavily. Quickly, Peer's rivals at Columbia, Paramount, and Victor followed suit with their own "race" series.[88] Although race records always represented a small percentage of the companies' overall sales (perhaps 5 percent), by 1927 the companies released nearly ten race records per week. They were sold in record shops, mail-order catalogs, saloons, book stores, barber shops, drug stores, furniture stores, and cigar stands, and they quickly became important elements in African American community life.[89]

In June 1923 Ralph Peer went to Atlanta, looking to record black talent for the Okeh company. While Peer was there, Polk Brockman, who sold Peer's race records in the phonograph department of his grandfather's furniture store, convinced him to record a white North Georgian performer named Fiddlin' John Carson, who had built up something of a local following on Atlanta's WSB radio. Peer found Carson's rough singing distasteful, and although he agreed to send Brockman five hundred copies of the record to sell in his store, he issued the record "uncatalogued, unadvertised, unlabeled and for circulation solely in Atlanta," says Malone. By late July, though, the first five hundred copies had sold, and Peer realized he had stumbled onto a potentially rich find.[90] He summoned Carson to New York to record more songs and began to look for rural white as well as black musicians on his future field-recording expeditions. In 1925 Peer recorded Al Hopkins's string band and dubbed them the "Hill Billies," a term that eventually grew to apply to the whole genre of rural white commercial music.

As had happened with race records, Okeh's competitors—Columbia, Paramount, Brunswick, the American Record Company, Gennett, and Victor—soon followed Peer's lead in searching out hillbilly music. In the late 1920s, companies did fieldwork in thirteen states. When recording in an area, they would establish headquarters in the nearest large city, usually setting up a temporary recording studio at the local radio station, concert hall, or (as when Peer first recorded Jimmie Rodgers) an old warehouse. Usually, recording scouts tried to book a full recording schedule in advance, relying on local agents to gather likely prospects or, occasionally, on a timely news article or advertisement announcing their recording plans. Upon arrival, the recording team would take down as many songs as possible in a few days and then pack the fragile wax discs in dry ice, ship them back to the company factory, and move on to another town.[91] The discs, meanwhile, were pressed into records and shipped to market. Aside from mail-order catalogs, distribution in the 1920s was largely regionalized. Whereas early books of folk songs such as the spirituals collected by Allen, Ward, and Garrison, the cowboy songs of John Lomax, or the mountain music of McGill, Wyman, and Brockway sought a diffuse middle-class market, commercial companies in the 1920s aimed hillbilly records at a distinct niche—primarily southeastern, working-class whites.[92]

This system seems to have worked well, for sales of hillbilly music boomed in the mid- to late twenties. Historian Charles Wolfe estimates

that the Columbia hillbilly series alone sold eleven million records between 1925 and 1932, and he adds that if the other companies "did only
half as well in sales in the South, probably as many as sixty-five million
old-time song or tune performances flooded into the culture" in this
period. Even if these figures are somewhat inflated, they show that the
commercial record companies were, in a numerical sense, far more successful at popularizing their vision of American folk music than had
been Cecil Sharp, Olive Dame Campbell, and the other documenters of
the Child canon.[93]

In addition to being more commercially viable, the record companies'
canon of folk music differed in other key ways from that of the ballad
enthusiasts who had explored the rural South before them. Not invested
in having a British-centered canon, the commercial companies could
record a wider range of contemporary vernacular music. Whereas ballad
enthusiasts collected almost exclusively from the older, more static domestic singing tradition, commercial collectors recorded the relatively
newer and more fluid repertoire of songs played in public gatherings.[94]
The commercial workers' canon also extended much more easily to include a variety of African American music. Race-record listings included
not only spirituals and sermons but blues, jazz, work songs, and story-
telling sessions; if it would sell, companies would record it. This economic imperative, though, did not drive the companies to treat African
American and white folk music as parts of a shared or interconnecting
tradition. Even though blacks' and whites' songs were often recorded by
the same people on the same field trips in the same cities, every company
in the twenties treated its race and hillbilly selections as completely independent series that had separate numbering systems, separate advertise-
ments, and separate markets.

Aside from including African American music, the commercial companies also differed from the proponents of the Child canon in their
orientation to white music. Early folklorists like Sharp climbed mountains searching for unaccompanied ballads, the form they considered the
most authentic and pure. The first commercial record scouts, however,
mostly recorded instrumentals, especially fiddle tunes, which the companies saw as a safer sell.[95] In the later 1920s, the commercial companies
did begin to focus on vocal music, but for the most part they still stayed
away from the unaccompanied British ballad. They did so not out of
antipathy for America's British heritage but because they had no use for
a conception of the past as rigidly circumscribed as that set out by the
Child canon.

As the case of Peer illustrates, the record producers recognized that hillbilly music's popularity depended on its connection to a sense of tradition, but they preferred to leave this tradition murkily defined. On his field trips, Peer portrayed himself as looking for old-time traditional singers. In a 1927 interview with a Bristol, Tennessee, reporter, for instance, Peer signaled to area performers what sort of music he and the Victor company wanted: "In no section of the South have the pre-war melodies and old mountaineer songs been better preserved than in the mountains of East Tennessee and Southwest Virginia . . . and it was primarily for this reason that Victor chose Bristol as its operating base."[96] Peer recognized, though, that old-timey music need not actually be old, and certainly not as old as a fourteenth-century ballad. Primarily he wanted to record artists who were comfortable enough with traditional music to sing songs in the older *styles* that attracted hillbilly music's audiences. Rather than insisting that his performers sing specific songs from a certain period, Peer focused on getting singers who generated a certain sound that he felt would be popular. As a result, historian Nolan Porterfield notes, performers such as Jimmie Rodgers and the Carter Family (both of whom Peer "discovered" and frequently recorded) drew on both "old half-forgotten relics of the past" and "original songs that sounded like the old ones."[97] In Peer's canon, these types were equally acceptable. His eclecticism signaled an important shift from his folk-collecting predecessors: instead of enshrining specific songs as "authentic," Peer looked for adept and appealing practitioners of certain styles and elevated them into stars.

Peer and the other record company executives were able to take this new direction because, unlike previous collectors, they were not self-consciously trying to pursue and popularize a specific canon. They simply sought profits. Peer, for instance, above all concerned himself with copyrighting material. When the Victor company tried to hire him to build up its hillbilly catalog, he wrangled with them not over salary or artistic control but over song rights. Later he recalled, "I had considered the matter very carefully and [realized] that essentially this was [a] business of recording new copyrights and that I would be willing to go to work for them for nothing with the understanding that there would be no objection if I controlled these copyrights." Victor accepted Peer's terms, so his music-publishing firm, Southern Music Company, owned the rights to all the songs he chose to record.[98]

Peer's financial stake in the songs he recorded led him to adopt collecting methods that would have horrified a rigorous folklorist. To draw royalties, for instance, Peer insisted that his artists copyright the arrangements of the traditional songs they sang, even if the songs themselves were in the public domain. Peer's focus on copyright led him to encourage his performers to compose new songs, which drew higher royalties than traditional tunes. Peer recalled, "I always insisted on getting artists who could write their own music." Indeed, Peer relates that when he first recorded Jimmie Rodgers, "we ran into a snag almost immediately because . . . he was singing mostly songs originated by the New York publishers—the current hits. Actually he had only one song of his own." Peer "told Jimmie what I needed to put him over as a recording artist," and Rodgers promised to write a dozen new songs before their next session. Peer's stress on original material bore fruit. In the late 1920s Rodgers became a star—a "household name" in the small-town South— not for his versions of traditional songs but for his own hits such as "T for Texas" and "My Lovin' Gal, Lucille."[99]

Peer had no qualms about moving hillbilly musicians into the realm of popular music. In fact, he often tried to give a more pop-sounding accompaniment to Rodgers's songs. In one inauspicious effort he backed him with a lush sextet from New York, what Rodgers called an "uptown ork [orchestra]." Rather than belittling popular music, as did most folklorists, Peer saw the riches of the popular field as his ultimate goal. "I was always trying," he recalled, "to get away from the hillbilly and into the legitimate music publishing field. . . . What I was doing was to take the profits out of the hillbilly and race business and spend that money trying to get established as a pop publisher." At the end of 1928, Peer transferred control of his Southern Music Company to Victor and included in the agreement a clause whereby Victor agreed to assign him rights to all songs "of popular nature that might be recorded."[100]

With their indifference to British ballads, their openness to recent and original compositions, and their emphasis on copyrighting and selling what they collected, Peer and the other recording scouts represented a significant break from Child's academic folkloristic legacy. Even so, these commercial recorders launched trends that influenced more folkloristic song collecting. By breaking with Child's British-ballad orientation, they opened up the world of African American music and showed the diversity and richness of indigenous white folk music traditions. Equally important, their lack of interest in canon building suggested a new purpose for recording technology. Before, recording had been treated purely as a documentary convenience. Howard Odum may have recorded Mississippi blacks as early as 1904; Charles F. Lummis had recorded almost four hundred Spanish American songs in California by 1905; John Lomax used a recorder to take down cowboy songs in 1910; and Cecil Sharp, too, experimented with (and abandoned) recording in

Britain in the early 1900s.[101] All these collectors, though, primarily used the recording machine as a tool that let them take down a song and transcribe it accurately later; it enabled them to produce finer, more precise song texts.

Commercial scouts like Peer, however, had no interest in publishing a book of texts. To them, recordings were an end, not a means. When they recorded a song, they did not see it as an incremental addition to a larger canon. They were, as Bill C. Malone says, "unwitting folklorists," who saw recordings as products—products that could be mass-produced and marketed and pushed into popular culture.[102]

Most of the more academic folk song collectors studiously ignored the work of the commercial recorders.[103] But increasingly they could not avoid confronting the implications of the commercializers' work. In the late 1920s, as Al Hopkins and the Hill Billies entertained President Calvin Coolidge at a press reception (1926) and Jimmie Rodgers starred as "The Singing Brakeman" in a nationally distributed movie (1929), two folk song collectors were at work, each of whom understood better than most the possibilities and the perils involved in setting aside the Child canon and capitalizing on the vogue that "the folk" were beginning to enjoy in popular culture.[104] One was Carl Sandburg, the poet, journalist, and biographer fresh from the rich success of *Abraham Lincoln: The Prairie Years* (1926), the first two parts of what would become a classic six-volume biography. Sandburg had collected songs since, as a restless nineteen-year-old, he had left his Galesburg, Illinois, home on a romantic hoboing journey west (he hoboed back four months later).[105] On the trip, Sandburg had begun taking down song lyrics in a pocket notebook, using his own notation system to catch the melodies. By the 1920s he was in the habit of gathering songs from friends, labor leaders, folklorists, and the people who attended the endless series of lectures he gave at universities and civic clubs across the country. He usually closed each program with a quarter- or half-hour set of music, giving what he called "verbal footnotes with each song."[106] In 1926 he began work on a volume that would capture and preserve the rich variety of songs he had heard and collected. The following year he published *The American Songbag*.

At the same time, another, less popularly renowned collector was at work. Robert Winslow Gordon had first collected folk songs as an undergraduate at Harvard, where he had been a freshman in 1906, the same year John Lomax did graduate work there. Gordon went on to pursue graduate work under Lomax's mentors George Lyman Kittredge and Barrett Wendell, working for eight years on a folklore dissertation that he never finished. In 1923 he became the editor of the "Old Songs That Men Have Sung" column for *Adventure*, a middlebrow action and adventure pulp magazine. Gordon used the column to solicit and print folk songs from readers around the country, and over the next four and a half years he received more than four thousand letters.[107]

Gordon's dream, though, was to be free from any job besides song collecting. No collectors up to that point had managed to dedicate themselves so single-mindedly to the task, but in 1925, funded by his salary as an *Adventure* correspondent, a contract for ten articles from the *New York Times*, and a twelve-hundred-dollar Sheldon Fellowship from Harvard, Gordon went to Asheville, North Carolina, and began recording. Over the next three years, despite perpetual financial hardships, he made almost a thousand recordings, mostly in North Carolina and Georgia. His most significant achievement in this period, though, was to convince the head of the Library of Congress's Music Division, Carl Engel, to raise funds for a national folk song repository. In 1928 Engel announced the founding of the Archive of American Folk-Song in the Library of Congress and named Gordon its first director.[108] For the first time, America had an institution devoted solely to preserving its vernacular music.

Both Sandburg's and Gordon's work suggested the possibility of combining self-conscious effort to define an American folk song heritage (a goal absent from the work of commercial collectors like Peer) with a determination to reach a broad popular audience (an aim largely foreign to Child and his followers). Sandburg's *American Songbag*, for instance, clearly aims at a popular audience. In presenting its 280 songs, it completely ignores academic standards. It does not list the folk sources from whom Sandburg collected the songs, nor does it specify which songs came from other collectors. Instead Sandburg frames each piece with a homey note and occasional line drawings of galloping horses or a hangman's noose. More than academic precision, Sandburg cared about producing a book of "*singable* songs."[109] Accordingly he included piano accompaniments for every tune so that the book, as his publisher Alfred Harcourt wrote, "could be stood up on the piano in fraternity houses and homes for ordinary folk to play the accompaniment and the rest of the crowd to sing."[110]

Gordon shared Sandburg's interest in popularizing and in fact spent three days with the poet contributing songs for *American Songbag*. After these sessions, Gordon excitedly wrote to Carl Engel about his hopes for future work with Sandburg: "What we have in mind is directly in line with my theory that scholarship *can* and *should* combine with general popularity. . . . One of the curses of the past has been, I think, that real contributions have been hidden away in recondite journals where they were seen only by those who needed them least."[111] Gordon certainly was not dismissing the importance of scholarship—he favored what he called a "popular-scholarly" synthesis—but he, like Sandburg, envisioned an expanded audience for folk music.[112]

The key to broadening folk music's appeal, both Sandburg and Gordon felt, was to spread the word that America had an indigenous musical tradition, that American music was more than British music recycled. Neither man rejected the Child canon out of hand. On the contrary, *American Songbag* includes "Barbara Allen," "Lord Lovel," and several other Child classics. In 1927 Gordon wrote an article for the *New York Times Magazine* entitled "The Old Ballads" in which he praises ballads as "the unquestioned aristocrats of the folk-song world. They have the most poetry, the highest literary values." Even so, both Sandburg and Gordon stressed the need to move beyond the Child canon. In the same article, Gordon referred to ballads as songs whose remnants "linger" but have "no real life in them." He saw them as "not fully representative" of America's folk song heritage: "They are true folk-songs but of a limited and peculiar type," he wrote. "They occupy one tiny corner of an immense field." In a 1926 letter he described it as a "disgrace to our national scholarship" that American songs were accorded less respect than British examples. Gordon set out to rectify the balance in his series of *New York Times Magazine* articles, doing pieces on, among other forms, American banjo tunes, outlaw ballads, lumberjack songs, and fiddle tunes.[113]

Sandburg, too, stressed the need to awaken Americans to the richness of their country's heritage. In his introduction to *American Songbag* he pointedly called the book an "All-American affair" and lamented that "there are persons born and reared in this country who culturally have not yet come over from Europe." Sandburg tried to reel in these cultural expatriates by showing that America's songbag overflowed not just with British ballads but with "Prison and Jail Songs," "Hobo Songs," "Mexican Border Songs," and "Bandit Biographies."[114] The effort to awaken a sense of native heritage among Americans took on the tenor of a crusade for Sandburg. In 1928 he wrote to H. L. Mencken about *American Songbag*'s success: "My gratification about the book is merely that of a patriot who has seen his duty and done it."[115]

In expanding beyond the Child canon, though, the most significant move Sandburg and Gordon made was to include African American songs in their vision of America's musical heritage. Whereas Child's followers had ignored black music and commercial companies had segregated it in separate "race" labels, both Sandburg and Gordon treated African American songs as central to the tradition they outlined. *American Songbag*'s exuberant text never directly addresses where exactly blacks belong in the "wide human procession [that] marches through these pages," but the book matter-of-factly includes a section on African American "Blues, Mellows, Ballets," and it intersperses other black songs in the categories "Railroad and Work Gangs," "Prison and Jail Songs," and the "Road to Heaven."[116]

Gordon worked more explicitly to define an African American folk song tradition. He recorded hundreds of black tunes in the South, and he included articles on Negro shouts, chants, work songs, and spirituals in his *New York Times Magazine* series. Gordon treated African American music as a coherent tradition. He praised Negro spirituals, for instance, as "the most extensive and varied body of folk-song that is alive and growing in any civilized country today." In a significant step he placed African Americans at the center of America's folk song heritage, noting that "the negro of the South is perhaps our best folk-singer."[117]

Even as Gordon worked to move black folk song in from the margins of America's folk song canon, he was not willing to depict African Americans as the progenitors of American musical forms. Although he was continually impressed by black musical expressions, he tended to depict them as having emerged out of styles that whites had originated. Of the Negro singer Gordon wrote, "Some of his [song types]—perhaps most of them—he derived in the beginning from the whites, for he is a marvelous assimilator." To buttress this theory, Gordon focused much of his early fieldwork on looking for the "white roots to black spirituals." In 1927 he concluded,

> In their basic structure such songs are not distinctively negro, but white. In the white churches were sung "spiritual songs" of the identical type before the earliest date yet definitely ascertained for any negro spiritual. The negro adopted, assimilated, made over. But his basic technique, very many of his actual words and couplets, even in certain cases his original tunes, he undoubtedly obtained from listening at white church meetings. In fact he took the very name "spiritual" from whites.[118]

Even though he embraced black music, there were limits to Gordon's acceptance of racial difference.

Overall, Gordon's and Sandburg's more inclusive canon of American song illustrates how much had changed since Child formulated his academic, manuscript-derived, text-based canon of white, British ballads. But Gordon's unwillingness to credit fully blacks' creativity points to a pattern that runs through both his and Sandburg's work: as far-reaching as Gordon and Sandburg were, each remained in some ways wedded to the traditional ways in which folk song collectors had worked since before the turn of the century. Old-fashioned aspects latent in their work in the end prevented them from moving folk song out of the insular world of academics and antiquarians and into popular culture.

In their approach to preserving American folk songs, both Gordon and Sandburg represented a complicated mixture of innovation and anachronism. Gordon, for example, was perhaps the first collector to recognize the phonograph's potential as a tool in building a folk song canon. In a grandiose proposal to "survey the entire field" of American folk music, Gordon recognized that such a trip would be worthwhile only if he returned not with texts but with "actual phonograph recordings of the songs in the exact dialect and intonation of the singers."[119] The future of collecting, he saw, lay with recordings because they were the only means by which he could secure a present-day hearing for the songs he collected and leave an accessible legacy to the future. Gordon's ambitious plans for his field trip fell apart, undermined by both fundraising problems and the technological limits of contemporary recording equipment, but he continued restlessly to tinker with recording technology, hoping to find "something that [was] capable not only of reproducing acceptably for an audience" but a form that would be "permanent."[120] Within a decade, after advancements in recording technology made portable recorders more feasible, the phonograph began to realize the potential that Gordon had foreseen for it.

Technological limitations and tight wallets, though, only partly account for the failure of most of Gordon's projects to get off the ground. Gordon had trouble winning backers for his far-reaching plans because he had not mastered the modern tools of promotion. Despite his avowed interest in popularizing folk song, Gordon showed a singular inability to publicize and rally support for his causes. Like Francis Child, Gordon remained oriented toward improving and expanding his collection. In his few interactions with popular audiences, such as his stint with *Adventure*, Gordon tended to focus less on sparking their interest in folk song than on gathering from them material for his collection.[121] He had not grasped what Ralph Peer, as shown by his careful handling of Jimmie Rodgers, plainly had—that in a modern media culture, for folk music to gather momentum and to take on a life of its own, it needed a star. A canon based on anonymous songs and texts was too bloodless, lacking the human element that could turn a scholarly enthusiasm into a revival. Gordon treated collecting as a private obsession instead of a popular crusade.

Gordon's absorption in his own collection translated directly into difficulties as chief of the Library of Congress's Archive of American Folk-Song. He arrived in Washington completely focused on using his new-found position as a salaried archivist to collect songs with the freedom for which he had yearned. As his biographer, Debora Kodish, writes, when Gordon came to the library, "he remained occupied with the same kind of research that had brought him this far. He believed he had earned the right to do things his own way" and held onto his "aims, goals, methods, and principles intact."[122] Gordon, therefore, made no effort to put the library's bureaucracy to work for him. For long stretches he pursued his own projects on his own timetable and neither updated his superiors on his progress nor tried to galvanize his small staff. Gordon felt that the importance of his work justified such independent habits, but in a bureaucratic institution like the library, these habits began to jeopardize the very work Gordon treasured.

Although under the aegis of the Library of Congress, the Archive of American Folk-Song in its early years depended entirely on private funding.[123] When the Great Depression hit, funds began to dry up. The library was having trouble convincing new donors to fund the archive's work, and Gordon did little to help the cause. He almost forced the archive to forfeit a grant from the American Council of Learned Societies because he ignored the ACLS's schedule for completing a recording and photostating project. The head of the music division, out of money, frustrated with Gordon's behavior, and under the impression, rightly or wrongly, that Gordon was doing little in the archive, informed him in March 1932 that he would not be retained at the end of the fiscal year.[124]

Unlike Gordon, Sandburg was a master of self-promotion. He realized that in trying to popularize American folk songs, presentation was at least as important as substance. Even though 180 out of 280 songs in *American Songbag* had been published previously by other collectors, Sandburg gave them fresh appeal by arranging them under lively headings—"Picnic and Hayrack Follies, Close Harmony, and Darn Fool Ditties," "Lovely People," "Tarnished Love Tales or Colonial and Revolutionary Antiques"—and by using an evocative writing style to place each song in a setting as vivid and dramatic as a film's. He introduced "The Midnight Train," for instance, with an image of "railroad trains hurtling with smoke, fire, and thunder across peaceful landscapes at night, rushing remorseless as fate along the iron rail pathways." To set up "Turkey in the Straw" he wrote, "On mornings when frost was on the pumpkin and the fodder in the shock, when nuts were ripe and winter apples ready for

The folklorist as media personality: Front cover of Carl Sandburg's American Songbag, *1927. (Yale Collection of American Literature, Beinecke Rare Book and Manuscript Library)*

picking, it echoed amid the horizons of the Muskingum river of Ohio and the Ozark foothills of Missouri."[125]

Vibrant writing alone, though, could not deliver Sandburg's folk tunes into mainstream popularity. Unlike Gordon, Sandburg seems to have realized that he needed a star to serve as the exemplar and expositor of folk traditions. He chose himself. In the steady stream of poetry, journalism, film reviews, biographies, children's stories, and songbooks he produced in the 1920s, Sandburg constructed himself as the plain-speaking common man—the "voice of the Middle West," said British novelist Rebecca West—who "has learned his country by heart." He traveled the country on his lecture tours, spouting homespun yarns, poems, Lincoln anecdotes, and, of course, songs. The Lincoln biography, published in 1926, propelled him to new levels of popularity for a literary figure. In its first year, the 962-page two-volume work sold forty-eight thousand copies at ten dollars each and made Sandburg a national celebrity. Instead of recoiling from this rush of fame, Sandburg employed new image-building media to capitalize on it. In 1926 he gave a half-hour radio speech in Chicago for Lincoln's birthday. That same year he both took advantage of the Lincoln book's success and promoted the forthcoming *American Songbag*, by making a recording of Lincoln songs for RCA Victor.[126] Sandburg the folk song collector helped Sandburg the folk song popularizer by being folk singer and folk hero as well. When *American Songbag* came out in 1927, it did not have a quaint log cabin on its cover but a picture of Sandburg.

Although he had a sure instinct for modern publicity and promotion, Sandburg remained decidedly old-fashioned in his song-collecting methods. Unlike Gordon, he failed to see that the future of collecting pointed toward new technologies. In his methods Sandburg was still fundamentally part of the old songbook tradition. In gathering songs, he either drew on published sources, solicited donations from friends, or scribbled down notes and lyrics as he heard a folk singer sing them. Then he published his collection in a book aimed at amateur pianists. Sandburg's 1926 recording of Lincoln songs indicates that he understood that phonograph records could enable a popularizer to reach a mainstream audience, but he does not seem to have foreseen the power recordings could have when used in fieldwork. For him, collecting remained a writing-based task. He did not realize that if field collectors pursued recordings, not song transcriptions, new possibilities opened up for popularizing folk traditions. With the unprecedented sense of immediacy that field recordings provided, audiences could embrace not just specific folk songs but the folk themselves.

By the late 1920s, Ralph Peer and the commercial race and hillbilly series, Robert Gordon and the Archive of American Folk-Song, and Carl Sandburg and his best-selling *American Songbag* had all made some inroads into America's popular culture. As the thirties began, though, not one of them had managed at the same time to articulate a canon of American folk music, use modern technology to document systematically and preserve this body of song, and employ the techniques of modern mass communication to popularize his vision of America's musical roots.

CREATING THE
CULT OF AUTHENTICITY
THE LOMAXES AND
LEAD BELLY

The winter of 1932 was bleak for John Lomax. In the past year his wife had died, and, with personal distress compounded by the strain of the depression, he had been forced to leave his bank job, telling his boss that he could no longer fulfill his duties adequately.[1] Needing a fresh start, he resolved to return to the vocation he truly loved, collecting American folk music. He decided to do a lecture tour to reintroduce himself into folk song circles and to promote his *Cowboy Songs* book, which, although more than twenty years old now, had been reprinted in 1929. By the spring, after a desperate letter-writing campaign to hundreds of colleges, high schools, and clubs around the country, he had enough engagements to justify a car tour. He enlisted his son John Jr., then twenty-four, to accompany him and aid in driving, selling books, and setting up camp.[2] In March 1932 they left from Dallas. Following the lecture schedule Lomax had arranged, and accepting whatever new engagements presented themselves along the way, they made their way by June to New England, where they picked up Lomax's youngest son, seventeen-year-old Alan. The three Lomaxes then embarked on a cross-country tour that would last the rest of the summer and would lay the groundwork for an American folk music revival.

The Lomaxes' experiences on this trip are preserved in a logbook that first John Jr. and then Alan kept throughout the journey. Its frontispiece shows the handwritten title, "30,000 miles by Cowboy song." On the adjacent page, John Jr., who seems to have brought his thesaurus along for the ride, wrote, "Herein are set down the experiences of the Lomaxes who peregrinated in 1932."

Peregrination can be hard. Book sales were sluggish on the trip—three sold here; four there; only occasionally as many as six. Inevitably, there were also strains between father and sons as the three spent months together in close quarters. After a day of driving and many flat tires, Alan wrote, "The tension between us grew almost too great to endure." These stresses were compounded by a current of political tension that pitted the elder Lomax, an Old South conservative, against his youngest son. The journal is dotted with references to heated debates in the car about "Alan's Communist friends" and his supposed "communistic activities."[3]

For all these difficulties, the Lomaxes seem never to have doubted their devotion to the music they were promoting. Indeed, for young Alan the trip was an eye-opening experience that introduced him to folk music's emotional power. A performance at the Taos Pueblo particularly moved him. In the logbook he wrote: "First we heard the tom-tom, distantly thumping, beaten by hands out of darkness. Then a strong man's voice in a wolf-shout began a tune; others took it up in harmony. They sang in perfect unison. Down the creek another group began a different tune that blended with and accentuated the first. [Through] both ran the rhythm thread of the tom-toms. The music was old and stirred one to fight, to make love violently." The Lomaxes did not have a recording machine with them on this trip, but even in his state of excitement, young Alan's thoughts turned to preserving this music for posterity. He wrote, "The rough, powerful voice of the men chanting in harmony from the gloom of the thickets on the creek howls excited men all over the pueblo. They shouted and joined in the chant.—Someday Alan will come with his recording outfit and can that music."

By August the three reached Los Angeles, where they took a few days off to watch the 1932 Olympics. Pasted into the logbook are black-and-white photos, taken from the stands, of a tiny figure crossing the finish line. The handwritten caption notes Babe Didrikson winning the fifty-yard low hurdles in world record time. The underlying strains within the family surfaced briefly in the two-hundred-meter dash. Alan wrote,

"Tolan and Metcalfe, black, loaf . . . and still break World's and Olympic records that have stood for 28 years. Father was half-chagrined, half pleased. Alan triumphant. The two negros settled the race problem for that afternoon." As the Lomaxes turned back toward Texas, though, these tensions for the most part did not intrude. They arrived home at least as committed to folk song as when they had left. But they were not significantly more well known or better established professionally. In the logbook's last entry Alan wrote, "Father and Alan know nothing of the future, even ten days ahead. They are homeless, jobless, and have no expectations. Let the curtain fall upon this woeful last scene. So ends this log."[4]

This doleful ending, though, turned out to be only the beginning for what would become the most spectacularly successful and innovative folk song–collecting team of the twentieth century. Unbeknownst to the Lomaxes themselves, the summer expedition of 1932 amounted to a test run. Over the next decade, John Sr. and Alan would travel tens of thousands of miles and make thousands of recordings.[5] They did so not with the detachment of academics but with the zeal of proselytizers. Eager to promote their vision of America's musical past, they recognized early on the power of enlisting living vernacular musicians—"actual folk"—to aid their cause. In a pioneering move, the Lomaxes began to promote not just the songs they gathered but the singers who sang them. In doing so they produced a web of criteria for determining what a "true" folk singer looked and sounded like and a set of assumptions about the importance of *being* a "true" folk singer. In short, they created a "cult of authenticity," a thicket of expectations and valuations that American roots musicians and their audiences have been negotiating ever since.

When Alan Lomax gave his woeful assessment of his and his father's prospects in 1932, he left out one potential bright spot. In June, John Lomax had persuaded the Macmillan publishing company to contract for a book of folk songs.[6] In 1933 Lomax used this contract to draw support for a collecting expedition. The American Council of Learned Societies and the Library of Congress's Archive of American Folk-Song contributed funds that enabled Lomax to order one of the first portable electronic recording machines for the trip. The archive, now leaderless, having dismissed Robert Gordon, agreed to be the official repository for the materials Lomax gathered.[7] Having again enlisted Alan as his assistant, in June 1933 Lomax loaded his Ford with "two army cots and bedding, a cooking outfit, provisions, [and] an infinite number of 'etceteras.'" After a delay, the Lomaxes added to this miscellany the 350-

Recording equipment in the back of John Lomax's car, probably late 1930s.
(Library of Congress)

pound "portable" Dictaphone recorder, which they built into the back
seat. It came with two seventy-five-pound batteries, a microphone, cables, and piles of blank aluminum and celluloid disks.[8] Carrying this load,
the Ford lumbered off, and the Lomaxes began their hunt for America's
folk songs.

The Lomaxes had a complicated agenda for this expedition. Their
collecting methods and attitude make the trip, from today's perspective,
seem part talent search, part sociological survey, and part safari. Primarily they sought traditional folk music in the "eddies of human society," self-contained homogeneous communities cut off from the corrupting influences of popular culture.[9] Mainstream communities, the
Lomaxes feared, had lost touch with their folk roots. As historian Joe
Klein writes, "Instead of listening to Grandma sing 'Barbara Allen' on
the back porch, the kids—and often Grandma too—were listening to
Bing Crosby on the radio." The Lomaxes hoped to find the old styles
"dammed up" in America's more isolated areas. They collected from
remote cotton plantations, cowboy ranches, lumber camps, and, with
particular success, southern segregated prisons. John Lomax believed
that prisons had inadvertently done folklorists a service by isolating
groups of informants from modern society. On their 1933 trip, the Lomaxes recorded in the penitentiaries of five states, as they sought to

document "the Negro who had the least contact with jazz, the radio, and with the white man. . . . The convicts heard only the idiom of their own race."[10]

Recording in a prison was not a simple proposition. Usually Lomax would write the warden in advance, soliciting likely prospects.[11] Upon arrival, though, the Lomaxes would audition as many singers as they could. Lomax painted a vivid picture of this process in a letter to his future second wife, Ruby Terrill. He wrote that he was listening to the prisoner nicknamed "Lifetime" sing while "over in a corner . . . Alan is trying out a heavy-jawed negro, appropriately named Bull-dog (we test out voices and songs before recording the songs). The interested and curious men in stripes crowd around, while the guards look on conde-scendingly, sometimes with amused tolerance."[12]

After selecting the best singers, the Lomaxes would set up their re-cording equipment and, usually with Alan manning the controls, have the prisoners sing for the machine. The recording session might take place under a shady tree or in a barn with bales of hay improving the acoustics.[13] Sometimes, though, conditions were more difficult for both the Lomaxes and the prisoners. John Lomax recounted to Ruby Terrill their experience at the Parchman Convict Farm in Mississippi: "The men convicts work from 4 a.m. until dark. Thus our chance at them comes only during the noon hour or at night before the lights are turned out at 9 o'clock. These periods are strenuous for us, for each group is timid, suspicious, sometimes stubborn and of no help whatsoever." At the end of their day the Lomaxes often would return to their car, either to drive by night to a new recording site or to camp by the roadside.[14]

Early on in the 1933 trip the Lomaxes were convinced of the value of their efforts. One of the first people they recorded was an African Amer-ican singer and guitarist named Huddie Ledbetter, or "Lead Belly."[15] The Lomaxes "discovered" Lead Belly, roughly forty-four years old at the time, in Louisiana's Angola prison, where he was serving out a sentence for murder. Lead Belly astonished the Lomaxes with the variety of songs he knew and the verve and virtuosity with which he played them. He seemed to be a living link to traditions that were slipping away, a store-house of old-time songs greater than they had thought possible to find in the twentieth century. John Lomax would later write, "From Lead Belly we secured about one hundred songs that seemed 'folky,' a far greater number than from any other person." Although Lead Belly did know some popular songs, the Lomaxes felt that "his eleven years of confine-ment had cut him off both from the phonograph and from the radio."[16] The Lomaxes had stumbled upon the folk song find of their dreams.

Prison Compound No. 1, Angola, La., 1934. Lead Belly appears in the middle foreground to the left. (Library of Congress)

Lead Belly inspired such excitement in the Lomaxes because he confirmed their most basic assumptions about American folk song, assumptions that may now seem commonplace but that in the early thirties represented decisive blows against the still powerful Child canon. The variety of songs that Lead Belly knew, for instance, nicely illustrated for the Lomaxes that America did have a folk song heritage independent of Britain. Even more so than Carl Sandburg and Robert Gordon, the Lomaxes were determined to praise America's indigenous music, refusing to apologize for its supposed inadequacy.[17] In *Our Singing Country* (1941), they wrote that America's artists "have created and preserved for America a heritage of folksongs and folk music equal to any in the world."[18]

As an exemplar of the African American song tradition, Lead Belly vividly illustrated that one need not be an English peasant to sing folk songs. On the 1933 trip, John Lomax was quite aware that in recording African American music he and Alan were displacing the Anglo-dominated folk music canon. He wrote Ruby Terrill about a "handsome

Lead Belly in prison (Angola, La.), July 1934.
(Library of Congress)

mulatto woman" who sang a spiritual for them in Texas: "Soon Alan had recorded the music and, possibly, a new musical theme had been added to our small American stock; for, to me and to Alan, there was depth and grace and beauty; quick power and dignity; and a note of weird almost uncanny suggestion of turgid, slow-moving rivers in African jungles."[19] Setting aside for the moment Lomax's sensationalized style, for him to

John A. Lomax, portrait by J. Anthony Wills, ca. 1964. (John Avery Lomax Family Papers, CN 10042, The Center for American History, University of Texas at Austin)

locate black songs in the center of America's folk song canon marked a significant step in the early thirties. In the book that resulted from their 1933 trip, *American Ballads and Folk Songs* (1934), the Lomaxes stated matter-of-factly that blacks created "the most distinctive of folk songs— the most interesting, the most appealing, and the greatest in quantity."[20]

Beyond illustrating the richness of America's musical traditions, Lead

Belly's immense repertoire lent credence to the Lomaxes' assertions that these traditions remained very much alive in contemporary America. Challenging Child and Sharp, they dismissed notions that an authentic folk song must be hundreds of years old and that only fragments of true folk culture survived in contemporary society. The Lomaxes depicted a much more robust folk tradition. They argued that traditional American music remained vibrant, creative, and essential to American life. Alan Lomax urged Americans to fight "the tendency . . . to begin to regard [folk] culture as static—to leave out of consideration its living quality (present and past)." In a lecture to the Progressive Education Association in 1940, he told the audience of his desire "to convince you and to convince you so that you could never be unconvinced that there is, was, and will be something here that is in American folk music to be looked into; and . . . that there is enough to go around for a long, long, time."[21] Lead Belly allowed the Lomaxes to make such statements with confidence and to illustrate them dynamically. Because he sang indigenous American songs, was rooted in the precommercial past, and yet was vibrantly connected to the present, he personified the Lomaxes' challenge to the Child canon.

The Lomaxes succeeded as canon makers, though, not just because they embraced performers with the repertoire and style of Lead Belly. At least as important as how they defined the new American folk canon were the ways in which they preserved and popularized its exemplars. First of all, the Lomaxes rejected Child's manuscript-based collecting and instead relied almost completely on fieldwork. A living oral tradition, they believed, could not be captured in a Harvard library. One must go out among the folk to find folk songs.

In an extension of this desire to collect directly from folk sources, the Lomaxes turned to the recording machine. Folklorists such as Robert Gordon and John Lomax himself had used recorders before, but in the 1930s the Lomaxes employed superior technology, recorded far more widely, and embraced the recording medium with more passion than previous collectors. No written document, the Lomaxes felt, could capture the full flavor and intricacy of a folk performance, and the process of transcription relied too much on human skill and judgment to be accurate. Even dedicated transcribers like Sharp, they concluded, could not do justice to the subtlety and emotion that a Lead Belly brought to his songs. On their trips, the Lomaxes relied exclusively on the recording machine to take down songs, always experimenting with new techniques and technologies in the hope of achieving a less distorted sound. The recorder, they believed, removed the collector as a source of bias and captured all of a song's nuances. Instead of a scholar's representation of a song, the machine preserved a folk singer's entire performance, unadulterated. As Alan Lomax recalled, using the recorder on the 1933 trip "meant that for the first time there was a way to stick a pipeline right down into the heart of the folks where they were and let them come on like they felt."[22]

Aside from producing more lifelike renditions of songs, then, the recording machine enabled the Lomaxes to downplay their role in the collecting process. John Lomax accentuated this point, stressing that he was "innocent of musical knowledge, entirely without musical training." He saw his ignorance as a distinct advantage, recalling that the head of the Library of Congress's music division had urged him, "Don't take any musicians along with you: what the Library wants is the machine's record of Negro singing, and not some musician's interpretation of it." At the end of his first summer of recording, Lomax concluded that he had successfully maintained his studied detachment from the recording process. He saw the 150 tunes he had come home with as "sound photographs of Negro songs, rendered in their own element, unrestrained, uninfluenced and undirected by anyone who had his own notions of how the songs should be rendered."[23]

In idealizing the recording machine, the Lomaxes tapped into what historian William Stott has called the "documentary motive" of the thirties. As George E. Marcus and Michael M. J. Fischer explain, "There was a hunger for reliable information, a widespread suspicion that newspapers were manipulating the news, . . . and a simple unavailability of public facts."[24] In this context, the recorder appealed as an incontrovertible source of truth. How could a recording machine lie?

In addition to making more effective use of the recording machine, the Lomaxes began to realize the potential of the Archive of American Folk-Song. Like Gordon, the Lomaxes had secured the archive as a repository for the recordings they collected. But the Lomaxes had a much stronger sense than their predecessor of the power and possibilities that the archive offered collectors. Gordon had used his position at the archive primarily as a base from which to pursue his own private collecting work. The Lomaxes, though, realized that government backing for their enterprise could give it added credibility. They used the archive not simply as a storage place for their recordings but as a credentializing institution, a way to link their personal musical tastes to a sense of national mission. Having the Library of Congress behind them made it easier for the Lomaxes to attract folk musicians to record and to secure a hearing for the music after they recorded it. When requesting permission to collect in prisons, for example, John Lomax always emphasized his position as honorary curator at the archive. His association with the nation's library gave him access that might otherwise have been denied.

The Lomaxes' Washington links impressed not only prison officials but folk informants as well. In a time in which the federal government under President Roosevelt played such a visible role in Americans' lives, any connection to the capital had considerable power. Alan Lomax later recounted the story of an African American singer in 1933 who refused to sing in advance the song he wanted the Lomaxes to record. Normally the Lomaxes tried to conserve blank cylinders by auditioning singers first, but this man said, "No sir, you are going to have to have this right from the beginning." The Lomaxes eventually agreed, and the man sang,

Work all week
Don't make enough
To pay my board
And buy my snuff.

After a few more stanzas, the man said, "Now, Mr. President, you just don't know how bad they're treating us folks down here. I'm singing to you and I'm talking to you so I hope you will come down here and do something for us poor folks here in Texas."[25] Harnessing the power and appeal of the recording machine and of the federal government, the Lomaxes succeeded in collecting thousands of folk songs in the thirties.

Beyond the Lomaxes' considerable skill at collecting vernacular music, what truly separated them from their predecessors was their ingenuity at popularizing it. In the twenties, Ralph Peer and Carl Sandburg had been attentive to the possibilities of using publicity to generate interest in old-time music. But Peer, for all his influence, had not articulated a unified vision of American music—he had not tried to shape the way America remembered its musical past. And Sandburg, for all the hype he generated, had not recognized the fascination that folk figures could generate in a modern industrialized culture—he had chosen himself to be the star figure who would personify folk traditions. The Lomaxes were the first to use "actual folk" to promote a coherent vision of America's folk music heritage. To promote their canon they relied not on a popular interpreter of folk songs but on exemplars from the folk culture itself. They enlisted the full array of mass media—newspapers, radio, movie newsreels, concerts, and records—to transform rural folk musicians into celebrities. In effect they spread their vision of American music by integrating folk into mass culture.

The Lomaxes' efforts to popularize representatives from folk culture added an element that became central to the folk music revival of the thirties and to every burst of interest in roots music since then—an impression of authenticity. In some ways, of course, this appeal was nothing new. The supposed purity and simplicity of the music had been what attracted the earliest collectors of roots music and what interpreters like Sandburg had capitalized on. But by dispensing with the second-hand interpreters and foregrounding the rural musicians who created the folk music, the Lomaxes added a new source of authenticity—the performers themselves. Purity now was attributed not just to specific folk songs (e.g., Child ballads) but to the folk figures who sang them. Audiences and critics began to assess roots musicians with new standards.

The Lomaxes' handling of Lead Belly helped spur this fascination with a folk performer's authenticity. Lead Belly was released from prison in 1934. A popular story, spread widely by the Lomaxes in the thirties and forties, says that Lead Belly was freed because the Lomaxes delivered his stirring musical appeal to Louisiana's governor, who was moved to commute his sentence. The Lomaxes did make a second visit to Lead Belly in prison in June 1934, and they did record his "Governor O.K. Allen" song, but prison documents show that Lead Belly actually won his release for good behavior.[26] Upon his release, Lead Belly was eager to pursue a postprison musical career, and the Lomaxes, having found a living example of the noncommercial tradition they prized, could not stand to allow their discovery to remain in the Louisiana backcountry. Early in 1935, therefore, the Lomaxes took Lead Belly to New York City.[27] There they recorded scores of his songs for the Archive of American Folk-Song, booked appearances for him at concerts, took him on a lecture-recital tour of eastern colleges (in which John Lomax explicated the songs Lead Belly sang), and arranged commercial recording sessions for him.

Most striking, upon arriving in New York the Lomaxes launched a publicity blitz, promoting Lead Belly as the folk song find of the century. This media campaign essentially relied on two strategies to establish Lead Belly's authenticity—strategies seemingly at odds. On the one hand, the Lomaxes depicted Lead Belly as the living embodiment of America's folk song tradition, a time capsule that had preserved the pure voice of the people. Often this strategy involved counterposing Lead Belly's "pure" music to its inferior modern descendants. At Lead Belly's New York debut (at a hotel luncheon for University of Texas alumni) John Lomax explained: "Northern people hear Negroes playing and singing beautiful spirituals which are too refined and unlike the true southern spirituals. Or else they hear men and women on the stage and radio, burlesquing their own songs. Lead Belly doesn't burlesque. He plays and sings with absolute sincerity. . . . I've heard his songs a hundred times, but I always get a thrill. To me his music is real music." The press picked up on this strain of Lead Belly's appeal. An article chronicling his March 1935 appearance at Harvard observed: "There is but slight resemblance between his singing and that of the stage and radio singers. There is a deep primitive quality to Lead Belly's songs." The *New York Post*, likewise, praised his music's "perfect simplicity."[28]

Often this emphasis on Lead Belly's musical purity extended into broader statements about his cultural authenticity. The *World Telegram*, for example, proclaimed that Lead Belly was "living history," while the *Post* dubbed him "a new American original." A 1935 *March of Time* newsreel used symbolism to make the same point. At the end of the dramatization, in which Lomax and Lead Belly reenact Lomax's "discovery" of the singer, a heavy voice-over announces that "Hailed by the Library of Congress . . . Lead Belly's songs go into the archives of the great national institution." The camera shows the Archive of American Folk-Song and then, as the music fades out, moves to a close-up of the Declaration of Independence.[29]

At the same time, though, that the Lomaxes ennobled Lead Belly as an authentic folk forefather, they thoroughly exoticized him. Their publicity campaign depicted him as a savage, untamed animal and focused endlessly on his convict past. Long after Lead Belly had been freed, Lomax had him perform in his old convict clothes, "for exhibition purposes, . . . though he always hated to wear them."[30] At the Modern Language Association Lomax arranged for Lead Belly to sing his "raw folk songs" while "seated on the top center of the banquet table," a performance, Lomax noted, that "shocked his hearers into attention."[31] The posed photograph on the frontispiece of the Lomaxes' 1936 biography, *Negro Folk Songs As Sung by Lead Belly*, shows Lead Belly in overalls rolled up to reveal bare feet, with a handkerchief tied around his neck. Sitting on canvas sacks, he is playing guitar, with his head tilted back, eyes wide, and mouth open to show a tooth missing.

In describing Lead Belly, John Lomax consistently stressed his rapacity. Shortly before taking Lead Belly to the North, Lomax wrote a letter previewing his coming attraction for the papers: "Leadbelly is a nigger to the core of his being. In addition he is a killer. He tells the truth only accidentally. . . . He is as sensual as a goat, and when he sings to me my spine tingles and sometimes tears come. Penitentiary wardens all tell me that I set no value on my life in using him as a traveling companion. I am thinking of bringing him to New York in January."[32] Similarly, in *Negro Folk Songs* the Lomaxes stress that Lead Belly "had served time in a Texas

Lead Belly, shown in the frontispiece to Negro Folk Songs as
Sung by Lead Belly, *1936. Exoticizing the singer only added to his authenticity.*
(Photograph by Otto Hesse)

penitentiary for murder; . . . he had thrice been a fugitive from justice; . . .
he was the type known as 'killer' and had a career of violence the record
of which is a black epic of horrifics." When Lomax first arrived in New
York, he introduced Lead Belly to reporters by explaining that he "was a
'natural,' who had no idea of money, law, or ethics and who was pos-
sessed of virtually no restraint."[33]

Lead Belly, 1942. Contemporaries recall Lead Belly as an immaculate dresser.
(Library of Congress, Charles Todd Collection)

Others who worked with Lead Belly in the thirties and forties dispute this portrait of him. Most people who met him commented on his gentleness. Pete Seeger remembers him as soft voiced, meticulously dressed, and "wonderful with children." Seeger found it "hard to believe the stories we read of his violent youth."[34] Producer Moses Asch recalls that his first impression was Lead Belly's "overall aristocratic appearance and demeanor."[35] Lead Belly had enough of an "idea of money," moreover, to demand that John Lomax give him control over the revenues from his concerts. For the first eight months or so that he was with the Lomaxes, they used him as their chauffeur and house servant. He drove the car on their collecting expeditions and to and from concert engagements, and he did chores around the Lomax home in Wilton, Connecticut. The Lomaxes kept two-thirds of Lead Belly's concert earnings and deducted room and board from the remainder. Lead Belly angrily challenged this arrangement (brandishing a knife) in March 1935, and a shaken John Lomax put him on a bus back to Shreveport, Louisiana. Lead Belly promptly hired a lawyer to press for compensation. Lomax eventually paid a lump sum to settle the matter.[36]

Regardless of the inaccuracies in their portrayal, the Lomaxes' emphasis on Lead Belly's "Otherness" seems to have been strikingly effective. The *New York Herald-Tribune* responded to the Lomaxes' publicity campaign with the headline "Sweet Singer of the Swamplands Here to Do a Few Tunes between Homicides," prompting John Lomax to reflect that "his criminal record was securing a hearing for a Negro musician" and that "the terms 'bad nigger' only added to his attraction." The next year the *Tribune* followed up with "Ebon, Shufflin' Anthology of Swampland Folksong Inhales Gin, Exhales Rhyme." Routinely the press in the thirties described Lead Belly with epithets like "two-time Dixie murderer," "[Lomax's] murderous protégé," or "two-time killer, who twice sang his way out of jail." In a typical story, the *Brooklyn Eagle* announced Lead Belly's wedding (a major media event organized by the Lomaxes) by reporting, "Lead Belly, the Louisiana swamplands Negro equally proficient with knife or guitar, is happy today in the knowledge that Martha Promise . . . , who sheltered him between prison sentences, is with him again." Such excesses were by no means confined to tabloid presses. In his 1936 ode to Lead Belly, published in the *New Yorker*, the poet William Rose Benét (Stephen Vincent's older brother) marveled,

> He was big and he was black
> And wondrous were his wrongs
> But he had a memory travelled back
> Through at least five hundred songs.

In reviewing *Negro Folk Songs*, the Texan folklorist J. Frank Dobie offered a particularly striking description of a Lead Belly performance:

> His way before an audience [was] to sit quiet and relaxed, this man
> of terrible energy, turning over in his mind God alone knows what

thoughts; then at the signal, to let loose his hands and his voice. He crouched over his guitar as he played, . . . and he sang with an intensity and passion that swayed audiences who could not understand a single word of his songs. His eyes were tight-shut so that between his eyebrows there appeared deep furrows of concentration curving back like devil's horns.[37]

In his public persona, then, Lead Belly seems to have been cast as both archetypal ancestor and demon—and to have been convincing as the real thing in each role. These conflicting personas illustrate a dynamic that has characterized the cult of authenticity ever since. Revival audiences yearn to identify with folk figures, but that identification is premised on difference. Roots musicians are expected to be premodern, unrestrainedly emotive, and noncommercial. Singers who too closely resemble the revival's middle-class audiences are rejected by those audiences as "inauthentic." Generally, then, the most popular folk figures— those with whom revival audiences most identify—are those who have passed a series of tests of their "Otherness."

The Lomaxes' handling of Lead Belly resonated with a current of primitivism that ran through early-twentieth-century modernism. Avantgarde writers, artists, and intellectuals used "the primitive" as a source of imagery, metaphors, and behavior patterns that fulfilled personal longings and enabled cultural critiques. Picasso and the cubists incorporated the stark geometries of African sculptures in their work. Art collectors and intellectuals (including Freud) sought out these sculptures for their galleries and studies. In *Heart of Darkness* (1913), Joseph Conrad used a ride down the Congo to signify his exploration of the darkest depths of the human soul. Both the 1893 Columbian Exposition in Chicago and the 1904 World's Fair in St. Louis put "primitive" tribes on display. Beginning in 1912, Edgar Rice Burroughs masterfully moved the fascination with the primitive into popular culture with his wildly successful series of Tarzan novels.[38] Often these appropriations of the primitive were based on extremely limited knowledge of non-Western societies. The modernists' representations of the primitive said as much about their own artistic visions and personal fantasies as about the people whose culture they purported to depict. "The primitive" became a symbol that could encompass violence, sex, irrationality, and, at the same time, noble innocence and childlike naïveté.

While modernist artists tended to discover the primitive without leaving their studios, turn-of-the-century anthropologists took the search more literally. In the late 1800s, extended fieldwork became more expected within the profession, and extended sojourns with isolated peoples became rites of passage for young anthropologists.[39] After the turn of the century, such missions increasingly set out to undermine the racist assumptions that had so often underlain depictions of non-Western societies. Columbia University professor Franz Boas, in particular, pioneered a relativistic approach to culture. Dominating the anthropological discipline for much of the first half of the century, Boas and his students attacked dichotomies between "savage" and "civilized" as simplistic divisions based on artificial Western values. They favored looking at each society on its own terms, charting cultural roles and rituals without passing judgment on whether they were "primitive" or "advanced." The relativists' goal, historian George Stocking summarizes, was to "account for human variability in all its aspects."[40]

The Boasians, though, were hardly dispassionate data gatherers. Their interest in documenting variability was very much counterposed to what threatened that variability—the spread of Western, industrialized culture across the globe. Margaret Mead recalled that as an undergraduate in 1922 she chose anthropology (rather than psychology or sociology) because fellow Boas student Ruth Benedict convinced her that "anthropology had to be done *now*. Other things could wait."[41] Boas and his followers saw their work as a cultural salvage mission.

The Lomaxes, then, in pursuing culture in the "eddies of human society" (and in expressing both fascination and fear at what they found there), were engaging in an exploration of "Otherness" that had deep roots. Emerging from these antecedents, the search for the "primitive" took on an especially rich and idiosyncratic inflection during the Great Depression. Many Americans in the period mistrusted business and political leaders and blamed them for the hard times. Henrietta Yurchenco, a public radio producer in the thirties, remembers feeling that "in the cataclysmic climate of the Depression, who was foolish enough to trust government spokesmen, the rich and powerful who had a stake in the status quo?"[42] In this environment, the Lomaxes' depictions of Lead Belly as both everyman and outlaw tapped into what one might call the "outsider populism" of the period—a tendency in the thirties to locate America's strength and vibrancy in the margins of society. The depression had caused many Americans to reevaluate what forces in society were good, powerful, and sustaining. The economic collapse had led to speculations about weaknesses in the national character, questions about whether the country had lost touch with the spirit that had once, many Americans felt, made it great. Many romanticized a mythical time in the past when Americans were more vigorous, more honorable, and more self-sufficient.

In this atmosphere, middle-class Americans were drawn to people who seemed to exist outside the modern industrial world, able to survive independent of its inhumane economy and not lulled by its superficial luxuries. Figures of the outcast, the folk, the impoverished, and the dispossessed fascinated Americans. The common person was glorified in a wide variety of media in the thirties—in novels such as Steinbeck's *Grapes of Wrath*, in the Chicago School's urban sociology, in plays such as Clifford Odets's *Waiting for Lefty*, and in the post office murals commissioned by the Works Progress Administration. Most poignantly, perhaps, the documentary photography of the Resettlement Administration, the photojournalism of *Life* and *Look* magazines, and the "I've-Seen-America" books of Margaret Bourke-White and James Agee and Walker Evans portrayed the strength and forthrightness of downtrodden men and women who leveled their steady gaze at the camera.[43]

There is, of course, an oxymoronic quality inherent to "outsider populism": how can one build populism around those outside "the people"? The outsiders appealed, though, because they reminded Americans of themselves—or of how they wanted to see themselves: independent, proud in the face of hardship, straightforward, beholden to no special interests. Images of the folk attracted Americans because they suggested sources of purity and character outside the seemingly weakened and corrupt mainstream of society. Ironically, then, to highlight a person's marginality in relation to the mainstream helped authenticate him or her as an exemplar of American grit and character. For the Lomaxes to depict Lead Belly as an exotic animal added to his appeal. They realized that if they wanted Lead Belly to achieve mainstream popularity his very incompatibility with mainstream society was his greatest asset.

This realization led the Lomaxes to manipulate not only Lead Belly's image but also his music. As the Lomaxes knew, Lead Belly's commercial strength depended on the perception that his songs were "pure folk." But they also recognized that popular audiences would not necessarily appreciate the folk style unadulterated. So, even as the Lomaxes worked to preserve Lead Belly's "authenticity," they encouraged him to make his singing more accessible to urban audiences. Alan Lomax recalled that white audiences found Lead Belly's southern dialect impenetrable until he "learned to compromise with Northern ways and 'bring his words out plain.' "[44] The Lomaxes may also have urged Lead Belly to insert spoken comments in the middle of his songs, a technique for which he is famous. Spoken sections made a song easier for a neophyte to understand by outlining its plot, explaining obscure words and symbols, and providing transitions between verses. Folklorist John Minton cites a Library of

Congress recording of "Scottsboro Boys," in which Alan Lomax "asks Lead Belly in mid-performance to expand on the song's theme." Minton speculates that "the interpolated narrative was already a part of Lead Belly's style, but it was obviously encouraged by the Lomaxes."[45]

A close look at one Lead Belly song, "Mister Tom Hughes' Town," illustrates how Lead Belly's musical style evolved in the years after he left prison. "Tom Hughes" was a signature piece in Lead Belly's repertoire, one that he recorded six times between 1934 and 1940 and twice more at his final recording sessions in 1948.[46] He first recorded the song for the Lomaxes on July 1, 1934, while still an inmate in the Louisiana State Penitentiary in Angola.[47] This version is a hard-edged, sometimes bawdy tale that recounts Lead Belly's desire as a youth to flee home and enjoy the illicit pleasures of Fannin Street, the red-light district of Shreveport, Louisiana, where Tom Hughes was sheriff.[48] To an outsider, the song is stirring but can sound opaque, full of arcane slang and local references. Over the next six years, as Lead Belly moved from prison to freedom, from Louisiana to New York, and from field recordings to the commercial studio, he made a series of alterations to the song. Some changes were subtle and some dramatic. Some innovations surfaced just a few months after he left prison; others evolved gradually over years. Some reappeared in each subsequent version of the song, while others dropped away forever as soon as they were introduced. The changes to "Tom Hughes" do not, then, reflect a complete transformation in Lead Belly, but they do suggest a trend—a shift toward a less rough-edged style that, presumably, he hoped would attract wider audiences.

Even by the fall of 1934, only months after Lead Belly had left prison, "Tom Hughes" differed from the original field recording he had made for the Lomaxes. The second version of the song, which was recorded by John Lomax as he and Lead Belly traveled in Arkansas, makes changes that help clarify the seemingly fractured story line of the original recording. It adds a spoken narrative that guides the reader through the tale. While the original prison version of the song featured high-pitched moans without explanation, here Lead Belly sets them up by saying, "I broke Martha's heart, and she turned around, and she started to cry. . . . I walked away from her, and here's what she said. [Moaning begins]."[49] On subsequent versions of "Tom Hughes," Lead Belly tended to start with long spoken introductions that set out the song's premise and previewed its plot ("Here's a song I composed about Mr. Tom Hughes' town, better known as Shreveport, Louisiana.").[50] At times, he used the spoken asides to translate key terms. In his 1948 version, he sings about rambling with "Buffalo Bill" and adds parenthetically "a bad man," so as to account for his mother's distress at their friendship.[51]

In addition to making more effort to explicate the song's story, Lead Belly's postprison versions of "Tom Hughes" considerably changed the story's outcome. In the first field recording, the narrator leaves for Shreveport, ignoring the pleas of his mother to stay at home, and adopts a licentious lifestyle about which he is remorseless, even boastful. Subsequent versions, though, add lyrics in which the narrator falls on his knees and begs his mother to forgive him for his past behavior.[52] Most striking, most of Lead Belly's postprison renditions omit two suggestive verses that appear on the first field recording. In these verses Lead Belly refers to a woman who earns her living by "[workin'][53] up her tail," and he exclaims that she has "somethin' lawd / I sure would like."

The taming of Lead Belly's narrator is also reflected in changes in his performance style. First of all, most of Lead Belly's subsequent versions of "Tom Hughes" are slower in speed than the original field recording, a change that makes the narrator sound less frenzied.[54] Lead Belly has more time to sing the words, and they come out more clearly than in his first session, in which he runs many words together. Similarly, Lead Belly's voice is more emotive on his first recording of the song. While all the versions of "Tom Hughes" feature Lead Belly humming a melody in a moaning voice, in the first version he uses a sharper attack on the moans, giving them a piercing quality that most subsequent versions lack.

These transformations appear even more dramatically in a 1940 rendition of "I'm on My Last Go-Round," a song that uses the same tune and a variation of the Tom Hughes refrain.[55] This recording session was Lead Belly's first with a major record company, and Alan Lomax arranged and supervised the session.[56] In this version Lead Belly's singing has lost all the bite that it had on the initial field recording. The song is considerably slower than on earlier versions, and Lead Belly's usually rough voice sounds almost mellifluous. Light, delicate strummings have replaced his once fierce guitar work.

One can suppose that the Lomaxes and the commercial producers of Lead Belly's records played a direct role in reshaping "Tom Hughes," but it would be a mistake to presume that Lead Belly himself resented the advice. He had a notable interest in popularizing his music and a willingness to alter his songs. The evolution of "Tom Hughes" does not necessarily chart the crass exploitation of a "pure" folk artist. More accurately, the ebb and flow of his style illustrates how contact with the Lomaxes and the world of commercial recordings affected Lead Belly's sense of what would appeal to white audiences. In addition, the changes give us a glimpse of the musical dilemmas Lead Belly faced as he tried to find his niche in the folk revival. How much should he adapt his style, and in what direction? What appealed to audiences as an honest-to-goodness rough-edged sound and what struck them as abrasive? What was the boundary between "mysterious" and scary? Throughout his career, Lead Belly struggled to translate his persona as a musical throwback into popular success.

The strategy of smoothing out Lead Belly's music while promoting him as an outsider did win Lead Belly some audiences in the mid-thirties. His story generated significant publicity in popular newspapers and magazines, and his music was disseminated via radio, record, and even newsreel. This publicity blitz likely reached millions of Americans, but it generated by far the most intense response from the political Left, the core constituency for the folk revival of the thirties and forties.

Folk-styled music had been a part of leftist culture since well before the thirties. In the first decades of the 1900s, both the Socialist and the Communist parties encouraged efforts to create a body of proletarian music, songs that would encourage solidarity among the workers and inspire them to challenge their oppressors. In its early attempts to create a people's music, the Left relied on a decidedly different style of music than would the folk song enthusiasts of the late thirties. For the most part, leftist music organizations before the thirties either ignored or disparaged traditional American songs. Instead, early agitprop music, such as the Industrial Workers of the World songbooks from the early part of the century, relied either on European or original composed melodies.[57]

In large part the Left was uninterested in American music because, before the thirties, most of its supporters were foreign-born and the vast majority did not speak English fluently. The primary musical outlets for these members were the workers choruses that the Communist Party (CP) sponsored in the 1920s and early 1930s. Drawing on a decades-old tradition of workers' choral groups in Europe and America, the CP intended for these choruses to inspire the masses to devote themselves to the movement. Certainly they had a sizable constituency, as groups such as the American People's Chorus, the Daily Worker Chorus, and the Jewish *Freiheit* ("Freedom") Chorus proliferated on the left. But their lack of connection to American musical traditions precluded a broader influence. Since most of the singers were Eastern European immigrants, the choruses sang few of their pieces in English. The groups also assumed a degree of familiarity with high-art musical traditions that likely would have intimidated most American workers. Their songs tended to be technically difficult and to require rehearsals under a conductor's baton to achieve an acceptable degree of precision.[58]

With the advent of the CP's doctrinaire Third Period in the late twenties and early thirties, the party began making a more conscious effort to politicize the arts. In 1931 the Workers Music League was founded to oversee the workers choruses. It organized their efforts and provided them with appropriate revolutionary compositions, still mostly European-styled.[59] The league delegated its most important compositional work to the Composers' Collective, a subset of New York's Pierre Degeyter music club, which had been named after the composer of the "Internationale." The collective was made up of classically trained composers such as Charles Seeger, Elie Siegmeister, and, occasionally, Aaron Copland. They took to heart the party's request for politically charged music and seem to have believed that they could write songs that would spark the revolution. In the *Daily Worker*, Seeger wrote, "Music is propaganda—always propaganda—and of the most powerful sort."[60]

Despite this hard-hitting attitude, the members of the collective proved to be singularly unsuccessful at reaching out to Americans. Making no effort to assess popular taste, they decided that music for a revolution should be musically revolutionary, and they composed songs designed to challenge listeners' rhythmic and harmonic expectations. Many of their compositions were inspired by the German composer Hanns Eisler, a student of Arnold Schoenberg, who hoped to use dissonance and rhythmic variation to create a politically charged alternative to symphonic music. As Seeger recalled, "Everything we composed was forward-looking, progressive as hell, but completely unconnected with life, just as we were in the Collective."[61]

In effect, then, the collective took a top-down approach to creating proletarian music, offering the masses the music that they, as composers, deemed most suitable. Although Seeger would go on to be an important folk music advocate, at this stage he and the collective scorned traditional songs as politically unaware and musically simple minded.[62] "Many folksongs," he wrote in the *Daily Worker*, "are complacent, melancholy, defeatist, intended to make slaves endure their lot—pretty but not the stuff for a militant proletariat to feed on."[63] The collective's high-art biases were clearly revealed when a few of their meetings were attended by Aunt Molly Jackson, a renowned ballad singer and strike organizer from Kentucky. She sang some of her strike songs, which were based on traditional melodies, and the collective's members in turn presented some of their own compositions. Each found the other's music impenetrable. As Jackson's bewilderment illustrates, even workers allied with the Left rejected the music the collective wrote for them. *Daily Worker* columnist Mike Gold quoted a worker who dismissed the collective's tunes as "full of geometric bitterness and the angles and glass splinters of pure technic . . . written for an assortment of mechanical canaries."[64] The Composers' Collective's music may have been intended for the populace, but it showed scant awareness of popular tastes.

The Left began to change its approach to vernacular music in 1935, when the Communist Party announced its Popular Front policy. The party's advocacy of a united stand against fascism brought with it a new attitude toward American culture. Rather than preaching mass revolution, the Popular Front urged Americans to embrace cultural diversity and to bond together in common cause. Culture came to be seen less as a didactic tool for arousing class conflict than as a force for fostering community and revealing people's shared humanity. The party's composers and musicians, therefore, could stop trying to transform popular taste and could focus instead on understanding it. They became fascinated with music that seemed to speak in the voice of the people, and folk songs enjoyed party approval. In 1936 the American Music League, a Popular Front organization, included among its published goals "to collect, study, and popularize American folk music and its traditions." Historian Robbie Lieberman writes that "folk song, more than any other cultural form, expressed and reaffirmed the Popular Front spirit. It was simple and direct; it invited mass participation; it expressed the concerns of the common person."[65]

With the party's new attitude, folk music became an established part of left-wing functions, and folk performers enjoyed quite a vogue among the white radicals and intellectuals who sustained the CP.[66] Lead Belly, from Louisiana; Aunt Molly Jackson, Sarah Ogan, and Jim Garland, from Kentucky; and (after 1940) Woody Guthrie, from Oklahoma, all became folk celebrities among the Left in a vibrant New York City–based scene. The singers were in demand for the political meetings, parties, and benefits that the Left sponsored. Henrietta Yurchenco recalls that these musicians were "the answer to left-wing prayers. Through their songs, life among poor whites of Appalachia, oppressed southern blacks, and dust storm victims came alive far better than in all the articles in the *Daily Worker* or the *New Masses*."[67] With these homespun folk associated with their movement, party regulars could feel that perhaps they could be accepted by "the people" after all and that their hopes for a mass following might one day be fulfilled.

Despite their popularity among leftists, though, the urban folk revivalists had little success at attracting broader mass-culture audiences.

Again Lead Belly serves as an example. Even with the adaptations he made to his style, he never enjoyed significant popularity in his lifetime. His records, even those on commercial labels, sold little, and he forever struggled with financial hardship. For much of the thirties, in fact, he and his wife depended on assistance from the New York Department of Welfare. In 1949 when he died of amyotropic lateral sclerosis, or Lou Gehrig's disease, Lead Belly was well known enough to generate an obituary in the *New York Times* but not popular enough to have achieved a broad-based following or any kind of financial security.[68] Americans found Lead Belly fascinating, it seems, but they kept him at arm's length.

Lead Belly's commercial career sputtered because of the contradictory demands placed on him by the folk revival. The outsider populism impulse that made Lead Belly and the other folk singers so intriguing to thirties Americans trapped them between the conflicting demands of purity and commercialism. Fundamentally, these singers' appeal depended on their folkloristic purity. They faced significant pressure, therefore, to sing only timeless songs that had been passed down (but not altered) through generations of oral transmission. This notion, though, of a pristine and unchanging traditional music fundamentally misrepresented the reality of folk culture. As the Lomaxes well knew, the folk tradition had always depended on its adaptability.[69] Lead Belly himself, for example, continually altered his songs. In concert he often varied his lyrics to mention the city in which he was performing, and he adjusted his repertoire to the tastes of his audience.[70]

No roots musician, moreover, was as isolated as the entrepreneurs of the folk revival wished. Although he had spent his whole life in the rural South, much of it confined in prison, Lead Belly was quite well versed in popular culture and saw no reason to shut himself off from it. He was renowned for his openness to all kinds of music, including Tin Pan Alley. In an interview he recalled, "I learned by listening to other singers once in a while off phonograph records. . . . I used to look at the sheet music and learn the words of a few popular songs." Similarly, Lead Belly did not share John Lomax's fears about the radio's corrupting influence on his repertoire. He so much enjoyed listening that while in New York he wrote a tribute song called "Turn Your Radio On," singing, "You listen in to tell what's goin' on in the world."[71]

Lead Belly's receptiveness to different kinds of music led to some striking juxtapositions. He was fascinated, for instance, with singing cowboy Gene Autry. He liked to sing Autry's songs, went to his movies, and was thrilled early in his stay in New York when Autry, dressed in white, stopped by to see for himself what a twelve-string guitar was all about. Lead Belly was also known to do a dead-on imitation of hillbilly star Jimmie Rodgers's yodeling.[72] He was, in short, an old-fashioned "songster," the term the African American community used to describe eclectic musicians able to sing practically any type of song. He performed everything from work songs to dance tunes to blues to cowboy ballads to popular hits. Literary critic Daniel Hoffman observes, "As he was a folksinger, not a folklorist, all of these [were] equally admissible to his canon." As one might guess, the Lomaxes found Lead Belly's attraction to ersatz cowboys and crooning balladeers disquieting, and they did their best to restrict him to his traditional repertoire. John Lomax wrote, "For his programs Lead Belly always wished to include [Autry's] 'That Silver-Haired Daddy of Mine' or jazz tunes such as 'I'm in Love with You, Baby.' . . . He could never understand why we did not care for them. We held him to the singing of the music that first attracted us to him."[73]

The revivalists, though, were not consistent in their emphasis on purity. Even as they warned folk singers not to add popular tunes to their song lists, they encouraged other changes in the singers' repertoire. In the spirit of the Popular Front, for instance, the Left was eager for Lead Belly to compose political songs. Some historians speculate that Alan Lomax helped compose "The Bourgeois Blues," Lead Belly's protest against segregated housing in Washington, D.C.[74] Lead Belly also wrote political material like "Jim Crow Blues," "Hitler Song," and "Scottsboro Boys" after being discovered by the Lomaxes.[75] Radicals found these songs more palatable than many of those Lead Belly chose to play if left to his own devices. In the mid-1930s, for instance, left-wing composer Earl Robinson invited Lead Belly to play at Camp Unity, the CP's summer retreat. The first night, Lead Belly performed songs like "Ella Speed" and "Frankie and Albert" that featured gun-toting gamblers, cheating husbands, and murderous wives. "The camp was in an uproar," Robinson recalled. "Arguments raged over whether to censure him, me, or both of us." Before the next performance, Robinson explained to Lead Belly that the party expected exemplars of the Negro race to express more high-minded sentiments. That night Lead Belly charmed the crowd with "Bourgeois Blues" and "Scottsboro Boys."[76]

If selecting songs to play was so complicated, choosing the style in which to play them must have seemed especially bewildering to the folk revival singers of the thirties. The singers' appeal to the cult of authenticity depended on the notion that they had a "natural" sound—a style unsullied by the encroachments of popular culture. But, as the case of "Tom Hughes" suggests, a singer's style often was altered in an effort to reach popular audiences. Folk performers were encouraged to moderate the pitch of their voices, enunciate clearly, and slow down their songs. Singers like Lead Belly and Josh White took these lessons to heart in an effort to broaden their music's appeal.

Performers who did make stylistic adjustments, though, soon found that adapting their sound jeopardized their standing in the eyes of the folk revival's core following. Purists denounced them for selling out their pure heritage. Folklorist Charles Haywood thought Lead Belly a "sad spectacle" by the end of his career, charging that he had changed to fit "night clubs and popular taste": "In the place of strong rhythms the guitar was toying with delicate arpeggi and delightful arabesques, filling in between verses with swaying body movements, marching up and down the stage, swinging the guitar over his head, instrument upside down, or behind his back. This was a sad and tragic sight, cheap vaudeville claptrap." Lead Belly attempted to adapt to the commercial market, and as a result, says Sven Eric Molin, "folklorists shake their heads over his recordings and distinguish between an 'earlier' and a 'later' Leadbelly, for . . . the singing techniques and the choice of materials changed, and Tin Pan Alley had its perceptible influence."[77]

The Lomaxes had encouraged Lead Belly to adjust his style, but they, too, spoke wistfully of his "purer" past. As early as January 1935, John wrote to his wife that he and Alan were "disturbed and distressed at [Lead Belly's] beginning tendency to show off in his songs and talk, when his money value is to be natural and sincere as he was while in prison. Of course, as this tendency grows he will lose his charm and become only an ordinary, low ordinary, Harlem nigger."[78] Alan Lomax found that "Lead Belly recorded his songs for a number of companies though never so beautifully as he had first sung them for us in Louisiana." He described Lead Belly's 1940 recordings as "not complete authenticity, but . . . the nearest thing to it that could be achieved away from the prison farms themselves."[79]

Lead Belly did not have the same yearning for the purity of the prison farms, but he does seem to have internalized the confusing standards that the Lomaxes and folk song revivalists set for him. In a 1940 letter to Alan Lomax, Lead Belly wrote: "If your Papa come I would like for Him to Here me sing if He say i Have Change any whitch i Don't think i have and never will But to Be [sure] to get his ideas about it i would feel good over what ever he say about it." Lead Belly's predicament arose from the conflicting demands the folk revival placed on him. As Joe Klein writes, folk singers who tried to make it in urban society while remaining "true to their roots" ended up like "museum pieces, priceless and rare, but not quite marketable in the mass culture."[80] The folk revival tried to use idealized conceptions of authenticity to achieve its dreams of reaching mass audiences. But the tensions in this agenda left performers like Lead Belly caught in limbo between folk and popular culture.

Like many roots musicians, Lead Belly found his way out of this limbo only after his death. Within months of his death at the end of 1949, the Weavers, a singing quartet featuring Pete Seeger, issued their version of Lead Belly's "Goodnight Irene." It eliminated from the song a verse about taking morphine, changed the ominous-sounding lyric "I'll *get* you in my dreams" to "I'll *see* you in my dreams," and added lush vocal harmonies. It became a number one hit.[81]

The Weavers' "Irene" was only one in a series of efforts by Lead Belly's allies in the folk revival to advance his legacy after his death. At the end of January 1950, Alan Lomax organized a tribute concert for him in New York's Town Hall. After Lomax moved to England that year, he produced a radio series that introduced British audiences to Lead Belly's music. (In 1956, Lonnie Donegan, a British banjo player, returned the favor by making Lead Belly's "Rock Island Line" a top-ten hit in America.) Moses Asch, who had recorded scores of Lead Belly songs for his Folkways label between 1941 and 1948, kept all of Lead Belly's albums in print and, in 1954, issued *Lead Belly's Last Sessions*, a set of three double albums featuring more than ninety songs and stories that Lead Belly had recorded in 1948 at the home of jazz historian Frederic Ramsey, Jr. A series of books, too, helped bring Lead Belly to new audiences. In 1959 Alan Lomax published a collection of Lead Belly songs, followed in 1962 by a songbook that he issued in collaboration with Asch. In 1965 Pete Seeger issued a manual on how to play twelve-string guitar in the style of Lead Belly. Meanwhile, in concert after concert, Seeger performed Lead Belly's music and recounted his story.[82] As folk-styled music surged in popularity in the late 1950s and 1960s, a new generation found Lead Belly. His music became a staple at coffeehouses and folk festivals across the country. The 1960s folk revival did more to cement Lead Belly's reputation than had all his own efforts while he was alive.

Recent decades have witnessed a series of affirmations of Lead Belly's place in the canon of roots musicians. He was inducted into the Rock and Roll Hall of Fame (1988), the Blues Hall of Fame (1986), and the Nashville Songwriters Association International's Hall of Fame (1980). In 1988 Columbia Records issued a tribute album, for which Beach Boy Brian Wilson, rock and roll pioneer Little Richard, and country legend Willie Nelson covered Lead Belly songs. In 1993, a few months before the suicide of lead singer Kurt Cobain, grunge-rock superstars Nirvana performed a Lead Belly tune for an MTV "Unplugged" album.[83]

On the face of it, such tributes are the stuff of tragedy. If only Lead Belly had lived long enough to see his dreams fulfilled![84] At the same time, the posthumous nature of Lead Belly's success has an air of inevitability to it. It is questionable to what extent he could have reaped the fruits of fame even if he had lived. Lead Belly's renown in the decades after his death certainly derived in part from his considerable artistry, but it was equally driven by the same dynamics that had frustrated and constrained him while he lived—the romanticized (and racialized) life story that had been constructed for him, the primitive emotiveness attributed to his music, the notion that he somehow existed out of time, or at least before the time in which artifice and superficiality had permeated popular culture. In his day, these myths brought Lead Belly momentary popular attention, but they hamstrung his efforts to advance within popular culture, leaving him a folk-revival darling who struggled desperately to make ends meet. The real tragedy, perhaps, is that Lead Belly could flourish in public memory—as a posthumous folk forefather—in a way that he never could have as an active performer. With the "real" Lead Belly buried in Louisiana, each generation could "discover" him for itself, much as the Lomaxes had decades before. Successive cohorts of middle-class, almost exclusively white audiences could become entranced by the Lead Belly myth, revel in the bracing foreignness of his songs, and, eventually, reinterpret the songs as their own. After his death, then, Lead Belly himself became an authenticating agent, one who could bestow legitimacy on performers and fans searching for a sense of roots in the midst of ephemeral pop culture.

In his lifetime, Lead Belly was stymied by the tensions within the cult of authenticity—between rural African American traditions and an emerging set of white cultural brokers, between field recordings and the commercial record industry, between folklore and the modern mass media, between raw naturalism and calculated promotion. In the realm of memory, though, these oppositions that had trapped him became the source of his appeal and his achievement as a roots musician. Haltingly, often painfully, Lead Belly brought together forces that his successors would deploy to powerful advantage.

MASTERING THE
CULT OF AUTHENTICITY
LEONARD CHESS, WILLIE DIXON,
AND THE STRANGE CAREER OF
MUDDY WATERS

The Lomaxes could not manage to make Lead Belly a star in his own time, but the experience did nothing to slow their hunt for the great American folk singer. In 1941 the quest took Alan Lomax to Mississippi's Coahoma County, where the Library of Congress and Fisk University were cosponsoring a field study. Lomax and Fisk professor John Work were trying to survey the full range of African American folk song in the county. In August 1941, they recorded bluesman Son House, who had taught the spectacular singer-guitarist Robert Johnson. At House's suggestion, the pair next visited Stovall's Plantation near Clarksdale to hear one of House's more recent pupils, McKinley Morganfield.[1]

Morganfield was a tractor driver on the plantation and, on the side, a moonshiner whose cabin on the weekend became a juke joint for drinking, dancing, and music. He was also gaining a reputation in the area as a guitar player who performed at local parties, sometimes in the houses of the white overseers. At these parties, he would play alone or, sometimes, join with the Son Simms Four, a string band that backed his vocals and guitar with a violin, mandolin, and second guitar.[2] When Lomax and Work began recording Morganfield's songs at ten dollars apiece for the Library of Congress, they credited him by his full name, but to everyone in the Clarksdale area, Morganfield was Muddy Waters.[3]

The day Waters sang for Lomax in that summer in 1941 marked the beginning of a forty-year recording career. In that span, Waters's persona shifted from downhome folk bluesman to downhome commercial singer to commercial pop star to old-time roots musician.[4] These twists and turns illustrate that the cult of authenticity is not a fixed and static entity. Rather, it takes on different configurations according to when, by whom, and to whom it is applied. For Waters, authenticity was a mantle that he variously cast off and embraced, donned whole cloth and cut to fit. Working with powerful cultural brokers, Waters ensured that for him, unlike for Lead Belly, his status as "the real thing" captured the popular imagination without taking hostage his creative flexibility. Waters mastered the cult of authenticity before it mastered him.

As Alan Lomax tells the story fifty years later, the twenty-six-year-old Waters came to their first recording session shoeless, so the twenty-six-year-old Lomax took his shoes off, too.[5] Then, Lomax set up his recording equipment and gave Waters the go-ahead signal. Accompanying himself on a guitar that he fretted with a bottleneck, Waters recorded three songs that day. First he played his "Country Blues," an amalgamation of Robert Johnson's "Walking Blues" and Son House's "My Black Mama." He followed this up with another of his blues, "I Be's Troubled," before finishing the session with "Burr Clover Farm Blues," a song he had written to support his boss in a soil-improvement experiment.[6] Lomax was impressed with Waters's emotive voice and singular lyrical touches. Early in 1942, after getting a polite reminder from the singer, Lomax sent Waters two copies of a Library of Congress disc that included "Country Blues" and "I Be's Troubled." Waters proudly put one on the jukebox in his joint.[7]

The next summer Lomax came back to Stovall and recorded Waters on another dozen or so songs, this time with the Son Simms Four backing him on several of them. Lomax included Waters's "Country Blues" and "I Be's Troubled" on the initial five-album set of American folk song that the Library of Congress issued in 1941. "This was the first time," he recalled in 1988, "that a government had ever published its sort of unwashed authentic folksingers on records." These albums, while landmarks in the history of field recordings, did not generate any interest in Waters. Alan Lomax clearly admired Waters's artistry and urged him to "keep in practice," but he continued to busy himself with his myriad of other folk song projects and did not bother to return to Stovall again. In fact, he didn't see Waters for another decade. When he did, he found Waters sitting behind the wheel of a Cadillac, comfortable in his role as the driving force behind the Chicago blues sound.[8] Lomax had let one of the most influential roots musicians of all slip out of his grasp.

In the absence of Lomax's influence, Waters went his own way, propelled by his own musical vision and by a series of other entrepreneurs and impresarios. One Monday in May 1943, Waters asked his overseer for a raise from twenty-two and a half to twenty-five cents per hour. When his request was rejected out of hand, Waters began to think more seriously about moving on. Once before he had left the plantation for St. Louis, but he had been unable to find his niche in the big city.[9] This time, though, it would be different. On Friday he sent word to the overseer that he was sick. Carrying his Sears Silvertone guitar and a suitcase containing one set of clothes, he caught the 4:00 P.M. train in Clarksdale, heading to Chicago.[10]

Waters was certainly not alone in moving north in 1943. Spurred by World War II, the second great black migration (the first having come between 1910 and 1930) was running full tilt. Census figures suggest that between 1940 and 1950 at least 154,000 southern blacks arrived in Chicago, roughly half of them from Mississippi. When he got off the Illinois Central train at 9:30 Saturday morning, then, Waters was entering a thriving subculture. From the train station, Waters took a taxi to his sister's house, where he would sleep on the couch for his first week in town. Within a few hours of his arrival, Waters had a job, working the three-to-eleven shift unloading trucks in a paper factory. After a few weeks he discovered he had cousins on Chicago's West Side, and he moved to an apartment next to them. When Waters picked up his guitar, therefore, he found himself playing for friends, relatives, and fellow southerners—first at informal gatherings, then at rent parties, and eventually in small clubs.[11]

Waters, like almost everyone in the music business in the early 1940s, did not initially recognize the significance of having such a rich slice of Mississippi culture relocated in the Windy City. Instead of capitalizing on his ties to the southern culture of the migrants, Waters adapted his music to his preconceptions about big-city culture. The songs he played in these early years on the Chicago club circuit, therefore, differed significantly from those he had recorded for Alan Lomax a few years before. As he tried to make his way to bigger venues with larger audiences, Waters determinedly modernized his sound. As Waters later told critic Robert

Palmer, "I wanted to be nationally known and I worked on it." Initially, working on it meant imitating other, nationally known acts. To reach a popular audience, Waters felt sure, he had to stop sounding like a country bluesman. His sister had told him when he arrived in town, "They don't listen to that kind of old blues you're doin' now, don't nobody listen to that, not in Chicago." This bleak assessment, likely, was not much of a surprise to Waters. Even in Mississippi, the old-style blues were being crowded by new sounds. In August 1941, just after he had finished recording "I Be's Troubled," John Work had asked him, "Are there many of these country blues around this neighborhood?" "No sir," Muddy had replied, "ain't so many round here." "Do the people round here like them?" Work continued. "Yes, they're crazy about them," Muddy asserted.[12] The downhome blues still had a devoted following, it seems, but already other styles were cutting significantly into their popularity.

A look at Clarksdale's jukeboxes told a similar story. As part of the Fisk University–Library of Congress project, folklorist Lewis Jones documented all the tunes appearing on the boxes in five local music joints. Analyzing the lists, blues historian Tony Russell concludes that of the 108 songs, only 20 are blues, and only 2 of those can be called country blues. Instead, the song lists indicate the popularity of newer, urban styles. Louis Jordan, Count Basie, and Fats Waller appeared on all five jukeboxes. These artists were heavily influenced by blues, but really their styles represented a synthesis between blues and jazz. Jordan's polished and energetic "jump blues" style, Basie's "swing" feel, and Waller's boogie-woogie-tinged piano (along with the crooning of Nat "King" Cole) nicely capture the range of influences working to reshape the contemporary African American music.[13] As Waters set out to launch his career, he was well aware of these artists' successes, and he determined to follow their lead.

Waters was by no means the first to try to adapt rural blues styles to contemporary sounds. When he arrived in Chicago, a group of established bluesmen had been experimenting with jazz- and pop-influenced blues for almost a decade. Mostly these performers had come to the city on earlier waves of the southern black migration. They included Big Bill Broonzy, born in Mississippi; Tampa Red, from Georgia; Roosevelt Sykes, of Arkansas; Lonnie Johnson, born in New Orleans; and Tennessee's Sonny Boy Williamson and Memphis Minnie. All these musicians recorded under the supervision of a white talent scout, record producer, and music publisher named Lester Melrose.

Born in Illinois in 1891, Melrose had run a music store in the 1920s that had grown into a publishing company. With an eye toward expanding his holdings, he had begun to move into recording. From the mid-thirties to 1951, Melrose was in charge of blues recordings for Blue-bird and Okeh, the race-record subsidiaries of RCA Victor and Columbia.[14] Along with Decca, these labels dominated the black music market through much of the thirties and forties.[15]

Essentially, Melrose and the other giants of the race-record industry were working to create a black pop music—a style that could reach large, diverse audiences simultaneously, would yield financial benefits that the companies could control, and could be easily produced and re-produced. Each of these mandates encouraged Melrose to create a less rough edged, more regimented blues sound. Eager to appeal to as wide a public as possible, he selected singers who could moderate their distinctive dialects and sing smoothly and evenly. He also tended to use songs that did not indulge in the rural blues' penchant for local references. Why unnecessarily limit one's audience? In order to control the profits these songs generated, Melrose made effective use of copyright laws. He enlisted the musicians he worked with to write dozens of songs, the rights to which he bought for small fees.[16] Aside from generating significant royalties for Melrose, this practice discouraged free-form improvised blues. In order to copyright a song, it had to be "original," a requirement that worked against rural blues singers' practice of piecing together songs from "floating stanzas" that they picked up from other performers and recordings. With the advent of race records in the late 1920s, therefore, commercial bluesmen gradually shifted toward inventing their own lyrics, which they used, essentially unchanged, each time they performed a given song.[17]

In his recording methods, too, Melrose exercised a modernizing influence. He showed a striking willingness to incorporate other contemporary styles into the blues form. Taking a cue from contemporary jazz, for example, he began recording with expanded instrumentation, using not only vocalist and guitar (the traditional downhome combination) but also bass, piano, drum, and, occasionally, saxophone or clarinet and harmonica. This beefed-up ensemble carried what historian Sam Charters has called the "Bluebird beat," a heavy, driving pulse with a swing-influenced feel. Melrose used this beat on everything from blues and jazz to novelty songs. As the phrase "Bluebird beat" suggests, Melrose's style had a formulaic aspect. As he worked out the elements of a successful black pop sound, he was determined to be able to replicate that sound at will. He therefore kept a stable of musicians at hand, in effect pioneering the concept of a studio group for the blues. These players functioned almost as interchangeable parts, appearing on one another's recordings and ensuring a striking degree of stylistic consistency across Bluebird's catalog.[18] Melding rural blues styles with urban-derived rhythms and instrumentation, Melrose was creating a new musical synthesis for the city.

As Waters worked to update his downhome blues style, many of the changes he made incorporated Melrose's innovations. He began, for example, to add more instruments to fill out his spare sound. Of course Waters had played with other musicians before—Lomax had recorded him with the Son Simms Four—but mostly he had performed solo on Stovall's Plantation and at the Chicago house parties.[19] As Waters began playing in Chicago's clubs, though, he increasingly worked with other musicians and gained exposure to new combinations of instruments. Initially as a sideman (a backup musician), he frequently played in groups that combined two guitars with harmonica, drums, and, often, piano and bass. By the mid-forties, Waters was leading his own band in area clubs.[20] In addition to playing with new combos, Waters revamped his guitar style in his first years in Chicago. He abandoned his bottleneck technique as old-fashioned and sought a smoother, more melodic sound. In a style reminiscent of jazz guitar, Waters experimented with distinct single-note lines instead of the heavy strummed chords and sliding bottleneck of the Delta style.[21]

The most dramatic step that Waters made to modernize his sound actually marked a break from Melrose's practices: he plugged in. Electric amplification had first appeared around 1940 and had quickly caught on among Chicago guitarists eager to be heard over the laughing, shouting, and, sometimes, fighting with which they competed in the blues clubs. Waters had tried playing his acoustic in the clubs but with poor results. He recalled, "When I went into the clubs, the first thing I wanted was an amplifier. Couldn't nobody hear you with an acoustic. . . . You get a more pure thing out of an acoustic, but you get more noise out of an amplifier." Finally, in 1944 Waters's uncle gave him a cheap electric guitar, which he soon used almost exclusively.[22]

Curiously, Melrose did not fancy the new electric sound. Bassist Willie Dixon recalls that Melrose's performers had electric instruments but that Melrose recorded with their volume "turned down to sound acoustic-style."[23] Whatever Melrose's misgiving about amplification, by the fall of 1946 Waters had adapted his sound enough and had become well enough known on the local music scene that Melrose invited him and his electric guitar to join two other performers at a September recording session date for Columbia Records. Waters recorded three of his own songs at the session. A closer look at one of them, "Hard Day Blues," reveals how far he had come in the five years since he and Alan Lomax had sat barefoot in his Mississippi cabin.[24]

In its basic form, "Hard Day Blues" resembles Waters's Library of Congress recordings. Like almost all the songs he sang for Lomax, "Hard Day Blues" follows the twelve-bar form basic to the vast majority of downhome blues: four four-beat measures rooted in the tonic chord (the chord built on the first note of the major scale); two measures based on the subdominant chord (built on the fourth note of the scale); two more measures based on the tonic; two more on the dominant (the chord built on the fifth scale degree); and, finally, two more measures on the tonic before the entire pattern is repeated. "Hard Day Blues" also carefully follows the A-A-B pattern of lyrics fundamental to most twelve-bar blues: an initial statement over the first two measures (A), followed by a two-bar instrumental response; an almost exact repetition of the statement (A), followed again by an instrumental response; and then a third, this time different statement (B), followed by an instrumental fill that covers the last two of the twelve measures. Over the first twelve-bar grouping in "Hard Day Blues," Water sings:

Had some hard days, out in the falling rain
[instrumental response]

Yes I had some hard days, out in the falling rain
[instrumental response]

Well you know I didn't have nobody to love me, people wasn't that a cryin' shame
[instrumental response].

If it is clear that "Hard Day Blues" follows the downhome blues formula, it is equally obvious from the beginning of the song that Waters's country style has undergone a dramatic transformation during his time in Chicago. Waters begins the song familiarly enough—with a bluesy chord poised tensely between the major and minor third. He repeats the chord three times (three eighth notes) to serve as a pickup or introductory cue to lead into the song. Immediately, though, it is evident that despite this traditional effect Waters is not the same musician he was in Mississippi. The chords have a brightly amplified and sustained ring, indicating instantly that Waters's acoustic guitar was packed away back home and the electric Waters was on the way. To any of Waters's Mississippi friends who had not heard from him since he boarded the Illinois Central, what comes next in "Hard Day Blues" would have been equally surprising: a heavy drum on the downbeat and a high-hat cymbal

Muddy Waters, ca. 1960s.
(Courtesy MCA–Chess Records Files)

on the offbeat, a walking bass line complementing the drum, and then, at the end of the first measure, a quick run by the piano into a measure of rapidly struck sixteenth-note chords. Waters was playing electric blues with a modern *band*.

To play blues in a group with this instrumentation marks a departure from Mississippi Delta traditions, but what makes the contrast particularly striking here is the jazz- and boogie-woogie-influenced sound the band produces. Rhythmically, the song has a strong swing feel. The bassist and drummer carry the tune forward by playing on each beat, and the drummer accents the offbeats (two and four) with the high-hat cymbal to create the propulsive feel so characteristic of swing. The piano frequently adds boogie-woogie figures in the two-bar breaks between Waters's lines: in the eleventh measure of each twelve-bar grouping, for instance, the pianist plays chugging sets of triplets, moving chromatically from the major third to the dominant (fifth scale tone).[25]

Waters's guitar work, too, reflects an effort to modernize his style. First of all, he has left his bottleneck back home with his acoustic guitar. Instead of the sliding pitch and rough timbre the bottleneck produces, Waters's playing has the cleaner tone that comes from using one's fingers (rather than the bottleneck) to fret the strings. Waters tends, moreover, to eschew the rough, strummed chords of the rural Delta style in favor of spare single-string lines characteristic of the urban blues.[26] In fact, Waters uses such restraint that his guitar seems almost to disappear on "Hard Day Blues." While the pianist plays rolling, rhythmic patterns during the two-bar instrumental-response sections, Waters relies on a tentative, almost cute, three-note fill eight separate times in the song.[27] In the solo section of the song, too, Waters's guitar playing seems much more restrained than in his older rural style. The piano, not the guitar, dominates here. The pianist bangs out open chords in fast sixteenth notes, a boogie-woogie motif that would later be popular among rock and roll stars like Fats Domino and Jerry Lee Lewis. Waters uses a heavier timbre in this section, but simply to outline a boogie-woogie bass line to support the pianist.

The final element of Waters's transformation in "Hard Day Blues" is his singing style. For Alan Lomax, Waters sang in volumes ranging from a mutter to a shout, and his timbre ranged from a tight nasality to a ringing, full-throated call. On "Hard Day Blues," though, Waters has eliminated the extremes from his vocal repertoire. He tends to sing in the middle register with a moderately full tone. Likewise, he has dropped the more dramatic variations in his pronunciation. On his Library of Congress recordings he often would roll over a word so that it was barely intelligible or, alternatively, chop it into several sharp syllables. His pronunciation was shaped by his desire for rhythmic expression more than a concern for literal communication. Certainly Waters's diction remains expressive on "Hard Day Blues." He draws out "hard" into "haard"; opens "out" into "owwt"; and at the end of a phrase truncates "shame" into a soft "shai." Nat "King" Cole he is not. But overall, Waters plainly makes an effort to sing loudly enough to be heard and to enunciate clearly enough to be understood.

The jazz and urban blues elements that Waters employs on "Hard Day Blues" are the most immediately striking changes from his down-home style; but, ironically, just as indicative of his break with Delta tradition is the rigidity with which "Hard Day Blues" adheres to the traditional blues formula. In the rural blues tradition, elements such as the twelve-bar stanza and the A-A-B lyrics pattern were guideposts more than rules. Downhome singers had considerable freedom to stretch the form. Waters's Library of Congress (LC) recordings suggest some of the formal options available to Delta blues singers. Of the thirteen different songs Waters recorded for Lomax in 1941 and 1942, five do not conform to the A-A-B pattern.[28] The way in which Waters sings his LC songs further accentuates the irregularity and idiosyncrasy of his style. Even songs that strictly follow the twelve-bar, A-A-B pattern sound fluid and mutable because of his flexible technique. Tempo, for example, fluctuates continually on Waters's LC recordings. "Take a Walk with Me" begins at a leisurely 84 beats per minute, but almost immediately the tempo begins to edge upward—to 88 beats per minute after the first line, to 92 after the second, to 96 by the beginning of the second verse, to 104 by the end of that verse, dropping back momentarily to 96 before surging to a peak of 112 per minute by the end of the tune.[29] In most of the songs that Waters recorded for Lomax, tempi ebb and flow within a general tendency to accelerate. The tempo on "I Be's Troubled," for example, is almost constantly in flux, but overall it progresses from 100 to 126 beats per minute. "Burr Clover Farm Blues" (#1) and "Why Don't You Live So God Can Use You," likewise, both move from 84 to 112; "Burr Clover" #2 shifts from 76 to an eventual 104; "32-20 Blues" progresses from 80 to 96; and "Country Blues" accelerates from 72 to 96.

Compared with these free-ranging tempi, the "Hard Day Blues" that Waters recorded for Melrose starts to sound like a march. For the first three verses the beat never strays from the 92–96 range. It increases moderately to 100 during the pianist's solo and then settles back to 96 for the final verse. "Hard Day Blues" treats tempo like a marking to be followed more than as an expressive element to be varied.

A similar contrast surfaces when one compares Waters's vocal technique on the LC recordings and on "Hard Day Blues." In the earlier songs, Waters sings even the most straightforward lyrics in a loose and uneven (although controlled) way that makes the lines seem to straddle the beat, parts of them landing ahead of it and parts behind. It is difficult to notate the way in which Waters sings across the beat on these recordings, but perhaps a look at "You're Gonna Miss Me When I'm Gone" (#2) can give some sense of his technique. In this song Waters's phrases are extremely uneven in length. In the beginning of the third verse, over a tempo of 80 beats per minute, Waters fits a stunning number of words into a four-beat measure. Each of the lines below corresponds roughly to one measure (including the pickup to the first measure):

1. Well you know I been feelin' blue I been feelin' blue baby ever since the
2. Sun went down
3. I just been sitting here thinkin' wonderin' why don't you
4. Drive in this town, but hey.

The next verse, at 84 beats per minute, begins with even more of a mouthful:

1. Well I know you don't want I know you don't want me gal, 'cause your best friend
2. Best friend told me so
3. But that's all right gal I can get along almost
4. Anywhere I go, but hey.

The point is not that Waters showed an unusual ability to sing quickly but rather that he assumed an elastic relationship between his lyrics and a song's underlying beat. On his LC recordings, Waters's phrases are almost never evenly divided, and rarely do words fall neatly on the beat. Even when singing songs built on short phrases, Waters uses an irregular, rhythmic delivery. No matter how many or how few words he utters in four beats, they do not seem rushed: instead of sounding compressed into a four-cornered box, they give the sense of being lightly draped over a four-post support. On "Hard Day Blues," Waters stretches the beat somewhat on his vocals, but the overall effect differs significantly from his LC technique. All the phrases on "Hard Day Blues" are approximately the same length, and they are evenly spaced in two-measure clumps throughout the tune. Moreover, although the song does feature syncopation, the words land solidly on the beat more frequently than in Waters's earlier work.

On multiple stylistic levels, then, "Hard Day Blues" represents a concerted attempt by Waters to adapt to contemporary urban styles. Having managed to record his new sound with a producer as established as Lester Melrose, Waters might well have felt that "Hard Day Blues" was a surefire bet to be a commercial breakthrough. If so, he was wrong. Melrose shelved "Hard Day Blues," and it remained unissued for twenty-five years.[30] Like Alan Lomax, the king of field-recorded blues, Melrose, the king of commercial blues, had let the future Father of the Chicago Blues pass him by.[31]

Almost by default, then, the opportunity to launch Waters's career fell to an unknown Polish immigrant, Leonard Chess. Chess was born Lazer

Shmuel Chez in 1917, two years after Alan Lomax and Waters. His family had lived in a shtetl of Motol, part of a largely Jewish region of Poland that was at the time controlled by Russia. In the early 1920s, Chess's father sought to escape anti-Semitism and poverty by sailing for America. A few years later he had saved enough money from his work as a carpenter to send for his wife and three children. On Columbus Day, 1928, eleven-year-old Leonard and his family arrived in Chicago. Chess seems to have adapted easily to America. After graduating from a technical high school, he held a series of odd jobs before entering the liquor business with his younger brother Phil in the early 1940s. They soon owned several liquor stores and bars, where they found that featuring black musicians increased the flow of customers. In 1946, when one of these musicians got an offer from a Hollywood producer to cut a record, Chess decided to do the job himself. He launched Aristocrat Records.[32]

At first, Aristocrat recorded mostly jazz and black pop (which in the forties was becoming known as "rhythm and blues," or "R & B"), but in 1947 the company considered moving into blues and invited the pianist Sunnyland Slim to the studio.[33] When the session needed a guitarist, Slim called in his friend Muddy Waters, who risked his job delivering venetian blinds by passing the rest of the day's deliveries on to a friend and rushing to the studio.[34] Slim began the session by singing two songs, but then Waters got the chance to sing two of his own, "Little Anna Mae" and "Gypsy Woman." These tunes represent Waters's continuing effort to perfect his commercial blues sound. Like "Hard Day Blues," they are tightly organized blues that prominently feature a rolling, boogie-woogie-style piano and Waters's somewhat tentative single-string guitar work. "Gypsy Woman" has a somewhat harder edge to it, and its occult subject matter foreshadows an important motif in Waters's later work. Overall, though, both of these tunes are attempts by Waters, still clearly in the Melrose mold, to create a smoother urban sound. Like Melrose, it seems, Chess was unconvinced by Waters's adaptation, and he held the recordings for months before releasing them and even then did little to push them.[35]

Early in 1948, though, Waters got invited back to record again for Chess, a session that would mark a dramatic turning point in his career. Frustrated, perhaps, that his new urban blues sound had yielded so few results, Waters this time brought his bottleneck slide to the studio and set aside his newer repertoire in favor of familiar Delta blues songs. Two of the three songs that Waters cut that day he had previously recorded for Alan Lomax—"Country Blues" (which Waters now called "I Feel Like Going Home") and "I Be's Troubled" (now "I Can't Be Satisfied"). With no great expectations, Chess released these songs as a single in April 1948, delivering them to the Aristocrat company's usual outlets—South Side Chicago's porters and Pullman conductors, barber shops, beauty shops, five and dimes, and record stores. The first pressing sold out within twelve hours. Chess quickly pressed more, and soon Waters and Chess had a legitimate hit on their hands. Waters later recalled, "All of a sudden I became Muddy Waters. You know? Just over night. People started to speakin', hollerin' across the streets at me. When they used to hardly say good morning, you know. I could walk down the street—'Hey, Muddy! Hey, Muddy! There go Muddy!' I'd been walking around them same people five years, they wouldn't say 'Good morning.' "[36] In the first of many ironies in Waters's career, he had finally broken into the urban commercial blues market by singing the old-fashioned tunes he had sung in Mississippi for years.

Why would "I Feel Like Going Home" and "I Can't Be Satisfied" prompt such a hearty "Good morning" from Chicago blacks? How can we account for the sudden popularity of these Delta-styled tunes? The most straightforward explanation is nostalgia. The thousands of migrants from the Mississippi Delta, struggling to make their way in the big city, grasped on to the old familiar sounds of home. A closer look at "I Feel Like Going Home," though, shows that there was more behind Waters's popularity than homesickness. Instead of literally re-creating the old-time blues style, with "I Feel Like Going Home" Waters forged a new hybrid of downhome and urban elements.

"Feel Like" certainly does sound more like Waters's Library of Congress recordings than any of his previous Chicago recordings. In remaking "Country Blues," Waters returned to the harsher vocal effects he had used when singing for Lomax.[37] He punches his words perhaps even more heavily on "Feel Like" than on "Country Blues," and at one point he jumps into falsetto, a familiar Delta effect. Throughout "Feel Like," moreover, he plays with pronunciation. On "Hard Day Blues" Waters had clearly enunciated almost every word, but on "Feel Like," as on "Country Blues," he alters, stretches, or clips words to increase their intensity. He also exhibits again his rhythmic facility as a vocalist, singing irregular, syncopated lines over and around the beat.

"Feel Like," therefore, is immediately recognizable as a Delta blues, a linear descendant of Son House's, Robert Johnson's, and Waters's own earlier versions of the song. Equally apparent, though, is that this off-spring has taken root in new ground. Waters's guitar work gives the clearest indication of a hybrid between old styles and new. In many ways Waters seems, on "Feel Like," to have returned to his original instrumental technique. He eschews the delicate single-string style of "Hard Day Blues" in favor of heavy, repeated chords in the Delta style (and when he does play a single string he insistently repeats the same note twelve times). Because Waters now uses an electric guitar, though, these down-home techniques produce very different effects than on his LC recordings. His heavy chords gain a new shimmering quality as he lets the amplified overtones ring. His bottleneck work, too, acquires a fresh character. The amplifier adds an echoing overtone to his shaky vibrato and to the slides he executes into notes from below.

Similarly, the spare arrangement on "Feel Like" seems on the face of it to suggest a return to the old style. Instead of using a full ensemble, Waters is accompanied only by bassist Ernest "Big" Crawford. Nonetheless, "Feel Like" follows a much more rigid tempo than "Country Blues." Individual verses show some small variations, but as a whole the tempo remains the same throughout the song (around 80 beats per minute). The steadier tempo also encourages a heavier beat than on "Country Blues," as Crawford firmly establishes a solid pulse.[38] With its electrified sound and strong rhythmic base, then, "Feel Like" reconfigures the Delta blues for audiences familiar with the jump blues heard in urban clubs.

On a more subtle level, too, "Feel Like" represents an adaptation for the new migrants from the South. The new title that Waters gives the tune implicitly signals a new relationship between the narrator and the song's lyrics. Son House had titled his version of the song "My Black Mama," and Robert Johnson had called his "Walkin' Blues," but when Waters recorded the tune for Alan Lomax in 1941, he had dubbed it "Country Blues." This title fit the LC song's lyrics, which express the narrator's frustration at being trapped in an isolated rural area without his lover. He has "the worried old blues," he sings, and "minutes feel like hours and hours seem like days." He has "been mistreated," and he is ready to take action: "I'm leaving this morning if I have to ride the blinds" (that is, in a train's baggage car). In the second version of "Country Blues" that Waters sang for Lomax (1942), he concretized these threats and added some thinly veiled sexual references:

Yes, I'm goin' back to St. Louis, I'm goin' to have my, my little
    churnin' done
I can't find no country woman can make my low-down, my little old
    butter come.[39]

On his 1948 version for Chess, Waters calls the song "I Feel Like Going Home," a title that implicitly places the narrator at a distance looking back longingly to his country roots. Although this title does not correspond directly to the song's lyrics, Waters makes a few lyrical adjustments that subtly shift the song's focus. On "Feel Like," Waters eliminates two verses that had appeared on his first version of "Country Blues"—the verse in which the narrator complains of the "worried old blues" and the one in which he threatens to "ride the blinds." The latter verse, especially, no longer had the same power for Waters and his listeners. They already *had* ridden the blinds, so to speak, and escaped the South.[40] Without this verse, the song becomes a more generalized lament about a mistreating woman and her "evil" and "lowdown ways" and about the passage of time.[41] With the subtraction of some of its specific thrust and the addition of the element of longing implicit in its title, Waters's new version of the song takes on an additional level of meaning. Beyond being an angry denunciation of a woman, it becomes a bittersweet reminder of the times and places in which such songs were sung.

On "Feel Like," Waters by instinct and effort synthesized old and new into a form that met the current needs of his African American peers. This was the sort of synthesis that Lead Belly lacked the cultural freedom to achieve. No matter how technically skilled Lead Belly may have been in modern styles (such as urban blues, cowboy crooning, or Tin Pan Alley popular song), to perform in these styles would have been inconsistent with his public persona as an old-time singer. Since the cult of authenticity painted him as a living anachronism, Lead Belly could not modernize his sound without facing a backlash. At this stage in his career, Waters did not face such constraints. As a commercial musician, his task was to represent a contemporary culture, not an intellectually idealized one from the past. He was singing primarily about and for a culture group of which he himself was a member, southern African American migrants in the city. His popularity did have a retrospective component—it depended in part on his canny recognition of blacks' attraction to the country roots they had left behind—but at this point Waters remained largely unencumbered by the cult of authenticity that had stymied Lead Belly.

Leonard Chess's outlook toward the blues contributed to Waters's relative freedom. Chess decidedly was not in the memory business. He was an entrepreneur who focused determinedly on the present and had little interest in preserving the past or shaping the inheritance of the future. A longtime engineer for Chess recalled him saying, "If shit is gold, we'll sell shit." Chess's interest in African American blues arose not from any expertise but from the realization that African American audiences would buy them. When Chess first heard Muddy Waters sing the Delta blues at that April 1948 recording session, he supposedly exclaimed, "What's he singing? I can't understand what he's singing." Waters later recalled that it was the Chess brothers' partner, Evelyn Aron, who understood his music and convinced Chess to release "I Feel Like Going Home" and "Can't Be Satisfied." "Chess didn't like my style of singing; he wondered who was going to buy that. The lady said, 'You'd be surprised who'd buy that.' He was dead down on our material." In another interview Waters added, "Leonard Chess never did dig me. He didn't dig me then. . . . She dug me."[42]

With the startling sale figures for Waters's first release, though, Chess began to dig the blues with a vengeance. Soon a steady stream of blues musicians were being recorded in Chess's studio. Chess proved to be highly skilled at introducing these artists into the black record market. He did so by constructing an elaborate distribution network. On Chicago's South Side alone the Aristocrat company had 180 small outlets, most of which the Chess brothers laboriously maintained through face-to-face contacts. Beyond Chicago, the market extended to the other portals of the northern black migration (Gary, Indiana; St. Louis; Detroit) and back to the migration's source, the South. The company's promotional efforts became particularly ambitious after the Chesses bought out Aron's share of Aristocrat in 1950 and launched Chess Records.[43] From 1950 to 1955, Leonard Chess periodically embarked on treks to nurture his southern markets, logging five thousand miles every three months. On these trips Chess worked to expand his network of contacts. He introduced his records to local record store owners, disc jockeys, and distributors; picked up tips about budding talent from area talent scouts and producers; and, occasionally, recorded a promising artist with the wire recorder he carried with him.[44]

In later years, the Chesses described these trips in romantic tones reminiscent of the Lomaxes' evocative accounts of their 1930s fieldwork. Just as there are canons of folk musicians, there are canons of folk music collectors. As they looked back on their work, the Chesses seem to have been eager to be remembered as pioneer discoverers of unvarnished rural songsters. In a story reminiscent of John Lomax's 1932 cross-country journey with young Alan and John Jr., Leonard Chess recollected that on his southern swing he would sometimes bring his young son, Marshall. "He was only eight," Chess recalled, "and I remember how he used to get tired and start to complain so I'd put a tag on him and put him on a plane for home." Like Alan Lomax, Marshall went on to follow in his father's career path, working at Chess all through his teenage years and becoming a company executive by his early twenties. Marshall's actual field experience may have been somewhat fractured, but in later years he had little trouble recounting the family lore about his and his father's adventures: "We'd stop off at a farmer's and record some guy out in a cotton field. He'd be set up on a couple of bales and my father would record him on the wire recorder—a *wire* recorder, not even a tape in those days! . . . I was ten or eleven." Recalling the isolated setting in which he set up his machine, Leonard Chess proudly noted, "I always paid for the electricity."[45]

Such documentarian moments, though, must have been exceedingly rare for the Chesses. They found the vast majority of their artists through straightforward commercial connections. Either the Chesses heard them in Chicago clubs, learned about them through their network of Chicago musicians, or discovered them waiting on the doorstep of their studio hoping for an audition. Often Chess bought the rights to artists or songs from other independent producers or small labels, usually in the South.[46]

In addition to romanticizing their role as discoverers of musicians, the Chesses shared other conceits with folklorists. Basically, the Chesses had no interest in connecting music to broader cultural or political ideals. Although they recorded African American music almost exclusively, they rarely saw themselves as preserving endangered cultural forms or demonstrating the dignity of the Negro race. The Chesses seem to have prided themselves, however, on having unusual empathy with African Americans. For most folklorists, being accepted by blacks was a major source of self-esteem. Over his career, Alan Lomax has sometimes gone to elaborate lengths to demonstrate his bond with his informants, from simply taking off his shoes when Muddy Waters entered the room barefoot to donning blackface when recording with Zora Neale Hurston in Florida, posing as a black reverend when conversing with a blind beggar in Mississippi, and recounting proudly that his singing of a prison song may well have convinced a group of bluesmen that he, too, had served time in a southern pen.[47]

The Chesses did not go to the same extremes as Lomax, but they did try to make themselves seem in touch with African American culture. "It was like a family," Phil Chess stressed. To fit in with his artists, Leonard adopted ghetto slang and learned to swear at them with casual proficiency. When historian Peter Guralnick visited the Chess company a couple of years after Leonard's death, he was struck by the extent to which Phil Chess had adopted the mannerisms of African American blues culture in dealing with his artists: "He can call a bluesman a motherfucker with great aplomb," Guralnick wrote, "and when he's conducting business negotiations he can play the dozens without even batting an eye. At times like these he no longer seems the mild-mannered, soft-spoken, almost self-deprecating man who appears in interviews. . . . If you look away for a moment, it is often difficult to distinguish the voices of the two men talking, the black man and the white one, cursing each other out in the harsh, elliptical, almost poetic language of the ghetto."[48]

Feeling strongly connected to African American culture, the Chesses at times tried to apply their insights during recording sessions. A studio drummer for the company, Odie Payne, recalls that in the studio Leonard Chess would work to transport himself into the mind-set of African American audiences. "Chess would sit there," Payne remembered, "with his eyes closed in the booth. If it hit him, he'd say 'that's it man,' but I heard him say many times, 'Man, you got to make me feel it.' The man would say 'I doing the best I can' and [Leonard] would say, 'Yeah, but I don't feel nothing.' . . . [Chess was] trying to be as a Negro. . . . Trying to feel you." In an oft-repeated story, Chess pushed aside Muddy Waters's drummer, who was fumbling with the beat on "She Moves Me," and played the bass drum line himself.[49]

The frequency with which this authenticating tale has been repeated suggests how rare such moments were. When recording, Chess generally relied not on his specific musical knowledge but on his vague sense of what sounds had worked before. "The Chess brothers didn't know A from Z in a beat," Etta James recalled.

> Leonard Chess would get in the booth with me while I was recording, and when I would get to a part where he thought I should squawl [*sic*] or scream "wheeawow!" he'd punch me in the side. I mean literally *punch* me. Or he'd pinch me real hard, so I'd go "yeeeow." And what-ever tune had the most "ooooch" or "eeech" or whatever, that's the tune he thought was going to be the hit.

> Then he'd sit there and listen to the playback, and he wouldn't pat his foot until I'd seen him sneaking a look at *my* foot. . . . And if he couldn't see it patting, he'd say, "Etta, I don't think that tune's any good." And then I'd wait until some old jive tune that wasn't anything came on, and I'd pat my foot and say, "How do you like that one?" And he'd say, "That's it! That's going to be the hit record! Believe what Leonard tells you!" He knew nothing about it.

Willie Dixon echoes, "Leonard didn't know one thing from another; he'd accept the other people's word for it if it sound good. But he didn't know any[thing] about it."[50] Likely some of the complaints by former

Leonard Chess, ca. 1960s.
(Courtesy MCA–Chess Records Files)

artists about Chess's musical ignorance stem from his notorious stingi-
ness with royalties. The fact remains that most of the performers criticiz-
ing Chess somehow managed to score the biggest hits of their careers
under his watchful eye.

James's story probably exaggerates Chess's lack of musical sense,
then, but its central insight rings true: in building a multimillion-dollar
business, Chess was savvy enough not to rely on his own musical in-

stincts but to keep a close watch on the reactions of his African American market. Before he released any record, he sent it to four people within the company. One was Willie Dixon, who, as I discuss below, made many of the decisions about song arrangements and instrumentation for Chess in the fifties and sixties. The others, though, had no specific musical background. They were Cary Sanders, a black woman in the accounting department; Dotty Lange, a southern white also in the accounting department; and Sonny Woods, who worked the stockroom. Dick Lapalm, a promotion consultant for the company after 1958, recalled that Woods was "the best because he was very blatant—he'd listen to something and go, 'This ain't shit,' or 'Put that motherfucker out.'"[51] As a businessman, Chess realized that these were the people whose opinions mattered and whose tastes he wanted to match. Above all, he was searching for a formula that generated consistent sales. When he found a winning combination, he stuck with it.

Chess's eagerness to re-create effective formulas accounts for his handling of Muddy Waters in the years immediately after the success of "I Feel Like Going Home" and "Can't Be Satisfied." Stunned by the sales of these rural-inflected blues, Chess insisted that Waters reproduce this downhome-flavored style as exactly as possible on subsequent recordings. For two years after "Feel Like," Chess resisted recording him with the full band that Waters was using on his club gigs. Instead, Chess basically limited the accompaniment to Waters's own guitar and Big Crawford's bass, the same pairing as on the "Feel Like"/"Can't Be" disc. These recordings also feature the same vocal inflections and downhome-tinged electric guitar riffs as on "Feel Like" and "Can't Be."[52]

In song selection, too, Chess stuck as close as possible to what had worked on the "Feel Like"/"Can't Be" disc. Indeed, "You're Gonna Miss Me," which Waters recorded in 1950, was a remake of "Can't Be" with new words added to the same bass and guitar parts. In this same period, Waters recorded Robert Johnson's "Walking Blues" (1950), on which "Feel Like" had been based, and other traditional songs.[53] He also continued to make explicit appeals to the migrants' nostalgia for the South. On "Down South Blues" (1948), he sang, "Goin' down south child / This weather here's too cold," and on "Where's My Woman Been" (1949) he added,

> Well my home is in the Delta
> Way out on that old farmer's road
> Well I'm leaving Chicago
> People I sure do hate to go.

"They were trying to make a Lightning Hopkins out of me," Waters lamented, "—an old-time blues cat."[54]

Only gradually did Chess let Waters adjust the "Feel Like"/"Can't Be" formula. In the summer of 1950 Waters recorded for Chess with two of his bandmates from the clubs, the young harmonica standout Little Walter Jacobs and the guitarist Jimmy Rogers. It took several more months before Chess would add a drummer. Through most of 1950 and 1951, Chess used each of the band members at one time or another, but he resisted using them all at once, choosing instead to rotate players in and out of the group. Similarly, Chess waited until the summer of 1951 to record Little Walter on the amplified harmonica, even though Walter had been performing amplified in clubs since the mid-forties.[55] Having found an audience for a spare, downhome sound, Chess was unwilling to risk losing it.

It was not Leonard Chess but Willie Dixon who, in the early 1950s, brought to the Chess company a more finely honed understanding of Waters's appeal. Dixon recognized that Waters's listeners were responding less to a specifically remembered Delta sound than to the overall vibrancy and emotional punch they associated with downhome blues. As Dixon began to exert more influence on the recording process at Chess, he made available to Waters a less rigid conception of tradition.

Dixon, like Waters and Alan Lomax, was born in 1915, the seventh of fourteen children (seven of whom survived) in Vicksburg, Mississippi. He left for Chicago in 1936, hoping to make it as a professional boxer. Although he won the Illinois Gold Gloves Championship as a heavyweight in the novice division and sparred with Joe Louis, his career stalled soon after he turned pro. Gradually, Dixon turned his full attention to his other love, music. From the beginning, he showed a sensitivity toward the pop sounds of the day. Dixon first recorded in 1940, as part of a quintet called the Five Breezes, for whom he played bass and sang. The group featured tightly rehearsed four- and five-part harmonies modeled after such popular groups as the Ink Spots and the Mills Brothers.[56]

Early in 1946, Dixon helped found the Big Three Trio (a timely reference to the wartime Roosevelt-Churchill-Stalin triumvirate), which consisted of a pianist, a guitarist, and Dixon on bass. Again the group was a highly professionalized ensemble. It specialized in pop standards and light blues, singing in tight harmony with an easy, swinging feel. Most popular among whites, the trio scored some significant hits in the mid- to late forties and received numerous bookings for its polished concert act at comfortable venues throughout the Midwest.[57] Meanwhile, Dixon was sitting in as a studio musician for Lester Melrose, playing bass behind many of the urban bluesmen Melrose was recording. This work caught Leonard Chess's attention, and late in 1948 he began hiring Dixon for recording sessions. When the Big Three broke up in 1951, Dixon started working at Chess full-time. Although he continued to play bass on sessions, his work behind the scenes started to over-shadow his role as a performer.

Chess would later describe Dixon as "my right arm." Dixon recalled that at one time or another he did everything from "packing records to sweeping the floor to answering the telephone to making out orders." Chess especially depended on him for his talent at selecting and arrang-ing material for other artists. "The artists would come," Dixon remem-bered, "and the first thing they would be sent to me." They would be told to " 'See Willie and what he thinks about it.' They told me if I thought it was a good thing to let them know and get it together and they would decide whether they would record it or not. They were going to do what they wanted to, anyway, but I would kind of approve them first." Dixon's influence was being felt at almost every stage of the production process in the early 1950s. Not until January 1954, though, was Dixon's portfolio complete. Only then did Chess begin to recognize Dixon's talent as a songwriter. Dixon had been writing songs since his youth in Missis-sippi—"I must have had 150 songs, a whole bagful"—but Chess had no interest until one day Dixon told him he had the perfect tune for Muddy Waters. That January, Waters went into the studio and recorded "I'm Your Hoochie Coochie Man."[58] It became a major hit that redefined Waters's sound, his style, and even his persona.

"Hoochie Coochie Man" actually built on and extended changes in Waters's recordings that had begun a few years earlier. Starting late in 1950 and especially in 1951, coinciding approximately with Dixon's ar-rival as a full-time producer at Chess, Waters's tunes began to edge away from the formula that "Feel Like Going Home" and "I Can't Be Satis-fied" had established. In part, the change involved adapting his song selection. Waters recorded fewer remakes or direct variations on classic Delta blues tunes and concentrated more on "original" compositions of his own. The style in which Waters recorded these songs began to evolve as well. As Chess slowly let him bring more musicians into the studio, Waters moved closer to putting on record the heavy, vibrant sound his band produced at club gigs. The new repertoire and fuller sound quickly brought results. The first tune to feature Little Walter on harmonica ("Louisiana Blues," 1950) became Waters's first to move beyond a re-gional record market (the northern black-migration cities and the Deep

Willie Dixon, ca. 1960s.
(Courtesy Ray Flerlage / MCA–Chess Records Files)

South) and enter the national R & B charts. Waters followed this break-through with a string of successful songs, all his own compositions and most showcasing Little Walter. On "She Moves Me" (July 1951), Walter finally got to record with his harmonica amplified, achieving a sustained, eerily distorted effect. The song cracked the R & B top ten.[59] After these successes, Chess at last let Waters use his full band. By the fall of 1952, Waters was recording backed by harmonica, piano, guitar, and drums.[60] Chess and Waters, likely with Dixon's help, were learning that adapting Waters's electrified Delta style could actually improve his sales. They began to realize that Waters's audiences did not have as simple an attraction to the old-time sound as they had supposed.

Waters's hits from the early fifties, though, represented essentially cautious experiments. Much like "I Feel Like Going Home," they remained securely within the traditional Delta blues style. Almost all the songs were slow, twelve-bar blues that followed the A-A-B lyrics pattern. Waters was writing mostly new material and updating his sound with talented band members, but basically he was resting his commercial hopes on variations of the same sorts of songs he had played for Alan Lomax a decade before. Before "Hoochie Coochie Man," Waters was still essentially a downhome bluesman. "Hoochie Coochie" made him, briefly, a pop star.

The difference was built into the very form of the song. Dixon had a savvier conception of commercial blues than either Waters or Chess. He recognized that the vast majority of record buyers in the early and mid-fifties did not judge blues songs by exacting standards of authenticity: they did not have a firm set of criteria by which they distinguished "real" blues from "fake." Within the genre of "blues," Dixon realized, he had immense latitude. He began to break away from the traditional twelve-bar blues style, writing songs that drew on commercial pop forms.

Like most pop songs, "Hoochie Coochie Man" divides neatly into eight-bar chunks. It also borrows from pop tunes the technique of the recurring chorus, an element foreign to most Delta blues songs. After every eight measures of new lyrics, the singer sings an eight-bar refrain:

Well, you know I'm here
Everybody knows I'm here
Well, you know I'm a hoochie coochie man
Everybody knows I'm here.[61]

The most striking aspect of "Hoochie Coochie Man," its distinctive arrangement, also marks a departure from traditional downhome blues. The song opens with a strong, rhythmic burst in the guitar, drums, and harmonica—da-*Da*dada-*Da*—followed by two full beats of silence. When Waters begins singing, he fills in the silence, completely unaccompanied. The repeated rhythmic figure and Waters's a cappella vocals alternate throughout all the eight-bar segments aside from the refrains. This pattern, very unusual in Delta blues, derives instead from the New Orleans jazz technique of stop-time, in which a band suddenly breaks and leaves an opening for a short instrumental solo. This technique spread from New Orleans jazz into the boogie-woogie piano and Texas blues styles that together helped shape the post–World War II urban blues.[62]

In addition to its musical form, the lyrical content of "Hoochie Coochie Man" also reflects Dixon's eagerness to adapt to pop styles. More than previous bluesmen, he embraced the notion that a song should tell a coherent story. Certainly this was not a completely foreign idea to downhome blues singers. The more polished blues artists had always tended to center their songs around a certain mood or theme, and this practice had become more widespread as the commercial pressures to copyright had discouraged improvised lyrics. But even if blues performers learned to repeat their lyrics the same way each time (and many resisted this practice), their work tended to retain a free-associative aspect. Images might follow one from the other, but often it would be hard to see how those from the first verse connected to those in the fifth or fifteenth. The absence of a chorus encouraged this discontinuity. Singers could introduce new ideas without having to tie them back to a constant refrain.

Muddy Waters had come out of this improvisatory blues tradition. Significant lyrical differences had surfaced, for instance, whenever Alan Lomax had recorded a song of his twice. By the early 1950s, though, Waters had become quite skilled at more formal composition. His hits for Chess in this period have set words, and, for the most part, the lyrics center clearly on a subject announced by the song's title. Still, the songs include verses that only loosely connect to the main theme. "Long Distance Call" (1951), for example, begins with a stanza that clearly matches the song's title. The narrator begs a lover to call him on the phone. In the second verse, though, Waters shifts to a much more generalized statement of longing, one that could just as easily be part of a blues having nothing to do with long-distance relationships:

> One of these days
> I'm gonna show you how nice a man can be
> I'm gonna buy you a brand new Cadillac
> If you only speak some pretty words about me.

Certainly the two verses make sense together, but they do not seem inextricably bound.

A similar pattern is evident on "She Moves Me" (1951). The song opens with the agonized and awe-struck statement of a man under the spell of a powerful, selfish woman: "She moves me man / Honey now I don't see how it's done." At this point, however, Waters shifts to describing how the woman insults him by calling him a "dumbbell" and a "square," a vaguer plaint that could appear in practically any blues about a wrong-doing woman. This stanza does not specifically follow up the first verse's idea that the woman has a supernatural hold on the narrator. In the next verse, though, Waters returns to this theme in a much more specific way than before, recounting her unearthly abilities to make the dead run, the dumb speak, and the blind see. Such discontinuities do not prove that Waters was a sloppy writer but rather that even in songs with carefully wrought, "original" lyrics, he had a tolerance for lines that only obliquely connected to each other or to his song's central theme.

Dixon's songs, in contrast, reflect a much more rigid conception of structure and thematic development. He was eager to do more than create a mood or spin out a series of evocative images: he wanted to tell a tale with a beginning, middle, and end. This desire for narrative cohesion helps explain why Dixon adopted formal elements from pop songs, such as opening introductions, refrains, and bridges.[63] As Dixon explained, "In dealing with twelve-bar music you could never get a chance to express everything or tell a complete story. And so I started writing introductions to these songs and also middles and changing ideas within it."[64]

In Dixon's work, each verse builds on the previous one, corroborating and elaborating on what came before; and the refrain serves as his chance to hammer home the moral of the story. "Hoochie Coochie Man," for example, verse by verse traces a story from past to present to future. It begins in a time before the narrator's birth, when a fortune-teller foretold great things for him:

The gypsy woman told my mother
Before I was born
You got a boy child comin'
He's gonna be a son of a gun
He's gonna make pretty women
Jump and shout
Then the world want to know
What this was all about.[65]

Next comes the refrain, which moves the story into the present. The narrator boldly asserts that the gypsy prophecy has come true and that he is a supernaturally powerful man:

> But you know I'm here
> Everybody knows I'm here
> Well, you know I'm a hoochie coochie man
> Everybody knows I'm here.

The next verse continues in the present, with the narrator boasting that he has the power of several voodoo charms rolled into one: the black cat bone, the John the Conqueror root, and the mojo hand (a perfumed, red flannel bag with mystical powers).[66] In the middle of the verse, though, the story looks to the future as the narrator makes a prophecy of his own, that he will win the woman he is eyeing and be recognized for his virile power:

> I got a black cat bone
> I got a mojo, too
> I got the John the Conqueror
> I'm gonna mess with you
> I'm gonna make you, pretty girl
> Lead me by the hand
> Then the world will know
> The hoochie coochie man.

When the chorus returns, therefore, the proclamation "I'm here . . . I'm a hoochie coochie man" means more than it did before. Now the listener has a stronger sense of what powers the narrator claims to have and of the extent of his ambitions for them. The final verse recapitulates the whole narration from the past to the future:

> On the seventh hour
> On the seventh day
> On the seventh month
> The seventh doctor say
> He was born for good luck
> And that you'll see
> I got seven hundred dollars
> Don't you mess with me.

The narrator boasts that he was born under good omens (the string of lucky sevens), stresses the successes he is already enjoying ("I got seven hundred dollars"), and cautions against any future attempts to sidetrack his plans ("Don't you mess with me").

Dixon's lyrical choices reflect an overarching concern with how individual parts connect to form a whole. In both music and lyrics, therefore, his "Hoochie Coochie Man" sits closer to the pop song genre than to the downhome blues traditions on which Muddy Waters had based so much of his appeal. How, then, can we explain why the song enjoyed extraordinary success among blues audiences and became an established standard in the blues repertoire?

Part of the answer, of course, is that for all its borrowings from pop forms, "Hoochie Coochie Man" retains significant blues elements. Like most blues, it confines itself to the tonic (I), subdominant (IV), and dominant (V⁷) chords and makes extensive use of the flatted third and sevenths so characteristic of the so-called blues scale. What most separates "Hoochie Coochie Man" from the pop songs of the day is the persona that its narrator projects. Every line in the song works to locate the narrator in the exotic world of the blues. It describes a culture ruled by omens, charms, and supernatural occurrences; a world where virility is prized and repeatedly proven; an emotional, expressive, dangerous world, with a rich idiosyncratic language and colorful customs. Clearly, Dixon is describing the rural South that he and Waters and their audience remember so well.

Or is he? The lyrics of "Hoochie Coochie Man" are so chock-full of mystical and sexual references that they start to seem stylized and exaggerated. Certainly there was some basis in reality for these references. Many African Americans in the South did believe in voodoo, and, as in any culture, sexual exploits were a familiar topic of gossip and speculation in African American communities. In fact, several downhome blues songs dealt with the voodoo theme, and innumerable ones were laden with sexual metaphors. But Dixon took this established part of the blues tradition and fixated on it in such a concentrated way as to sensationalize it. The song became almost a litany of the elements of rural African American culture that would seem most colorful to outsiders. It created a supercharged version of southern culture, a world ruled by violence, sex, and the supernatural.

The song's admixture of pop-influenced blues and juiced-up downhome lyrics proved explosive. It became Waters's biggest seller to date, hitting number three on the R & B charts in March 1954 and remaining in the top ten for thirteen weeks. An ecstatic Chess urged Dixon to write more songs like it, and Dixon happily obliged. That same year he wrote two more songs for Waters, "I Just Want to Make Love to You" and "I'm

Ready." Both draw on the formula suggested by "Hoochie Coochie Man." They combine blues chords and scales within pop song structures and use stop-time riffs. Strikingly, both songs also build on the swaggering, macho persona that "Hoochie Coochie Man" had introduced to such effect. "Make Love to You" is the wooing song of a man who knows what he wants, feels no need to hide his desire behind social pleasantries, and does not expect to be refused: "I don't want you to be no slave / I don't want you to work all day / I don't want you to be true / I just want to make love to you."[67] "I'm Ready" pursues a similar theme with the same confidence and further outlandish boasting:

> I gotta axe handle pistol
> On a graveyard frame
> That shoots tombstone bullets
> Wearing balls and chain
> I'm drinkin' TNT
> Smokin' dynamite
> I hope some screwball
> Start a fight.
>
> Because I'm ready
> Ready as anybody can be
> I'm ready for you
> I hope you're ready for me.

"Make Love to You" and "I'm Ready" were powerful hits for Waters, each reaching number four on the national R & B charts.[68]

In part, Dixon's and Waters's 1959 successes represented the fruits of Leonard Chess's system of regional distribution. They also derived in part from Chess's grasp of "payola," the pattern of bribes for services that determined radio airplay. In the fifties, as today, record sales depended heavily on radio exposure. Until Congress intervened in 1960, though, disc jockeys often would play a tune only if the record companies paid them to do so. The Chess company unabashedly relied on such payoffs to boost sales in the 1950s. Leonard Chess recalled, "Payola was standard practice in the industry. . . . At least *I* was doing it honestly—make a deal with them [the DJs] and send 'em a check and at the end of the year report it on a 1099 form."[69]

Chess's talent for distributing and promoting his product, though, cannot fully account for the public response to Dixon's songs. As with most mass-culture successes, the songs' popularity to a great extent derived from their ability to contain different meanings for different people. In the mid-1950s, even more than in previous decades, the notion of a single "blues audience" was illusory. Even among the African American migrants from the South, clear divisions had emerged. Dixon's tunes sold so well, perhaps, because as syntheses between blues and pop, old and new, they were cultural products that disparate groups could adapt to fit their own needs.

In the mid-1950s a good portion of the blues audience remained southern migrants who had only very recently arrived in Chicago. Between 1940 and 1950 the African American population in Chicago had grown from 277,000 to 492,000, an expansion of 78 percent. From 1950 to 1960 it surged to 812,000, a growth of another 65 percent.[70] At one point in the 1950s, 2,200 African Americans were moving to Chicago each week, the vast majority of them from the South. By the end of the decade, Chicago contained over half a million more African Americans than two decades before. This overwhelming influx of new residents strained the city's peacetime economic capabilities and pushed against traditional neighborhood boundaries. When "Hoochie Coochie Man" was released in 1954, demobilization from the Korean War (which had ended the previous summer) was producing massive black unemployment.[71]

The newest arrivals to the city endured the worst hardships first. As the laborers with the fewest skills and least experience, they had the hardest time finding jobs and tended to be the first fired. The recent migrants also had difficulties finding adequate housing. Chicago's South Side, the settlement point for the vast majority of previous African American migrants, no longer could offer affordable shelter to all the newcomers. In the early 1950s, therefore, African Americans began to edge into other, previously all-white neighborhoods, especially on the West Side. Whites eager to preserve their neighborhood's racial homogeneity and its perceived land values hurled insults, rocks, and firebombs. The chaos, fanned by real estate speculators, caused property values to plummet and whites to flee for the suburbs. One West Side neighborhood, Lawndale, shifted from 13 percent African American in 1950 to 91 percent in 1960. Facing economic deprivation and enjoying little social standing, then, the most recent migrants found that their lives differed the least from what they had left behind in the South. The same was true culturally. Following the classic pattern of assimilation, recent arrivals were the most likely to hold on to the foodways, religious beliefs, and rituals of the "home country."[72]

To these migrants, Dixon's songs offered some of the same consolation that Waters's statements of yearning in "I Feel Like Going Home" had provided for earlier settlers. Joining familiar, downhome holdovers with new urban styles, the tunes achieved formally the sort of juxtaposition that the migrants themselves were grappling with in their own lives. To hear evocations of their southern customs in the context of the vibrantly urban sound appealed to their longing for all they had left behind and their eagerness to merge the old and new.

Like Waters's early Chess recordings, therefore, Dixon's songs offered much to the homesick migrant fresh from the farm. But the differences are more striking than the similarities between Waters's homesick blues of the late forties and Dixon's outlandish mid-1950s evocations of the South. Dixon's songs could appeal to newcomers from the South, but his language and imagery suggest that he was primarily speaking for and to migrants who had been settled in the North longer.

These more established migrants led lives that were very dissimilar from those of African Americans just arrived from Mississippi, and they were well aware of the differences. By the mid-fifties, more than a full generation had passed since the first wave of African Americans had arrived after World War I, and the harbingers of the second great migration had been in town for fifteen years. These groups had made Chicago's South Side a mecca of African American culture whose cultural richness and community strength rivaled the Harlem of the early decades of the twentieth century. The South Side had more than its share of putrid slums, but as the home to black-owned businesses, community organizations, and public institutions, it was a source of African American pride and envy. The South Side was seen, in journalist Nicholas Lemann's words, as "the seat of civilization," and part of its community identity involved condescension toward recent arrivals striving to achieve what the South Siders already had. Lemann writes, "The South Side looked down on the West Side, and thought of it as made up wholly of rural people from Mississippi who had proceeded directly there from the Illinois Central station. South Side families did not approve of romances between their children and young West Siders; children on the West Side dreamed of moving to the South Side when they grew up."[73] In this schematic division between newcomers and old-timers, Dixon and Waters belonged securely to the more established group. Their lives had essentially followed an upwardly mobile arc since they had left the South. Certainly they faced prejudice within the industry, and they probably never earned their fair share of royalties, but on the South Side they were well-known entertainers assured of finding a paying audience for their music. They acknowledged their downhome southern roots, but they had become Chicago urbanites.

This context sheds some light on Dixon's depiction of rural African American culture in his songs. His lyrics describe the South from the perspective of someone who has moved on and is now looking back from a distance. The explicit longing that Waters expressed in "I Feel Like Going Home," "I Can't Be Satisfied" ("Goin' back down South, child / Don't you wanna go"), or "Down South Blues" ("I'm going down South child / This weather here's too cold") is absent from "Hoochie Coochie Man," "I'm Ready," and "I Just Want to Make Love to You." In these newer songs, bittersweet yearning has been replaced by the easy recollections of glory days gone by. Dixon's lyrics sound like chuckling memories of the rowdy, humorous, even violent exploits of one's youth, or like oft-told and oft-exaggerated stories about *other* people's youths. The songs suggest a past that, over the years, has slowly been converted from a jumble of visceral feelings into a collection of finely honed anecdotes. Nostalgia still surfaces strongly in these stories, but there is little sense of regret or remorse. The tellers of these tales look back on the old days from a distance, accepting that they can never turn back the clock.

Both Dixon and Waters were explicit about feeling that they no longer belonged in the southern culture of their youth. They treated their downhome past as a resource to be drawn on, a memory that they could share with their audiences. They saw no contradiction in reveling in these memories while having no desire to return to the culture of the past. Dixon, for example, filled his tunes with supernatural references but openly scorned occult practices, characterizing them as "a kind of weakness to a majority of the [southern, African American] people." He invoked the old days not to advocate its belief system but to communicate with his audiences. "I found out," he explained, "[that] by using some of the past it fitted a lot of the people and fits also our hopes for the future."[74] Waters, likewise, recalled that he had believed in voodoo magic while living in the South ("We all believed in mojo hands," he remembered) but that after a few years in Chicago he had dismissed it as a racket that duped uneducated blacks: "It's just a con game on people's heads, you know, gettin' the fools. And these mojo doctors was drivin' big cars owned big homes, 'cause the peoples was brainwashed." Nonetheless, Waters felt comfortable employing voodoo culture as a common reference point with listeners: "You know, when you're writin' them songs that are coming from down that way, you can't leave out somethin' about that mojo thing. Because this is what black people really believed in at that time. We played so many times, 'I'm goin' down to Louisiana / Get me a mojo hand' [in "Louisiana Blues"], and I tried to make it a picture so you could see it, just like you're lookin' at it. When I was singin' it I didn't believe in it no way."[75]

Of the established South Side migrants who helped make Waters's 1954 recordings hits, most probably shared his disbelief in mojos, just as most probably did not approach women and say, "I just want to make love to you." Although they may not have literally subscribed to the sentiments Dixon expressed in these songs, his tone and the imagery rang true for them. The energetic, flamboyant culture that Dixon's songs evoked reminded them of how they liked to remember the South they had left behind. Whether Dixon's depictions of African American culture were strictly accurate or not, they tapped into (and helped shape) African Americans' emerging collective memory of southern culture. More than Chess or Waters, Dixon had realized that blues audiences were not wedded to the traditional Delta formula and were not necessarily seeking literal depictions of the South they had left behind. Songs could succeed, he showed, if they evoked the spirit and vibrancy that blues audiences ascribed to southern culture.

Waters and Chess were quick to grasp Dixon's lesson, and they worked to follow up on the successes of 1954. Waters wrote a series of tunes over the next few years that to a remarkable degree mimicked the style that Dixon had introduced on "Hoochie Coochie Man," "I'm Ready," and "I Just Want to Make Love to You." Songs like "Mannish Boy" (recorded in 1955), "Got My Mojo Working" (1956), and "Evil" (1957) borrow many musical techniques from Dixon's work—eight-bar verses, repeated choruses, stop-time, and the like. In fact "Evil" uses the same da-Dadada-*Da* riff that appears in "Hoochie Coochie Man," and "Mannish Boy" uses a variation of the same figure.[76] Waters seems also to have made a concerted effort to match the number of allusions to downhome mysticism and sexual prowess that appeared on Dixon's hits. "Mannish Boy" outlines a prophecy narrative that closely follows the plot of "Hoochie Coochie Man." As a boy of five, Waters sings, his mother had foretold that he would become "the greatest man alive." Swelling with pride, the singer announces the prophecy fulfilled: "Now I'm a man. . . . I'm a hoochie coochie man." With similar swagger "Evil" announces, "Oh so evil / Evil as a body can be / Well you know I'm the hoochie coochie man / Don't nobody mess with me." "Got My Mojo Working" echoes with "Going down to Louisiana / Get me a mojo hand / Gonna have all you women / Fetched under my command."[77] Waters is credited as composer of these tunes, but Dixon's involvement in producing songs for Chess no doubt accounts for some of these similarities. Regardless of who contributed what, however, Waters, Chess, and Dixon are plainly trying to recycle the elements that had produced hits in 1954.

Contemporary accounts suggest that in his stage shows, too, Waters assumed the feral persona that Dixon's songs had created for him. In the late fifties Paul Oliver, a pioneering blues historian from Britain, heard Waters play at the F & J Lounge in Gary, Indiana, a club frequented by African American steelworkers and servicemen. Oliver was awestruck by the display Waters put on, describing him as

> stamping, hollering, his whole body jerking in sheer physical expression of his blues. He would double up, clench his fists, straighten with a spring like a flick-knife, leap in the air, arch his back and literally punch out his words whilst the perspiration poured down his face and soaked through his clothing.

> The effect was stunning. And frightening, too. The sheer physical drive of band and blues singer chilled the spine. Muddy roared, leaped, jerked in fierce and violent spasms. When he came off the stage [at 4:00 A.M.], he was in a state of near trance and the sweat poured off him. It was close on half an hour before he unwound. . . . For most of the following day, he lay in a shaded room with an icepack on his head.[78]

This description, as I discuss below, probably says as much about Oliver and white critics' conceptions of the blues as about Waters; but the account does, perhaps, suggest the image that Waters was trying to project in this period.

Dixon, of course, was eager to follow up "Hoochie Coochie Man" himself, and he wrote several songs in the mid-fifties that Waters and other artists recorded for Chess. Almost as soon as it had achieved success, though, the Chess-Dixon-Waters hit-making formula began to lose its potency. In 1956, wanting more complete artistic control and better pay, Dixon left Chess for Cobra Records, a short-lived Chess rival based in Chicago. Dixon wrote the label's first single, "I Can't Quit You Baby," which became a top ten R & B hit for the young bluesman Otis Rush.[79] Cobra's financial and administrative problems, though, soon left Dixon just as dissatisfied as he had been before, and he returned to the Chess company early in 1959. He wrote some moderately successful songs over the next few years for Waters (e.g., "You Shook Me" and "You Need Love," both recorded in 1962) and for Waters's rival on Chess, Howlin' Wolf (e.g., "Little Red Rooster," "Back Door Man," and "Spoonful"). But none generated strong sales. Between 1960 and 1969 Waters, Wolf, and their fellow Chicago bluesmen Little Walter and Sonny Boy Williamson combined for only two chart hits.[80]

Overall, then, the decade after the mid-fifties was a period of commercial decline for Dixon, Waters, and the rural-inflected Chicago blues style they had forged. The year 1954 may have marked Waters's commercial breakthrough, but it also proved to be the culmination of his commercial career. He never matched the popularity of these three hits, and after 1958 he dropped from the R & B charts permanently.[81] Even as it represented his peak, 1954 also signaled the arrival of the force that would knock Waters from his perch as an R & B star. Willie Dixon had brought Waters new heights of commercial success by fusing pop and traditional forms; but in the way of such syntheses, it was very much of the moment. When the cultural balance tilted, Dixon's timely synthesis would soon look outdated. Tilt it did—and shake, rattle, twist, and shout. In April 1954, the day before Waters recorded "I Just Want to Make Love to You," Bill Haley and the Comets recorded "Rock around the Clock" in New York. The next year it soared to number one on *Billboard*'s pop charts and number three on the R & B charts. The rock and roll craze had begun.[82]

As Haley's hit sold millions of copies and his concerts drew thousands of screaming fans, record companies quickly recognized its central lesson: there was a massive audience of white teenagers that could be reached with the right type of R & B–tinged pop song. Naturally, the Chess brothers set out to capitalize on this new dynamic. As Leonard Chess remembered, "The kids wanted the big beat, cars and young love. It was a trend and we jumped on it." In the summer of 1955, the company released a single called "Maybellene," by an unknown singer-guitarist from St. Louis, Chuck Berry. While in New York on business, Leonard Chess took the record directly to Alan Freed—the powerful DJ who in 1952 had coined the term "rock and roll"—and urged him to play it. For his trouble, Freed got co-credit and royalties as songwriter (as did Russ Fratto, the man who printed up Chess's record labels). Soon the Chess company had a major national hit. "Maybellene" reached number one on the R & B listings and "crossed over" to number five on the pop charts. That same year Chess launched a significant, if not quite as dramatic, crossover career with Bo Diddley's "I'm a Man" and "Bo Diddley."[83] The Chess company had demonstrated once and for all that African American performers could tap into the commercial power of the white youth market.

Muddy Waters and Willie Dixon were not blind to the potential for crossover. Through a chance encounter, in fact, it was Waters who had directed Chuck Berry to the Chess brothers. Waters's "Mannish Boy" (1955), moreover, drew directly on Diddley's "I'm a Man" (although the lines about the hoochie coochie man and his mother's prophecy were Waters's own). Dixon, especially, did not turn his back on the new styles. He was involved in producing "Maybellene," working with Berry to juice up what was initially a country-and-western-styled song.[84] Dixon played bass on the cut and on most of Berry's recordings into the 1960s. Dixon also wrote several of Bo Diddley's more successful tunes (including "You Can't Judge the Book by Its Cover" [1962] and "Pretty Thing" [1959]) and played bass on several of Diddley's sessions.[85]

Despite Waters's and Dixon's contacts with the emerging rock and roll styles, they and most of the Chess bluesmen found it extremely difficult to cross over themselves. In the late forties and early fifties they had transformed country blues into urban blues, but adapting to the white youth market proved to be more difficult. In the late fifties many of the same elements that had enabled the bluesmen to reach urban blacks hamstrung their ability to move beyond this audience. Suddenly Waters's allusions to southern culture, his use of African American argot, and his references to raw sex and voodoo mysticism ceased to be assets. White teenagers preferred to hear stories about their lives or, more typically, the lives they liked to imagine for themselves—ones full of true romance and spirited high jinks. In their fantasies about cruising in T-Birds they did not carry mojos.

Beyond the lyrical gap, Waters's songs had a different rhythmic feel than rock and roll tunes. His blues lacked the same propulsive drive as "Maybellene" or Little Richard's "Tutti Frutti." They did not fit with the new dances like the stroll and the fish and the steady stream of new steps that Dick Clark began introducing on "American Bandstand" in 1957. By the mid-fifties Waters was a forty-year-old bluesman and the victim of something of a generation gap. His lyrics, his sound, and even the persona he projected were not in step with the culture of the newly powerful young white audiences, and he was no match for younger stars like Chuck Berry and Chubby Checker who duckwalked and twisted their way to teen-idol status. As music historian Peter Guralnick writes, "[Around 1955] the race music which Chess had been recording up until that time would suddenly become an anachronism."[86]

Whites, of course, had never been a central part of Waters's constituency, but as the fifties progressed, the same factors that limited Waters's appeal among rock and roll audiences began to affect his popularity among African Americans as well. Part of the problem stemmed from broader cultural shifts taking place in African American culture at this time. As the civil rights movement emerged, many African Americans began to associate the blues with the Jim Crow era they were trying to leave behind. Waters's feral persona and downhome allusions began to strike them as inappropriate in an era that prized integration and racial dignity. Music historian Charles Keil has described African Americans in this period as reluctant "to be identified with that 'nasty,' 'gutbucket,' 'bottom,' 'in-the-alley' music 'from slavery days.' " In the late fifties, Waters began to lose ground with younger African American audiences.[87]

Waters retained his core following among somewhat older black urbanites, but rock and roll had brought about changes in the recording industry that made this audience almost irrelevant. White audiences were so much larger and more lucrative that the traditional R & B labels began to devote themselves almost completely to trying to achieve crossover. Marshall Chess recalls that the economics of the decision were simple: "When we started selling Chuck Berry and Bo Diddley to whites, the volume was an immense difference. A blues would do 20–30,000 copies, nothing in comparison, and that would be a hit." Blues performers stopped getting the promotional attention they would have needed to nurture new audiences and sustain old ones. After "Rock around the Clock," Alan Freed and other early rock impresarios staged a series of well-hyped tours in which black R & B and white country singers alike were promoted as rock and roll stars. Chuck Berry, Little Richard, LaVern Baker, Jimmy Reed, and Fats Domino could make this transition and gained valuable exposure; but old-fashioned blues artists were excluded. Record companies no longer were devoting their energies and their payola to pushing blues performers, and Alan Freed's example had shown disc jockeys that rock and roll could bring them fame and fortune. Stations began dropping blues from their play lists. By the late fifties, says Willie Dixon, "when we took a record to someone, no one would play it."[88]

The Chess company both reacted to and helped create this climate of retrenchment for blues artists. The label dropped all but its major singers from its roster. Although it continued to record Waters and Howlin' Wolf, primarily it focused on moving away from the blues into other, more profitable genres. The company expanded its jazz output and even released some comedy albums, but the major new frontier was soul music. In 1961 Chess hired twenty-four-year-old Detroit native Roquel "Billy" Davis as its new A & R (artist and repertory) director and staff producer and gave him considerable authority to direct the label's efforts to capitalize on this new urban black sound. Dixon retained primary influence over blues recordings at Chess, but these were no longer as central to the company's agenda.[89] Rock and roll was such a powerful musical synthesis that, within just a few years, it had pushed its predecessors to the margins.

Whether by instinct or design, in the late fifties Willie Dixon began carving out a new, dramatically different niche for the blues, one that would prove more enduring and powerful than Bill Haley's or Chubby Checker's personas as teen idols. Facing the decline of urban blues as a commercial pop music, Dixon began to repackage it as a roots music, presenting it to largely white audiences as both an alternative to and the progenitor of rock and roll. In effect, he shifted his focus from mass markets to collective memory. It proved to be his savviest marketing move of all.

This new phase of Dixon's career began with an effort to jump-start his own flagging career as a performer. In 1957 he had formed a duo with Memphis Slim (Peter Chatman), a pianist who had recorded for Lester Melrose's Bluebird label in the forties and had led a seven-piece jump blues band including two saxophones. Gigs in Chicago proved to be so scarce that, in desperation, Dixon and Slim decided to leave the area and tour in places with fewer competitors. "Slim and I worked here and there in America," Dixon recalled, "and it was our intention to promote the blues. We played in California and Seattle and all the way up and down the West Coast, just trying to promote the blues."[90] This tour did not draw well, but in attempting to draw neophytes to the blues it prefigured future successes. Perhaps unknowingly, Dixon had joined an emerging cluster of folklorists, performers, record company executives, and buffs working to launch a blues revival.

Within efforts to preserve and popularize the blues in the fifties and sixties one can distinguish two currents, one that took a folkloristic attitude toward the music and one that adopted a looser, less purist conception of the material. The first current came out of the Lomaxes' work, particularly their mission to preserve the last vestiges of "traditional" African American music. Its advocates treated the blues as a venerable rustic style and set out to preserve it before it slipped away.

The decade from the early forties to the early fifties had been a time of decline for folklorists. The profession had endured the dismantling of the New Deal's arts programs, a damaging alliance with the failed Henry Wallace presidential campaign, and the blacklisting of many of its eminent members during the Red Scare (during which Alan Lomax fled to England).[91] Even as McCarthyism was at its height, though, a few folklorists and enthusiasts were laying the groundwork for a powerful resurgence of interest in collecting rural African American music. This rebirth came out of efforts to understand the roots of jazz. In the forties, when the vigorous bebop sound was only just emerging, the popular swing style had struck many performers and critics as too calcified. To understand and reinvigorate the contemporary scene, many had turned to jazz's roots, sparking a revival of the 1920s Dixieland style.[92] In the early fifties, collectors and critics began trying to take the story one step further back—to unearth the roots of Dixieland—and became enthralled with the downhome blues.

Connections between jazz and blues, of course, had been made long before the fifties. From the Original Dixieland Jazz Band's "Livery Stable Blues" (1917), to Louis Armstrong's "Gut Bucket Blues" (1925), to Count Basie's "Good Morning Blues" (1937), a bewildering variety of jazz tunes had claimed allegiance to the form. Jazz impresario John Hammond had been one of the first to make an explicit historical connection between the two styles. His "From Spirituals to Swing" concerts at Carnegie Hall (1938 and 1939) had drawn a line from rural singers like Sonny Terry and Big Bill Broonzy to contemporary jazzmen like Basie and Benny Goodman.

Like Hammond, the collectors of the fifties initially sought to understand blues as a jazz precursor, but they pursued the quest with unprecedented zeal. Samuel Charters, having moved to New Orleans to study jazz in 1950 (at age twenty-one), gradually worked his way back to the rural blues and became one of the most important collectors of the next two decades. His 1959 book *The Country Blues* was the first full-length treatment of the topic, and its evocative style inspired thousands of whites to explore the music.[93] Frederic Ramsey Jr., who recorded *Lead Belly's Last Sessions* in 1948, also came to the blues in an attempt to understand New Orleans jazz, and by the early fifties his interests, too, had mushroomed. Between 1951 and 1957 Ramsey conducted five field trips, funded by a Guggenheim fellowship, in a regional survey of rural African American styles. Such expeditions established that traditional rural music could still be found in the South, two decades after the Lomaxes had feared for its survival and a decade after the Library of Congress had stopped sponsoring field trips.[94] Their success helped inspire a series of other field trips in the late fifties. Harry Oster retraced the Lomaxes' steps by recording the prisoners at Louisiana's Angola Penitentiary, where they had found Lead Belly; Mack McCormick did extensive work in Texas; and Alan Lomax returned from Britain to lead southern swings in 1959–60 that produced a series of albums on Atlantic Records.[95]

To an extent, the work of these midcentury collectors differed from that of their 1930s predecessors. Not surprisingly, for instance, the hardships the Left had endured in recent years led the 1950s folklorists to adopt a less explicitly political agenda for their work. Unlike the younger Alan Lomax and more radical thirties collectors such as Lawrence Gellert, collectors of the 1950s did not connect their efforts to organized movements against oppression and injustice. In addition, the midcentury folklorists showed a much greater openness to commercial blues than had early revivalists. Some of the greatest "discoveries" of the period were actually the "rediscoveries" of bluesmen who had made race records as far back as the 1920s and 1930s and then had disappeared from the record business. Folk music enthusiasts had become fascinated with old commercial recordings after Folkways Records released Harry Smith's *Anthology of American Folk Music* in 1952, a six-LP sampling of commercial songs from the 1920s. In the late fifties and early sixties, collectors such as Charters supervised a series of blues reissues and, most dramatic, began to hunt for the singers of their favorite old recordings. Through years of effort in some cases, they located long-forgotten performers such as Son House, Mississippi John Hurt, Skip James, and Sleepy John Estes.[96]

Beneath these differences lie fundamental similarities between the work of the collectors from the thirties and fifties. In their methods for collecting and popularizing, for example, the midcentury folklorists followed the strategy pioneered by the Lomaxes with Lead Belly: they documented as much of a given singer's repertoire as possible and presented him or her to northern audiences as a pure vestige of a dying culture. Despite their openness to commercial recordings, the blues revivalists by no means set aside earlier folklorists' notions of the "authentic," noncommercial folk singer. Lightning Hopkins, for example, had made many commercial recordings in the late forties and early fifties on which he played electric guitar and fronted a band. After a five-year search, Charters found him in 1959. Soon Hopkins had unplugged his amplifier and assumed the style of the traditional acoustic folk bluesman. Between 1960 and 1965, he recorded approximately thirty acoustic albums for blues revival audiences.[97]

Ideologically, too, the revivalists of the thirties and fifties shared a decidedly antiestablishment bent. The fifties collectors were not explicitly political, but by identifying themselves so strongly with rural African Americans, they linked themselves to other nonconformist movements of the time. The Beats, for example, embraced African American music (especially jazz) as part of a broader challenge to what they perceived as the rigid conformity of the Eisenhower age of the organization man.[98]

As with the thirties revivalists, the midcentury collectors' conception of African American culture was decidedly romanticized. Disillusioned with what they perceived as bourgeois culture's corrupt materialism and constraining standards of propriety, they depicted bluesmen as the embodiments of an antimodern ethos. At the end of *The Country Blues*, for instance, Samuel Charters describes Lightning Hopkins as "one of the last of his kind, a lonely, bitter man who brings to the blues the intensity and pain of the hours in the hot sun, scraping at the earth, singing to make the hours pass. The blues will go on, but the country blues . . . will pass with men like this thin, intense singer from Centerville, Texas."[99] Mack McCormick, too, depicts Hopkins as a counterpoint to the emptiness of contemporary society. Hopkins, he writes, "is a fascinatingly complete man: even the least of his routine actions seem in tune with the earthy cynicism that characterizes his songs. A man with a tribal sense of belonging to his culture, he is outside the modern dilemma."[100] Collectors like Charters and McCormick, then, approached African American culture with much the same mix of yearning and regret as had previous folk music enthusiasts.

The idealized standards and mawkish language of the midcentury collectors may have been nothing new, but in the late fifties and early sixties the strategy of presenting authentic bluesmen began to produce considerable results. Encouraged by the work of collectors like Charters, plus the efforts of folk song advocates like Pete Seeger, a growing number of young whites were exploring alternatives to the increasingly formulaic rock and roll sound.[101] The blues revival was under way.

With their folkloristic attitude, Charters and the early blues revivalists were not particularly fond of Willie Dixon's pop-oriented songs. But since Dixon was one of the first established bluesmen to understand the need to introduce the blues to white audiences, he was in a position to take advantage of opportunities that began to emerge. Still paired with Memphis Slim, Dixon worked out a performance routine designed to appeal to the revival. "He learned a vast quantity of folk material," blues historian Mike Rowe writes, "and included in his act little homespun homilies calculated to please [white concertgoers]." Slowly the duo began to acquire bookings. In the late 1950s they were among the first bluesmen to appear at the Newport Jazz Festival, and in 1959 they played the first annual Newport Folk Festival. They also were among the earliest to take advantage of the emerging overseas market for the blues, touring in Europe for several months in 1959.[102] In 1960 a chance encounter with a club owner from Haifa led to an extended stint in Israel for the duo. At around this time, Slim and Dixon began to make their way onto the record labels that were fueling the folk-blues revival. Dixon recalls that John Hammond recorded them first. This session was quickly followed by one on the new Bluesville label, a subsidiary of the Prestige jazz record company that primarily released field recordings by collectors such as Charters and Pete Welding.[103] The duo also made several recordings for Moses Asch's Folkways Records, including a live album recorded at New York's Village Gate with Pete Seeger (1960).[104]

As Dixon and Slim were beginning to make their way into the folk-blues revival, Muddy Waters began to feel its influence as well. He first encountered the possibilities and constraints that the revival presented when, a year or so before Dixon, he went to England. Arriving in 1958, Waters was certainly not the first African American vernacular musician to perform in Europe. During World War I, James Reese Europe led a band that performed orchestral arrangements of ragtime and popular songs in Paris; New Orleans saxophonist Sidney Bechet played in a band that performed in London in 1919, and he lived in Paris off and on for years afterward; Louis Armstrong caused quite a sensation with a series of European tours between 1932 and 1934, after which a reasonably steady flow of American jazzmen made their way to the Continent. The first to introduce Europeans to rural African American styles was Lead Belly. Shortly before his death in 1949 he played the Paris Jazz Festival (as did Miles Davis and Charlie Parker that year). Lead Belly's concert was poorly attended, but in 1950 another product of the 1930s folk revival, Josh White, toured the Continent to considerable fanfare.[105]

The immediate precedent for Waters's British tour was Big Bill Broonzy. In the thirties and early forties, Broonzy had made hundreds of recordings with urban blues combos for Lester Melrose, but in the late forties and fifties he had become popular among whites (especially on the left) as a downhome country singer with quaint stories and an acoustic guitar. Broonzy brought this act to Europe in 1951 and was an instant hit in London and Paris. Billed as the last of the great blues singers, he appealed to Europeans as a vestige of the roots of jazz. For some years Broonzy encouraged the notion that he was the final remnant of the old style, but a few months before he died of cancer in 1958, he began introducing Europeans to other downhome performers. That spring, two of his friends, the folk bluesmen Sonny Terry and Brownie McGhee, arrived in Europe and joined Broonzy on a highly successful tour with Chris Barber's Dixieland jazz band. Before Broonzy died in August, he passed Muddy Waters's name on to some of his English fans.[106] That fall Waters and his pianist, Otis Spann, arrived in Britain.

Waters was unsure what to expect from his tour abroad ("I didn't have no idea what was going on," he remembered), but he could not have foreseen that six thousand miles from Clarksdale he would again run into Alan Lomax. This time the encounter was indirect. After coming to England in 1950, Lomax had begun lobbying the BBC to pay more attention to traditional music. At his urging the network sponsored several song-collecting expeditions and, in 1951, funded a radio series called *Ballads and Blues*. Produced by Lomax and British revivalists Ewan Mac-Coll and A. L. Lloyd, the show featured music from England, Scotland, and the United States. For the American segments, Lomax either sang himself or enlisted Broonzy or Appalachian singer Jean Ritchie. The show enjoyed astounding success. Its initial six segments were repeated four times, and eventually it took over BBC's prime-time Saturday evening slot, where it drew more than fourteen million listeners.[107]

This surge of interest in traditional music produced a curious phenomenon in Britain, skiffle. Skiffle was a hybrid of African American blues, Anglo folk songs, and traditional jazz. A large part of its appeal was that young fans could easily re-create the style themselves, since skiffle bands mainly featured simple lines on acoustic guitar, string bass (often homemade from a broom handle and plywood tea chest), washboard, and kazoo. In 1956 Lonnie Donegan, formerly the banjo player in Chris Barber's Dixieland band, released his skiffle version of Lead Belly's "Rock Island Line." Overnight, the song became a major hit in Britain, and it went on to reach number eight on the *Billboard* chart in America. Over the next two years skiffle was a national craze in Britain, spawning scores of professional and amateur imitators (including a sixteen-year-old John Lennon) who played clubs and cafés around the country, doggedly working their way through every Lead Belly song they could find.[108]

Waters arrived, then, in a country conditioned to understand the blues as old, rural, and acoustic. Even without his full band, his amplified Chicago blues shocked British audiences. Touring with the Chris Barber band, Waters and Spann gave their first performance in Leeds. The next day, Waters remembered, the headlines read "Screaming Guitar and Howling Piano." He turned down the volume for subsequent performances, and the tour went well. "Now I know that the people in England like soft guitar and the old blues," he told *Melody Maker* as the tour ended. "Next time I come I'll learn some old songs first." He learned them sooner than he might have expected because he came back to an

America in which the folk-blues revival had taken hold. Word of his success overseas had reached the United States, and he began to get offers to play for white audiences. In April 1959, for example, he appeared at the Carnegie Recital Hall with Memphis Slim and harmonica player James Cotton.[109]

As Dixon and Waters began to enjoy some success within the folk-blues revival, Chess sought to take advantage of the trend. In late summer 1959, he recorded *Muddy Waters Sings Big Bill Broonzy*, on which Waters covered ten songs associated with the older bluesman. Gone was the savage Hoochie Coochie Man persona. Although backed by an urban blues–styled ensemble (piano, bass, harmonica, and guitar), Waters sang with more restraint and used simpler arrangements than on his mid-1950s hits. Most striking, the album came with liner notes in which Studs Terkel vouched for Waters's authenticity as a rural bluesman in the great Broonzy mold. Terkel cited Broonzy as saying, "Muddy, he can *really* sing the blues. I mean the country, wide open blues. He ain't like those pretty boy singers who dress up the blues so you don't know what it is. . . . Oh yeah, Muddy's a *real* singer of the blues."[110] The folklorists' conception of the blues—as old-fashioned, intuitive, and unadorned— had penetrated the commercial music industry and, once again, remade Muddy Waters.

Muddy Waters Sings Bill Broonzy signaled how much had changed for Waters in the five years since "Hoochie Coochie Man." Now he was being packaged as an old-time authentic bluesman for white audiences. In many ways, *Muddy Waters Sings* was a shrewd move on Leonard Chess's part. He recognized that with the advent of the folk-blues revival certain music had commercial appeal to whites precisely because it seemed noncommercial. Even so, the album represented a cautious approach to America's musical past, one to which Waters was not particularly suited. In his eagerness to capitalize on a hot trend, Chess conformed to it more rigidly than he needed to. *Muddy Waters Sings*, with its antiquated repertoire and backwoods rhetoric, essentially placed Waters outside the narrative of American pop music, an isolated position to which he had never aspired. As his British tour had shown, Waters was willing to go along with any repackaging that would help him reach new audiences. But he remained uncomfortable in the role of the old-time country folk singer. Echoing his complaint about his early Chess recordings ("They were trying to make a Lightning Hopkins out of me"), Waters recalled that the folk-bluesman mantle had not sat easily with him on the British tour: "They thought I was a Big Bill Broonzy—which I wasn't."[111]

What Muddy Waters "was," of course, remained up for grabs throughout his career, but at every stage he resisted being cast as the endpoint of a dying tradition. The Broonzy tribute album portrayed Waters as the inheritor of Broonzy's title as the "last great blues singer." This sort of link to the past certainly can be powerful for a performer. The notion of recovering a "disappearing" culture continued to drive some of the most visible aspects of the folk revival in the 1960s, and even today collectors traipse the South looking for "lost" practitioners of the old-time styles.[112] But as the case of Lead Belly illustrates, being the heir of an obsolete style is an inherently confining role. Filling that niche entails cutting oneself off from contemporary commercial trends, conforming to outsiders' conceptions of traditional music, and resisting the urge to update one's style. *Muddy Waters Sings* sought to distance Waters from the commercial realm in order to boost his sales; but the image of Waters it projected limited his freedom to adapt.

Even as *Muddy Waters Sings Big Bill Broonzy* was issued to an indifferent response, a second current in the blues revival was emerging, one that had a more elastic conception of the blues than the folkloristic camp.[113] As the new outlook took hold, it helped recast Waters's role from an inheritor, the recipient of an inert tradition, to a forefather, a precursor to further innovations. Once again, Willie Dixon played a key role in charting the new direction.

Dixon's tours with Memphis Slim had attracted a growing reputation among American music aficionados overseas. In 1962 a pair of jazz concert promoters from Germany, Horst Lippman and Fritz Rau, contacted him. They had organized a series of European jazz concerts, beginning with the Modern Jazz Quartet in 1957, and now they wanted to stage a tour that would explore jazz's roots in the blues. Lippman recalled, "We like[d] blues because we liked jazz and always thought that the blues was the foundation of jazz." Out of this impulse came the American Folk Blues Festival (AFBF), which brought bluesmen to the Continent annually into the 1970s.[114] Dixon was a major force in producing the festival each year. He played bass on each of the first three tours, but his main influence came in selecting the artists who would perform. To assemble the festival's lineups, Lippman traveled each year to Chicago. Using Dixon's house as his base, he drew heavily on the bluesman's network of contacts as he selected performers to travel overseas. Dixon also handled a variety of administrative and personnel duties for the festival, from tracking down birth certificates for the older bluesmen, to informing artists of their contractual obligations and benefits, to serving as the unofficial mediator of disputes among the artists.[115]

Part of what made the American Folk Blues Festival innovative was its format. It pioneered the concept of a blues "package" tour, in which large "all-star" troupes traveled from city to city. More important, the AFBF marked a departure in the type of music it presented. On its promotional flyers the festival billed itself as "A DOCUMENTARY OF THE AUTHENTIC BLUES," but it had a much more elastic conception of "authentic" than the folkloristic revivalists. Whereas the first phase of the blues revival had privileged rural, old-fashioned styles, the AFBF's rosters included an eclectic mix of downhome and big-city performers. The 1964 festival, for example, featured Lightning Hopkins and Sleepy John Estes, "rediscovered" bluesmen who were mainstays of the folkloristic revival. But the program also showcased some of the biggest stars of the commercial urban blues—Sonny Boy Williamson, Howlin' Wolf, Dixon, and Chess R & B singer Sugar Pie Desanto. In the mid-fifties Dixon had used "Hoochie Coochie Man" to prove that African American audiences would accept a more pop-oriented sound as legitimate blues. Ten years later, he was making a similar point with the AFBF, demonstrating that the Chicago sound could gain acceptance among white blues revivalists as an authentic roots music. Consistently the festival was dominated by the biggest figures from the Chicago scene, almost all of whom had made their reputations recording commercially for Chess. In addition to the urban bluesmen from the 1964 tour, the AFBF in the sixties featured Muddy Waters, Little Walter, Junior Wells, and the leading lights of the second generation of electric blues, Buddy Guy and Otis Rush.[116] The AFBF, then, was a direct attempt to appropriate for urban blues the aura of authenticity that was driving the folkloristic blues revival. It worked.

As its organizers had hoped, the American Folk Blues Festival caused a considerable stir, but it did so among an unanticipated audience. The jazz fans whom the AFBF had expected to attend stayed away, but in Britain an emerging group of music lovers infatuated with the American blues came in full force. At the core of this new constituency were young people who had discovered the blues from recordings. American soldiers had left some blues discs behind in Britain after World War II, and British labels had repackaged some others, but blues records were not easy to find in Britain in the late fifties and early sixties. Mostly the diehard fans who came to the AFBF had stumbled across the music by chance and through word of mouth. Mick Jagger, twenty years old when the AFBF came to England in 1963, had been introduced to the blues as a teenager when a friend had played him recordings by Muddy Waters, Howlin' Wolf, and Jimmy Reed. Soon he was hunting in specialty record shops for the rare albums and sending away for more from the mysterious Chess company. On a train one day around 1960, Jagger and a young art student named Keith Richards struck up a conversation over some albums Jagger was carrying by Chuck Berry, Little Walter, and Muddy Waters. Within a couple of years, they had founded the Rolling Stones, named after a Waters tune, and were performing covers of their favorite blues songs.[117]

The early blues bands in Britain took their blues seriously. In 1962 when *Jazz News* announced the name that Jagger and Richards had chosen for the band, it included a quote from Jagger worrying, "I hope they don't think we're a rock and roll outfit." Commenting about this period in 1968 he said, "We were blues purists who liked ever so commercial things but never did them on stage because we were so horrible and so aware of being blues purists." On the emerging British scene, "pure" blues meant Chess blues. Giorgio Gomelsky, one of the first patrons of both the Stones and the Yardbirds (another early blues rock band from Britain), recalled that "for all the young musicians, Willie Dixon and Muddy Waters were great great heroes." Since Gomelsky was also the English representative for the AFBF, he gave the Stones and a dozen or so other struggling blues musicians free tickets in the front row when the festival first came to Britain. They sat there, Gomelsky recalls, "worshipping."[118]

The urban bluesmen on the AFBF tour had stumbled into rich terrain. Dixon, especially, worked to take full advantage of the situation. Most directly, he offered the young British musicians his songs, both old ones and new. He sang the musicians his tunes in private homes, left them tape recordings before he returned to the States, and urged them to record his material. Over the next few years, British bands included Chess blues songs on a series of albums. In 1963 the Rolling Stones issued their first single, a cover of Chuck Berry's "Come On" on one side and Dixon's "I Want to Be Loved" on the other. In 1964 they released their first album, featuring Dixon's "I Just Want to Make Love to You," along with Jimmy Reed's "Honest I Do" and Berry's "Carol." Their 1965 album included Dixon's "Little Red Rooster," Bo Diddley's "I Need You Baby (Mona)," and Berry's "You Can't Catch Me."[119] Many other British bands recorded Dixon's songs in this period, including the Yardbirds, Cream, and Led Zeppelin.

Dixon, though, passed on more than song material to the British band members. In his personal interactions with them, he encouraged their romantic attraction to the blues. Mostly skinny white youths, just leaving their teens, the British musicians were fascinated by Dixon, a gregarious black man who weighed well over three hundred pounds and had fathered eight children. To the British musicians, he represented the archetype of the bluesman. His physical bearing and manner reinforced their notions that the blues represented a dynamic alternative to bourgeois British culture. Dixon's lyrics, with their aggressive, sexually charged tone, certainly added to this impression. Long John Baldry, who sang for one of Britain's first blues bands and led a group of his own called the Hoochie Coochie Men, recalls being drawn to Dixon's personal magnetism. Likening Dixon to a "guru," Baldry recalls that he was "responsible for injecting the whole mystique of the blues into many of us."[120] Dixon also helped ease whatever doubts the British bands had about the legitimacy of their efforts to play in the blues idiom. By welcoming their efforts to use their songs, he in effect gave them clearance to move freely into an African American cultural form without doubting the authenticity of their efforts.

When British bands began touring America, they did not hesitate to pay their respects to the bluesmen who had showed them the way. When the Beatles arrived in America in 1963, they expressed their desire to see Muddy Waters and Bo Diddley. "Where's that?" a reporter is said to have replied. "Don't you know who your own famous people are here?" Paul McCartney responded.[121] A few months later, when the Rolling Stones began their first American tour, they made a pilgrimage to Chicago to record an album at Chess studios. Willie Dixon, Muddy Waters, and Buddy Guy frequently visited the recording sessions to chat and offer pointers. The Stones titled one of their original compositions on the album "2120 South Michigan Avenue" in honor of the Chess company's Chicago address, and immediately after the session, the band held a press conference outside 2120 in front of screaming fans. When the Yardbirds came to America, they made Chicago their base as they toured the country, and in 1965 they, too, recorded at Chess.[122] That same year the Paul Butterfield Blues Band, a white-led group out of Chicago, released its self-titled debut album, a hard-driving blues-rock synthesis that paid tribute to urban blues traditions even as it broke new ground. The notion of the Chicago blues as a roots music was taking hold.

One might think that as urban blues became celebrated as an elemental part of America's musical heritage Muddy Waters's career would take off. In the early sixties he was being glorified by a young generation of white rock stars and their fans as a driving force behind the contemporary pop sound. Young musicians were flocking to Chicago to learn from the forefather of rock and roll. To capitalize on this role required something of a balancing act, but it was one that would seem to come easily to Waters, given his history of adapting his music. He needed to demonstrate his connection to the contemporary music but, befitting an elder statesman, also retain a healthy distance from its vicissitudes. The Muddy Waters albums that Chess issued in these years, however, exhibited none of the moderation and constancy necessary to achieve this balance. Chess showed a singular lack of understanding of the powers and demands that went along with Waters's move into American public memory. The company's recordings of Waters veered from antiquarian attempts to capitalize on the folkloristic blues revival to gaudy efforts to mimic the latest rock and roll fads.

As the urban blues began emerging as a roots music, the Chess label's shrewdest effort to take advantage of Waters's new status was initiated from outside the company. In 1960 George Wein, the producer of the Newport Jazz Festival, decided to pay tribute to the roots of jazz with a blues program. That same year Nesuhi Ertegun, jazz producer and vice president of Atlantic Records, heard Waters in Chicago and, enthralled, recommended him for the session.[123] Waters closed the festival (which had been hosted by Langston Hughes) to tumultuous applause. Noting this response, Chess issued an album of Waters's Newport performance that sold surprisingly well and generated an especially strong response in England.[124] As on *Muddy Waters Sings Big Bill Broonzy*, the album's liner notes presented the music as pure old-time fare. They quoted Studs Terkel's observation (not borne out over the next decade) that young urban blacks, who had recently scorned Waters's music as "that old stuff," were now returning to the music and "finding in this 'old stuff' [their] hitherto undiscovered roots." Terkel went on to praise Waters's "unadorned blues" and his "outgrowing healthiness and earthiness."

This rhetoric evokes the romance of the backcountry blues, but the songs Waters and his band actually played that afternoon in Newport were solidly in the urban blues style that Dixon and Waters had crafted in the mid-fifties. Indeed, three of the eight songs on the album were by Dixon, including "I'm Your Hoochie Coochie Man," "I Got My Brand on You," and Waters's then current Chess single, "Tiger in Your Tank." Moreover, on the album (as at the performance) Waters performed his Dixon-styled song "I've Got My Mojo Working," *twice*. The enthusiastic response to these song selections illustrates the emergence of the less folkloristic wing of the blues revival. Waters's audiences had no interest in holding him to a traditional country-blues repertoire or performance style. They didn't need him to be Big Bill Broonzy (although, just in case, the Chess album cover showed Waters holding a large acoustic guitar, belonging to John Lee Hooker, instead of the red electric model that he had used in the performance).[125] Revival audiences were seeking authenticity, but they were not using folkloristic standards to define it.

Chess does not seem to have grasped the dynamic that made *Muddy Waters at Newport* a success. Waters's popularity as a roots musician depended on his ability to occupy the boundary between folk blues and rock: to move decisively into one domain or the other would sap his appeal. Over the next decade, though, Chess repackaged Waters to match each successive trend in the record industry. In 1962, for example, Chess followed up the Newport album with the "Muddy Waters Twist," seeking to capitalize on Chubby Checker's hits "The Twist" (1960) and "Let's Twist Again" (1961). In 1963 and 1964, the folk-blues revival gained publicity as Mississippi John Hurt, Son House, Skip James, and Bukka White were "rediscovered." Chess responded with *Muddy Waters, Folksinger* (1964), which once again depicted Waters as a simple folk bluesman. Waters's electric guitar is banished from this album, as is his band.[126] The album closes with Waters, unaccompanied, revisiting "Feel Like Going Home."

In his liner notes to *Folksinger*, Ralph Bass, the album's producer, begins by speciously lamenting the day when "record companies discovered they could sell more records by appealing to a broader buying public and labeling country and blues folk music." Even as he denies the need for such labels, he goes on, in a contradiction-ridden statement, to make clear that Waters is the genuine article: "We should treasure the few real folk singers and at least make the distinction between the real and the pseudo. So whether we label Muddy a blues singer or folk singer is not important. What is important is that we give full recognition to the greatness of Muddy Waters as one of the last of his breed." For his part, Waters remained ill at ease in this role, complaining, "They tried to put me over in another bag, but I just don't fit no other bag."[127]

The stylistic shifts in Waters's Chess recordings were just as extreme in subsequent years. *Muddy, Brass, and the Blues* (1966) recast him as a soul singer and left him, Jas Obrecht writes, "competing with heavy organ and honking overdubbed horns." The effort to adapt to the latest sounds became even more intense in the late sixties when the young Marshall Chess began producing many of the company's blues albums. Marshall was determined to reach the young rock market, reflecting, "We get a lot of criticism for making it different, but that's like saying keep the spade a cotton picker all his life, keep him a nigger, don't let him progress into something that's different or new."[128] To tap into the psychedelic rock scene, Chess released *Electric Mud* in 1968. It featured classics like "I'm Your Hoochie Coochie Man" and "I Just Want to Make Love to You" plus a cover version of the Stones' "Let's Spend the Night Together," all submerged under a cloud of distortion and a hail of drums. For the album's publicity shots, Clarence Peterson reported in 1969, Waters was reluctantly "freaked up" by the hair stylist. Around 1970 Waters noted with disgust that the album's array of special effects made it impossible to perform live—"now what the hell do you have a record for you can't play it the first time it's out. I'm sick of that. That's out."[129]

While it is difficult to gauge with certainty how audiences reacted to these albums, it seems clear that the Chesses did not get the response for which they had hoped. None of their post-1960 attempts to manufacture hits for Waters cracked the pop or R & B charts.[130] Moreover, the albums tended to sound dated within only a year or two. The Chesses' obsessive focus on the latest fads was inherently shortsighted: they were creating disposable products by an artist whose public persona was defined by his endurance, his links to tradition, and his influence on successive generations of musicians—in short, his place in the country's musical memory.

Even as Chess ignored the realm of memory, other people in the music industry continued the task that Dixon had begun in the late 1950s, working to solidify the standing of urban blues as a roots music. Festival promoters like Horst Lippman and George Wein included more and more urban bluesmen after the mid-sixties, as did a proliferation of new festivals that were devoted exclusively to the blues. Dedicated fans founded blues magazines such as the British publication *Blues Unlimited* (1963) and the American magazine *Living Blues* (1970). Popular scholars like Paul Oliver and Peter Guralnick continued to imbue the blues with an aura of romance and integrated urban bluesmen into a narrative about the creation of American popular music. Public radio and television stations came to embrace the blues as a historically significant, indubitably American art form that still resonates with contemporary audiences. Record company executives and collectors like Chris Strachwitz, Pete Welding, and many others supervised the reissue of a stream of blues recordings, a stream that turned into an avalanche of albums and hefty box sets after the advent of the CD. And an unending succession of rock musicians, whether to acknowledge musical debts or to gain stature by association, made cover versions of urban blues songs and spread the word about the style in their liner notes, concerts, and interviews.[131]

Dixon himself, of course, continued to be a powerful advocate for the blues, involving himself in almost every aspect of the revival. In the late sixties and seventies he managed and booked artists (such as Koko Taylor); launched two short-lived record labels; briefly ran his own studio; founded a touring group called the Chicago Blues All-Stars; and con-

tinued to write and produce songs and to assemble lineups for the American Folk Blues Festival.[132]

In the decade before his death in 1992, Dixon moved even more
directly into the memory business. In 1982 he founded the Blues Heaven
Foundation, a nonprofit organization designed to foster respect for the
legacy of the blues, encourage the perpetuation of the tradition among
younger generations, and help older artists claim the financial benefits
due them for their role in pioneering the form. Several of the foundation's projects implicitly canonized urban blues musicians. When it (in
cooperation with the Yamaha Corporation) secured donations of musical instruments to inner-city schools in Mississippi, the gifts were made
in name of the memories of Howlin' Wolf and Little Brother Montgomery (a blues pianist whom Lester Melrose had recorded regularly).
The organization also sponsored an annual Muddy Waters scholarship
to give financial aid to young music students in the Chicago area. At
the same time, the foundation worked to identify and recover missed
or past-due royalty payments and to educate musicians about how to
avoid future exploitations. Among its clients were Buddy Guy, John Lee
Hooker, Koko Taylor, and the estates of Howlin' Wolf, Jimmy Reed, and
Muddy Waters.[133] In 1993, aided by a donation from rock star John
Mellencamp, Dixon's heirs bought the old Chess building at 2120 South
Michigan Avenue to serve as the headquarters of the Blues Heaven
Foundation.

Beyond the ambitiousness of its agenda, though, perhaps the most intriguing aspect of Blues Heaven is the language Dixon used in setting out
its mission. Reminiscent of his stance within the revival, Dixon worked
to define the blues as both an antecedent and a contemporary form. On
the one hand, he adopted a folkloristic tone, depicting the blues as an
endangered historical treasure that deserved to be praised and protected:
"Blues Heaven is a historical thing. The blues are a part of the history
and heritage of our people and these things are supposed to be known
through the rest of history. . . . Pretty soon, you'll find generations that
will judge you on the past. Your past helps you on your present and your
present helps on your future. If you don't have a past to look back to,
what are you living on in the present and why should you live in the
future?" "The blues are the roots and other musics are the fruits," Dixon
summarized. "Without the roots, you have no fruits, so it's better keeping the roots alive because it means better fruits from now on."[134]

On the other hand, in keeping with his pragmatic, eclectic style as a
producer for Chess, Dixon refused to shield the music like a purist.
"Change" was not a fraught term in his lexicon: "As you change the time,

it changes the blues. Every time you change the news, you got to change the blues because the news ain't always the same. The blues changes just like everything else changes." Instead of yearning to freeze the style, Dixon favored adapting it and trying always to look ahead: "The only thing you can go through is what's popular as of now, that people are interested in. . . . I made blues yesterday about the things of yesterday and what would be the hopeful future of today. Today I make blues about today and what the hopeful future of tomorrow is."[135]

In the latter stages of his career, Muddy Waters seems to have had a more conflicted attitude toward change than Dixon. Sometimes he expressed confidence in the resiliency of the blues: "They'll always be around," he said in 1972. "Long as people hurt, they'll be around." And Waters seemed eager to keep the blues sounding contemporary. In a 1964 interview he said, "The blues have to change because the people're changing so fast nowadays. They're learning all new ideas, and if you are a blues singer you have to be right *now* in this business."[136]

Even as Waters stressed the importance of letting the blues evolve, though, he at times took a defensive stance against alterations to the old-time styles and invoked more rigid standards of authenticity. In the same interview with Welding, he worried, "Is it good for the blues to change like this? I don't think so. I really think that the blues, the *real* blues, is just what I was doing when I made my first recordings." Naturally, this attitude affected Waters's response to the white imitators of his music: "I think they're great people," he told Peter Guralnick, "but they're not blues players. Really what separates them from people like Wolf and myself, we're doing the stuff like we did way years ago down in Mississippi. These kids are just getting up, getting stuff and going with it. . . . It's not real." In the late 1970s, Waters even invoked his longtime anti-type, Lightning Hopkins, to make the point: "Ain't too many left that play the real *deep* blues," he reflected to Robert Palmer. "There's John Lee Hooker, Lightnin' Hopkins. . . . Ain't too many more left."[137]

Whatever pangs Waters may have had in his later career about moving away from the old styles, he continued in these years to do what he had done ever since he arrived in Chicago: adapt to the changing times. Beginning in the mid-sixties, though, as interest surged in urban blues as a roots music, Waters's style of adaptation shifted. Following Dixon's lead, he tried to take advantage of his emerging status as a musical forefather. In 1962 Waters had hired a manager for the first time, Bob Messinger, who had been in charge of bookings for the Jazz Workshop in Boston. Messinger was determined to sell Waters to white audiences, and after the Rolling Stones came in 1964, he began to succeed. Initially, to build exposure, Messinger and Waters accepted any offers to play in front of whites, regardless of the pay. Waters gradually accumulated engagements at festivals, coffeehouses, and colleges (he even played the Illinois Governor's Ball and New York's Museum of Modern Art) until he had roughly one hundred gigs a year, almost all of them outside Chicago and almost none for African American audiences.[138] Even as Chess worked to record him as a pop commodity, then, Waters was touring as a roots musician, bringing "downhome" styles to whites.

This disjunction between Waters's live appearances and his recorded output began to break down somewhat at the end of the 1960s, a time of turmoil for the Chess company. In 1969 a weary Leonard Chess sold the company for ten million dollars to the General Recorded Tape corporation. He planned to continue running the business during a one-year transition period, but that October he suffered a heart attack in his car and died in the resulting crash.[139] Two months before he died, the Chess company issued *Fathers and Sons*, an album that signaled a savvier, if still somewhat contrived, conception of how to present Waters to the commercial market. The album cover mimics Michelangelo's painting from the Sistine Chapel, *The Creation of Adam*; in this case, though, the gift of life passes from a black man's fingertip to a white man's. The double-length recording paired Waters with Paul Butterfield and Michael Bloomfield, two young white Chicago bluesmen whom he had mentored. Subsequent Chess releases over the next few years, while erratic, continued to show a greater awareness of how to take advantage of Waters's status as a blues forefather. *They Call Me Muddy Waters* (1971) was a compilation of releases from 1951 through 1967. It won a Grammy award for Best Ethnic/Traditional Recording, as did two of his other releases from this period, *The London Muddy Waters Sessions* (1972) and *The Woodstock Album* (1975), which he recorded with the folk-rock group the Band.[140]

The albums that most effectively tapped into Waters's appeal as a roots musician were made after Waters left Chess for CBS Records in 1976. Between 1976 and his death in 1983, he released four albums, all of them produced by Johnny Winter, a young white albino blues-rocker and guitar wizard from Texas. A longtime fan, Winter consciously worked to re-create Waters's "Chess sound" from the 1950s. He drew heavily on Waters's prime Chess repertoire, used a full blues-band accompaniment, and recorded with a live "back to mono" approach. Whatever the musical merits of these decisions, they struck a chord in the American music world. The albums generated much publicity and elicited gushing praise from reviewers, fans, and, since then, blues historians (Jas Obrecht's

Fathers and Sons *album cover, 1969. When Muddy Waters recorded with white disciples Paul Butterfield and Michael Bloomfield, the album cover depicted a black man passing the creative gift to a white man, à la Michelangelo. (Courtesy MCA–Chess Records Files)*

1983 comment that "Johnny Winter . . .—praise God—understood Muddy's music" is fairly typical).[141] Audiences seem to have been drawn to the interracial and intergenerational dynamic behind the releases and, most of all, thrilled to hear what they thought of as the "real" Muddy Waters back at last. In his last years, Muddy Waters enjoyed strong album sales, won three consecutive Grammies, and in 1977 performed for President Jimmy Carter and his White House staff. Several years after this official commendation, American popular culture followed suit with ceremonial recognition of its own. In 1987 Muddy Waters was inducted into the Rock and Roll Hall of Fame.[142]

In part, certainly, one can attribute Waters's canonization as a roots musician simply to longevity. He lived long enough to influence many musicians and enjoy their gratitude. But this explanation does not adequately account for Waters's exalted status. Nor does the notion—true though it is—that Waters benefited from the liberalizing of white American ideas about race and the toppling of Jim Crow. To cite the improved racial climate is akin to pointing to improvements in recording technologies and distribution methods. These factors, among others, were necessary, but they are not sufficient to explain how Waters moved beyond the commercial realm of *Billboard* charts and radio play lists into the rarefied domain of public memory.

Waters's career suggests that the realms of commercialism and memory, while inextricably connected, are nonetheless distinct. People like Lester Melrose and Leonard Chess could take Waters only so far. They might bring him sales and, for a while, even fame, but they could not secure for him a role in the narrative of the genesis of American music. They tried to catch every new swell in popular culture, riding the waves of boom and bust; but Waters's eventual position in the sea of American popular culture would be determined by those who attempted to sense (and direct) the underlying current. This was the domain of memory workers, people like John and Alan Lomax and Sam Charters, or, in Waters's case, Dixon, Lippman, Messinger, and Winter—folklorists, collectors, writers, promoters, and producers who advanced visions of America's musical past. The diversity of this group—and the many ties its members had to the commercial music industry—illustrate that memory creation does not occur only in specific cultural locations. What these brokers shared, rather, was a drive for rootedness and a penchant for reinterpreting and renewing cultures. At base, memory work is a set of goals and cultural strategies—an effort to string lines between past, present, and future.

The Lomaxes pioneered what proved to be one of the most powerful memory-shaping strategies of this century, deploying what I have called the cult of authenticity. Presenting Lead Belly as "the real thing" brought him a dedicated audience and, eventually, an honored place in the canon of American folk music. But the Lomaxes' construction of authenticity also left Lead Belly culturally constrained, with little room to adapt to changing times. Waters's career, too, depended on being perceived as authentic, but the label in his case proved to be more elastic. Early in his career he drew on the power of authenticity only implicitly: he was a commercial performer who appealed to African American listeners as an honest and telling expositor of their condition. Without jeopardizing his standing as a bluesman, therefore, he could adjust to match the shifting cultural outlook of his audience. Even during the blues revival, though, when Waters's status as an "authentic" bluesman became more explicit and central to his success, Waters's persona left him a good deal of flexibility to adjust his sound. To a great extent, he owed this breathing room to Willie Dixon. The portrait of the "true bluesman" that Dixon created left space for performers to remain generative artists with strong connections to contemporary culture. Dixon showed that a roots figure could be "Other" without being marginalized, "traditional" without being static, and "archetypal" without being obsolete.

SEARCHING FOR FOLK
MUSIC'S INSTITUTIONAL NICHE
ALAN LOMAX, CHARLES SEEGER,
B. A. BOTKIN, & RICHARD DORSON

In the 1930s, even as the Lomaxes struggled to promote vernacular music within popular culture, their efforts began to attract support from a surprising source, the nation's "official culture"—the culture sustained, sanctioned, and deployed by the federal government. On the face of it, one might have expected the government to feel threatened by the depression-era vogue for marginalized Americans. After all, America's fascination with folk culture challenged the status quo: it registered dissatisfaction with the emptiness of mass culture and the sterility of high culture, the corruption of power politics, and the vicissitudes of the industrial economy. Faced with this broad-based challenge, though, the government did not attack but appropriated the folk vogue. By the end of the 1930s, the celebration of the marginal, which had emerged out of disenchantment with America, had become the basis for a new style of patriotism celebrating America. The folk became figured not as failures or malcontents but as embodiments of America's strength through diversity. Many people within the official culture began to treat folk forms as part of a resilient cultural core that, they hoped, would see the country through the depths of the depression and the perils of war.

The federal government's move to embrace America's marginal populations was signaled first by Franklin and Eleanor Roosevelt. In marked contrast to Herbert Hoover's administration, the Roosevelts worked in both their rhetoric and actions to move rural whites and minorities to the forefront of the nation's consciousness. This attentiveness to the people who had been hardest hit by the depression marked a significant shift in attitude. Hoover had chosen not to focus on America's marginal populations, preferring not to spotlight people whose extreme poverty so clearly illustrated the depths of the country's economic crisis. The Roosevelt administration, though, made the nation's migrants, sharecroppers, and mountaineers the centerpieces of official culture, emphasizing not their desperation but their character, dignity, and strength.

As part of this new official attitude toward ordinary Americans, the Roosevelts embraced folk songs as America's true musical heritage. They did so, in part, by staging a series of largely ceremonial and symbolic events. As early as 1933, the first lady attended the White Top Folk Festival in Virginia. The festival, founded in 1931, had drawn almost four thousand people the year before Mrs. Roosevelt's visit, but as she listened to mountaineers sing and play dulcimers and banjos, the crowds around her swelled toward twenty thousand. The festival's organizer commented that "a lovely dignity was lent to the festival by the presence of the First Lady of the Land."[1] The president, too, did his part to bestow respect on folk music. He posed for photos with a string band in Warm Springs, Georgia; named "Home on the Range" his favorite song; and, as a collector of sheet music on nautical themes, was known to favor in particular old sea chanteys. The Roosevelts sponsored a series of nine concerts of folk music and dance in the White House between 1934 and 1942. Among the performers were the Hampton Choir singers, the Spirituals Society of Charleston (who sang in the Gullah dialect), bluesman Josh White, banjo picker Bascom Lamar Lunsford, and chantey singer John M. "Sailor Dad" Hunt. Concerts by opera singers and classical musicians still far outnumbered those by folk performers, but the infusion of traditional music at the White House was unprecedented and taken quite seriously by the Roosevelts. When the king and queen of England visited in 1939, they were treated to an evening of fiddling, cowboy songs, and square dancing.[2]

The Roosevelts' sponsorship of folk music, though, went well beyond symbolic gestures. Under their watch, the federal government became involved as never before in the preservation of traditional cultures. New

Franklin Roosevelt poses with local musicians, Warm Springs, Ga., January 1933.
(Courtesy Franklin D. Roosevelt Library)

Deal agencies such as the Resettlement Administration, the Federal Writers' Project, and the Federal Music Project all devoted resources to folk song, and, in a key move, in 1937 the Library of Congress's Archive of American Folk-Song received government funding for the first time. This flurry of activity represented both continuity and change. In some ways, governmental funding for folk song was the culmination of what folk song enthusiasts had been working toward since the turn of the century: at last people in power were acknowledging that America had indigenous cultures of beauty and significance that needed to be preserved before they were overwhelmed by industrialization. Many aspects of the New Deal folk song programs, therefore, differed in scale more than in kind from what had preceded them. Having found an ally that could give them funds to do their work, folklorists pursued projects that had long preoccupied them. Like Cecil Sharp or Robert Gordon before them, they saw their task as preserving traditional rural music, and they worked to achieve this goal by going on field trips to remote areas and searching out the oldest and most isolated residents.

For the Archive of American Folk-Song, for example, government funding most directly enabled an expansion of the sort of collecting trips that had heretofore been funded by outside grants. In the years immediately before government support, the archive, under the Lomaxes, had certainly not been idle. In 1935 Alan Lomax, assisted by a young anthropologist from Columbia University named Zora Neale Hurston, had recorded in Florida, the Georgia sea islands, and, in a significant expansion of the archive's reach, the Bahamas. The following year, Lomax had spent his honeymoon on a five-month recording expedition that included pioneering work in Haiti. John Lomax, meanwhile, had gone on another major expedition to southern penitentiaries in 1936. By June 1936 the Lomaxes had single-handedly contributed more than seven hundred discs to the archive, each containing between two and twelve performances.[3]

When government funding arrived, the archive built on these precedents more than it diverged from them, launching a series of ambitious collecting expeditions. John Lomax used improved recording equipment on a sixty-five-hundred-mile trek through the South; Alan explored the coal-mining region of the Appalachians; and for the first time Alan took the archive's recording equipment into Indiana and Ohio. The archive also added significantly to its collections by acquiring recordings made by other New Deal folklore programs, established a recording equipment loan program to help outside folklorists launch expeditions, and constructed an in-house recording laboratory so that the archive could duplicate recordings made by other folklorists and commercial companies.[4] With government funding, then, the archive expanded its efforts to gather and preserve the nation's folk music.

The programs initiated by the New Deal made significant contributions to this goal. The Federal Writers' Project, for instance, sent fieldworkers to gather spirituals, blues, and work songs in North Carolina and Mississippi, Creole and Acadian songs in Louisiana, Indian songs in Oklahoma, and Spanish American songs in New Mexico. Under Charles Seeger, the Resettlement Administration, too, sent field-recording expeditions to the South, as did the Federal Theater Project. Even the Federal Music Project, primarily a make-work program for classical musicians, joined in pursuing folk music. Particularly after Charles Seeger became assistant director late in 1937, it sponsored a series of song-gathering projects.[5]

Significant aspects of the New Deal folk music programs, then, continued to treat folk music like an endangered relic on the verge of obliteration. To emphasize only the traditionalism of the government-sponsored projects, though, obscures the extent to which the New Deal folklore workers brought a new attitude to the materials they studied. The Roosevelt administration's backing not only enabled an expansion of traditional fieldwork but also brought to the forefront a group of folklorists who took a more contemporary-minded, activist stance toward folklore. Figures such as B. A. Botkin of the Federal Writers' Project, Charles Seeger of the Resettlement Administration and later the Federal Music Project, and Alan Lomax of the Library of Congress represented an emerging "folk establishment" in Washington, and they were eager to use their positions to launch folk music into the public sector.[6] Their agenda was grounded in new ideas about what constituted authentic folklore, how to preserve it, and what role it should play in contemporary society. Building on these ideas, the New Deal folklorists carried folk song from a largely left-wing circulation to a position in the nation's official culture—a position that brought unprecedented respect to folk culture but, as the folklorists soon discovered, had decided limits.

The New Deal folklorists' efforts to carve out a niche within official culture were very much shaped by a powerful current in contemporary anthropological scholarship, functionalism. Pioneered by British anthropologists Bronislaw Malinowski and A. R. Radcliffe-Brown in the 1920s, functionalism exerted great influence in academic circles through the 1950s and beyond. It postulated that all cultural forms in a given society—from superstitions to rituals of economic exchange—existed because they served functions in that society. This notion represented a fundamental challenge to two schools of anthropological thought. First, it dealt the final blow to an already beleaguered evolutionary doctrine that had dominated nineteenth-century scholarship. Evolutionists believed that culture progressed in a stepwise fashion and that folklore represented the earliest, most primitive stage. Functionalists rejected the notions, implicit in evolutionism, that the present day was superior to all that came before and that any remaining traces of the past were anachronistic "survivals" that had little function in contemporary society.[7] Second, functionalism challenged the proponents of diffusionism, a more contemporary school of thought derived from the work of Franz Boas. Its proponents methodically mapped the diffusion of cultural forms across the world and across time. Although this approach sometimes identified rich cross-cultural links (Malinowski praised Boas's work in this regard), the functionalists felt that it also encouraged an overly literary and ahistorical pursuit of isolated similarities across time. Such comparisons, Malinowski charged, "suffer from a lifeless and inorganic view of culture and treat it as a thing which can be preserved in cold storage for centuries, transported across oceans and continents, mechanically taken to pieces and recompounded."[8] To the functionalists, neither the evolutionists nor the diffusionists adequately recognized that culture is a living system, not a collection of isolated elements, and that traditions survived because they were integral to that system.

Such a message had direct import for the study of folklore, and the New Deal folklorists eagerly grasped functionalism's implications. Writing in 1937, B. A. Botkin lamented "the tendency . . . to treat folklore from the evolutionary and historical rather than the functional approach." The evolutionists, he felt, wrongly treated folk traditions as "fossils and artifacts" from primitive cultures, instead of as vibrant elements of contemporary societies. "Even when the notion of savagery is not present," he wrote, "the tendency has been to restrict the folk to the backward, ignorant, and illiterate members of society and to emphasize the anachronistic and static, the useless and so meaningless aspects of folklore to the neglect of its living and dynamic phases." Happily, Botkin concluded, the "functional view of folklore is now generally accepted."[9]

Among New Deal folklorists, functionalism encouraged a much more robust conception of American folk culture. Pioneering collectors such as Child, Sharp, and even John Lomax had tended to study folk song to demonstrate the vitality of America's *past*. They had offered little sense of present-day possibilities for these cultural forms. Rather, they had decried modern culture for overwhelming the folk forms they cherished. Folk song, in this conception, was a delicate remnant from a bygone era, and the folklorist's job was to preserve it from being trampled by the pernicious forces of change. Functionalism, in contrast, encouraged the New Deal folklorists to see vitality in folk forms. If Appalachian mountaineers sang ancient British ballads, they did so because the songs helped them cope with problems they faced in their lives; and there was no reason to expect a song to cease performing this function anytime soon. To the New Deal folklorists, therefore, the survival of a form of folk expression was not a remarkable fluke but a sign of that form's extraordinary vitality and cultural utility. Where early collectors had seen brittle relics, the New Dealers saw healthy regeneration. As Botkin wrote, "Folklore is not something far away and long ago, but real and living among us."[10]

This sense of folklore's resilience led the New Deal folklorists to define a new role for the folklorist in relation to his or her material. Since they conceived of folklore as fundamentally vibrant, not endangered, the folklorists no longer saw themselves as mounting a desperate rear-guard preservation effort. They moved away from the notion of folklore as a matter of collecting what Botkin called "dead or phony stuff" and instead concentrated on the role folklore played in society and the process by which it evolved. As Charles Seeger summarized three decades later, this new attitude marked a split within the profession between the more literary, academic folklorists, "with their loyalty to ancient value in shrinking repertories, and the functionalists, with their vision of expanding, blending, ever-creative tradition." The "functional view," Botkin wrote, encouraged folklorists to pay attention "not only to survivals but also to folklore in the making. . . . Folklore becomes germinal rather than vestigial."[11] Influenced by functionalism, therefore, the New Deal folklorists shifted the profession's mission from preserving cultural relics to exploring the processes by which culture was created and transmitted.

The effects of this philosophical shift extended into almost every aspect of the New Deal folklorists' work. Alan Lomax's embrace of functionalism, for example, subtly transformed the songbooks he published with his father based on the material they collected on their field trips. The contrasts between *American Ballads and Folk Songs*, published in 1934, and *Our Singing Country*, published in 1941, illustrate a transition from the antiquarian, vaguely evolutionist assumptions that had persisted in John Lomax's work since the beginning of the century to the new notions implicit in functionalism. Significantly, as historian Jerrold Hirsch points out, these two volumes also quietly announce a generational passing of the torch within the Lomaxes' partnership. In the introduction to *American Ballads*, John Lomax's name comes before Alan's, but in the preface to the later, more functionalist work, Alan's name precedes his father's.[12]

Most basically, these two volumes reflect different conceptions of what constitutes legitimate folk song. In their introduction to *American Ballads* the Lomaxes keep the focus on old-time rural songs. Clearly they want to show that these traditions are still vibrant. "New songs spring up," the introduction asserts cheerily, "and almost every version of a current song shows interesting changes." This optimism, though, is undercut by statements that depict folk singing as a beleaguered, premodern tradition. In the midst of twentieth-century industrialization, it would be hard for a folk song devotee to take much reassurance from a statement like "Although the spread of machine civilization is rapidly making it hard to find folk singers, ballads are yet sung in this country." And when the authors add that "a life of isolation, without books or newspapers or telephone or radio, breeds songs and ballads," one senses the extent to which *American Ballads* defines authenticity in opposition to contemporary realities.[13]

Our Singing Country, in contrast, reflects functionalism's more flexible standards of authenticity. In *American Ballads* the Lomaxes had marveled at but feared folk song's adaptability, worrying that the form would be corrupted by modern-day society; but *Our Singing Country* suggests that the Lomaxes have become fascinated by the process of adaptation. "A piece of folklore," they write in their preface, "is a living, growing, and changing thing." Befitting this emphasis on fluidity, in *Our Singing Country* the Lomaxes no longer hold folk tunes up to standards of purity but instead analyze the roles they play in singers' lives. The songs of the American folk singer, the introduction notes, "have been strongly rooted in his life and have functioned there as enzymes to assist in the digestion of hardship, solitude, violence, hunger, and the honest comradeship of democracy."[14] Instead of treating folk songs as remnants from America's rural past, *Our Singing Country* shows them to be adaptive tools, continually reshaping themselves to match contemporary needs.

This functionalist emphasis on what songs do for the singers shaped the organization of *Our Singing Country*. *American Ballads* had matter-of-factly divided its chapters on the basis of either the subject matter of songs or the origins of their singers. Songs about the sea had become "Sailors and Sea Fights"; tunes about the Erie Canal had gone into an "Erie Canal" chapter; songs collected in the mountains had fit nicely into "Songs from the Mountains." Essentially the book had treated the songs like antiques from the past—quaint, evocative, perhaps even beautiful, but no longer having an evident utilitarian purpose.

Our Singing Country includes many of the same song types and even retains some of the same categories as *American Ballads*, but it adds an organizational superstructure that gives new meaning to the song groupings. The book's twenty chapters are divided into six broad headings that highlight the songs' societal functions. As in *American Ballads*, therefore, sailor songs remain a significant chapter heading, now grouped with military songs into "Soldiers and Sailors"; but in *Our Singing Country* this chapter appears under the heading "Men at Work," along with other chapters on miners, cowboys, railroaders, farmers, lumberjacks, and teamsters. Likewise, mountain songs remain well represented in the book, but many of them are grouped under a chapter title ("Old-Time Love Songs") and a section heading ("Social Songs") that highlight their function. And the chapter's introduction pointedly resists depicting the songs as Old World relics, instead stressing their present-day relevance in mountain culture: "The people of America who preserved these songs and the rural people who still sing them have never felt that these ancient ballads, called by scholars English and Scottish popular ballads, were

Charles Seeger with his family (Ruth Crawford Seeger, Mike Seeger, Peggy Seeger) at their home in Washington, D.C., ca. 1937. (Courtesy Mike Seeger)

particularly ancient; nor have they valued them as such. Instead, as we have tried to point out in our notes, they have kept these songs because they felt the near and moving reality of them."[15] Folklore had moved far away from the antiquarian treatment of folk materials advocated by Francis Child and his followers.

The move toward functionalism, naturally, also affected the way folklorists conducted their fieldwork. With their optimism about the vitality of the folk song tradition and their fascination with the process of folk song creation and dissemination, the New Deal folklorists did not share their predecessors' drive to record in the most technologically isolated areas possible. Certainly they did not ignore rural America—they still mainly recorded traditional rural tunes—but they did so without feeling that *only* the purest old-time songs were worth hearing and without the sense of being engaged in a doomed race against time. Field trips became not a chance to record the last whispers of a dying culture but an opportunity to examine how a culture sloughed off or adapted the old and incorporated the new into a constantly revitalizing mixture. Functionalism encouraged an interest in documenting cultures in transition. Charles Seeger, for example, praised American music as "a dynamic folk art," for "while it continually loses old songs, it continually adds new ones." This process, exactly what had frightened and depressed folklorists like Cecil Sharp, excited the New Dealers. By the early forties, Alan Lomax discussed alterations in traditional cultures in the language of an intrigued scientist more than an outraged advocate. He found that "perhaps the most hopeful characteristic" of contemporary American communities "is that they are now in [the] process of quite rapid change." He urged that these communities be treated as "folklore laboratories in which we can see recognizable old patterns from the past subjected to new strains and stresses, growing, decaying, proliferating." As Botkin wrote in the preface to his *Treasury of American Folklore* (1944), "If folklore is old wine in new bottles, it is also new wine in old bottles. It says not only 'Back where I come from,' but also 'Where do we go from here?' "[16]

This attitude led the New Deal workers to be far more omnivorous in their collecting efforts than previous folklorists. Sidney Robertson, who was a field-worker under Seeger in the Resettlement Administration, recalled her instructions as "Record EVERYthing. . . . Don't select, don't omit, don't concentrate on any single style. We know so little! Record *everything!*" Thirsting to understand the folk process, folklorists began to break away from the fetishization of folk purity. Seeger, at the "Conference on the Character and State of Studies in Folklore" (1942), unabashedly defined Stephen Foster's composed, popular songs as folk songs. Noting that they had passed into the oral tradition, he concluded, "To me they were folk songs, even though they are only quasifolksongs." And in a move that would have made Sharp cringe, Seeger even accepted commercial hillbilly music, dubbing it a "super-hybrid form of some genuine folk elements which have intruded into the mechanism of popular music." Botkin concurred that " 'hillbilly' has its place in the hierarchy of American folk styles" and matter-of-factly stated that "folk music is not a pure but a hybrid activity which is a fusion of 'folk,' 'art,' and 'popular' idioms and tastes."[17]

This openness to mixed styles prompted the New Deal folklorists, in a striking departure from their predecessors, to seek out the culture of the city. Previous folklorists had treated cities as anathema to folklore (even though many of them lived in them), blaming urbanization and industrialization for destroying traditional cultures. The New Deal folklorists, though, were fascinated by the new forms that urban communities created to meet their cultural needs—forms that Botkin called "the folklore of the metropolis." Botkin believed that "machinery does not destroy folklore," and he and his colleagues devoted considerable energy to studying and preserving culture produced by people whose lives centered around technology. Under the Works Progress Administration (WPA), collectors worked to gather the songs and stories not just of Cumberland mountaineers and African American sharecroppers but also of New York Jewish needleworkers, Connecticut clockmakers, Pennsylvania steelworkers, Montana copper miners, and Chicago railroaders.[18]

Much of this urban work was done through the Federal Writers' Project (FWP), which, under Botkin's leadership, established what it called "Living Lore" units in New York City, Chicago, and New England. These units were staffed by writers, many of them borrowed from the FWP's Creative Writing Unit, who lacked background in folklore but were fascinated by the hidden cultures of the city.[19] They haunted the hiring halls, locker rooms, and picket lines, engaging workers on their lunch breaks or between shifts and asking them for stories and songs. In this manner the New York Living Lore unit recorded stories from construction workers building the Queens Midtown Tunnel, jokes from members of Compressed Air Local No. 147, and songs by Clyde "Kingfish" Smith, the "singing fish man of East One Hundredth Street." Explaining the WPA's attentiveness to urban materials, Botkin noted that "the Negro street cries of Harlem are work songs, just as surely as the southern Negro's songs of the cotton, cane, and tobacco fields, road-construction saw mill and turpentine camps, and chain gangs. And they have social significance."[20]

Botkin's claim of social significance points to a key consequence of functionalism and one of the sources of its appeal in the thirties. By emphasizing "living lore" and insisting that modern society did not preclude quality folk expression, functionalism allowed folklore a political potential. Folklore could move beyond its associations with the past and actively and powerfully address the needs of the present. With the dislocations of the depression and the rising threat of fascism overseas, the notion that collecting songs could have political utility was tremendously reassuring to American folklorists in the thirties, and it permeated their rhetoric. Charles Seeger, for example, urged workers at the Resettlement Administration to select music on the basis of utilitarian as much as aesthetic criteria. "The main question," he asserted, "should not be 'is it good music,' but 'what is the music good for?'" Botkin shared Seeger's pragmatism, noting in his report on the WPA that the agency's folklore research was premised on a connection between "bread and song." "Throughout," he wrote, "we stress the relation between art and life, between work and culture. . . . The WPA looks upon folklore research not as a private but as a public function and folklore as public, not private property."[21]

With this idealistic agenda for folklore, it is not surprising that the New Deal folklorists strove to extend their reach beyond the traditional limits of their profession. Doing fieldwork and publishing song collections remained priorities, but the government folklorists saw folk song as too important a tool for social betterment to be confined to the scholarly realm. They worked to move from studying and preserving folk music to reintroducing it, with a hero's fanfare, into parts of society that had lost touch with the country's folk heritage.

The most utopian effort along these lines was mounted by Seeger and the Resettlement Administration (RA). The RA had been established in 1935 with a novel approach to aiding impoverished small farmers and industrial workers. It settled them in planned communities where they could have access to modern housing, better land to grow food, and, the RA hoped, a fresh start in a new community. But the diverse residents in these model communities did not share the RA's idealism about community spirit. The new settlers mostly ignored one another or fell into petty disputes, and the worried RA sent an expert to decide what should be done. She recommended music and drama programs to relieve stress and to encourage community bonding.[22]

Seeger, as head of the RA's Special Skills Division, took on the task of creating the music program. He set up a plan to send three hundred musicians to thirty-three RA communities within six months.[23] These musicians, Seeger hoped, would in effect serve as folk music facilitators, unearthing old-time songs that the residents knew, writing new songs based on traditional materials for local occasions, and encouraging people to sing music from their folk traditions instead of commercial music. Seeger had lofty hopes for this program. Alerting the homesteaders to the vitality of their folk song heritage, he felt, would spark pride in their culture, awaken them to the dangers that the mass media posed to their traditions, and encourage them to band together to protect their collective self-interests.[24]

Seeger's agenda quickly ran into trouble. In 1936 he sent ten musicians to ten communities. For the most part, they met with a lukewarm response from town residents. In no small part the fault lay with the musicians themselves. Seeger recalled ruefully that the consultants "simply couldn't do what they were supposed to do. They were supposed to get out and learn how to sing the songs that the people sang in the community and they didn't do it."[25] Seeger found that the consultants often hindered acceptance by taking the songs the residents sang and making elaborate classicized versions of them. One employee essentially ignored local folk materials and instead performed a series of Italian arias.

Even RA projects that tried to respect the integrity of the local music came up short. The music program produced a series of song sheets, for instance, that gave the words and music to traditional songs and featured rustic pen-and-ink drawings of rural people by Charles Pollock (Jackson's older brother). Township residents, though, seem to have resented the implications that their culture was behind the times. They saw Pollock's drawings as caricatures, and many, especially young people, expressed their preference for pop music over folk songs. This cool reception, plus charges in Washington that the RA's goals for the townships were communistic, doomed Seeger's program. When the RA was reorganized into the Farm Security Administration in 1937, the Special Skills Division was reduced, and Seeger left the agency.[26] His dream of 300 folk music consultants fell 290 short.

Seeger's goals for the RA proved out of reach, but in the late thirties and forties, the Washington folk establishment held on to its idealism about the social utility of its work. The Library of Congress's Archive of American Folk-Song, for example, started to see itself as more than simply a repository for traditional materials. Instead of just gathering folk music, the archive began to consider how to reinject it into the national culture. The driving force behind this new approach was Alan Lomax. Lomax, of course, had been involved in folk song collecting since the early thirties, but as the decade progressed, he began to forge a professional identity distinct from his father's. In 1937, when the Archive of American Folk-Song for the first time received government funding and could hire a full-time employee, the library chose Alan Lomax. At twenty-two he replaced his father as the head of the archive, with the title of assistant in charge (John Lomax remained honorary curator).[27]

Alan Lomax continued to use the archive to launch field trips, many of which he himself headed, but he also involved the archive in new efforts to popularize their results. Under Lomax, for example, the archive participated in an innovative Library of Congress effort known as the Radio Research Project. This project, funded by a Rockefeller Foundation grant in January 1941, was designed to use radio to open up the library's resources to the American populace. In the span of thirteen months, the project produced fifty educational programs (all for a price "less than the budget for the Eddie Cantor show for one single week," the project's chief proudly noted) that aired over both local and national networks. Some were transmitted over shortwave radio to Europe, Asia, and the Pacific. Although not government-funded, these broadcasts were produced out of the library's facilities. The project chief was Philip H. Co-

Promotional photo of Alan Lomax, ca. 1940.
(Library of Congress)

Alan Lomax, 1941.
(National Archives)

hen, formerly radio production director of the United States Office of Education, and Alan Lomax served as "music and folklore editor."[28]

The Radio Research Project launched a series of programs that amounted to a trial run for an alternative vision of network radio. Its shows combined the populism of the New Deal and functionalism's openness to contemporary folk culture with advances in recording and broadcast technology. The show's producers felt that network programs were shaping a national culture dominated by metropolitan centers and emphasizing artifice and uniformity. They wanted to demonstrate that commercial radio could create stronger, more interesting programs if it drew on regional culture, not just urban; on ordinary people, not just actors; and on the actual events of the country's rich history, not just the tired material of situation comedies and variety shows. Alan Lomax, for one, set out to prove that "local radio stations can one day produce programs with as much color and drama as the big network stations and we believe with a thousand times more honesty and meaning."[29] The project's goal, in effect, was to turn on its end the process by which radio technology was creating a national culture: instead of envisioning culture as diffusing from urban centers to the rest of the country, the project wanted to decentralize the process of cultural dissemination so that diverse local and regional sources could contribute as equal partners to a multifarious national culture.

This goal was ambitious and not without its ironic aspects. The project's organizers were devoted to preserving the nation's diversity, but they were trying to promote this diversity with shows produced from a single, urban-based, government-controlled, centralized source. They were determined to shield pockets of localism from homogenizing forces but were equally eager to knit these diverse elements into a cohesive whole. These tensions—between localism and nationalism, idiosyncrasy and unity—surfaced in the shows the project produced.

Some of the programs called attention to the nation's diversity in a raw, simplistic way, highlighting all the weird and unfamiliar cultures to be found in America. "The Ballad Hunter," for instance, a series of ten recorded programs narrated by John Lomax, emphasized folk song's exoticism, primitiveness, and nostalgic appeal. Much as Lomax had in his work over the previous three decades, these shows took an old-fashioned approach to traditional cultures, stressing the disjunction between them and the rest of America. In each program, the opening introduction established this theme. As that day's musical piece played lightly in the background ("Pick a Bale of Cotton," perhaps, or "Rock Island Line"), the announcer asserted the show's populism: "In each of these programs the Library of Congress presents John A. Lomax, the Ballad Hunter. For more than thirty years Mr. Lomax has been gathering the songs of the American People—songs that were not written down or learned from books—but folk songs of the people." As the rest of the introduction makes clear, "the people," for Lomax, existed only in the most isolated and out-of-the-way places: "To collect these songs Mr.

Lomax has ridden night-herd with cowboys, visited ballad-singers far back in the Ozark mountains, gone to dances in the country, spoken to tenant farmers in the Deep South and *yes*, he has gone into crowded cell-blocks in penitentiaries in many parts of the United States." Following this introduction, Lomax would relate a titillating story from one of his field-collecting expeditions, interspersing it with musical examples. He might tell about the time in the Sugarland, Texas, prison where the "self-important" convict Clear Rock, with a haughty "Ready right now," "pushed through [a] jam-packed room," nearly destroying Lomax's recording machine, and started singing "Dat's All Right, Honey." "You can hear his big hands beating the time," Lomax told listeners as he played the recording. Or the time at the Arkansas Penitentiary, where the prisoners exclaimed, "Get your diamond blades, boys, we'll set him afire," and then broke into "Rock Island Line" as they "sung and swung their axes—their diamond blades—[and] shouted to each other in sheer ecstasy—the blood running warm in their veins."[30] Folklore, to the Ballad Hunter, had the romantic appeal of something foreign. It spoke to the nation's simpler past, not to the struggles Americans faced in their daily lives.

Befitting his attraction to functionalism, Alan Lomax's work for the Radio Research Project focused on contemporary folk communities. Radio, Lomax believed, could do more than simply allow more people to hear the old-time music he and his father had recorded: it could enable the voices of the folk to be heard across America, and therefore it could be a powerful democratizing force. With this agenda in mind, Lomax played a central role in creating what was probably the Radio Research Project's most original programming, its documentary series. In these shows, Lomax worked to alter the traditional relationship between the documenter and the documented. Instead of sending experts into an area and asking them to do interviews and report on their findings, Lomax and his colleagues envisioned a documentary in which ordinary people would tell their stories themselves. These documentaries, Lomax said, would point to "a new function for radio; that of letting the people explain themselves and their lives to the entire nation."[31]

The centerpiece behind this scheme was a new technique for editing field recordings, introduced to the Radio Research workers by Jerome Wiesner, a recording engineer at the Library of Congress who would later become president of the Massachusetts Institute of Technology.[32] Wiesner assured the staff that in the Library of Congress's new recording laboratory one could cut and paste field recordings with such precision that edited interviews would sound like a single, seamless conversation.

Inspired by this possibility, Radio Research staff members devised a documenting process that suggested a whole new approach to fieldwork. They would send recording machines, sometimes in the Library of Congress's new recording truck, to areas in which particularly human dramas were being played out. The field-workers would record interviews, speeches, and songs of the people they encountered, and then when they returned to Washington, they would splice them into a script, add a narrator and background music, and present an "authentic" portrait of the nation as constructed by the words of ordinary Americans. This approach was first used in May 1941 to document rural Americans' views of the war in Europe. Folklorist Charles Todd and Alan Lomax used the same technique to convert field recordings that Todd and folklorist Robert Sonkin had made in California Okie camps into a program about the Okie migration. Lomax headed a team that documented the effects of the Tennessee Valley Authority (TVA) on a rural county in Georgia, recording the county doctor, lawyer, and newspaper editor, along with "farmers' meetings, family reunions, [and] revivals." A young writer on staff named Arthur Miller did fieldwork and wrote a script about the effects of the defense-related boom on the shipbuilding town of Wilmington, North Carolina.[33]

Implicit in these shows was a new conception of folklore, one that drew on New Deal folklorists' openness to contemporary materials and on their eagerness to connect folklore to social activism. Plainly the Radio Research workers did not see folklore as a matter of rescuing remnants of primitive cultures. "The folk," in their conception, had been reconfigured into "people like your own neighbors—1941 Americans." And the culture the project was trying to document was not firmly anchored in the historical past but was fluid and continuous with contemporary America. "The record is not finished," Alan Lomax summarized at the end of one the shows. "Living history never is. . . . This will be not only a record that men of the future may study. It is a record from which men of the present may have much to learn."[34] Far from being antiquarians, then, the Radio Research Project workers positioned themselves as facilitators of a multiregional, multiethnic discussion among the American people, a discussion in which the people themselves set the agenda. Those Lomax informants from the early thirties who had imagined themselves singing directly to President Roosevelt no longer seemed so naive.[35] Folklore was now being used to inject the voices of the voiceless into a national conversation.

Some of the Radio Research Project's less technologically innovative programs also tried to facilitate a dialogue among the American people.

The project's "Hidden History" series, for example, worked to involve Americans in the country's history. Each of these twenty-six programs, broadcast in 1941 over NBC, drew on archival materials from the Library of Congress to tell the story of ordinary people's involvement in a key event in American history. One episode, for instance, looked at the origins of "Yankee Doodle," while another told the story of the various towns that claim to have been first to declare independence from Britain. Regardless of the topic, each episode strove to show the human side of history and stressed that listeners could play an active role in shaping how historians interpreted the subject. The show, one staff member wrote, worked to say "in dramatic form that history is found not only in books and manuscripts in public libraries but in the minds and memories of the people; in attics and trunks hidden away and belonging to the people." Accordingly, the shows resisted the temptation for complete closure and historical certainty. Instead the announcer ended each episode by saying, "There are many stories about [the origin of Yankee Doodle, the declarations of independence, and so on]. Perhaps you, or someone in your family, has materials about [this topic]. If so, send it to the Library of Congress."[36] History, the program stressed, was ever changing and elastic, open to being shaped and reshaped by ordinary people, not just by great leaders. In much of its programming, then, the Radio Research Project avoided assuming an authoritative, expert voice in favor of a more open-ended, contingent stance that left room for the diverse voices and opinions of the people.

Even as the folk establishment began advancing its vision of a fluid folk populism, it faced mounting pressure to adopt a more didactic tone. In the late thirties, as the country began moving toward war, government programs increasingly had to prove their usefulness to the war effort to get funding. Rather than chafing under this utilitarian mandate, the leaders of the government-sponsored folklore programs embraced it. The Lomaxes and Harold Spivacke, the head of the Library of Congress's Music Division, argued that the Archive of American Folk-Song was a defense-related institution and requested a 100 percent increase in funding. Charles Seeger wrote excitedly of folk song as "a weapon in war—and at that not only . . . a defensive weapon for the home front but an offensive one in the armed services!"[37] This eagerness to be involved stemmed in part from the New Dealers' determination to see social significance in their work and in part from straightforward patriotism: the folklorists were strong supporters of the Allied effort, particularly after Hitler's invasion of Russia. In addition, the government folklorists no doubt recognized that their positions in the government's official culture depended on establishing the necessity of their work in this time of crisis. Their efforts to solidify their role in the official culture during the war highlight both the extent to which folklore had established a niche in official culture and the unsteadiness of its position.

To some extent, New Deal folklorists found that targeting their work for the war effort was a simple extension of the sort of work they had been doing already. All along, certainly, the folklore establishment's projects had been strongly pro-American. The oppositional element that had made folk song so appealing to the Left had already been deemphasized in the folklorists' government work. The New Deal folklorists found that some war-related efforts jibed easily with their emphasis on giving voice to ordinary Americans. On December 8, 1941, for instance, the day after Pearl Harbor, the documentary section of the Radio Research Project sent telegrams to its field-workers in ten different areas and asked them to begin documenting local reactions to war's outbreak immediately. Over the next three days Alan Lomax, John Lomax, Robert Sonkin, Charles Todd, and other staff members stopped people on street corners, interrupted games at pool halls and haircuts at barbershops, everywhere recording people's reactions to the coming of war. Exemplifying their belief in the power of contemporary folklore, Lomax and the others were treating the people they interviewed both as informants whose responses would interest future generations and as citizens whose opinions needed to be heard by the policy makers of the day. This program was broadcast over the Mutual Broadcasting System, and parts of it were rebroadcast by the Office of Emergency Management.[38]

Other war-related efforts, too, were extensions of the New Deal folklorists' interests in contemporary folklore. Early in 1941, for example, Alan Lomax outlined a proposal to Archibald MacLeish, the librarian of Congress, for an Army Music Program to be operated out of the Archive of American Folk-Song. When visiting the army camp near Washington, he had observed "an enormous and basic interest among the white soldiers . . . in 'hill-billy music,' that is in contemporary American folk song." Lomax wanted funds to document the songs the soldiers sang and to respond to their requests for instruments and musical materials. "Very few have instruments of their own," he noted, "and those that do are afraid to bring their instruments to camp." Moreover, he added, "Few know as many verses and tunes as they would like to know." Lomax proposed to address these deficiencies by providing army barracks and camp recreation centers with a wide variety of stringed instruments and with song sheets that would give the words to a range of cowboy, hillbilly, popular, and folk songs.[39] Once a month, to follow up on these donations, he would send a field recording team to the camps "to record the best programs by the men and the songs they have themselves made up."[40]

Lomax's interest in the army camps, though, went beyond a desire to document the emerging folk culture. His proposal shows him to have been equally concerned with influencing the form the culture would take. Instead of simply targeting soldiers who already had an established interest in folk music, he advocated making a special effort to reach soldiers who had no experience with traditional music. Along with sending instruments, Lomax suggested providing instruction books and recordings "by folksong virtuosos who play these instruments to be used as instruction records by the men." And significantly, despite suggesting that the program "follow the desires of the men," Lomax was not interested in encouraging all of the soldiers' musical interests. He was willing to give them the words to some popular songs along with his folk materials, but he clearly had a vision of the sorts of music it would be appropriate for them to play. The instrument shipments would be confined to "all types of stringed instruments," not trumpets or saxophones. Indeed, in the first draft of this proposal, Lomax explicitly recommended that there "should be a center in camps for this type of music as opposed and as counter distinction to jazz and other types of music played from written music and with complicated arrangements."[41] Lomax moved easily from documenting to shaping culture.

As the recipient of this proposal, MacLeish seems to have been in step with Lomax's thinking. The day after Lomax's letter was dated, MacLeish was quoted in a *Washington Post* article entitled "Folk Songs May Inspire America's Soldiers." MacLeish, the reporter noted, "hopes that the Army morale service will wish to ask for [the Archive of American Folk-Song's] extensive materials and have them made available in recordings and text." He was quoted as saying that "these songs are great 'democratic indoctrinators.'"[42]

MacLeish's language points to a tension in the folk establishment's wartime projects. As war fervor rose within the government, the folklorists increasingly realized that for their work to have significant impact on the mobilization effort (and for it to receive institutional support) it needed to do more than document the American people's culture; it had to begin trying to *shape* this culture in ways that the war machine would recognize as helpful to its cause. As wartime patriotism rose, therefore, a new style of populism began to surface in folklorists' efforts. Their projects became less oriented to providing a forum for the expression of the diverse and multifarious voices of ordinary people; more, they focused on melding these discordant voices into a single united chorus of nationalism. Folklore moved into the realm of propaganda.

This new emphasis was increasingly visible in the Radio Research Project's later work. Elements of a more didactic style had been evident even in the project's earliest and most innovative programs. Alan Lomax's documentary shows, for example, were not as free-form as his rhetoric suggested. For the initial programs the project's workers made field recordings and edited them into a script, but eventually the show decided that the technique worked best the other way around: "A rough script should be written [first]," Lomax decided, "and recording should be done within the confines of the script."[43] This technique likely encouraged the stilted dialogue that one hears in some of the documentary programs.

Working from a preexisting script also gave the producers more freedom to shape the overall moral to which each show pointed. Sometimes a show's final message seemed to diverge from the spirit of the dialogue spoken by the ordinary people the program interviewed. For his show on the TVA, for example, Lomax conducted lengthy interviews with Paul Ledford, a well-off Georgia farmer whom Lomax had selected because he was "a good talker." For much of the time that Lomax spent with him, Ledford talked about how angry he was at the TVA. The dam it was building was forcing him to give up the old house his family had lived in for three generations. He was losing his family home, his land, and the nearby spring where, Ledford noted fondly, the "cold water bubbled out cold enough to make your teeth hurt like drinkin' ice water." When Lomax asked Ledford to look down on his farm from a hilltop and say goodbye, Ledford's voice rang with pain and bitterness at what had been done to him. On the show, though, Lomax followed this speech with a conclusion that must have made Ledford's head spin. The local farmers, Lomax noted, were "sick at heart" about having to pull up their roots, but they were not, he intoned, angry at the TVA: they understood the need for "more power for more aluminum for national defense." This rhetoric says more about the effort to mobilize for World War II than about the views of the distraught Mr. Ledford.[44]

Elements of this didactic approach also surfaced in a series the project produced occasionally in 1941, "Report to the Nation." Broadcast over CBS, the program was intended to take the American people behind the scenes of the American government, with an eye toward making them feel informed and empowered. As one episode explained to listeners, the show "aims to bring you the story of the biggest business on earth—the United States Government—a business in which you are a stockholder." One episode outlined for listeners what went on in the Library of Congress, while another described the work of the Radio Research Project itself. The show's rhetoric, though, suggests that being involved in the government entailed fulfilling an obligation more than exercising options. "*Attention, citizens,*" began the October 7, 1941, report. "You, the people of the United States, have in Washington a government which is your agent in the conduct of your interests. It is a government of, by and for *you* . . . and it is your *duty* as well as your privilege to know how this government is operating."[45]

Not surprisingly the Radio Research Project adopted this more propagandistic style of patriotism most decisively after the attack on Pearl Harbor brought America formally into the war. The project's leaders clearly understood that the new situation demanded that they adapt their agenda. Philip H. Cohen, for example, decided that the "Hidden History" programs were unnecessary in the current environment. Writing to Archibald MacLeish in February 1942, he noted that the series had "made a great deal of sense when it was presented; [but] it is doubtful that that sort of program would be of value at this moment. . . . If the Radio Project is carried on in any form, it must concern itself with the problems that face the American people at this moment."[46] Cohen's misgivings about "Hidden History" did not simply reflect a discomfort with producing shows about the American past. On the contrary, the project's most successful shows in the months after Pearl Harbor focused directly on history. They offered, though, a very different vision of the country's heritage than "Hidden History." Instead of focusing on common people and small-scale events buried in the sediment of history, they dealt with the venerated heroes of the past and their monumental accomplishments. And instead of portraying history as mutable and indeterminate, they treated it as a source of moral instruction.

A look at the history programs the Radio Research Project did produce after Pearl Harbor illustrates how the war caused it to readjust its goals. In terms of popular reaction, probably the biggest success the project ever had was a patriotic show celebrating the 150th anniversary of the adoption of the Bill of Rights. In producing this program, eventually entitled "We Hold These Truths," the Radio Research Project had a more indirect role than usual. Archibald MacLeish, who had recently become director of the Office of Facts and Figures (OFF), engaged the project's core staff members (including Philip Cohen, Alan Lomax, and Jerome Wiesner) as a planning committee and charged them with deciding how to celebrate the anniversary. Not surprisingly, they suggested a radio program. The Radio Research staff, though, did not have the authority to produce the show on its own. The head of the OFF's radio division, William Lewis (the former head of CBS), had lobbied the committee to consider a radio show, and when the committee accepted his suggestion, he selected a producer with whom he had experience, Norman Corwin. The Radio Research staff helped gather material for the show, but Corwin wrote the script and exercised most of the control. Corwin was a thirty-one-year-old writer, producer, and director of middlebrow radio dramas who had worked with Lewis at CBS and whose career had just begun to take off. "We Hold These Truths" proved to be an important stepping-stone. The program was broadcast over all four major networks and, one historian estimates, reached sixty million listeners, a number equal to half the population of the country, making it "the largest audience ever to hear a dramatic performance."[47]

"We Hold These Truths" achieved this success through a combination of luck and savvy calculation. The show received an unforeseen boost in the public eye when, a week before it was to be broadcast, the Japanese bombed Pearl Harbor. Corwin had a sufficient flair for the dramatic to know how to take advantage of the crisis. "We Hold These Truths" features an even more exaggerated and maudlin version of the sweeping populism toward which the Radio Research Project's work had been moving. It did not attempt to offer a diverse, multifaceted portrait of the American folk, as the early Radio Research shows had tried to do. In "We Hold These Truths," this many-hued vision of Americans has been displaced by an idealized everyman character known as "the Citizen." Somber and dutiful, he leads the listeners through an explanation of each of the ten amendments in the Bill of Rights, explaining their contemporary significance, painting stark pictures of what life would be like without them, and soliciting testimonies about their greatness from figures like "Farmer," "Worker," "Mother," and even "Okie." These archetypes of the American people are brought on stage less to represent individual factions than to attest to the possibility of eliminating all factions; above all, "We Hold These Truths" preaches the importance of unity. "Citizen," for instance, hears "the voices of Americans together now, together in a new way, in a strange new way . . . a way that men have never lived together in before . . . proud men, unsuspicious, trusting men, their fighting over and their living just begun, their building, and their working and their singing just now getting started. . . . A hundred thirty million people . . . working in a mighty unison to prosecute a war."[48] History, in "We Hold These Truths," is not a way of locating one's individual place in the nation but a source of icons around which differences may be elided.

One scene in the play illustrates the approach. As in the "Hidden History" shows, "We Hold These Truths" envisions Americans visiting the Library of Congress. In this case, though, they are not coming to contribute a story they know about the origins of "Yankee Doodle"; instead, figured as "the Citizen," they climb the library's marble stairs to pay homage to the original copy of the Constitution, preserved behind glass. The populism of "We Hold These Truths" promotes reflexive devotion to the nation, not questioning and introspection about one's relationship to the past

This agenda shaped not only the script but also the production style of "We Hold These Truths." Above all, the show's producers wanted even widely diverse audiences to be able to identify with its characters. This goal not only encouraged the producers to construct the show's characters as anonymous archetypes but also, paradoxically, led them to enlist big-name stars to play these characters. The "just folks" style of "Hidden History" and of the Radio Research Project's documentary programs seemed inappropriate given the weighty themes "We Hold These Truths" wanted to address and the broad appeal it hoped to garner. With a big budget, full government backing, and a national crisis at hand, Corwin could attract an impressive cast of celebrities, among them Lionel Barrymore, Rudy Vallee, Walter Huston, Walter Brennan, Marjorie Main, Edward G. Robinson, and Orson Welles. For the central role of "the Citizen," Corwin landed Corporal Jimmy Stewart, who, as a star whose appeal rested on his "everyman" image, was an ideal choice. And, as a final addition to the momentousness of the occasion, President Roosevelt agreed to conclude the program with a short speech. On December 15, the show began by broadcasting live from CBS's Hollywood affiliate, then switched directly to a live remote from the White House for Roosevelt's speech, and concluded with a final switch to New York, where Leopold Stokowski directed the NBC Symphony Orchestra playing the national anthem.[49] The Radio Research Project's focus on quirky folk simplicity had been displaced by a gala style that pounded its message home.

The folk establishment was never again involved in an extravaganza of the same magnitude as "We Hold These Truths," but the stylistic shifts the show represented were not momentary aberrations. In February 1942, the Radio Research Project produced a celebration for Lincoln's birthday, entitled "Lincoln Speaks to the People and to the Soldiers," in which the former president offered patriotic exhortations to contemporary Americans. Broadcast over NBC's Blue Network, it, too, opted for a star-studded cast, including Walter Huston and Douglas

Fairbanks Jr. That same month the Almanac Singers, a group that included Pete Seeger, Woody Guthrie, and Bess Lomax (Alan's sister), wrote a folk-styled song for Corwin's nationally broadcast radio drama, "America at War!" Entitled "Round and Round Hitler's Grave," it featured the chorus:

> Round and round Hitler's grave
> Round and round we go.
> Gonna let that feller down
> He won't get up no mo'.

(For subsequent verses, the chorus was adapted for "Musso's grave" and "Hito's grave.") The show, part of a thirteen-part series ("This Is War!"), was broadcast on the most extensive national hookup ever used for a radio series (700 out of the nation's 924 stations) and sent via shortwave around the world. In 1945 Corwin reused the song for his program celebrating victory in Europe ("On a Note of Triumph!"), this time sung by the country-pop singer Johnny Bond and a trio. In 1944 Alan Lomax tried his own hand at the more didactic style of radio drama. Along with his wife, Elizabeth, he wrote and arranged to have broadcast "The Martins and the Coys." It featured such performers as Guthrie, Seeger, Burl Ives, Will Geer, and Sonny Terry singing antifascist songs, many of which were written to traditional mountain tunes ("Round and Round Hitler's Grave" also made another appearance). In the plot, the two West Virginia families resolved decades of feuding and went off together to fight Hitler.[50] The folk had become sources for a morality play.

To some extent, the folk establishment's willingness to adapt its populist style to wartime exigencies enabled it to hold on to a place in official culture during the war. Alan Lomax, for example, left the Archive of American Folk-Song in the fall of 1942 and began working for the recently organized Office of War Information (OWI), the government's propaganda wing.[51] Within the OWI, Alan, along with Elizabeth and his sister Bess, worked for the music department of the Voice of America.[52] Throughout the war, the Lomaxes pushed the OWI to include as much folk-styled music as possible in its propaganda efforts. In 1943 Lomax, with the Czech folklorist Svatava Jakobson, produced a songbook for the OWI entitled "Freedom Songs of the United Nations." According to one estimate, one hundred or more hours of the agency's programming featured the singing of folk song luminaries like Seeger, Guthrie, and Ives, along with traditional folk singers in various languages.[53]

There were other signs, too, that the federal government was taking folk music seriously. In 1941 Charles Seeger edited the *Army Song Book*, which was published by the Adjutants General's Office and the Library of Congress. It included patriotic classics such as the "Star-Spangled Banner" and "America the Beautiful," military winners like the "Song of the Army Engineer," and a smattering of rural folk tunes like the "Boll Weevil Song" and "Old Joe Clark." That same year Eleanor Roosevelt threw her support behind Lomax's and MacLeish's notion of a folk music program for the military camps. Writing in her "My Day" newspaper column about the recent folk music concert at the White House, she stressed folk song's importance as a tool in the war effort. "I hope these songs spread through all the branches of the service. I would like to see musical instruments available and records of these songs in the recreation centers and in every community center near a camp throughout the country. I think it would make us conscious of our rich background of folk literature and music."[54]

Getting a sympathetic hearing, though, did not always translate into actual accomplishments. Although the folk music establishment was involved in many branches of government culture during the war, the crisis ultimately revealed its position in the official culture to be somewhat precarious. Many of the most ambitious plans of the government folklorists never came to fruition. Archibald MacLeish, for example, although a folk music advocate, rejected the Lomaxes and Spivacke's request to increase the archive's funding as a defense-related institution. Despite the first lady's endorsement, moreover, no folk music program was ever instituted at the U.S. military camps. As Lomax recalled, "The Pentagon considered the morale of the armed forces a strictly military matter." Similarly, in February 1942 the chief of the Radio Research Project, Philip Cohen, pleaded, "It is of utmost importance not to end the Project now when we have just learned the possibilities of the work that can be carried on here," but the project lost its funding that month anyway. Support instead went to more straightforwardly propagandistic organizations like the OWI.[55]

The war mobilization effort also revealed that the federal arts relief programs, which had funded so much folklore work, had only shaky backing. In the late thirties, opponents of the New Deal in Congress and the press targeted the arts programs, sensing they were easy prey. They were right. In August 1938, the House Committee to Investigate Un-American Activities, chaired by Martin Dies, opened hearings to investigate charges that the WPA arts programs (known as Federal One) were dominated by Communists and were using their government funding to propagandize against the American political system. Dies claimed that the Federal Writers' and Theater Projects were "doing more to spread

Communist propaganda than the Communist party itself," and he orchestrated a procession of ill-informed and often grudge-bearing witnesses to prove it. Although the administrators and staffs of these programs expressed outrage, Dies's charges initially brought little response from either the Roosevelt administration or the American public. Even the leaders of the WPA ignored the accusations. The head of the Federal Theater Project, Hallie Flanagan, recalled that the agency was working under "the supposition that if you do not answer an attack, the attack will cease."[56]

The attacks continued, though. The Dies committee ended its hearings in December 1938, but early in 1939 the arts programs were targeted for investigation by the House Committee on Appropriations. In the meantime Federal One had lost its most powerful advocate within the administration, Harry Hopkins, who, in an effort to position himself to run for the presidency, had resigned as director of the WPA and become the new secretary of commerce. His successor had little interest in the arts programs.[57]

With such limited political support behind Federal One, its opponents succeeded in significantly scaling back the federal government's commitment to the arts. In the summer of 1939, Congress eliminated the Federal Theater Project completely and mandated that the other WPA arts programs secure state sponsorship to continue their work. The Federal Writers' Project (now renamed the Writers Program) succeeded in lining up sponsors to keep the project afloat in almost all states, but it had to make personnel reductions and pursue its goals on a smaller scale. Primarily it worked on completing its acclaimed state guidebook series and on producing small publications for sponsors. After Pearl Harbor, the Writers Program became the Writers Unit of the War Services Subdivision, and all projects that did not directly contribute to the war effort were set aside in favor of ventures like bomb-squad training manuals and recreational guides to the areas around army camps.[58]

The Federal Music Project, too, had to scale back drastically and reorient its programs for the war. Historian Barbara Tischler finds that "as long as [Federal Music Project] units performed for USO gatherings, gave concerts at defense plants, for bond drives, and at military installations, and generally offered their instruments and voices to the cause, the Project was able to continue its relief efforts, albeit on a severely limited basis." Encapsulating the pragmatic attitude government officials took toward the arts during the war, one member of Congress challenged an appropriation for the New York City Music Project by saying, "Isn't it time to quit fiddling around? The money for this music project would be enough to buy three bombers."[59]

By the spring of 1942, the arts programs were almost completely moribund. To guarantee that staff members tailor their projects to the war effort, the WPA issued a set of guidelines that explicitly prohibited a variety of non-defense-related pursuits. Among the banned projects were "creative music activities; collecting, annotating, and recording folk music; music surveys and research activities."[60] Officially, the Writers Unit held on into the winter of 1943, and the WPA was not liquidated until that June, but the commitment to using federal relief agencies to explore indigenous American arts had faded long before.[61]

The folk establishment's standing in official culture, therefore, proved to be less secure than its leaders might have expected. Since the mid-thirties they had pushed hard to achieve an activist role for folklore within the official culture, and with the advent of World War II they had shown a willingness to adapt their work to match the needs of the official culture. These efforts had won them more official patronage than American folk music had ever before enjoyed, but even so, the niche they had secured during the depression proved to be transitory.

After World War II, few institutional vestiges remained from the various government projects folklorists had launched. The Archive of American Folk-Song, which predated the depression, continued to operate; but the Radio Research Project, the music programs of the Resettlement Administration and of the Office of War Information, and the collecting efforts of the Federal Writers', Music, and Theater Projects all disappeared. Marking a symbolic close to the period of folk music's ascendancy in the official realm, the death of President Roosevelt put an end to folk concerts at the White House. The Trumans preferred classical music.[62] With their institutional support gone, most of the major players in the folk establishment ended up working outside government after the war. After the cutbacks in the Federal Writers' Project, Benjamin Botkin had taken over from Lomax as head of the Archive of American Folk-Song, a position he had held from 1942 to 1945. As the war ended, though, Botkin resigned and spent the rest of his career writing with no institutional affiliation. He edited a series of highly popular folklore anthologies in the forties and fifties.[63]

Alan Lomax, too, ended his association with the government after the war. In the late forties he was the director of folk music for Decca Records, a commercial company. In 1948, though, the end of Lomax's efforts to find a niche within America's official culture was marked by a woeful coda. After the war, Lomax was on the board of directors of

People's Songs, the folk music organization that Pete Seeger and other of the former Almanac Singers founded in 1946. The organization threw its support behind the 1948 presidential campaign of Henry Wallace and his Progressive Party. Wallace had been vice president under Roosevelt and secretary of commerce under Truman but had been asked to resign the latter position for advocating partnership and peaceful coexistence with the Soviet Union. This stance and his support of civil rights and of the more populist aspects of the New Deal—he had challenged Henry Luce's notion of the "American Century" by proclaiming the "Century of the Common Man"—earned Wallace the backing of Roosevelt's more left-wing supporters and of the Communist Party itself.[64] The members of People's Songs were particularly enthusiastic, and, as had the Almanac Singers during World War II, they determined to make folk song central to the cause.

Alan Lomax took charge of planning music for the campaign, excitedly proclaiming it "the first singing campaign since Lincoln's." He helped arrange for performers to accompany the candidate on campaign swings, and, along with Pete Seeger, Guthrie, and others, he wrote songs to rally supporters. Often the songs consisted of new lyrics grafted onto familiar tunes. Lomax's output included the memorable "I've Got a Ballot," meant to be sung to the tune of "I've Got Six-Pence." It's a "magic little ballot," the song lilts, that can "bring a higher wage" and "pension my old age" and "make a little home for kids and wife."[65]

Such songs remained highly visible throughout the course of the 1948 campaign. Pete Seeger, for example, sang at the Progressive Party's convention in Philadelphia and at a huge Wallace rally in Yankee Stadium. But the singers' excitement at their role turned to foreboding as Wallace's campaign floundered. Put off by his left-wing associations, labor unions refused to back him, and Wallace's conciliatory attitude to the USSR drew hostile, sometimes violent audiences. Although the songs cheered Wallace's staff, they seemed to mean little to the public they were intended to reach.[66]

In the end, Wallace made a disastrous showing at the polls, finishing fourth, behind the segregationist candidate Strom Thurmond. The result completed the CP's expulsion from the New Deal coalition and prompted many within the folk music world to reassess their efforts to apply music to contemporary politics. Woody Guthrie was especially critical of the organization's misguided attempt to win over the American people. "Why," he asked, in a letter to People's Songs, "did our songs not reach in and touch deep enough to cause the hand to push the C Row handles in that voting booth?" By way of answering, he singled out

Lomax: "How a man with such a long road of sensible travels behind him . . . could expect such a shallow jingly and insincere number as 'I've Got a Ballot' to touch the heartstrings and conscience of the hard-hit masses, is a problem beyond me. I never did hear a living human being call his vote a 'magic little ballot.' People I have seen call their vote a number of things, none of which are nearly as cutiepie, as highly polite, as flippant, as sissy nor effeminate as this song."[67] By the beginning of 1949, People's Songs was bankrupt, and its disheartened leaders disbanded the organization. In 1950 Alan Lomax was cited in *Red Channels*, a blacklisters' handbook claiming to identify Communist influences in the media. He fled to Britain, where he lived the next eight years.[68]

Among the leaders of the New Deal folk establishment, only Charles Seeger retained an official role after World War II. In 1941 he had become head of the Pan-American Union's music division, a position he held until 1953. Founded in 1910, the Pan-American Union (PAU) was an international organization whose members included Latin American countries and the United States. The music division's goals were to foster the exchange of music, performers, and scholars among PAU member nations, a task for which the PAU assigned Seeger the largest budget of his administrative career. He arranged for the music of Latin American composers to be published, for North American composers and musicians to tour Latin America, and for an exchange of North and South American field-workers. Seeger also worked to use the PAU as an organizational wedge for introducing traditional music into American public schools. He tried to integrate folk tunes into music textbooks, enlisting the aid of American composers like Aaron Copland and Henry Cowell. On an even broader scale, Seeger used the PAU as a launching point for the creation of a worldwide music organization. He began by establishing the Inter-American Music Council (IAMC) within the PAU and becoming its director. After the PAU became incorporated into the Organization of American States (OAS) and affiliated with the United Nations, Seeger successfully pushed for a worldwide organization, the International Music Council (IMC), which was formed in 1949.[69]

Despite this degree of musical and organizational ferment, Seeger's time at the PAU was filled largely with disappointments and frustrations. He felt he lacked the organization's full backing, particularly after it merged with the OAS, a virulently anti-Communist organization dedicated primarily to fighting the Cold War. In the late forties, PAU officials did not come to his defense when the United Nations decided to eliminate his Inter-American Music Council. And, although he was known as the "father of the International Music Council," he felt increasingly marginalized by that organization as well. Delegates of the IMC, he found, lacked a deep commitment to traditional music and were more interested in promoting European classical music worldwide than in encouraging the people of the world to make their own music. In 1952 he complained that the IMC spent its time sponsoring conference sessions on "we know who great composers are" and "similar useless topics."[70]

This elitism galled Seeger and contributed to a feeling of despair about ever achieving his musical agenda within the IMC and the PAU. Seeger still clung to the notion that cultural forms, if sensitively applied, could ameliorate relations between classes and between nations. "The arts," he maintained, "are the prime vehicles of communication among men and indispensable to broad programs of public relations." Seeger stressed, though, that the arts could just as easily foster hostility as friendship: "They can be used equally well," he wrote, "to provoke war or to promote peace." Increasingly, Seeger felt that the international organizations, with their antipathy to folk cultures and their labyrinthine bureaucracies, were doing little to improve the world's cultural political situation. In 1953, frustrated by his position in these organizations and anxious about being employed in a government agency as the Red Scare mounted, Seeger retired from the Pan-American Union, left Washington, D.C., and, essentially, withdrew from public life.[71] He had worked to create permanent institutional outlets for his activist conception of folklore, but the institutions he had helped found had not fulfilled his hopes. After almost two decades, his career in government was over.

In the same decades that Seeger and the New Deal folklorists were attempting to carve out a niche in official culture, other American folklorists were working outside government to institutionalize a very different vision of folklore. Having little interest in folklore as a tool for reform, these folklorists took a more insular view of the field. They set out to legitimize folklore as an intellectual pursuit—to establish and codify its methods and standards in the hope that it at last would command the respect of other disciplines and, not incidentally, win the favor of foundations and government grant-giving agencies. They wanted, in short, to professionalize folklore. Instead of struggling for a toehold in government, they turned to the more inviting world of the American university.

Folklore, of course, had played a role on American campuses since before the turn of the century. Many of the earliest connoisseurs of folk ballads had been literature professors, and often they had integrated some folk materials into their course offerings. Francis James Child and George Lyman Kittredge, especially, had inspired generations of young ballad collectors at Harvard. As folklorists' interests had begun to extend beyond Old World ballads, so had the scope of their courses. From the 1920s until after World War II, historian and folklorist J. Frank Dobie had taught a popular course on the folklore of the American Southwest at the University of Texas. At New York University in the 1930s James Weldon Johnson had incorporated African American spirituals and blues into his course "Racial Contributions to American Culture," while Mary Elizabeth Barnicle had regularly brought Lead Belly in to sing for her course on folk song. By 1939, a nationwide survey counted sixty courses on folklore in twenty-five institutions, in departments ranging from English and German to anthropology, music, and sociology. In most of these cases, though, the folklore work a professor did was necessarily a sidelight to work in other disciplines.[72] Meanwhile, those few people who saw themselves as professional folklorists showed little inclination to take an academic approach to folk materials. Antiquarian folklorists concerned themselves mainly with collecting as much folk material as possible, while public folklorists such as the New Dealers focused on applying folklore to a pragmatic end. Neither of these groups saw themselves as scholars. Into the 1940s, few folklorists were preoccupied with defining folklore as a distinct discipline.

The push to professionalize folklore began with Stith Thompson, a professor at Indiana University. Thompson was born in 1885 (the year before Charles Seeger), and, like John Lomax, he studied with George Lyman Kittredge at Harvard and began his career by teaching at the University of Texas (1914–18). While in Austin, Thompson edited the first publication of the Texas Folklore Society, an organization that Lomax had helped found in 1914, and he even rented a room in Lomax's house. Thompson's career, though, quickly diverged from Seeger's and Lomax's. He showed little interest in music or, for that matter, field collecting. Instead, in the early 1920s, he landed a job in Indiana University's English Department, where he stayed until he retired in 1955.[73] In his academic career, Thompson published prolifically, pursuing what is known as the "historic-geographic approach," an offshoot of diffusionism. This approach rejected functionalism's emphasis on contemporary folklore and its penchant for social activism. Instead, Thompson and like-minded colleagues treated folklore largely as an art form devoid of context. One of their favorite pursuits was to catalog recurring motifs in folklore, often juxtaposing hundreds of versions of the same proverb or folktale in an effort to locate its archetypal form. Thompson made monumental contributions to this effort, including *The Types of the Folktale* (1928, revised in 1961), which expanded a landmark Finnish index, and his six-volume *Motif-Index of Folk Literature* (1932–36, revised in 1958). These works enabled scholars to identify the origins and track the migrations of folktales around the world.[74]

Thompson's weighty publications were only part of his efforts to solidify folklore's professional standing. In 1942 he organized the Summer Folklore Institute in Bloomington, in which professors and students spent eight weeks taking courses and forging professional bonds. These institutes were held every four years for two decades, and they served as the beginning point for a more ambitious step. In 1949, while dean of the graduate school, Thompson founded at Indiana the nation's first Ph.D. program in folklore. The first doctorate was awarded in 1953, the year that Charles Seeger resigned from the Pan-American Union.[75] Folklore, a profession fundamentally dedicated to the culture of the illiterate, had entered the world of letters.

Establishing a graduate program, of course, did not guarantee folklore's standing within academia. It was still necessary to make the program productive and profitable, to inspire other universities to form programs of their own, and, perhaps most important, to ensure that the professional standards the Indiana program inculcated would be the criteria by which all folklorists were judged. The drive to achieve this larger agenda was spearheaded by Thompson's successor as chair of Indiana's folklore program, Richard M. Dorson.

Dorson shared Thompson's desire to professionalize folklore, but more than Thompson he pursued this goal with a crusading zeal that, coinciding with the post–World War II boom in the American research university, brought unprecedented results. Born in 1916 (the year after Alan Lomax), Dorson from the very beginning of his career was an academic innovator, eager to redraw traditional departmental boundaries to make room for new disciplines. Dorson graduated from Harvard in 1937 with a major in American history and literature (Alan Lomax also attended Harvard that year). He then became part of the first cohort of doctoral candidates in the first Ph.D. program in American studies, Harvard's History of American Civilization.[76] After completing his dissertation in 1943, Dorson taught at Michigan State University before arriving to chair Indiana's folklore program in 1957. From the beginning Dorson recognized that his new position could be a powerful beachhead from which to advance his vision of academic folklore. He immediately set about to professionalize the discipline.

In part, Dorson led by example. A prolific scholar, he published two dozen books and more than two hundred articles in his career. In these writings, Dorson tried to present a model of disciplined yet far-reaching scholarship. He worried that folklore was a fractured, directionless discipline—"a helter-skelter domain" in need of rationalization. "Instead of the one standard vocabulary, the common frame of reference, and the accepted critical or empirical approach within which controversy arises [the folklorist] witnesses a kaleidoscope of activities and hears a multiplicity of accents," he lamented.[77] Above all, Dorson wanted to offer his fellow folklorists a methodology to guide their work, an agreed-on approach around which they could structure their research and writings.

"A Theory for American Folklore," which resulted from this ambitious goal, reveals both the daring and the limitations of Dorson's vision. In crafting the theory, Dorson set out to formulate a conception of folklore grand enough to stake a claim for the discipline at the core of American scholarship. Stith Thompson's work, therefore, while attractive to Dorson for its scientism, was too narrow in its intellectual reach to suit his purposes. Instead, Dorson found his role models among his former teachers at Harvard. Following the example of professors Perry Miller and F. O. Matthiessen (as well as a contemporary generation of consensus historians), Dorson concluded that the most noble pursuit for an American intellectual was to work toward defining "the American character." His theory, which he presented in 1957 at a joint conference of the American Folklore Society, the American Studies Association, and the American Anthropological Society, positioned folklore as central to achieving this sweeping goal. Dorson outlined the major historical forces that had shaped the national character (e.g., colonization, westward expansion, immigration) and showed how folklorists could enhance the understanding of each of them. "American civilization," he wrote, "is the product of special historical conditions which in turn breed special folklore problems." Folklore could offer unique perspectives on the questions that had preoccupied the great scholars of the twentieth century. Dorson urged his colleagues to embrace the possibility of answering such sweeping questions, to break out of their insular specialties and pursue a "whole civilization approach." If they did so, Dorson envisioned, greatness for the folklore profession would be at hand: "Ultimately American folklore will take its place alongside American literature, American politics, the history of American ideas, and other studies that illuminate the American mind."[78]

Dorson stayed committed to his theory for the remaining two dozen years of his career, but despite his grandiose hopes it won few adherents. In 1969 Dorson conceded ruefully that "the 'Theory' created about as much impact as a cherry blossom dropped from the summit of Mount Fuji onto a snowbank at the foot." In no small part, this tepid response stemmed from contradictions in the theory itself. As folklorist Dan Ben-Amos suggests, the theory assumes a degree of uniformity and coherence in the American experience that is belied by the very folk materials it champions. The myriad diversity of vernacular culture denies the validity of an overarching "American mind."[79]

Dorson was not entirely blind to this tension in his scheme. In response to criticism, for instance, he explicitly rejected the notion of a "monolithic, homogenized peasant class." The American folk, he noted, "cover a whole spectrum of world views." And even "a seemingly tight-knit ethnic, regional, or occupational group . . . is composed not of interchangeable units but of distinct individuals who share tradition yet think and act in unpredictable ways." Likewise, Dorson tried to distance himself from the elements of American exceptionalism implicit in his theory. He bemoaned the corrupting effects of "romantic nationalism" on American folklore and warned that folklore could be dangerous as a propaganda tool: "Folklore has served national interests of various sorts: the anxious pride of the small country seeking its cultural identity; the hubris of the racist state, glorying in the solidarity of the Herrenvolk; the aspirations of an emergent nation, hoping to crystallize its myths; the ideology of the socialist state, extolling the creative powers of the anonymous masses. . . . Today the well-equipped political state possesses its accredited historical records, its approved literary masterpieces, and its classified folklore archives." These disclaimers, though, instead of refining the theory, gutted it of its raison d'être. Dorson's notions of the "American character" and "American mind" depended on sweeping generalities and insistent nationalism. Without these terms his theory was an empty shell, and yet he could not reconcile them with the multiplicity of American folklore. In the fifties and sixties, therefore, folklorists continued the postwar trend toward the largely nonhistorical models that social science offered.[80] Dorson's theory for American folklore did not offer a coherent enough vision to deter them.

If Dorson's theories of how to conduct folklore study attracted few converts, his ideas about how *not* to study folklore had greater influence. As part of his drive to secure an academic niche for American folklore, in the fifties and sixties Dorson became a one-man crusader against what he saw as the shoddy and compromised work of folk popularizers. He particularly criticized the New Deal folklorists and their allies for trying to bring folk culture to mass audiences.[81] "Folklore started to become big business in the United States," he charged, "[in] the 1940s, when Botkin began issuing his treasuries, Alan Lomax took to the air and Burl Ives hit the night clubs. The cavernous maw of the mass media gobbled up endless chunks of folksiness, and a new rationale appeared for the folklorist: his mission is to polish up, overhaul, and distribute folklore to the American people." Dorson disparagingly referred to the popular-izers' work as "fakelore," a spurious, gussied-up imitation of the genuine article passed off as the real thing. He had no patience with such attempts to draw audiences, dismissing the popularizers as "the banjo-pickers, the newspaper sages, and the toddler titillators."[82]

Among the popularizers, Botkin in particular was the object of Dor-son's scorn. Dorson coined the term "fakelore" in 1950 especially for Botkin's work and over the next two decades attacked him relentlessly. What particularly galled Dorson about Botkin was his disregard for the professional standards that Dorson cherished. Dorson championed the importance of doing thorough fieldwork with untainted folk informants and the absolute necessity of transcribing informants' words literally. Botkin, though, did not share Dorson's obsession with pure primary-source material. In his anthologies, Botkin quite openly included songs, poems, and stories that came from published, not oral, sources. News-papers, books, and magazines were fair game to him along with field recordings. His *Treasury of American Folklore* featured stories that rural sharecroppers had told to Federal Writers' Project field-workers; but they also showcased tales written by folk popularizers like Mark Twain and Carl Sandburg.[83]

These easygoing methods incensed Dorson. He described Botkin's *Treasury of Southern Folklore* as a "rehash of rehashes." Botkin's research, Dorson charged in the *Journal of American Folklore*, involved "stripping all kinds of volumes of their frothy stories—often ones recently published and of a popular nature . . . and reshuffling them in his files under snappy headings." Dorson urged his colleagues to regard the treasuries as "suc-cessful publishing ventures but intellectually shoddy conglomerations," and he stressed that they have "nothing to do with folklore." "Some folklorists contend," he concluded, "that Mr. Botkin has considerably aided their cause, in getting folklore widely known throughout the coun-try. I say that he has greatly injured it, and lessened the prestige of the study in the eyes of scholars in other disciplines."[84]

As the venomous nature of Dorson's review suggests, the debate about Botkin's standards of scholarship was at the same time a fight to define the proper place of the folklorist in society. To Dorson, Botkin's efforts to fill his treasuries with material appealing to a wide public amounted to sabotage of Dorson's efforts to legitimize folklore within academia. "The hope for scholarly attitudes toward folklore," Dorson insisted, "and for general recognition of folklore as a field of scholar-

B. A. Botkin, ca. 1960s.
(Photograph by Fred Salaff; courtesy Dorothy Rosenthal)

Richard Dorson, ca. 1960s.
(Courtesy Indiana University Archives)

ship, rests with the universities." Botkin infuriated Dorson because he so neatly sidestepped the thrust of this injunction. He rejected stodgy scholarly attitudes to folklore materials, ignored academic standards, and dropped out of the world of the university (leaving the University of Oklahoma to head the Federal Writers' Project).[85] In effect Botkin made himself immune to Dorson's attacks by denying Dorson's criteria for judgment.

Indeed, Botkin never felt the need to respond publicly to Dorson's assaults, probably because he willingly conceded Dorson's charges against him; Botkin simply attached different value judgments to the practices Dorson abhorred. Dorson, for instance, depicted himself as a disengaged scientist, asserting at one point that he "always opposed ideology from the right as well as from the left," while pursuing "the search for truth and standards of excellence." Botkin, in contrast, embraced the ideological and subjective aspects of folklore practice. "There is an art as well as a science of folklore," he wrote: "The art consists in selecting and presenting aesthetically as well as socially valid expressions by folksayers." And having coined the term "applied folklorist," Botkin applauded its alloyed nature: "Whereas a pure folklorist," he explained, "might tend to think of folklore as an independent discipline, the applied folklorist prefers to think of it as ancillary to the study of culture, of history or literature—of people."[86] Botkin had no interest, therefore, in creating a hermetic, rationalized folklore discipline. He worked instead to highlight the irrational, human elements that drew people to folklore. He felt it more appropriate to weave folklore into a patchwork coat of many colors than to cloak it in the dignity of academic regalia.

Dorson may not have managed to rattle Botkin's commitment to his work, but he had extraordinary success in reshaping the rest of the folklore field. Indiana University's Folklore Institute was transformed under his leadership. When he arrived in 1957, the graduate program had only six students, and its faculty members were scattered across the campus. With the aid of Indiana's president, Herman B. Wells, Dorson worked tirelessly to expand the program. In 1963 he established folklore as an independent department at the university, and by the end of his career in 1981 the department enrolled more than 150 graduate students, employed fourteen full-time faculty members and seven associate fellows, and controlled a separate folklore collection at the library.[87]

In keeping with his emphasis on standards, Dorson worked to maintain as much personal control as possible over the university's program. He shaped the program's degree requirements, designed its curriculum, taught several of its key courses, and structured its comprehensive examinations. As a former student remembered, "He made himself the center of everything that happened. He had energy and style. . . . He convinced people that he had to be on every committee . . .—every decision, he was somewhere near it." Dorson maintained this degree of involvement in the program because his graduate students were central to his plans for folklore. As another student recalled, he wanted Indiana's graduate students to "seed the other programs, other universities; to go out from Indiana and be professional folklorists, publishing and teaching, training others to become professionals, *not* amateur folklorists." By the end of Dorson's career, according to some estimates, Indiana produced 50 percent of the nation's graduate students who went on to teach folklore.[88]

As Dorson had hoped, these "seeds" eventually bore fruit in the form of a new professional attitude among folklorists. Increasingly, folklorists showed respect for the academic standards that Dorson prized. Symptomatic of this emerging outlook, Benjamin Botkin's work fell into disfavor in the fifties and sixties. Although his 1944 *Treasury of American Folklore* had received glowing reviews from his peers, folklorists judged his later treasuries by the criteria Dorson had established and, like Dorson, found them wanting. Writing in 1986, more than a decade after Botkin's death, folklorist Bruce Jackson found that charges of shoddy research practices and "fakelore" continued to tarnish Botkin's reputation among folklorists.[89]

In perhaps the strongest sign of the ascendancy of academic folklorists, their standards began to penetrate even the popularizers' enclaves. As early as the late forties, there had been signs of academia's emerging influence over the remnants of the folk establishment. When Botkin resigned as head of the Archive of American Folk-Song at the end of World War II, he was replaced by an academically oriented folklorist, Duncan Emrich. Emrich's conception of the archive differed from Lomax's and Botkin's. He did not share their vision of the archive as a clearinghouse for gathering songs from the American people and funneling them back into popular culture. Instead, Emrich saw the repository as a resource for folklore scholars. In his eleven years at the archive, he ended its involvement in field collecting, reorganized the collections to make them more accessible to researchers, and worked to establish closer relations with universities and with the American Folklore Society.[90]

In the late fifties and early sixties, Charles Seeger, too, became increasingly oriented toward academia. Having given up on establishing a governmental niche for folklore, he turned his attention to scholarly pursuits, particularly those involving the emerging discipline of ethnomusicology. In collaboration with his oldest son, Charles Jr., he invented an electronic transcription machine called the melograph. Designed for ethnomusicological researchers, it was intended to enable objective tran-scriptions and to facilitate the notation of non-Western music. Seeger's work on the melograph brought him into contact with Mantle Hood, who had founded the ethnomusicology program at the University of California, Los Angeles, in 1954. In 1961 Hood expanded this program into the Institute of Ethnomusicology and appointed Seeger, then in his mid-seventies, to a post as a research musicologist.[91]

Over the next decade, Seeger used this position as the base for the final, most scholarly phase of his career. He became a driving force in the international effort to shape and define the discipline of ethnomusicol-ogy. He published prolifically, took part in high-powered seminars with UCLA faculty and graduate students, and was strongly involved in the professional associations that emerged to serve the growing field. He wrote the constitution for the Society for Ethnomusicology, adopted in 1956, and in 1960 was elected president of the organization. In 1967 he served as the first ethnomusicology delegate to the American Council of Learned Societies.[92]

Alan Lomax's work grew academic in the 1960s as well. He had re-turned from Britain in 1958 with a new determination to systematize his ideas about folk music. In 1960, having received a grant from the Ameri-can Council of Learned Societies, he spent a year traveling to universities around the country, consulting with anthropologists, musicologists, eth-nologists, and linguists. Based on these explorations Lomax, in collab-oration with anthropologist Victor Grauer, announced in 1961 a new approach to classifying world song styles. They dubbed the approach "cantometrics." For three decades Lomax directed the cantometrics project in Columbia University's Anthropology Department.[93]

In the broadest sense cantometrics represented an extension of the work Lomax had been doing since the 1930s. Like his earlier efforts, can-tometrics presupposed that people's songs offer windows into their lives, that song traditions remain vibrant and vital in contemporary society, and that the modern industrialized world has much to learn from these folk forms. Despite these continuities, though, cantometrics marked a transformation in Lomax's approach to these issues. Instead of dealing with folk music as a collector and popularizer, with cantometrics Lomax assumed the mantle of the scientist.

The cantometrics system was based on thirty-seven measuring scales with which Lomax could notate all aspects of song performance—from volume to nasality to glottal shake—along continua marked with from three to thirteen points. Lomax and his associates used these scales to diagram thousands of songs from hundreds of different societies around the world. They used these diagrams, in turn, to make cross-cultural comparisons and sweeping conclusions about the relationships between musical and social structures. Nasal singing, Lomax asserted, occurs more frequently in societies that repress the sexual behavior of girls and women, while "open-style singing" is usually found in sexually permissive cultures. Moreover, "songs from societies where infant stress is present [are] characterized by wider [vocal] range than songs from societies where infant stress is absent."[94]

Such conclusions may seem like risky leaps, but to Lomax they represented the fruits of hard science and, interestingly, a counterpoint to his functionalist past. In 1962 he wrote, "We have moved on beyond the crude analogies which functionalism has so far provided ethnomusicology—work songs, funeral laments, ballads, game songs, religious songs, love songs, and the like. On the whole, style, as a category, is superordinate over function." Lomax no longer felt comfortable classifying folk songs in terms of the various roles they played in singers' lives. Like Seeger, he had less interest now in directly applying songs to contemporary societal needs, preferring to focus on describing folk song in a quantified, scientifically reputable way.[95]

In the last decades of their careers, then, both Seeger's and Lomax's conception of themselves as folklorists moved closer to Dorson's view of the folklorist as scholar. It would be misleading, of course, to imply that Dorson converted the two erstwhile New Dealers into devoted followers. Both Seeger and Lomax, with some justification, saw themselves as pioneering their own innovative directions within the folklore profession, and neither expressed any particular respect for Dorson. Both men, in fact, were uneasy with insular notions of scholarship such as his. Seeger, for instance, liked to see himself as having a more generative role than a narrow-minded academic. "Strictly speaking," he wrote, "I do not regard myself as a scholar, I am a systematist. The two are very different. For one thing, the scholar is primarily interested in knowing everything he can of other people's work; the systematist, in appropriating everything he can lay his hands on in the continual task of fortifying his World View. The scholar may be a creator; the systematist must be."[96]

Lomax, too, would have chafed at being pigeonholed as an academic. Even as he focused on cantometrics, he continued to be actively involved in such nonacademic pursuits as producing television shows, making films, and issuing recordings. For his cantometrics work, too, Lomax was always eager to ascribe a purpose broader than the usual limits of scholarship. In 1977 he asserted that cantometrics could help foster what he called "cultural equity"—equal access to the world's airways for all cultures: "This parsimonious classification of musical styles into [geographic] areas makes planning for the cultural administrator—the defender of the principle of cultural equity—far easier." In the 1980s and 1990s, Lomax worked to convert his cantometrics data into a publicly accessible form. In 1994 he presented the first public demonstration of his "Global Jukebox"—a computerized reference tool that allows users to compare more than four thousand songs (and one thousand dances) from four hundred cultures around the world.[97] Both Seeger and Lomax, then, resisted being thought of as traditional academics. Nonetheless, by the early 1960s each of them had concluded that the university offered them the best chance to pursue their objectives, and each had begun tailoring his work to scholarly audiences.

After World War II, therefore, the pioneers of the depression-era folk programs gradually abandoned their efforts to use the federal government to nurture an alternative national culture. Had Richard Dorson's conception of folklore carried the field? Yes and no. The 1930s folk establishment was dismantled and dispersed, and the academic model came to ascendancy within the profession, but the dream of securing a presence for folklore in Washington was not dead.

Over the Fourth of July weekend in 1967, as opposition to the Vietnam War heightened, 430,000 people converged on the Mall in Washington. There was much singing and some speeches, too; but the throngs were equally captivated by basketweaving and blacksmithing. A few months later, when angry protesters marched on the Pentagon, they would be led by celebrities such as Norman Mailer. Here, though, the stage belonged to Norman Miller, a potter from Alabama, and to Homer Miracle, a carver from Kentucky, and Almeda Riddle, an Ozark ballad singer. The scene was the Smithsonian Institution's first Festival of American Folklife. Fifty-eight craftspeople and thirty-two musical and dance groups demonstrated their skills during the four-day extravaganza.[98] Their talents—and especially the scene of hundreds of thousands of people celebrating American culture—won the ear of official Washington and set forces into motion that would bring folk culture further than ever before into the marble halls of official Washington.

The first Festival of American Folklife was part of a broader effort by the secretary of the Smithsonian, S. Dillon Ripley, to enliven the Mall. Ripley was determined to attract larger audiences for Smithsonian activities and to secure broader popular support for the institution as a whole. In the years after he took office in 1964, the Smithsonian began offering evening hours for summer visitors, installed a carousel on the Mall, and sponsored free concerts, puppet shows, and a kite festival. Many of these ideas were spearheaded by James Morris, a cultural entrepreneur whom Ripley had hired in 1966 to inject life into the Smithsonian's public programs. In the mid-1960s, Morris had organized the short-lived American Folk Festival in Asheville, North Carolina. It was he who proposed to Ripley that the Smithsonian stage a similar event on a grander scale on the Mall.[99]

In one sense, to mount a folk festival on the Mall was a daring challenge to the Washington establishment. In the nineteenth century the Mall had been the site of a railroad depot and an odorous grazing ground for the National Zoo, but since the turn of the century it had been gradually reshaped into a landscaped boulevard, lined with museums attesting to the sophistication of American culture. To stage a party on the Mall and invite common folk as the honored guests threatened the decorum and, implicitly, the cultural hierarchy that the Mall celebrated. In some circles, the idea of a folk festival called to mind radical politics, coarse backwoodsmen, and, more recently, counterculture "love-ins." The Newport Folk Festivals of the period, for example, were seen, in historian Robert Cantwell's words, as "massive countercultural pow-wows." Indeed, the person whom Morris hired to plan the program for the first festival (at Alan Lomax's suggestion) was Ralph Rinzler, an impresario and producer who had been deeply involved in planning the Newport events.[100]

In another sense, though, the folk festival offered a comforting vision to the liberal establishment in Washington. On the one hand, the display of traditional artists and artisans on the Mall implicitly rebuked society for its crass consumerism, environmental negligence, and ethnocentrism; but on the other hand, the scene suggested a way to transcend the divisiveness that antiwar, countercultural, and civil rights protests had spawned. Let us look back, the festival seemed to say, and rediscover the deep cultural currents from which we all draw—not so much a fixed body of traditions (the festival certainly demonstrated America's pluralism), but a common appreciation for the local, the authentic, the handcrafted, and the heartfelt. Even as the festival challenged the established order, it nostalgically treated American culture as a source of pride—one that could bridge generation gaps and cross racial divides. Here was a counterculture that promised to knit the social fabric together, not tear it apart. The festival, in effect, was a living-theater demonstration of what a healed American culture might look like.

Organizers may have intended a darker message for the festival. Historian Cantwell finds a tone of foreboding and bitterness in a promotional film that the festival produced in 1968, its second year. The narrator urges viewers to reach back for "the feel of a world where no one hardly ever bought anything . . . a world when there was no litter problem . . . where nothing was ever wasted." Cantwell sees the film as having a "disconsolate and despairing view" of contemporary America. Indeed, Rinzler later described the festival in these early years as making "not just a statement of aesthetics, [but] a statement of politics, of working-class anger, and of rights."[101]

Contemporary observers, though, seem to have found the festival's message uplifting. Marveling at the live crafts demonstrations, the *Washington Post* praised the 1967 festival for demonstrating that "the folk craft tradition has not died. Yesterday it burst into life before the astonished eyes of hundreds of visitors on the mall." The *Washington Evening Star* exclaimed, "Thanks to S. Dillon Ripley, Secretary of the Smithsonian Institution, thousands of people have been having a ball on the Mall, watching dulcimer-makers, quilters, potters, and woodcarvers and listening to music." Certainly official Washington found the message heartening. Shortly after the festival ended, Representative Thomas M. Rees (D-Calif.) stood in the House and sang its praises: "In this day of the frug and jerk Americans need to be shown what their own culture has produced and continues to produce. . . . I hope to see it again next year when we may have an even bigger and better all-American Fourth of July Festival." The festival did indeed become an annual affair. In 1968 it featured Muddy Waters and his band as well as a tribute to the John A. Lomax family, attended by Alan and his siblings. By the mid-1970s, the festival was a treasured part of Washington culture. In 1976 it was extended from its customary four days into a twelve-week Bicentennial extravaganza. An estimated 4.4 million attended. By this point the festival had outgrown the Division of Performing Arts, which had staged it in previous years, so in 1977 the Smithsonian created the Office of Folklife Programs expressly to operate the festival.[102]

From the start, the festival served as a showpiece to which other folk-culture advocates pointed as they worked to advance their causes. In 1968 the festival spotlighted the folklife of Texas. A legislative aide to Texas senator Ralph Yarborough, Jim Hightower (whose wife worked for the festival), brought the senator to the Mall to see the show. Yarborough had a long-standing interest in his state's heritage (fanned by his boyhood purchase of John Lomax's 1910 book of cowboy songs), so he was a ready audience. Inspired by the scene, Yarborough and Hightower contacted Ralph Rinzler to discuss how to build on what the festival had begun and solidify folk culture's niche in Washington. In 1969 Yarborough sponsored legislation to create the American Folklife Foundation, a new agency to be housed within the Smithsonian. The foundation, the bill envisioned, would serve to stimulate research, collect folklife materials, generate programming, and award grants.[103]

Over the next several years, the legislation saw many incarnations, most of them overseen by Archie Green, a professor of folklore (and a former shipwright) who spent most of seven years in Washington lobbying for the bill. Within the folklore profession, some support came from familiar quarters. Alan Lomax gave an impassioned speech at the bill's Senate hearing in 1970, pleading that the Folklife Foundation would "fill an enormous and painful gap in the cultural structure of our country."[104] The driving force, though, behind the push for the foundation was a new generation of folklorists that had come to professional maturity in the 1960s. In mustering support for the bill, Rinzler, Hightower, and Green turned to folklorists such as Henry Glassie, Kenneth S. Goldstein, Richard Bauman, and Alan Jabbour, all of whom had both academic credentials and a demonstrated commitment to reaching beyond the academy. As Alan Lomax told the senators with pride, "Young social scientists are taking a new direction. They are insisting that social scientists should be advocates for the people they study, that their studies should go farther than the publication of learned papers. . . . This new breed of social scientists is looking for ways to do more than write about people. They wish to act, and particularly in behalf of the people and their aspirations."[105] Another generation had taken up the cause of Botkin, Lomax, and Charles Seeger.

Not surprisingly, some of the fiercest opposition, both to the young folklorists' public-minded outlook and to the Folklife Foundation in particular, came from Richard Dorson. At the 1970 hearings, Dorson challenged the public-oriented aspects of the proposed foundation: "I would certainly not agree that the scholar serves humanity by tying in his scholarship and his research with social causes. I think he functions in one realm as a scholar and he functions in another realm as a citizen. When you begin to mix these two, you debase the coin of scholarship." Senator Yarborough subsequently sent Dorson a letter chiding him for his "medieval" conception of the university's role in society. Recalling the letter in 1975, Dorson was unrepentant: "Maybe the medieval university is to be commended," he wrote, "in preference to the activist role we are asked to assume as applied folklorists." Again he expressed his fear that public support of folklore would compromise standards within the field: with a sidelong jab at his nemesis Botkin, he warned that "any kook can join the American Folklore Society and publish a book of fakelore and become a spokesman. A healthy discipline must be wary of federal and state subsidies."[106]

This time, though, the battle did not go Dorson's way. Aided by the patriotic spirit surrounding the Bicentennial, a revised version of the bill was signed into law by President Ford in January 1976. Some elements had changed since Senator Yarborough's initial proposal six years before. The agency no longer had the power to give grants (thereby appeasing the national endowments for the arts and humanities, which had feared competition); it was to be housed at the Library of Congress (since the Smithsonian's Board of Regents had declined it); and its name had been changed to the American Folklife Center.[107] The core of Yarborough's vision, though, remained intact. The act authorized the center to initiate and disseminate folklore scholarship, sponsor and create programming, and create an archive of folklife. In 1978 the Library of Congress's Archive of Folk Song, where Robert Gordon and John and Alan Lomax had led the push for federal support of folk culture nearly half a century before, was integrated into the American Folklife Center.[108]

At the same time that folk-culture advocates were lobbying for the Folklife Center, many of the same players, including Archie Green, were instrumental in creating a niche for folklore within the National Endowment for the Arts. In the early 1970s, as the Folklife Center bill inched toward passage, the NEA began to face the possibility of competing with another grant-giving institution for federal funds. In part to forestall this challenge, the head of the NEA, Nancy Hanks, decided to move into folk culture. In 1974 the NEA launched the Folk Arts Program, a grant-giving program designed to support arts organizations and individual artists who perpetuated folk traditions. The program was initially a small part of the NEA's Special Projects division, but in 1977 the NEA elevated it into a program in its own right, equal in status to the endowment's other artistic discipline programs. Over the next twenty years, the program distributed millions of dollars, mostly in the form of start-up funds to state and local folk-arts initiatives. Much of this support was allotted via state folk-arts agencies, organizations that hardly existed when the Folk Arts Program began. In 1977 only one state had a folk-arts coordinator; in 1993 fifty out of fifty-six states and territories had full-time coordinators.[109] Step by step, the Folk Arts Program had built a nationwide bureaucratic infrastructure for the folk arts.

By the late 1970s, then, the Smithsonian, the Library of Congress, and the NEA each had distinct administrative entities dedicated to folk culture. As each of these programs approaches the end of its first quarter century, one may wonder: Has the folk establishment arrived in Washington after all, half a century after Lomax, Botkin, and Seeger left town in frustration?

Perhaps folk "presence" rather than "establishment" more accurately characterizes the place of folk culture in contemporary Washington. There are moments, certainly, when the government appears eager to deploy the image of the folk. In 1992, following a narrow and divisive victory in the election, the staff of President-elect Clinton began planning for an "American Reunion" on the Mall to mark his inauguration. The reunion would be a chance for the American people to join together in celebrating a new era—a "people's inaugural festival," in contrast to the black-tie, closed-door affairs of old (although, of course, many such formal affairs were being planned as well). To give the event the common touch, the inaugural committee called in the Center for Folklife Programs, hoping to draw on the expertise the center had gained in producing the Smithsonian folk festival.[110] On January 16–17, 1993, between 500,000 and 600,000 visitors swarmed the Mall to sample the talents of African American gospel singers, Hmong embroiderers, and Cajun chefs. The program for the festival included a statement signed by the Clintons and Gores that celebrated the reunion's populist message: "We Americans . . . take pride in our own regional, ethnic, religious, and family identities, for these give us a sense of self. . . . Being American means bridging differences, not stamping them out. . . . Indeed, just as the creativity, genius and generosity of individuals enlarges our sense of humanity, so too can an appreciation of our diversity increase our sense of national accomplishment."[111] Folk cultures, it seems, are American culture, and vice versa.

Public triumphs such as the reunion, however, mask considerable instability in folklife's position within government. In 1995 the House of Representatives voted to eliminate all funding for the Library of Congress's American Folklife Center; friends in the Senate, though, prevented the cuts from taking effect, and in the fall of 1998 Congress authorized permanent funding for the center. The NEA as a whole was a key target of the so-called Republican Revolution. It was, in fact, slated to be eliminated at the end of September 1997. A compromise saved the endowment but could not forestall the loss of almost half of its staff and 40 percent of its budget. In the resulting reorganization, the Folk Arts Program, along with all the other disciplinary-based divisions, ceased to be defined as a separate departmental entity and was folded into a system of broad-based categories (for example, "Creation and Presentation" and "Heritage and Preservation"). Although most of the program's initiatives continue, they do so at a reduced level.[112] The Smithsonian's Center for Folklife Programs and Cultural Studies is somewhat better funded, and it continues to mount the Festival of American Folklife annually, but the center relies considerably on private support to sustain its activities. Indeed, the director of the center, Richard Kurin, characterizes all three of the federal folk entities as woefully short of government funds. He notes that the appropriations for each represent hardly drops in the bucket within the budgets of their parent institutions, and the appropriations for these parent institutions, in turn, are but tiny (yet constantly endangered) fractions of overall federal spending.[113]

At times, then, Washington seems more enamored of the *idea* of folk culture than of the institutions supposedly charged with perpetuating it. Nonetheless, despite facing significant instabilities, dozens of folklorists, archivists, educators, and administrators continue to work within the Library of Congress, the Smithsonian, and the National Endowment for the Arts to preserve and invigorate the nation's folk traditions. These folk bureaucrats may not have the clout to effect the broad-based social changes their depression-era forefathers envisioned, but for the time being at least, the voice of the folk continues to be heard in Washington.

PERFORMING THE FOLK
PETE SEEGER &
BOB DYLAN

In folk music circles, the story is well known and oft told. In the summer
of 1963, Pete Seeger and Bob Dylan stood onstage at the Newport Folk
Festival and sang "We Shall Overcome," joined hand in hand with such
luminaries of the folk revival as Joan Baez, Theodore Bikel, the Freedom
Singers, and Peter, Paul, and Mary. For Seeger the moment was the sweet
fruit of a quarter-century career. Indeed, he could legitimately see the
moment as the consummation of an effort begun by his mentors—his
father Charles, Alan Lomax, Lead Belly, and Woody Guthrie—the apo-
theosis of the Popular Front folk revival that had begun when Lead
Belly arrived in Greenwich Village. The focal point of Seeger's pride and
hopes was Dylan. The twenty-two-year-old sensation seemed to meld a
political conscience with a performance style, persona, and repertoire
firmly rooted in American folk traditions, and he was demonstrating
conclusively that this combination could be commercially powerful.
Thirteen thousand cheering fans at the Newport performance attested
to this power, as did thousands more like them in college dorm rooms
across the country who were bent over acoustic guitars, painstakingly

picking out "Michael Row Your Boat Ashore" or Dylan's "Blowin' in the Wind."[1]

In the summer of 1965, the story goes, the folk-revival kingdom crumbled. At that summer's Newport festival the final concert seemed at first to be unfolding beautifully. Seeger had started the evening by playing a recording of a newborn baby's cry. Jim Rooney, a folk revivalist from Cambridge, Massachusetts, recalled that Seeger had asked "that everyone sing to the baby and tell it what sort of world it would be growing up into"—a world with troubles, certainly, but ones that, in a rousing chorus, "PEOPLE would OVERCOME." Kentucky folk singer and banjo player Cousin Emmy had just performed a spirited "Turkey in the Straw," and there was anticipation as Bob Dylan came up next. But something went wrong. Dylan walked onstage in a bright orange shirt and black leather jacket, plugged in his electric guitar, and, backed by the five-piece Paul Butterfield Blues Band, let loose a deafening electric version of his song "Maggie's Farm."[2] Backstage, Pete Seeger was in a rage and, according to one account, ran to get an ax, threatening to chop the power cables. Theodore Bikel is supposed to have said, "You can't do that! Pete, you can't stop the future." Dylan finished his three-song set to a smattering of cheers and loud boos as (depending on who tells the story) people expressed their frustration at the shortness of the set, the inadequacy of the sound system, or the hellishness of the cacophony that had just assaulted them.[3] Dylan returned to play two acoustic songs, and Seeger managed to herd the festival's performers onstage for another rousing group-sing finale, but the scene of relaxed harmony rang false this time. The folk revival's old guard remained upset by Dylan's performance. Theodore Bikel encapsulated the reaction of Seeger, Lomax, and their generation: "You don't whistle in church—you don't play rock and roll at a folk festival." Peter Yarrow reflected, "It . . . was as if all of a sudden you saw Martin Luther King, Jr., doing a cigarette ad."[4] Most of Dylan's young audiences, though, did not take this purist stance, and over the next few years they eagerly followed Dylan into mainstream pop as he made a series of successful electric albums. By the late sixties, concludes the standard narrative, the rock revolution had triumphed, and the folk movement was over, having received a death blow from one of its own.

This story has elements of truth to it. Dylan's Newport appearance in 1965 did crystallize a shift in his style, and Seeger's backstage rage was real; but accounts that schematically describe a pre- and post-1965 Dylan to chart the downfall of the glorious revival are fundamentally off the mark. These narratives reflect a narrow definition of the folk revival and a misunderstanding of both Seeger's and Dylan's role within it. Dylan's

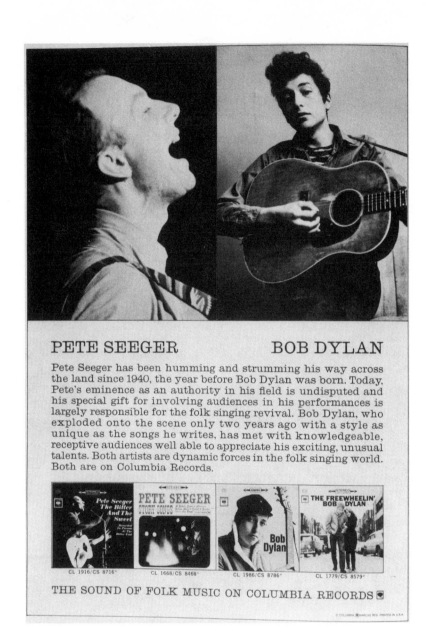

PETE SEEGER   BOB DYLAN

Pete Seeger has been humming and strumming his way across
the land since 1940, the year before Bob Dylan was born. Today,
Pete's eminence as an authority in his field is undisputed and
his special gift for involving audiences in his performances is
largely responsible for the folk singing revival. Bob Dylan, who
exploded onto the scene only two years ago with a style as
unique as the songs he writes, has met with knowledgeable,
receptive audiences well able to appreciate his exciting, unusual
talents. Both artists are dynamic forces in the folk singing world.
Both are on Columbia Records.

CL 1916/CS 8716°   CL 1668/CS 8468°   CL 1986/CS 8786°   CL 1779/CS 8579°

THE SOUND OF FOLK MUSIC ON COLUMBIA RECORDS ◉

Pete Seeger and Bob Dylan, advertisement appearing in Newport Festival program, 1963

sound did change in the mid-1960s, and Seeger did not like it, but Dylan's
post-1965 output (more than thirty albums) represents an extension, not
a rejection, of Seeger's work. Essentially, Seeger and Dylan represent
different manifestations of the same role within American popular music. Both have functioned as what one might call "folk stylists"—figures
who grew up outside the regional or ethnic traditions that produced

Pete Seeger at Newport Folk Festival workshop, 1964. (Photograph by Diana Davies; courtesy Center for Folklife Programs and Cultural Studies, Smithsonian Institution)

roots music but who became public performers of and emissaries for that music. Whereas "folk promoters" and "folk bureaucrats" had popularized other people's culture as "folk," Seeger and Dylan took on the voice of the folk themselves.[5] In doing so, they reached wider audiences than any previous revivalists and shaped more directly than ever before how Americans viewed the nation's musical traditions.

Bob Dylan goes electric, Newport Folk Festival, 1965. (Photograph by Diana Davies; courtesy Center for Folklife Programs and Cultural Studies, Smithsonian Institution)

Pete Seeger was the archetypal folk stylist, moving from a privileged background to become the personification of folk music to millions of Americans, an identification he reinforced in thousands of concerts, well over a hundred albums, and scores of books and articles. Born in 1919, Seeger grew up with a father who was a musicologist and an experimental classical composer (Charles Seeger did not discover folk music until Pete was about sixteen) and a mother who was a professional violinist (Charles's first wife, Constance). Mostly, though, Seeger's musical education took place away from home. He began attending upper-crust boarding schools at age four. When he was eight, his parents gave him a violin and a ukulele. "One was for 'good' music," writes Seeger's biographer, David Dunaway, and "the other was for fooling around." The violin gathered dust, but Seeger played the ukulele constantly. When he entered the Avon Old Farms high school in Connecticut, Seeger discovered a new instrument. A faculty member introduced him to the tenor banjo—a four-stringed instrument often used in Dixieland jazz—and Seeger was hooked. Soon he was playing in Avon's five-piece Hot Jazz Club, picking out jazz standards like "Night and Day" and "I Got Rhythm."[6]

In the summer of 1936, Seeger's interests shifted again, this time permanently. Having graduated from Avon, he was on summer break, preparing to complete his educational trajectory by entering Harvard in the fall (where he would join an ambitious young Bostonite, John Kennedy, in the class of 1940). Seeger spent most of his summer evenings in the new home of his father and Charles's second wife, Ruth Crawford Seeger. Charles Seeger had recently moved to the Washington area to begin his work in the Resettlement Administration. In 1936 John and Alan Lomax asked him to transcribe field recordings for their *Our Singing Country* songbook. Seeger recommended his wife, a talented composer. That summer she spent her evenings meticulously notating the recordings, sometimes playing a song a hundred times to get it right. Pete listened enthralled. Not realizing that the old-time banjo players were using five-stringed instruments, he tried to play along on his tenor banjo, but to his frustration he could not keep up. Finally his father noticed the problem. Charles Seeger recalled, "Pete had the four-string in his lap and I asked, 'What are you playing that for?' . . . Peter looked up at me and asked, 'Well, father, what *should* I play?'" Charles suggested a trip to Asheville, North Carolina, where they could attend banjo player Bascom Lamar Lunsford's annual Folk Song and Dance Festival, ask his advice, and see the fifth string in action. In a scene reminiscent of the Lomaxes' father-son expeditions, the Seegers loaded up their big blue Chevy and headed South to meet "the folk."[7]

For Pete, the trip brought a moment of awakening almost as dramatic as young Alan Lomax's had been in the New Mexico pueblo. He recalled, "I discovered there was some good music in my country which I never heard on the radio. . . . I liked the strident vocal tone of the singers, the vigorous dancing. The words of the songs had all the meat of life in them. Their humor had a bite, it was not trivial. Their tragedy was real, not sentimental. In comparison, most of the pop music of the thirties seemed to me weak and soft, with its endless variations on 'Baby, baby I need you.'" Lunsford lent the Seegers a five-string instrument for Pete to practice on, and the career of the next great folk revivalist was launched.[8]

In 1938, Seeger dropped out of Harvard and moved to New York City. Initially he had dreams of becoming a journalist, but he made better progress with his music. Through his father's connections to Alan Lomax (only four years Pete's senior), Seeger met Aunt Molly Jackson and Lead Belly and eagerly began learning their songs. In mid-1939, Seeger performed for three months with a traveling music-and-puppet troupe, putting on shows across New York State from a portable stage. When he got back to the city that summer, he had a job as a porter at the 1939 World's Fair when Alan Lomax invited him to come to Washington and work at the Archive of American Folk-Song. Seeger spent the next several months paying his dues to the folk tradition as the Lomaxes had constructed it. The bulk of the archive's holdings had been contributed by the Lomaxes, and as Seeger spent his days cataloging and transcribing the collection, he in effect retraced their steps on their pioneering field trips, apprenticing himself under their canon. "It was an ear-opening education for me," he recalled.[9]

From the beginning, Seeger worked to re-create these new sounds on his beloved banjo. In the period in which he worked at the archive, recalled Alan Lomax's sister Bess, Seeger played "almost continuously. . . . He played all night, and he played all day, and after a while you wanted to ship him off somewhere." In the early 1940s, he began to channel this energy into public performances. Seeger certainly was by no means the first outsider to build a career as a singer of American roots music. Minstrel singers, after all, had been playing stylized versions of African American songs since the 1820s, creating the most popular mass entertainment form of the nineteenth century. In the early 1930s, singing cowboys emerged, making recording and film stars out of "cowboys" from Mount Vernon, New York; Fresno, California; and Cincinnati.[10]

In its broadest outlines, Seeger belonged to this tradition, but he brought to his work a sense of mission that distinguished him from these predecessors. Seeger's performances and recordings were always driven by a didactic desire to convince Americans to embrace their folk music heritage. In pursuing this goal, Seeger followed more directly in the footsteps of Carl Sandburg and Alan Lomax. Sandburg often included folk songs on his lecture tours and also made a few recordings. Lomax, too, tried his hand at the folk stylist role. He sang and played guitar on his radio shows and at the White House when the king and queen of England visited. His knowledge of the folk repertoire was formidable. In the early forties he would spar with Woody Guthrie in informal song contests at Lomax's home. Each man would try to keep coming up with songs on a given topic—cows, floods, no-good women—until the other was stumped. Lomax took great pride in consistently winning these bouts.[11] But performing always remained a sidelight for both Sandburg and Lomax. Closer parallels to Seeger might be John Jacob Niles, Earl Robinson, Richard Dyer Bennett, or Burl Ives, all of whom built careers on performing folk songs. Ultimately, though, none could match Seeger's sustained devotion to folk materials or his popular reach. It was Seeger who gave the role of folk stylist its power. For more than half a century, Seeger strove to awaken interest in American roots music by pitching folk songs in his own voice.[12] This strategy was so successful that his voice defined the sound of folk music for generations of Americans, and indeed, his whole way of life became the prototype for thousands of other would-be "folk singers."

Given the pivotal role Alan Lomax played in introducing Seeger to folk music, it is not surprising that much of Seeger's work as a folk stylist was an extension of Lomax's efforts as a collector and promoter. Like Lomax, Seeger had as one of his primary goals to help establish a canon of American folk singers and folk tunes. At the top of his list were two performers strongly associated with Lomax—Woody Guthrie and Lead Belly.[13]

Early in his career, Seeger performed and socialized with both men. He learned twelve-string guitar from Lead Belly and spent many an evening at impromptu sing-alongs in Lead Belly's Lower East Side apartment. He was awed by Lead Belly's immense repertoire and by the energy he imparted in performance. Seeger was even more intimately associated with Guthrie. When Seeger was twenty-one, Guthrie invited him along to drive west to Oklahoma. Seeger often cited the trip as a turning point in his career. Guthrie introduced him to the expanse of America, the generosity and vigor of its people, and the power of song (at every stop they sang and played for food).[14] Seeger eagerly absorbed these lessons and tried to assimilate Guthrie's musical style—the simplicity of his tunes, the directness of his words, and the poignancy of the stories with which he introduced his material. Seeger performed frequently with Guthrie throughout the forties, and early in the decade both were members of the Almanac Singers, an agitprop group that lived communally in New York City.

Although Lead Belly's and Guthrie's influence on Seeger was immense, the period in which Seeger could share the stage with his mentors was relatively brief. Lead Belly died in 1949, and Guthrie was increasingly incapacitated by Huntington's chorea by the early fifties. For the bulk of his career, all Seeger could do was promote their memories. He did so at every turn. He made their songs the centerpieces of his repertoire, performing numbers like "This Land Is Your Land," "So Long, It's Been Good to Know You," "Midnight Special," and "Rock Island Line" thousands of times, recording them on countless albums, and including them in the many songbooks he issued. In the early 1950s, Seeger's pop-folk group the Weavers brought highly orchestrated versions of "Goodnight Irene," "So Long," and "Kisses Sweeter Than Wine" to the top of the pop charts, selling millions of copies.[15] Many of Seeger's efforts to canonize Guthrie and Lead Belly only indirectly involved their music. He wrote to Oklahoma's Senator Fred Harris (probably in the 1960s), urging him to erect a historical marker identifying Guthrie's boyhood home in Okemah. In the 1980s, when he built two old-fashioned sloops as part of his campaign to clean up the Hudson River, he christened one *Woody Guthrie*.[16] Perhaps most influential, in all his concerts, in all his books and articles and interviews, Seeger supplied a steady stream of anecdotes about Lead Belly and Guthrie. Everywhere he went he spread the legend of the straight-talking, hard-living, musical giants who walked in the common man's shoes.

Like Alan Lomax, as much as Seeger worked to introduce Americans to a pantheon of folk forefathers, he also strove to help them appreciate a discrete body of songs. Over the years, only a small percentage of the songs Seeger performed and recorded were his own compositions. In selecting the remainder of his repertoire, he was winnowing and augmenting the canon of American folk song. In 1965 he compared the process by which some tunes get selected over others to a war and acknowledged his involvement in the combat: "I realize this every time I select one tune over another to sing, whenever any artistic judgment is made, whenever a woman decides to buy one dress rather than another. A skirmish is won or lost."[17]

As in his embrace of Guthrie and Lead Belly, the canon of tunes that Seeger selected was essentially a continuation of the work of the Lomaxes. Like theirs, Seeger's canon was stunning in its eclecticism, encompassing everything from Child ballads to cowboy songs, spirituals, play-party tunes, and work songs. Seeger's debt to the Lomaxes' canon appears strikingly in the seminal series of albums that he recorded for Folkways Records between 1957 and 1962, *American Favorite Ballads*. This five-volume series offers a useful way of understanding the parameters of Seeger's folk music canon. Of the eighty-one songs in the set, more than half (forty-five) appeared in the Lomaxes' four songbooks: *American Ballads and Folk Songs* (1934), *Our Singing Country* (1941), *Folk Song: U.S.A.* (1947), and *The Folk Songs of North America* (1960). Given that one might expect a desire on Seeger's part to carve out a professional niche of his own with his anthology (he issued his own songbook based on the albums), this degree of overlap between Seeger's albums and the Lomaxes' books is striking.[18]

Of the songs that Seeger included that the Lomaxes did not, most fit securely within the confines of the Lomaxes' canon of folk song—a spiritual like "Mary Don't You Weep" (vol. 3); a miners' song like "Clementine" (vol. 3); a British ballad like "The Water Is Wide" (vol. 2); a Woody Guthrie original like "So Long, It's Been Good to Know You" (vol. 1).[19] Two types of partial exceptions, though, point to ways in which Seeger subtly broadened the Lomaxes' canon. One is highlighted by the appearance of "Wimoweh" and "Cielito Lindo" in Seeger's anthology. To include a South African and a Mexican song in a collection of "American favorite ballads" is a suggestive move, one that typified Seeger's canonization efforts throughout his career. He was eager for Americans to recognize the compatibility of all the world's musical genres and the possibility of uniting them into a single tradition. He expressed this ideal in an original song entitled "All Mixed Up":

> You know, this language that we speak
> Is part German, part Latin and part Greek
> With some Celtic and Arabic all in the heap
> Well amended by the man in the street
> Choctaw gave us the word "okay"
> "Vamoose" is a word from Mexico way
> And all of this is a hint, I suspect
> Of what comes next
> I think that this whole world
> Soon, mama, my whole wide world
> Soon, mama, my whole world
> Soon gonna be get mixed up.[20]

Throughout his career, this vision of "one world" permeated Seeger's concerts and recordings. A typical performance pattern, Seeger wrote, included "a few songs from other countries, hinting at the different types of people in this big world—but also good songs which will give us a feeling of friendship to them." On a given night, Seeger might play a sprightly tarantella on recorder or a pastoral tune using his chalil, a bamboo flute found in the Middle East, Africa, and eastern Europe.[21]

Seeger's albums, too, featured a crazy quilt of international styles. Throughout his career he championed foreign-language songs. In 1943 he recorded *Songs of the Lincoln Brigade* in honor of the American troop that had fought in the Spanish Civil War. The album included "El Quinto Regimento" and "Si Me Quieres Escribir." "El Quinto" later appeared in his 1964 songbook, *The Bells of Rhymney*, along with the German peasant song "Die Gedanken Sind Frei," the Japanese "Furusato," the French Canadian "Un Canadien Errant," the Yiddish "Tumbalalaika," and "El Dia de Tu Santo," from the pueblo in Taos, New Mexico. One of the Weavers' biggest hits was the Israeli folk song "Tzena,

Tzena" (released on the flip side of "Goodnight, Irene"), which they recorded in both Hebrew and English. In 1955 Seeger recorded *Bantu Choral Folk Songs* and *Folksongs of Four Continents*. His 1965 album *Strangers and Cousins* included not just "All Mixed Up" but "Manurah Manyah," "Ragaputi," "Malaika," and "Shtill Di Nacht."[22]

Seeger was certainly not the only folk revivalist intrigued by foreign-language songs. Charles Seeger's work at the Pan-American Union and the International Music Council had focused on international musical exchange. Alan Lomax spent much of the 1950s making field recordings abroad for Columbia Records' World Library of Primitive and Folk Music; and, of course, his cantometrics project had a decidedly international bent. Beginning in 1949, Moses Asch launched the Ethnic Folkways Library, an effort (overseen by anthropologist Harold Courlander) to issue recordings of indigenous music from around the globe. By 1963, Asch claimed to have documented the cultures of "600 peoples of the world."[23] Seeger took the notion of mixing and matching traditions to an extreme, but his internationalism was an extension of other folk revivalists' efforts in the decades after World War II.

In addition to reflecting the global scope of Seeger's canon, his *American Favorite Ballads* collection suggests that he was more receptive than the Lomaxes to American pop music. Of the tunes in the anthology that do not appear in the Lomaxes' songbooks, four would seem unlikely to be accepted as "folk" by the Lomaxes. They were composed relatively recently by professional songwriters with an eye toward commercial markets: "St. Louis Blues" (vol. 3) was written in 1914 by composer and publisher W. C. Handy, was a hit as Tin Pan Alley sheet music, and was recorded in a classic rendition by vaudeville blueswoman Bessie Smith in 1925; "T. B. Blues" (vol. 5) was written and recorded in 1931 by hillbilly star Jimmie Rodgers; "Summertime" (vol. 5) came from George and Ira Gershwin's 1935 Broadway musical *Porgy and Bess*; and "You Are My Sunshine" (vol. 4) was written in 1940 by popular country and western singer (and former history professor and future two-term governor of Louisiana) Jimmie Davis.[24]

The Lomaxes' books had included some songs that could, under rigid definitions, be considered pop instead of folk songs. Both *Folk Song: U.S.A.* and *American Ballads and Folk Songs*, for example, include sections on minstrel songs. The Lomaxes, though, did not unequivocally accept minstrelsy as a genre. They only considered as "folk song" those minstrel tunes that had broken free from their popular song-industry roots—songs that had been "taken over by the people, polished and changed by oral transmission to become folk songs."[25] By these standards, they felt, only two of Stephen Foster's tunes measured up.[26] The four pop songs that Seeger included had been on the lips of Americans for some years, but apparently they retained too much of their association with individual professional artists and Tin Pan Alley for the Lomaxes to include them in their canon.

The distinctions here are fine ones. Certainly Seeger's canon remains fundamentally in accord with the Lomaxes'. But the minor discrepancy over the four pop songs points up a broader difference in emphasis that more clearly distinguishes Seeger from the Lomaxes. For all Seeger's efforts on behalf of Woody Guthrie and Lead Belly, and for all his attention to building his repertoire, neither folk heroes nor folk songs were truly at the core of his cultural project. Unlike most folk advocates, he was not fundamentally concerned with preserving or reclaiming outmoded cultural products. At no point in his career did he show sustained interest in doing fieldwork to document obscure tunes before they slipped away; and at no point did he dedicate himself to rediscovering and reviving grizzled, long-forgotten folk singers.[27] Even as Seeger paid homage to old songs and old singers, he had a deeper allegiance to the folk process that had produced them: to the way in which ordinary people create new songs and alter old ones to fit their personalities and their individual and community needs. Seeger was less concerned with what songs people sang (cowboy ballads or Broadway show tunes) than with how they sang them (cautiously or confidently, painstakingly or playfully). Seeger's entire career can be seen as an effort to break down the passivity that often marks Americans' encounters with music. He chafed at the notion of people deferentially following the edicts of musical experts and strove to free amateurs to interpret songs loosely and make them their own.

Not surprisingly, this attitude led Seeger to adopt an extremely flexible definition of "folk music," or, rather, to resist defining it. "I try not to get in the argument over defining folk music," he wrote in the mid-sixties. Instead, he consistently emphasized the need for conceptions of folk song to evolve. "All definitions change with the centuries," he wrote in 1960. "What is called a 'play' nowadays is far different from what was called a 'play' in Shakespeare's time. The definitions of folksong and folksingers are liable to change also. Folks will insist on it." Seeger consistently tried to undermine purists' exclusionary conceptions of traditional music, asking, "Is a Greek-revival farmhouse (circa 1830) in New York State unauthentic [*sic*] because it is not an exact copy of a Greek temple? Of course not. It is authentically itself—and a fine period of U.S. architecture this was." "Face it," he said bluntly, "folk traditions will change as the folks who inhabit this earth change. . . . The person who beats his breast and says, 'I will sing nothing but a folk song' is either fooling himself or trying to fool someone else."[28] To Seeger, folk music was not a collection of old songs but a process by which new ones were assembled. In theory, at least, any genre of music could become "folk."

Seeger's broad conception of folk song directly shaped his recordings. His albums became less about trying to convince people to accept a canon of songs than about offering them raw material out of which they could build their own repertoire. This approach accounts for the inclusion of pop songs in *American Favorite Ballads*. To Seeger, pop music was neither inherently "folk" nor inherently "not-folk": "A mountaineer singing a pop song to some neighbors in his cabin," he asserted, "might have more folk music in it than a concert artist singing to a Carnegie Hall audience an ancient British ballad he learned out of a book."[29]

Pop songs like "Summertime" and "TB Blues," then, appear on *American Favorite Ballads* not because Seeger had decided that they were folk songs but rather because he wanted to demonstrate the process by which they could be *made* into folk songs. The way Seeger sings these tunes illustrates the point. He makes no effort to re-create the styles of the original pop interpreters. On "St. Louis Blues," for instance, he does not try to echo the mournful, moaning tone that Bessie Smith used on her recording. Nor does he mimic the looseness with which her lines fell across the beat. He also chooses not to adopt the slow, melancholy tempo or the jazz-based instrumentation of the 1925 recording.[30] Instead, Seeger plays "St. Louis Blues" self-accompanied on his banjo, gives it a bouncy tempo, firmly accents the words that fall on the beat, and sings them in his full-voiced tenor. Gershwin's "Summertime," too, becomes transformed in Seeger's hands. Played on the banjo over a loping beat, and again sung in Seeger's inimitable vocal tone, the tune sounds more like the next cut on *American Favorite Ballads*—"I've Been Working on the Railroad"—than like the slow hymnlike arrangement to which most listeners are accustomed.

In part, Seeger's mannered renditions of these tunes may stem from technical limitations on his part.[31] But even if Seeger had been able to do a dead-on impersonation of every style he tackled, it is doubtful that he would have done so. To mimic precisely the original rendition of a song would have contradicted the message he wanted to get across in singing "Summertime" and "St. Louis Blues." He expressly did not want to offer definitive interpretations of these tunes that his listeners would imitate. He wanted to demonstrate that it was legitimate to stray from the original recorded version of a song. He was offering personalized and intentionally idiosyncratic performances of pop tunes so as to help listeners recognize that any given song can be played in many different ways and to encourage them to create their own personalized interpretations.

One of Seeger's more adventurous recordings, his *Goofing-Off Suite* from 1954, imparts a similar lesson. The suite consists of Seeger playing excerpts from a stunning array of musical sources. Some of the items are familiar parts of the folk repertoire, such as "Sally Ann" or "Cindy"; others, such as "Woody's Rag" by Woody Guthrie, are more recently composed pieces that fit comfortably into that canon. But the suite also features Seeger playing a banjo version of the chorale from Beethoven's Ninth Symphony and whistling along. And it includes similarly arranged versions of Bach's *Jesu, Joy of Man's Desiring*, Edvard Grieg's *Peer Gynt* suite, and Igor Stravinsky's *Pétrouchka*. Seeger's goal, he wrote in the liner notes, was to spur "those who like to fool around with music, picking up tunes by ear, [to] take hold of some of these fragments and work them into something really worthwhile."[32]

In expanding beyond the traditional folk singer's repertoire, *American Favorite Ballads* and *Goofing-Off Suite* sidestep the question of whether Tin Pan Alley blues, Broadway show tunes, and classical art music are folk music. Instead of holding tunes up to an idealized definition of "folk song," these collections illustrate how such forms can be subjected to the folk process—or, rather, to Seeger's personalized folk process.

The concern for process also shaped Seeger's recordings of the more traditional folk repertoire. Again, Seeger did not want listeners to treat his renditions as the "correct" ones, and he was eager for them to become involved in creating and re-creating them on their own. This goal led to some quirky song arrangements on *American Favorite Ballads*. "Four Nights Drunk" (vol. 3) humorously chronicles the tale of a husband who each night discovers a new sign of his wife's infidelity (an unfamiliar horse in his stable, a strange hat on the hat rack, etc.). Each new verse opens with the husband saying, "The [first, second, etc.] night when I got home, drunk as I could be, I spied a . . ." Seeger sings the poor cuckold through the four nights of misadventures suggested by the song's title, but then he keeps going: "Well, the fifth night, I got home, drunk as I could . . ." There, in midsentence, the song ends. This abrupt cutoff serves as an invitation to Seeger's listeners, a signal that this sort of song can be extended endlessly and that they should pick up and continue what Seeger started.

Seeger's rendition of the Lead Belly classic "Alabama Bound" (vol. 2) also works subtly to elicit listener participation. This tune's catchy chorus goes:

I'm Alabama bound, I'm Alabama bound,
And if the train don't stop and turn around,
I'm Alabama bound.

Near the end of the song, though, Seeger begins truncating the lyrics, leaving his guitar to finish the lines without his vocals. He sings,

I'm Ala ——, I'm Ala ——
And if the —— don't stop and turn ——
I'm Ala ——, I'm Ala ——

Then he finishes the song with one chorus without any lyrics at all. The suddenness with which Seeger breaks off singing suggests that he is trying to drop out while listeners are singing along and give them a chance to hear their own voices. "Hey," he seems to want them to say. "I can sing this song myself. I don't need Seeger anymore." The bid to draw audience participation becomes more explicit on the *American Favorite Ballads* version of "Wimoweh" (vol. 3). Directly addressing his listeners, Seeger says, "Now this is kind of an experiment. I usually sing this song with a whole bunch of people. . . . [It] needs basses, altos, and tenors all joining in. It's not a very difficult part. But here I am all by myself, and frankly I can't sing it very well by myself. So I'm going to give you the parts." "First [of] all," he begins, "the low voices." "They sing like this," he says, demonstrating. "Now if that's too low for some of you, . . . you can take the high part that goes [he demonstrates]." Soon Seeger, alone in the studio, has cued an imaginary three-tiered chorus that is belting out its parts.

The sing-along is the musical technique for which Seeger is most famous, and it is the ultimate testament to his passion for the folk song process. At every concert, Seeger was determined to make everyone into folk singers *instantly*. "I'd really rather put songs on people's lips than in their ears," he said in a 1994 interview. "Many performers can turn on an audience as well as Pete can," wrote Gene Marine in *Rolling Stone*. "What they can't do is turn on *any* audience the way Pete can. . . . In Moscow— standing by himself on the stage of the Tchaikowsky Concert Hall . . . Pete had 10,000 people who didn't speak English singing four-part harmony to 'Michael Row Your Boat Ashore.' I doubt whether Barbra Streisand and Mick Jagger *together* could do that."[33] Seeger achieved these results not simply because he was a skilled judge of what repertoire would appeal to a given audience. Rather, he deployed a variety of deceptively simple techniques—many of which performers had been using for centuries—to encourage people to join in the singing. Seeger was adept, for example, at pitching a song within the range of untrained voices and at choosing tempi that were fast enough to allow people to sing lines easily in one breath but slow enough to keep them from getting tongue-tied. He also developed a way of feeding audience members the words of a song even while singing with them. At the end of a phrase he would quickly deliver the next line as the singers gathered their next breaths.[34] Finally, Seeger had a strong feel for what made a line catchy and accessible enough to entice an amateur to attempt it. Both in the songs he adapted and the ones he wrote, the lyrics tend to stick very close to the beat, with the key words on the all-important downbeat ("It's the hammer of *jus*tice"; "Where have all the *flow*ers gone?"). Often significant words appear on notes that are held for longer duration, creating points in a song that can serve as an anchors for unsteady singers ("Where have *allllll* the flowers gone"; "If I had a *haaaamer*").

"We Shall Overcome" is probably the ultimate Seeger sing-along tune, partly because its collectivist political message makes a large chorus so appropriate but also because its musical and lyrical construction makes it ideal for a group sing. Its tune is simple and divided into easy two-measure segments with room for a breath at the end of them. Its lyrics are uncomplicated, and the five syllables in each line fall directly on the beat. To make audience participation even easier, Seeger made an important change to the lyrics. When he first heard the tune in 1947, it was called "We Will Overcome." Seeger says, "I changed it to 'We shall.' Toshi [his wife] kids me that it was my Harvard grammar, but I think I like a more open sound; 'We Will' has alliteration to it, but 'We shall' opens the mouth wider; the 'i' in 'will' is not an easy vowel to sing well."[35]

This passion for audience involvement manifested itself not only in recordings and performances but in Seeger's vast array of publications. In decades of writing, Seeger produced a host of books, articles, album notes, and columns. Some of this work addressed the broadest philosophical questions confronting the revival, speculating on the political function of singing, the mutual obligations inherent in the relationship between artists and audiences, or the delicate balance between "folk" and "commercial." But a significant subset of his output worked primarily to give people the tools and the inspiration to make music on their own. One of Seeger's earlier works, for example, was a book called *How to Play the Five-String Banjo*. It gives readers only the sketchiest discussion of the instrument's history, its great masters, and its role in southern mountain culture. But it goes into great detail (and offers accompanying illustrations) about how to execute a basic banjo strum, how to read a fingering chart, how to cut one's fingernails to the proper length, and how to make a banjo case. Seeger mimeographed the first edition himself, typing the stencils while traveling with Henry Wallace's presidential campaign in 1948. To make it easier for the manual to circulate among would-be pickers, he did not copyright it.[36]

In the decades that followed, Seeger continued to work on imparting the nuts and bolts of music making. He published a pamphlet called "How to Make a Chalil," a book on how to sight-sing, and short pieces about everything from how to sing a gospel bass part to how to put together a "well-equipped washboard."[37] He also directly encouraged people to exhibit their newfound musical skills before audiences. In a piece from 1956, he urged young performers to organize community songfests or "hootenannies," and he offered some concrete recommendations for doing so. "The best hoot," he wrote, "would have an audience of several hundred, jammed tight into a small hall, and seated semicircularwise, so that they face each other democratically." The performers, he suggested, should range "from amateur to professional, from young to old," and should present everything from "Bach to bop." In another article, he offered advice about how to mount "youth caravans" modeled after the puppet troupe with which he had toured in 1939. Caravans, he suggested, could travel across rural areas, bringing "songs, skits, movies, exhibits, from town to town." He made a list of equipment that would be needed ("a secondhand car, public-address system, and spotlights"), gave tips for securing engagements ("[Dr]ive twenty or thirty miles away during the daytime, line up bookings for the following week, and return to perform at night"), and sketched out a timetable for a June start date ("In March you should be discussing the project. In April and May you should start rehearsing").[38]

In outlining these suggestions, Seeger hoped to create a burst of interest not just in reviving old-time music but in writing new songs in the traditions of the old. The folk tradition could not remain healthy, he believed, unless it maintained strong connections to the contemporary world. In 1954 he inaugurated his "Johnny Appleseed, Jr." column in *Sing Out!* magazine and dedicated it to "the thousands of boys and girls who today are using their guitars and their songs to . . . [create] a new folklore, a basis for a people's culture of tomorrow." "Every folk singer," Seeger asserted, "should consider himself or herself a songwriter on the side." Continuing the legacy of the Almanac Singers, Seeger especially pushed for topical songs—songs about the events and debates of the day. He was a major contributor to *Sing Out!*, which was dedicated to publishing topical songs (and had named itself after a line in Seeger's "If I Had a Hammer"), and he helped found the topical-song magazine *Broadside* in 1962.

"We must have an outpouring of topical song," Seeger wrote. "What does it matter that most will be sung once and forgotten? The youthful Joe Hills, [Rabindranath] Tagores, [Robert] Burnses and Shakespeares and Guthries can only thus get their training."[39]

The reasoning implicit in this exhortation is revealing: one should encourage contemporary political songs in the hope of spawning transcendent artists like Shakespeare and Guthrie. Throughout his career Seeger preached that songs could be politically transformative. Quoting his father, Seeger insisted in 1994, "The important thing is not, 'Is it good music?' [but] 'What is the music good for?'"[40] These political ideals, though, were closely intertwined with—and at times seemed subservient to—his allegiance to the folk song process. Seeger's plea for topical songs had as much to do with a desire to prime the pump of the nation's musical creativity as it did with his opposition to social inequities.

Seeger's involvement in the historic civil rights march from Selma to Montgomery, Alabama, suggests the extent to which his political idealism was driven by his longing for vibrant folk traditions. In 1965, at the invitation of Martin Luther King Jr., Seeger flew from New York to take part in the march. He joined five thousand demonstrators who were trudging along hot asphalt and keeping a nervous eye out for the segregationist state troopers and Selma's nefarious Sheriff Jim Clark. As they marched, the protesters began to sing. Some of the tunes were invented from scratch on the spot. Others were old hymns to which they added new words appropriate to the day's events. Younger marchers improvised civil rights lyrics to rock and roll tunes. For Seeger, the moment was the embodiment of his musical ideals: this was the folk song process in action. "All of us wish we'd had tape recorders," he wrote after his first day on the march. "The young singers and songwriters of Selma were creating one great song after another, right before our eyes. . . . Any folklorist would have found the day a fascinating experience in living folk music." Seeger spent two days in Alabama in a flush of excitement, happily scribbling down words and notations for all the songs he could. A fellow marcher recalled, "It was Pete Seeger's thing come true."[41]

Selma encapsulates Seeger's "thing" at more levels than one. Most directly the singing by the demonstrators exemplifies just the sort of folk song process that he idealized—firmly rooted in tradition yet contemporary, pragmatic, and applied. At the same time, his involvement in Selma throws into relief the curious and dynamic role he played in trying to invigorate this process. Seeger came to Selma as both an outsider and an insider. On the one hand, he hardly differed from Tony Bennett, Harry

Belafonte, Anthony Perkins, and the other celebrities who had been asked to join the march. They were recognizable figures whose involvement in the demonstration would draw TV cameras and, perhaps, the sympathy of other whites to the cause. They were concerned supporters on the sidelines. Seeger accentuated his outsider status by acting as a folklorist, identifying and documenting the products of the culture he encountered. On the other hand, Seeger was remarkably fluent in the southern African American culture he encountered in Alabama. Songs like "Jacob's Ladder" and "Lonesome Valley" had been part of his repertoire for years, and now that they had resurfaced as freedom songs, he sang out full voiced. Seeger had been one of the main carriers of some of the most rousing songs that had found their way into the marchers' repertoire, including "We Shall Overcome," "Which Side Are You On?" and "We Shall Not Be Moved." As a longtime singing activist, moreover, Seeger easily related to the demonstrators' instinct to make music in the face of adversity. Finally, Seeger was personal friends with some of the young leaders of the march, including Bernice Johnson Reagon of the Freedom Singers and Jimmy Collier, a singer and organizer under King.[42]

As an upper-middle-class white Yankee, Seeger certainly could not pretend that he was part of the aggrieved African American community. Yet he identified with it strongly and was adept at expressing himself in its idiom. What makes Seeger such an intriguing figure is his ability to cross the outsider-insider barrier without pretending to dissolve it—to become identified as a legitimate expositor of traditional cultures without disguising his status as an interloper. In sustaining this liminal status, Seeger modeled for young, middle-class, would-be folk singers a way in which they could legitimately enter the seemingly alien terrain of roots music. For all that his recordings, performances, and writings did to revitalize the folk song process, Seeger's most fully realized and influential product was, in the end, his life—a work of performance art that fused his personal and professional identities into a role that he performed day and night for his entire adult life.

On and off stage, Seeger worked endlessly to transform himself into the embodiment of the common man. Early in his career, for instance, his conception of the folk led him to affect overalls and stop bathing. When he stayed with an Alabama family in 1940, his hostess recalled that she "was worried about my bed, he was so dirty." In subsequent years, even after Seeger reconciled himself to soap and water, he kept his working-class uniform. When he met Lead Belly, he found the former convict wearing "a clean shirt and standard collar, well-pressed suit, and shined shoes"; but whether walking around the house or performing in concert, Seeger always wore blue jeans and an open-collared work shirt, usually with sleeves rolled as if he had been engaged in heavy labor.[43] While with the Almanac Singers, Seeger and the other group members worked at the idiomatic speech patterns of the folk, adopting what historian Robert Cantwell calls "a kind of method-actor's version of a southern accent, one made exclusively of linguistic markers like the usual 'you-alls' and 'I reckons.'" Seeger fleshed out the image in 1949 by moving from New York City to rural Beacon, New York. There, on a spot overlooking the Hudson River, he built a log cabin by hand, using notes he had taken on the subject at the New York Public Library.[44]

The stories Seeger told—short set pieces that recurred in his concerts and in his writings—further encouraged his identification with the folk. He fondly recalled his days hoboing with Woody Guthrie, or the time he broke his banjo jumping off a freight train, or how he stayed with a southern coal-mining family and "had cornbread and beans three times a day, with what they called 'bulldog gravy' to force it down" ("I would have felt embarrassed to be their guest, if I hadn't been just as broke myself").[45]

Seeger also, of course, adopted the politics of the common person—or rather, politics *intended* for the common person. The people in Peekskill, New York, in 1949 (who ruthlessly attacked the Communists at Paul Robeson's and Seeger's concert) or in Beacon in 1965 (who tried to ban Seeger from singing at the local high school) simply did not understand. Along with Seeger's proletarian identity went an effort to downplay his star status. "A person shouldn't have more property that he can squeeze between his banjo and the outside wall of his banjo case," Seeger used to say. Even if one makes allowances for Seeger's customized banjo cases, this seems like a problematic ideal, particularly for an entertainer whose income hit six figures by 1960.[46] Seeger tried, though, to assume the common touch, developing an attitude that fellow Weaver Lee Hays teasingly referred to as "arrogant modesty." As he grew more popular in the sixties, Seeger urged fans *not* to buy his albums, preferring that they sing the songs themselves. In 1966 he yelled "Who did this!" and ripped up a poster that announced his name in banner headlines. When he published a volume of his collected writings (*The Incompleat Folksinger*, 1972), he urged Simon and Schuster to limit its advertising efforts on the book's behalf. When a photographer asked him to pose for a shot to accompany a magazine feature, he said uneasily, "I can't—it's against my principle." "You really ought to write about Aunt Molly Jackson," he told his biographer at their first interview session.[47]

Even as Seeger went to such lengths to associate himself with the common folk, he never claimed to be an authentic folk singer. He acknowledged his privileged childhood, for example, and openly discussed his family's intellectual background, his parents' classical-music roots, and his years at prep schools and at Harvard.[48] He acquired some southern speech mannerisms, but he made no real effort to sing with a southern accent, letting his Yankee inflections remain out front. Likewise, despite his aversion to the star system, Seeger did not pretend to be cut off from the marketplace. In 1967 he related that a fan had approached him and said, "I'm so glad you haven't gone commercial." "I had to disillusion her," he wrote: "I've been commercial for a long time. In fact, you probably never would have heard me sing if I hadn't been." In a 1962 letter to the London *Times*, Seeger emphasized that he was not equipped to re-create the downhome sound of old field recordings: "It would not only be futile but completely wrong of a singer such as myself to try and produce exact imitations." Seeger acknowledged, in other words, that he came to the folk tradition as an outsider. If part of his persona involved telling romanticized stories about thumbing with Woody, it also included recounting with a chuckle how, as an overcitified, wannabe hobo, the first train he jumped never left the freight yard.[49]

At times, Seeger's self-consciousness could turn withering. In 1965 he published an article in *Sing Out!* (to which he signed his wife's name) that gave a blistering assessment of his career. "Taken all together," he wrote in a fit of third-person self-flagellation, his albums "form one of the most horrendously uneven bodies of recorded music that any performer could boast of, or perhaps be ashamed of." He continued, "Perhaps he has opened Young America's ears to new sounds and songs, but he has also given them a bad example: 'you, too, can sing in sixteen idioms.'" In *The Incompleat Folksinger*, Seeger enumerated his contradictions one by one:

> This man is advertised as a singer—but he obviously hasn't much
>   voice.
> He is a Yankee but sings southern songs.
> He sings old songs, but somehow his meanings are contemporary.
> He tries to talk simply but obviously has a good education and has
>   read widely.
> He sings about poor people, though I doubt he is poor himself.
> Altogether, he is a very professional amateur.
> I would call him a phony, except that I think he is just another
>   modern paradox.[50]

Seeger lived this paradox, and at times he bemoaned the effort required to contain its oppositions. He wondered whether it would have been easier to have adopted a less multifaceted public persona, even one blatantly false in its seamlessness. He daydreamed to his biographer about hiding behind a pseudonym: "I could be Pete Seeger/Uncle Zeke. The posters would say Uncle Zeke, and everybody would know Uncle Zeke is Pete Seeger; still, the posters wouldn't say Pete Seeger."[51] Seeger was tempted to ease the tensions in his life by neatly bifurcating it, dividing public from private and professional from personal. But instead of segregating the clashing elements within him, he openly displayed the internal discord, identifying and analyzing the disjunctions in his identity as both common man and aristocrat, amateur and celebrity, traditionalist and popularizer.

Ironically, laying bare his contradictions only made Seeger's synthesis between "nonfolk" and "folk" seem more of a tour de force and made him seem more "real" to the young Americans who idolized him in the 1950s and 1960s. As undergraduates, Ralph Rinzler (a doctor's son who would go on to spearhead the Smithsonian's Festival of American Folklife) and Roger Abrahams (a lawyer's son who would become one of country's most respected academic folklorists) heard Seeger perform in 1953 at Swarthmore College. They identified with him completely. Rinzler remembered that "everything fit together" in Seeger; "he seemed absolutely coherent." Rinzler and Abrahams immediately went out and bought banjos and embarked on their careers.[52]

It is doubtful that "Uncle Zeke" would have had the same impact on Rinzler and Abrahams. Much of Seeger's influence on middle-class youths depended on the fact that as he immersed himself in folk culture he never fully effaced his outsider roots. Even as he blazed a trail to an alternative culture, he left behind markers for those who would follow. Keeping his unlikely origins in view illuminated the cultural distance he had traveled and made the journey seem possible to others.

By the late 1950s, thousands of college-aged men and women like Rinzler and Abrahams had started down the path that Seeger had laid out. They were, in effect, an early wave of the 1960s counterculture, pushing against what they perceived to be the empty homogeneity of their suburban backgrounds, the hypocrisy of a government that saved the world for democracy and then launched the House Un-American Activities Committee, and the schizophrenia of a life filled with unprecedented abundance yet shadowed by fears of annihilation. For these young people, the possibility that Seeger held out of entering into the world of the folk appealed as a chance to build a richer, more morally grounded, more thoroughly integrated life.

For some, joining the folk revival in the late 1950s and early 1960s simply meant listening to acoustic music in coffeehouses or buying the folk-pop albums of the Kingston Trio. Hard-core revivalists took the search for an alternative lifestyle more literally. "I'm proud to report," Seeger wrote in *Sing Out!* in 1956, "partial success in my campaign to lead the younger generation astray by persuading them to hitch-hike around the country." Some students joined campus folk song clubs, and many more learned to play acoustic instruments. Guitar sales reached five hundred thousand in 1955. Seeger's banjo manual appeared in a second edition in 1954 and a third in 1961. In the 1950s the respected Vega company came out with a "Pete Seeger" model banjo.[53]

Seeger's imprint on the revival was visible in less direct ways as well. To a great extent, the folk fad of the late fifties and early sixties was an extension of the revival he and Alan Lomax had helped nurture under the Popular Front. As in the pre–World War II revival, Lead Belly and Woody Guthrie were revered as forefathers by the revivalists. Guthrie especially was held up as a role model for a coherent, more politically aware life.[54] Thousands of young people were listening to the traditional repertoire that Seeger and the Lomaxes had worked to popularize.[55] Most encouraging of all, as far as Seeger was concerned, was a loose group of musicians that began to emerge in Greenwich Village. Phil Ochs, Tom Paxton, Mark Spoelstra, Len Chandler, and Peter La Farge produced edgy, often angry topical songs about the news of the day and the state of the world.[56] In the early sixties they began to attract a considerable following. From the beginning, though, the star of the group was a baby-faced guitar- and harmonica-playing singer named Bob Dylan. Seeger fixed his hopes on him.

In the early sixties, Dylan seemed to be the consummation of all of Seeger's efforts over the previous quarter century. If Seeger had worked to demonstrate the accessibility of folk culture, Dylan seemed to have taken all his lessons to heart. The young Dylan was eager to identify himself with the folk, diligent in apprenticing himself to their music, and determined to apply what he learned by writing new, politically charged songs modeled on traditional styles. Dylan had been born Robert Zimmerman in 1941 in Duluth, Minnesota. When he was six, his parents, Abe and Beatty, moved the family to Hibbing, Minnesota, where his father ran a hardware and appliance store downtown and the family maintained a comfortable middle-class lifestyle. None of these facts, though, were part of the nineteen-year-old singer's persona when he arrived in New York City in December 1960. He came into town not only with a new name (which he had acquired the year before) but a whole new identity, or, rather, multiple identities.[57]

In his early years in New York, Dylan spun out a series of almost entirely fictitious tales about his background. Many of these stories contradicted one another, but in all of them Dylan sought to connect himself to the folk cultures that he admired and romanticized. In his brief stay at the University of Minnesota in 1959–60, Dylan tended to say he was from Oklahoma, but when he arrived in New York, he was an orphan from New Mexico who had been rambling for years. He claimed to have heard Woody Guthrie on the radio at the orphanage, and (when speaking to people safely outside Guthrie's circle of friends) he would say that he had met the Dust Bowl balladeer in California. He told one acquaintance (who recorded the remark in his journal), "I was in Carmel, doing nothing. During the summer, Woody impressed me. Always made a point to see him again." He told the same person, "Cowboy styles I learned from real cowboys. Can't remember their names. Met some in Cheyenne." In his first press interview, with the *New York Times*, Dylan said, "I was born in Duluth, Minnesota, or maybe it was Superior, Wisconsin, right across the line. I started traveling with the carnival. I cleaned ponies and ran steam shovels in Minnesota, North Dakota, and then on south." At times, Dylan seemed to be poking fun at the nebulousness of his identity. Early on in New York he said, "Hey, man, there a lot of things about my life I ain't told ya. Did I ever tell you I got my nose from the Indian blood in my veins? Well, that's the truth, hey. Got an uncle who's a Sioux." Despite this playfulness, though, Dylan, unlike Seeger, worked to conceal his true middle-class background as completely as possible. Some of Dylan's Greenwich Village friends realized the put-on, but they did not bother challenging him, and few outside his immediate circle knew the truth until the winter of 1963, when *Newsweek* discovered Abe and Beatty Zimmerman and exposed Dylan's past. Until then, some mutual friends maintain, Dylan's girlfriend thought he was an Italian orphan.[58]

Along with Dylan's efforts to create ersatz folk roots, he affected a look, a manner, and even a smell designed to establish his authenticity in folk circles. Many of his moves were reminiscent of the young Seeger two decades before. Like Seeger, Dylan acquired the fashion sense of a would-be working man, wearing dungarees and a wrinkled work shirt wherever he went. "I come onstage the same way I go anywhere," he told *Life* in 1964. "I mean, are all those people paying to see me look neat?" To this by then familiar look Dylan added a distinctive short-billed black corduroy hat that he wore everywhere in his early years in the city.[59] He also adopted a mannered twang and ungrammatical, elliptical speech patterns, which he had picked up from Woody Guthrie's recordings and writings. As Seeger had, Dylan further fleshed out his image by developing an aversion to grooming and bathing. His scruffiness, *Life* pointed out, served to distinguish him from the "new crop of well-scrubbed collegiate folk groups" that had proliferated since the clean-cut Kingston Trio had scored a pop hit in 1957 with "Tom Dooley." "We're not singing folk songs in order to sell soap," joked Dylan in *Sing Out!*. "Hell, we don't even buy soap!" Remembering Dylan's 1963 concert at New York's Town Hall, critic Robert Shelton writes that Dylan came onstage in "his hobo look": "With his jeans and head of hair that shouted unfamiliarity with barbers, Dylan resembled Holden Caulfield lost in the Dust Bowl." In the balcony, Shelton recalls, Pete Seeger "glowed benevolently."[60]

Seeger likely recognized some of himself in Dylan's cobbled-together folk persona, but what most of all prompted his affection that evening in New York was how seriously Dylan took folk music. Like Seeger, Dylan began his career by immersing himself in American roots traditions. Dylan did not have an apprenticeship as formal as Seeger's had been under Lomax at the Archive of American Folk-Song, but he did have his mentors, some voluntary and some involuntary. In 1959 Jon Pankake, coeditor of the folk song magazine *Little Sandy Review*, introduced Dylan to his extraordinary record collection. When Pankake left town for a weekend, Dylan entered Pankake's (unlocked) apartment and stole twenty or so choice albums, incurring Pankake's enduring wrath. In Dylan's early New York days, he studied the published collections of the Lomaxes, Francis James Child, and Cecil Sharp and, like most other young revivalists, listened devotedly to the *Anthology of American Folk Music*. He also embraced the blues, soaking up the sounds of Robert Johnson, Muddy Waters, Jimmy Reed, and many others.[61]

The strongest influence on Dylan's music was Seeger's friend and hero, Woody Guthrie. Dylan first encountered Guthrie's work around 1960 while in Minneapolis, and almost immediately he began to transform himself into a Guthrie look- and sound-alike. When Dylan arrived in New York City, one of his first objectives was to visit Guthrie. Early in 1961 he hitchhiked to Greystone Hospital in central New Jersey and met his idol, whose disease had progressed to such an extent that he shook uncontrollably and could barely talk. Nonetheless, over several visits he and Dylan seem to have developed a rapport. Dylan would sit by him and play Guthrie's songs back to him. An awestruck Dylan wrote a postcard to a Minneapolis friend, saying that he was seeing Guthrie four times a week and that "Woody likes me—he tells me to sing for him—he's the greatest, holiest, godliest one in the world." In this same period, Dylan spent time with friends of Guthrie's, Bob and Sidsel Gleason, who had taped roughly 90 percent of Guthrie's personal record collection. Dylan would hitchhike from New York to the Gleasons' East Orange, New Jersey, apartment and spend hours listening to the music, copying down words and chord progressions for songs he wanted to add to his repertoire. "He'd start in the morning," the Gleasons recalled, "and play tapes all day long, for days on end." When Dylan's first big break came, a chance to open at Gerde's Folk City, a popular club on the New York revival scene, Bob Gleason gave him one of Guthrie's suit jackets to wear for the occasion.[62]

The depth of Dylan's allegiance to roots music and the breadth of his influences are reflected in his self-titled debut album, released in 1962. It includes covers of southern white mountain songs ("Man of Constant Sorrow"), downhome blues (Bukka White's "Fixin' to Die" and Blind Lemon Jefferson's "See That My Grave Is Kept Clean"), Scottish ballads (a parody of "Pretty Peggy-O"), country standards (Roy Acuff's "Freight Train Blues"), spirituals ("In My Time of Dyin'" and "Gospel Plow"), and a modified bawdy-house song ("House of the Rising Sun," which had first been recorded by Alan Lomax in 1937). The only two original songs on the album are homages to Guthrie. "Talking New York" is a narrative based on several Guthrie tall tales, and "Song to Woody" is a direct tribute to his idol that appropriates its tune from Guthrie's "1913 Massacre."[63]

Seeger no doubt appreciated the commitment to old-time repertoire that Dylan showed on his debut, but it was really on his next two albums that Dylan began to fulfill Seeger's dreams for a revitalized, contemporary folk process. On *The Freewheelin' Bob Dylan* (1963) and *The Times They Are A-Changin'* (1964), Dylan worked within the folk song idiom to create new, timely songs with pointed political messages. Some of the most politically charged topical songs on these albums draw directly on folk sources. "Hard Rain," for example, strings together a series of apocalyptic images that, Dylan says in his liner notes, he wrote in the depths of the Cuban missile crisis; but the melody for this atomic-age warning cry comes directly from a Child ballad, "Lord Randal." "Masters of War," likewise, protests the hypocrisy of the military-industrial complex while (Robert Shelton speculates) using a tune from an old English mummer's play that was passed on via Appalachian singer Jean Ritchie. "Bob Dylan's Dream" shares its melody with the British song "Lord

Franklin," while "The Ballad of Hollis Brown" is derived from the Appalachian tune "Poor Man."[64]

Even the songs on *Freewheelin'* and *Times* that do not have immediate folk antecedents sound as if they belong in Pete Seeger's songbook. "Blowin' in the Wind," for instance, challenges society to confront the persistent injustices in the world, and it does so with a song structure ideal for sing-alongs. It has a simple melody that moves in slow, stepwise fashion with several repeated notes; it has a constant, loping four-four beat; and its key words fall on the downbeat and are held for longer durations:

> *Hoooow* many *rooooads* must a *maaan* walk down
> Be*foooore* you *caaaall* him a *maaan?*

Dylan directly attributed "The Times They Are A-Changin'," his call to arms for sixties activism, to the folk tradition, even if its melody was "original." The song, he recalled, "was influenced of course by the Irish and Scottish ballads . . . *Come All Ye Bold Highway Men, Come All Ye Miners, Come All Ye Tender Hearted Maidens.* I wanted to write a big song, some kind of theme song, ya know, with short concise verses that piled up on each other in a hypnotic way." Three other "protest" songs on *Freewheelin'* and *Times* came straight out of the Almanac Singers' tradition of writing songs from the newspaper's headlines. "Only a Pawn in Their Game" chronicles the killing of civil rights advocate Medgar Evers; "The Lonesome Death of Hattie Carroll" recounts the 1963 murder of a poor woman at the hands of a socialite; and "Oxford Town" tells the story of James Meredith, the first African American to attend the University of Mississippi.[65]

Like Seeger, Dylan in the early years of his career carried the political messages in his songs over into the rest of his life. He established an essentially seamless relationship between the persona on his recordings and his image outside the studio. In both arenas, Dylan presented himself as a young bard determined to use his art to fight political injustice. In a 1962 profile for *Sing Out!*, Gil Turner portrayed an idealistic man crusading against dishonesty: "Reality and truth are words that Bob Dylan will use often if you get him into a serious discussion about anything. They are his criteria for evaluating the world around him, the people in it . . . , songs to sing and songs to write." Dylan himself elaborated on the point: "I don't have to bs anybody like those guys up on Broadway that're always writin' about 'I'm hot for you and you're hot for me—ooka dooka dicka dee.' There's other things in the world besides love and sex that're important too. People shouldn't turn their back on 'em just because they ain't pretty to look at. How is the world ever gonna get better if we're afraid to look at these things?" With a directness and idealism reminiscent of Seeger, Dylan told the *New York Daily News* in 1963 that "the times call for truth . . . and people want to hear the truth and that's just what they're hearing in good folk music today. . . . There's mystery, magic, truth, and the Bible in great folk music. I can't hope to touch that. But I'm goin' to try." This fervor led Dylan to Greenwood, Mississippi, in July 1963, where he, Seeger, and Theodore Bikel worked to draw attention to scare tactics being used against the civil rights organization SNCC (Student Nonviolent Coordinating Committee) and its voter-registration drive. Dylan sang "Masters of War." At the 1963 March on Washington (during which Martin Luther King Jr. delivered his "I Have a Dream" speech), Dylan sang "Pawn in Their Game" on the steps of the Lincoln Memorial. In the winter of 1964, he delivered clothes to striking miners in Harlan County, Kentucky.[66]

With his folksy image, knowledge of American roots music, dedication to revitalizing folk music traditions, and political idealism, Dylan in the early sixties seemed to have bound up into a tight package all the elements that Seeger and the old-left revivalists most treasured. Excited observers frequently stressed the coherence and consistency they saw in him. "Bob's stage personality," Gil Turner noted in 1962, "is not a contrived, play-acted personality. One gets the impression that his talk and story-telling onstage are things that he thought you might be interested in." Irwin Silber, editor of *Sing Out!*, urged readers, "Compare the direct honesty of Dylan's songs to the pseudo-folksongs created on Tin Pan Alley and Hollywood boulevard . . .—songs which seemingly deal with Trouble, Poverty, Lonesomeness, Hard Times. . . . But it's all froth when you come to really examine the stuff. You can tell the difference between a Dylan song (or a Guthrie song, or an Aunt Molly Jackson song) and the hokey-folky pieces rather easily." In 1962 Harry Jackson, a cowboy singer, painter, and sculptor, succinctly expressed the prevailing opinion about Dylan: "He's so goddamned real, it's unbelievable."[67]

Seeger certainly was a true believer. Early on, Seeger proclaimed that Dylan "may well become the country's most creative troubadour." Seeger did all he could to make the prophecy come true. By the end of 1962, he was frequently performing Dylan's songs and, Robert Shelton notes, had "singled him out as the most important new songwriter of the time." Jon Pankake wrote that Seeger tended to be "hovering over" Dylan and some of the other young stars of the revival "as would an actual father." In these early years of his career, Dylan was graciously receptive to these overtures. In the fall of 1963, he wrote an open letter to *Broadside* magazine in which he described Seeger as "truly a saint / an [*sic*] I love him / perhaps more than I could show." In the "11 Outlined Epitaphs" that Dylan wrote to accompany *The Times They Are A-Changin'*, he again referred to "Pete Seeger's saintliness."[68]

These mutual tributes obscured the fact that at an important level Dylan's relationship with Seeger and the other leaders of the folk revival was based on a misunderstanding, one that both sides had encouraged. The older revivalists' burning hopes for a young standard-bearer and Dylan's willing posturing combined to exaggerate the extent to which Dylan was the seamless amalgam of traditional folk styles that he seemed to be. Apparently, in celebrating Dylan's creativity and coherence as a folk singer, no one in the folk revival had thought to ask him about Elvis.

Long before he had heard of Woody Guthrie, Bobby Zimmerman wanted to be a rock and roll star. A classmate recalls that when the fourteen-year-old Zimmerman first heard Bill Haley's "Rock Around the Clock" he shouted, "Hey that's our music! That's written for us!" By high school Elvis Presley and Little Richard were his heroes, and he played in a band that covered their tunes. In his senior yearbook, Zimmerman listed as his ambition "To join the band of Little Richard." While Seeger had dropped his high school pop-music ambitions after discovering folk music, Dylan never lost his rock and roll dreams. When Dylan was staying with the Gleasons, studying Woody Guthrie's record collection, he boasted to them that he had played piano on several of Presley's recordings. Even as he began to break into the New York folk scene in 1961–62, he still continued to play his Presley records "when nobody was around." Elvis also continued to be the reference point against which Dylan charted his dreams of success. After recording his first album, Dylan excitedly told an old friend, "John Hammond, he's the big producer, you know. Well, hey, he says I'm gonna be bigger than Presley. Bigger than *Presley!*"[69]

Dylan's love for rock and roll was only one of several factors that precipitated his break with the Seeger-styled revival around 1965. As his popularity increased, Dylan found that his topical songs were creating the expectation that he was going to serve as the political conscience of his generation. When he went out in public, one old friend recalled, people would approach him and ask searchingly, "What's life all about?" Other fans likened him to Jesus Christ. Dylan's politicized persona also began to constrain him artistically. By the time of the release of *The Times They Are A-Changin'* in 1964, Dylan had begun experimenting with drugs and associating with New York hipsters and Beat poets like Allen Ginsberg. These experiences encouraged a more free-associative and imagistic use of language than the journalistic style of topical songs. Dylan would later recall, "I had to hold a lot of things back before. People would never understand. . . . I couldn't go too far out."[70]

Dylan's break with the revival may also have come from a savvy sense in the mid-sixties that the political song movement had crested. As the Freedom Rides gave way to Black Power, and the Cuban missile crisis to Vietnam, the answers to the country's political crises seemed less clear-cut. Perhaps Dylan sensed that the protest singer's technique of painting stark dichotomies between right and wrong would seem anachronistic in the more fractious days ahead and that a less sententious, more equivocal language was needed. Or maybe Dylan simply realized with the onslaught of Beatlemania in 1964 that the folk-revival sound could not sustain its popularity.

For a combination of these reasons, likely, in the mid-1960s Dylan broke decisively with his folk-revival allies. Within the sixteen months between March 1965 and May 1966, Dylan debuted a raucous performance style at the Newport Folk Festival, released three groundbreaking electric albums, and unveiled a new public persona.[71] Together these moves transformed Dylan into what he has been ever since, a rock star.

On the face of it, Dylan's new style marked a complete rejection of all that Pete Seeger stood for. Most obviously, Dylan diverged from Seeger by performing with electric instruments. The extent, though, to which Dylan's embrace of the electric in itself represented a break with Seeger's revival has been exaggerated. Seeger was not intractably opposed to electric instruments per se. "Who knows," he speculated in February 1966, "the electrified guitar may prove to be the most typical folk instrument of the twenty-first century." Although he did not perform on electric instruments, Seeger was not averse to experimenting with them. Early in 1967 he wrote, "I like the 1966 electric guitars a lot better than the ones I tried playing in the 1930s. . . . Of course, me, I've been playing electrified music for a long time. Ever since I started using microphones." Beginning in the early 1970s, Seeger even recorded occasional albums with electric instrumental accompaniment.[72] It seems unlikely, then, that Dylan's decision to use electric instruments could, in itself, have prompted Seeger's rage in Newport that summer in 1965. In fact, it is hard to believe that Seeger was completely surprised to see Dylan take the Newport stage with his electric guitar. By the time of the festival, Dylan's *Bringing It All Back Home*, with its several electric songs, had been in stores for five months, accumulating strong sales figures behind its electric single, "Maggie's Farm." Moreover, Dylan had recorded with electric instruments as early as 1962. One of the two songs on his first single had been the electric "Mixed Up Confusion."[73]

If at some level the sight of Dylan on the Newport stage with an electric guitar did not completely shock Seeger, the sound he produced with it certainly did. The grinding, distorted roar that Dylan unleashed attacked the very core of Seeger's philosophy of performance—that a concert was an opportunity to build community. Seeger's sing-along techniques strove to engage audience members in a common cause— making music. He tapped into the alternative meaning of the word "concert": he wanted the spectators to join together as a single, united body, working together *in concert*. The blare of Dylan's guitar at Newport suggested a different conception of the spectators' role. The overwhelming volume precluded a group sing: audience members could not have heard one another, and, as Seeger said frantically, "Damn it, you can't hear the words!" Dylan's song set at Newport was a performance done for and perhaps to his audience, but he had little interest in allowing it to be done *by* them.[74]

Dylan's more distanced stance from the spectators at Newport signaled that in the mid-sixties he was beginning to conceive of the relationship between artists and audiences very differently than Seeger. Increasingly, Dylan tried to disentangle himself from the notion (a legacy of the Popular Front) that performers should try to shape public opinion. Dylan no longer had any interest in Seeger-styled "message music." He stopped writing topical songs and tried to shuck off the role of political spokesman. "My songs are just me talking to myself," he said on his 1965 British tour. "I have no responsibility to anybody except myself." In September 1965 he told *Newsweek* perversely, "I've never written a political song"; and in a direct hit on Seeger's idealism he added, "Songs can't save the world. I've gone through that."[75]

Dylan's albums in the mid-sixties did more than just avoid direct political positions; they implicitly undercut the legitimacy of taking a committed political stand. Some of the protest material on Dylan's earlier albums had attempted to spur listeners to unite behind a common cause. "Blowin' in the Wind," for instance, poses rhetorical questions that point directly to answers. In asking "How many times must the cannon balls fly / Before they're forever banned?" and "How many years can some people exist / Before they're allowed to be free?" Dylan offers clear, bottom-line positions. Ban the cannonballs! Free the people! On his mid-1960s albums, though, Dylan depicted a world spinning so beyond the reach of reason that any coherent principled stance was bound to crumble. The song "Highway 61 Revisited" (1965), for example, is a jumble of shattered narratives, opaque references, and answers that answer nothing:

> Well Mack the Finger said to Louie the King
> I got forty red white and blue shoe strings
> And a thousand telephones that don't ring
> Do you know where I can get rid of these things?

"Ballad of a Thin Man" (1965) not only denies the possibility of easy answers but casts doubt on the chances of understanding the questions:

> You raise up your head
> And you ask, "Is this where it is?"
> And somebody points to you and says
> "It's his"
> And you say, "What's mine?"
> And somebody else says, "Where what is?"
> And you say, "Oh my God
> Am I here all alone?"[76]

In the midst of such confusion, to sing a declarative song like "We Shall Overcome" would be ludicrous. Dylan's clattering disjunctions undermine the faith in vision and the possibility of order that fuels Seeger's songs of hope and protest. Dylan's liner notes for *Bringing It All Back Home* (1965) declare, "i accept chaos."[77]

Dylan's suspicion of cohesion and commitment not only reshaped his music but also led him in the mid-sixties to create a public persona that was almost the antithesis of Seeger's. In interviews, Seeger was given to earnest self-reflection, simple homilies, and pithy exhortations (Let's clean up this river!). Dylan, though, abandoned the idea that an interview should be an occasion for self-revelation or even communication. In a 1965 press conference in San Francisco, Dylan was asked, "Do you think of yourself primarily as a singer or a poet?"

> Dylan: Oh I think of myself more as a song-and-dance man. . . .
> Q: If you were to sell out to a commercial interest, which one would you choose?
> Dylan: Ladies garments. . . .
> Q: What's your new album about?
> Dylan: . . . all kinds of different things—rats, balloons . . .

In refusing to explain or reveal himself to his audiences, Dylan rejected the sort of merger between private and public self that Seeger had crafted. In effect, he chose the "Uncle Zeke" option about which

Seeger had daydreamed, openly and playfully making clear that his public persona was a matter of role-playing. On his 1965 tour of Britain, Dylan was asked, "When did you start making records?" Dylan (born 1941) replied, "I started making recordings in 1947. . . . A race record. I made it down South. Actually the first record I made was in 1935. John Hammond came and recorded me. Discovered me in 1935, sitting on a farm." "God, I'm glad I'm not me," Dylan said when reading a newspaper story about himself.[78] Coupled with Dylan's oblique and disrupted songs, this antipersona was perhaps the ultimate challenge to Pete Seeger's worldview. If Seeger's life was performance art that demonstrated how to gain access to "real life," Dylan's was a performance that challenged the existence of "real life" by playing on *in*accessibility and the *sur*real.

Seeger was well aware of the extent to which Dylan had rejected him. Shortly after the 1965 Newport festival, he tried to purge his feeling of betrayal in a journal entry. He paraphrased a poem he had written about cancer ("The Beast with a Hundred Claws") and used it to decry the effects of commercialism on his protégé. Likening Dylan to a corpse, Seeger wrote, "The fangs and claws sink swiftly deeper now / First the muscles, then the brain / The fangs reach for the heart, and victory is won / And when we reach for him, we have only the shrivelled corpse." Seeger's despair was so deep that, in an uncharacteristic move, he temporarily withdrew from public associations with the folk revival. He quit the Newport festival's board of directors; he resigned as director of the Woody Guthrie Children's Trust Fund; he suspended his column in *Sing Out!*. Seeger later referred to Dylan's Newport performance as "some of the most destructive music this side of hell."[79]

But Seeger should have listened more carefully to what Dylan was saying. At the deepest level, Dylan's move into the world of pop renounced one manifestation of the folk revival, not revivalism as a whole. Dylan broke with the Popular Front's agenda for folk song: he no longer treated music as a tool for social reform. But if one sets aside Dylan's antipolitical jibes and his jester poses, one sees that even after 1965 Dylan's approach to music retained basic similarities to Seeger's. Although Dylan's style had changed dramatically, he remained fundamentally committed to drawing on American roots music to produce vibrant new songs grounded firmly in tradition. Whether Seeger realized it or not, Dylan never abandoned his allegiance to the folk song process that Seeger so treasured. His post-1965 work represents a transmutation, not an abdication, of the folk-stylist role.

One constant in Dylan's pre- and post-1965 career was his allegiance to his folk heroes.[80] In the decades after 1965, Dylan repeatedly paid his respects to figures with unassailable reputations even among folk purists. His attraction to Woody Guthrie, for example, remained undiminished. In October 1967, when Guthrie died, Dylan had spent more than a year isolated from the public, recuperating from a near-fatal motorcycle accident and recording in his Woodstock, New York, home. But when he heard of the death, he suggested to Guthrie's longtime manager, Harold Leventhal, that a tribute be held. That winter Dylan made a triumphant return to the stage, singing covers of three Guthrie classics. Other traditional performers continued to appeal to Dylan as well. In a 1968 interview, he expressed his admiration for Appalachian singer Roscoe Holcomb and bluegrass pioneer Bill Monroe. In 1973 Dylan published a volume that included his entire oeuvre of song lyrics (*Writings and Drawings by Bob Dylan*). In his dedication he saluted "the magnificent Woody Guthrie and Robert Johnson, who sparked it off." Similarly, in the interview accompanying his retrospective *Biograph* box set (1985), Dylan urged, "You have to get past the keeping-up-with-the-times stuff. . . . The old trades are still the most useful. . . . To the aspiring songwriter and singer I say disregard all the current stuff, forget it, you're better off, read John Keats, Melville, listen to Robert Johnson and Woody Guthrie."[81]

Even as Dylan continued after 1965 to acknowledge his debts to icons of the folk revival, he also paid homage to musicians whose status within the revival was more uncertain. As he transformed his sound in the mid-sixties, Dylan expressed a willful disregard for rigid divisions between musical genres. The cover photograph for *Bringing It All Back Home* (1965) showed Dylan holding his cat (named Rolling Stone) while behind him were displayed albums by Robert Johnson, the soul group the Impressions, blues revivalist Ric Von Schmidt, classical singer Lotte Lenya, and, far in the background, Dylan's own previous album. In 1965 Dylan urged Nora Ephron and Susan Edmiston, "You gotta listen to the [gospel] Staple Singers, [and Motown's] Smokey and the Miracles, [and] Martha and the Vandellas." At times he could be petulant in demonstrating his resistance to hard-and-fast genres. He needled the *Village Voice*, "I consider Hank Williams, Captain Marvel, Marlon Brando, The Tennessee Stud, Clark Kent, Walter Cronkite, and J. Carroll Naish all influences." Dylan listed his favorite performers for an Austin, Texas, reporter: "Rasputin . . . Hmm . . . Charles de Gaulle . . . the Staple Singers."[82]

Even when he was speaking less flippantly, the musicians whom Dylan cited after 1965 cut across the usual boundaries. In 1969 he told John Cohen, "Those old songs reach me." He then rattled off a wide-ranging list of his favorites, including Kentucky hillbilly singer Buell Kazee; early Chicago bluesmen Scrapper Blackwell, Leroy Carr, Jack Dupree, and Lonnie Johnson; jazz pioneers Jelly Roll Morton and Buddy Bolden; Canadian folk-pop singers Ian and Sylvia; country singers Porter Wagoner and Charley Pride; and Irish song revivalists the Clancy Brothers and Tommy Makem. Early in 1969, shortly before the release of his country-flavored *Nashville Skyline* album, Dylan told *Newsweek*, "The people who shaped my style were performers like Elvis Presley, Buddy Holly, [and country singer] Hank Thompson." In 1978 he commented to Robert Shelton, "If it wasn't for Elvis and Hank Williams, I couldn't be doing what I do today." In 1985 Dylan told *Time* that his favorite songs were not only Guthrie's "Pastures of Plenty" but also the pop standards "That's All" and "I Get a Kick Out of You." In the *Biograph* interview that year he cited as influences not just Robert Johnson, bluesman Blind Willie McTell, and Guthrie but also pop singers Al Jolson, Jimmie Rodgers, and Judy Garland.[83]

Dylan, then, did not reject roots music after 1965 but rather seemed to embrace *everything* as a potential influence. In some ways, this eclecticism was in keeping with Seeger's approach to folk song. Just as Seeger had confidently absorbed music from all of America's regions and from countries around the world, Dylan moved easily into rural Appalachian and African American cultures to which he had no connection by birthright. Just as Seeger included pop songs from his youth in *American Favorite Ballads*, Dylan acknowledged the influence of the pop heroes of *his* younger days, Elvis and Hank Williams. Like Seeger, moreover, Dylan did not try to mimic exactly the original practitioners of the genres he embraced. Instead, in line with Seeger's commitment to evolution within the folk process, he customized roots traditions to fit his own personal needs.

Dylan's appropriation of roots music, though, differed subtly from Seeger's. Seeger tended to flit from style to style in an instant, hardly missing a beat as he moved from the minstrel song "Oh Susanna" to the Israeli folk song "Tzena Tzena." As he tried on different styles, they often remained decidedly ill fitting. Particularly when he extended beyond Appalachian traditions, Seeger tended to sound as if he were taking on diverse cultures for demonstration purposes. This awkwardness suited Seeger's message: "See, *anyone* can put on this style! Give it a try!"

Dylan, by contrast, implied that playing in a given style involved intense commitment and personal transformation. Whether experimenting with the Popular Front folk singing of Woody Guthrie, the country sound, or southern gospel, Dylan did more than dabble. He identified himself completely with the music he was exploring and with the public persona that went along with it, becoming a protest singer, a Nashville balladeer, or a born-again evangelist. He did not just sing "Tzena Tzena"; he converted. As Dylan reflected in 1984, "When I get involved in something, I get totally involved. I don't just play around."[84] More than rejecting Seeger's legacy, then, Dylan adapted it. Even after he moved away from the Popular Front's folk revival, Dylan continued working with roots music, cutting it to shape and embossing it with signature personal touches. He still wrote songs that alluded to and expressed his debts to roots traditions and presented these traditions in a contemporary and idiosyncratic light. The disjunction, therefore, between Seeger's "folk" style and Dylan's "rock" style in the mid-1960s was misleading. The sound had changed, and the times had changed, but Dylan, like Seeger, was modeling a process by which an "outsider" could work within roots traditions—a process, Dylan suggested, that involved both single-minded devotion and creative adaptation.

Dylan's effort to appropriate and personalize American roots music suffuses the songs he produced after 1965. One can demonstrate Dylan's engagement with roots traditions by looking at the extent to which his songs drew on four key genres: ballads, blues, country, and African American religious music. It would be a mistake, of course, to posit distinct and unchanging definitions for any of these styles. Each of them encompasses a myriad of divergent forms, and each tends to draw on and incorporate the others. One can identify traits, though, that, while not necessarily representative of everything produced within a given form, characterize many of its defining examples.

For all the diverse manifestations of the ballad, for example, one can still legitimately point to certain formal elements that recur within the genre: a concern with narrating a story, references to specific names and places, the reliance on a simple and repetitive melody, and the avoidance of repetition in the sometimes numerous lyrics. Many of the classics in this genre were established parts of Pete Seeger's repertoire. "Barbara Allen," "The Farmer's Curst Wife," and innumerable others chronologically trace the stories of individual characters from beginning to end.[85] Early on, Dylan wrote several songs that fit directly into the ballad genre, including "Ballad of Donald White" (1962) and "The Lonesome Death of Hattie Carroll" (1964).[86] Later in his career, Dylan still sometimes produced songs that straightforwardly narrated a story.[87] More frequently, though, he borrowed elements from the traditional ballad and applied them to a new sort of storytelling. After 1965, Dylan's ballad-styled songs no longer traced the story of specific characters and stories through a beginning, middle, and end. In a Dylan ballad the cast of characters fluctuates unpredictably, their individual identities are unstable, the chronology of the story is hopelessly jumbled, and narrative closure is continually undercut.

"The Ballad of Frankie Lee and Judas Priest" (1967), for example, begins traditionally enough by introducing the two main characters named in the song's title, calling them "the best of friends." Immediately, though, the story devolves into a web of surrealism, cryptic conversations, and empty aphorisms. Judas puts a wad of money on a footstool "above the plotted plain" and tells Frankie to take his pick. Frankie asks Judas where he can find him. "Eternity," comes the reply. "Though you might call it 'Paradise.'" Frankie finds Judas at a house in which a woman's face shows in every window. Frankie foams at the mouth and raves for sixteen days and nights and dies of thirst. In the course of this fractured story line, Dylan introduces two unaccounted-for characters: "a passing stranger," who bursts in to tell Frankie to meet Judas, and "the little neighbor boy," who carries Frankie to his grave, muttering, "Nothing is revealed."[88]

Dylan's "Desolation Row" (1965) dispenses with plot entirely and instead chronicles a phantasmagoric cast of characters that parade past the narrator and his "Lady." Each verse introduces several figures about whom one could have written a ballad. Dylan, though, combines them all in a narrative that cuts across temporal boundaries and revels in anachronism. The song features appearances by Romeo, Cain and Abel, the hunchback of Notre Dame, Dr. Filth, and "Einstein disguised as Robin Hood." Cinderella "puts her hands in her back pockets / Bette Davis style." Ezra Pound and T. S. Eliot are "fighting in the captain's tower / while calypso singers laugh at them."[89] Dylan has preserved the ballad form's historicity and its attention to setting and scene, but he has shifted its focus from chronicling events to spinning out a series of evocative allegorical images.

Even in his so-called rock period, then, Dylan continued to draw on the formal aspects of the folk ballad, but he reassembled these elements in ways that showed less concern with telling a story than with playing with the conventions of storytelling. His ballads featured personas that showed the plasticity of persona, morals that questioned the legitimacy of fixed morals, and narratives that demonstrated the breaking down of narrative.

One sees a similar interplay between appropriation and alteration in Dylan's relationship to the blues after 1965. Elements of the blues influenced countless other genres, but traits that are strongly associated with the style include the twelve-bar harmonic progression, the A-A-B lyrical pattern, a style of vocal delivery that is not rigidly tied to the underlying beat, and a vague mood that suggests melancholy and malaise (although not necessarily despair or protest).[90] For his part, Seeger never felt comfortable with the blues. He did include some examples of the genre in his songbooks and performances, but often (as in *American Favorite Ballads*) he relied on vaudeville blues (such as "St. Louis Blues"), which had a close relationship to Tin Pan Alley songs. Writing in 1965, Seeger noted that "some kinds of music . . . I admire but never could listen to for long at a stretch"; along with "real flamenco guitar playing," he included "blues, such as those of the great Robert Johnson. Why? Hard to put in words. Perhaps the aggressive sound puts me on edge. I just don't feel that aggressive."[91]

Dylan, apparently, had little problem mounting the requisite aggression. At the outset of his career, Dylan performed and recorded covers of several downhome blues songs. He certainly did not stop using the blues after he broke with Seeger's folk revival. Some of his efforts, in fact, follow the twelve-bar, A-A-B pattern quite rigidly and feature a vocal delivery and "feel" reminiscent of traditional blues.[92] Generally, though, Dylan approached the form more loosely after 1965—varying it, ignoring parts of it, and at times almost completely overhauling it.

"Outlaw Blues" (1965), for example, on the face of it fits securely into the downhome blues genre. It closely follows the A-A-B pattern and uses the blues chord progression (although it doubles the duration of each chord, producing stanzas of twenty-four instead of twelve bars). Its lyrics, though, have a surreal element to them that makes the tune sound like a parody of traditional blues:

> Ain't gonna hang no picture,
> Ain't gonna hang no picture frame.
> Ain't gonna hang no picture,
> Ain't gonna hang no picture frame.
> Well, I might look like Robert Ford
> But I feel just like a Jesse James.
>
> Well, I wish I was on some
> Australian mountain range.
> Oh, I wish I was on some
> Australian mountain range.
> I got no reason to be there, but I
> Imagine it would be some kind of change.

The disjointedness here tweaks bluesmen's penchant for obscure references and, at the same time, makes light of Dylan's status as outsider to the blues tradition (most blues do not dwell on Australia). The next verse mimics the prevalence of supernatural omens and occult charms in the blues:

I got my dark sunglasses,
I got for good luck my black tooth
I got my dark sunglasses,
I'm carryin' for good luck my black tooth.
Don't ask me nothin' about nothin',
I just might tell you the truth.[93]

The parody becomes more direct in "Sitting on a Barbed-Wire Fence" (1965). This song uses the A-A-B form and harmonically is even simpler than the twelve-bar blues progression (it repeats the same two chords over and over). The striking part of this song is Dylan's vocal technique. He uses the song's open-ended structure as a chance to show off his ability to sing over and around the beat in the way of blues titans like Muddy Waters and Robert Johnson. Over a brisk tempo, Dylan (perhaps improvising) begins by singing a particularly ungainly phrase over the first three measures: "I paid fifteen million dollars, twelve hundred and seventy-two cents." Then he lets the band riff for a few measures unaccompanied before adding a second line across two measures, playing with accents and alternately drawing out and clipping words along the way: "I paid one thousand two hundred twenty-seven dollars and fifty-five cents." After a break he completes the stanza with a final irregular line: "See my bulldog bit a rabbit / And my hound dog is sittin' on a barbed-wire fence."[94]

Songs like "Outlaw Blues" and "Barbed-Wire Fence" are essentially exercises, signs of Dylan experimenting with the imagery and performance style of the blues and stretching the form beyond its usual limits. The process, though, was more than just artistic muscle flexing. It produced songs that were coherent extensions of the blues form and could stand in their own right. "Subterranean Homesick Blues" (1965), for example, is both blues and not-blues. As its title suggests, the song is closely allied to the blues genre but offers a new, underground take on it. Structurally, the song only subtly varies the traditional blues form, following the standard harmonic progression exactly but extending beyond the twelve-bar format to an unusual eighteen (plus a four-bar instrumental break after each verse).[95] Lyrically, the song takes off in a completely new direction. Instead of using the A-A-B form, it pieces together a series of fragmented images that together offer an impressionistic look at 1960s youth culture. The song sketches out the drug scene ("Johnny's in the basement / Mixing up the medicine"), satirizes authoritarianism ("Look out kid," each verse nags), and captures the Vietnam-era cynicism about the military ("Join the army if you fail").[96]

Dylan's lyrics may be utterly contemporary on "Subterranean," but the way he delivers them suggests his debts to blues stylists. On first hearing, Dylan seems to sing all the words in a monotone. Except for the short "Look out kid" refrain, the song seems hardly to have a tune. But Dylan brings a spectrum of colors to the performance through his nuanced use of microtones, notes (common in African and blues music) that fall between the intervals on the Western scale. Like the voices of blues singers, his subtly rises and dips to enliven what could be drab, lifeless repetition. The rhythm of Dylan's delivery further adds to the effect. He stretches certain words ("I'm on the paaavement / Thinking about the gooovernment") and places others rhythmically off center. Lines such as "Don't wanna be a bum / You better chew gum" dance in and out of the beat.

More often than in most blues songs, words fall squarely on the beat in "Subterranean." Couplets like "*Walk* on your *tip toes* / *don't try 'No Doz'*" and "*God knows when* / But you're *do*in' it ag*ain*") have a repetitive emphasis reminiscent of a wagging finger in the face, an impression that highlights the picture of a scolding authority figure. Placing words so heavily on the beat is uncommon in blues, but the notion of adapting vocal delivery to the song's message is very much in step with the tradition. Like downhome bluesmen, Dylan here treats words as percussive elements whose placement can either add bite to a beat or loosen its hold. He is both drawing on and altering the downhome blues to create a personalized form that can communicate the messages he wants to convey. His blues have ceased being tributes to his idols and have become vibrant and expressive contemporary outlets.

In a similar way, Dylan adapted country music to his own ends. Country emerged shortly before World War II, drawing on Anglo-Celtic ballads, minstrel and medicine-show songs, blues, church tunes, Tin Pan Alley, and, most immediately, commercial hillbilly singing from earlier in the century. When dealing with such a hybridized form, any generic definition invites exceptions, but certain stylistic traits are prevalent in country. The music tends to feature the open-voiced, sometimes drawled singing of a simple, catchy melody. The singer is often backed by a mixture of electric instruments (such as steel guitar) and acoustic ones (such as string bass and fiddle). Background musicians tend to be muted and unobtrusive, usually anchored by a drummer who supplies a slow, steady beat. Lyrically, country songs draw heavily on rural imagery, often depict a hardscrabble life (rambling men, hard work, and prison are recurrent themes), and frequently invoke the myth of the cowboy and the American West. They also tend to use rich, if sometimes clichéd, imagery in telling tales (generally in the second person) of the promise and perils of romantic love. The songs country-music pioneer Hank Williams recorded in the 1940s and early 1950s project the unequivocal sentimentalism characteristic of so many love songs in the genre. On "Why Don't You Love Me?" he pleads, "Why don't you love me like you used to do? / How come you treat me like a worn-out shoe? . . . My hair's still curly and my eyes are still blue / Why don't you love me like you used to do?" Beginning in the 1950s such sentimental lines and their tuneful melodies were converted by professional songwriters and musicians in Nashville into a formulaic style. Spurred by powerful radio stations such as WSM (Nashville) and WSB (Atlanta) and by popular shows like *Grand Ole Opry*, country became a nationwide commercial bonanza.[97]

Pete Seeger was receptive to forerunners of country like hillbilly songs and cowboy ballads, and he certainly had no aversion to love songs, but he showed little interest in the cultural synthesis being forged in Nashville. After all, it was driven by professional songsmiths with an eye toward making money for a burgeoning commercial industry. Seeger included pop songs in *American Favorite Ballads* to demonstrate that they could become folk songs, but he always tried to distance himself from large-scale efforts to dictate popular taste for profit.

Dylan, though, saw country as another form of roots music and set out to appropriate it. His most direct effort to do so was his 1969 album, *Nashville Skyline*. It was recorded in Nashville with local studio musicians, and the song arrangements prominently feature the Dobro steel guitar (backed on "Lay Lady Lay" by cowbells and light bongos) and the lush sound and soft touch typical of country.[98] Most striking, Dylan seems to have adopted the relaxed persona of the country singer for *Nashville Skyline*. The bitterness and misanthropy so much a part of his earlier efforts have been displaced by a sunny openness. The album cover shows Dylan under blue sky, holding out his acoustic guitar and displaying a disarming smile as he tips his cap to the camera. Dylan's voice reflects this mood, his nasal, whining sound having given way to a open-throated, mellow, almost crooning tone.[99] The album's lyrics, too, place Dylan firmly in the country genre. Some of the songs refer directly to country-music themes. On "Country Pie," for instance, Dylan sings, "Listen to the fiddler play / When he's playin' 'til the break of day / Oh me, oh my / Love that country pie." More frequently, Dylan's debt to country surfaces in his romantic attitude toward love. These songs have no trace of Dylan's trademark sarcasm or surrealism. Instead he expresses pure yearning, lonesomeness, or joy. "Love is all there is," he sings on "I Threw It All Away": "One thing that's certain / You will surely be a-hurtin' / If you throw it all away."[100] The most illustrative track on *Nashville Skyline* is "Girl from the North Country," a remake of a song that had appeared on *The Freewheelin' Bob Dylan* in 1963, during his "folk" period. The song's words and melody are almost identical on the two versions, but the later one features Dylan's "new" voice accompanied by the archetype of that resonant country vocal style, Johnny Cash. Country, this remake seems to suggest, has been in Dylan's songs all along; *Nashville Skyline* just brought it to the forefront.

Indeed, one can see key elements of country songwriting even on Dylan albums that do not directly pay tribute to the genre. Western imagery, for example, recurs in songs from every period of his career. "John Wesley Harding" (1967) tells the tale of an altruistic outlaw who "trav'led with a gun in ev'ry hand." "Isis" (1976) opens like a scene from an old cowboy Western, as a restless husband leaves his wife and rides "straight away / For the wild unknown country."[101] Dylan made the connection to the movies explicit when he wrote the soundtrack for Sam Peckinpah's *Pat Garrett and Billy the Kid* (1973). Although Dylan's "country" voice mysteriously disappeared, love songs reminiscent of the sentimental country-music style appear on many albums from both before and after *Nashville Skyline*. "If Not for You" (1970) chirps,

> If not for you,
> Winter would have no spring,
> Couldn't hear the robin sing
> I just wouldn't have a clue.

And on "You Angel You" (1974) Dylan sings yearningly:

> Never did feel this way before.
> I get up at night and walk the floor.
> If this is love then gimme more
> And more and more and more and more.[102]

A final roots genre that Dylan appropriated was African American religious music—church songs (including gospel and its immediate predecessor, spirituals) that directly praise God and Jesus and generally offer an optimistic vision of salvation.[103] Spirituals were often sung a cappella, but with the advent of gospel around the 1930s, African American religious music became increasingly likely to have instrumental accompaniment (piano, organ, guitar, and perhaps even trumpet or saxophone) and a marked beat (whether by hand claps or drums).[104]

Seeger regularly sang several well-known spirituals and gospel songs, and his concerts and recordings did much to popularize them. He was especially drawn to the power of spirituals within the civil rights struggle. At no point, though, did religious music predominate in his repertoire, and rarely did he compose original religious music.[105] Dylan, too, for most of his career incorporated religiously oriented songs into a primarily secular repertoire. Both *Desire* (1970) and *Planet Waves* (1974), for instance, include songs that are essentially prayers ("Father of the Night" and "Forever Young"). The refrain of "Knockin' on Heaven's Door" features religious imagery over a hymnlike tune: "That long black cloud is comin' down / I feel like I'm knockin' on heaven's door." "God Knows" (1990) matter-of-factly declares that "God knows everything," adding that

God knows there's a purpose
God knows there's a chance
God knows you can rise above the darkest hour of every
    circumstance.[106]

The most striking instances of Dylan invoking religion, though, appear on the three albums he made after he became a born-again Christian: *Slow Train Coming* (1979), *Saved* (1980), and *Shot of Love* (1981). With these releases, Dylan took an approach very different from Seeger's interest in spirituals and gospel. Instead of just trying to understand and appreciate religious music, Dylan worked to enter into that tradition as an active participant and shape it to reflect his personal creed and spiritual needs.

In doing so, Dylan subtly altered the traditions on which he drew. In traditional gospel (predominant between the late forties and early sixties), singers tend to focus on celebrating their faith, exuberantly proclaiming their status as saved, and envisioning the benefits they will enjoy when the day of salvation arrives. On the classic "By and By" (as performed by the Davis Sisters), the narrator imagines that soon "This old soul of mine / Is going home to live with God / All my troubles will soon be gone / That's when I'll make a brand new start." On "Walk around Heaven All Day," the Caravans sing, "One of these mornings; it won't be very long / I'm going to a place where I'll have nothing, nothing, nothing to do / I'll just walk around heaven all day."[107]

Dylan's gospel albums, by contrast, take a more foreboding and less future-oriented stance than these classic gospel tunes. His songs devote less attention to the pleasures of faith and salvation than to the failings of the earthly world that make faith so necessary and so difficult to sustain. He points insistently to signs of social and moral decay in society and envisions apocalyptic punishment for humanity's sins. In "When You Gonna Wake Up?" Dylan paints a picture of ignorance and debauchery that is bleaker and more detailed in its attention to contemporary events than most gospel:

> Counterfeit philosophies have polluted all of your thoughts.
> Karl Marx has got ya by the throat, Henry Kissinger's got you tied
>   up in knots. . . .
> You got innocent men in jail, your insane asylums are filled,
> You got unrighteous doctors dealing drugs that'll never cure
>   your ills.

"Solid Rock," likewise, depicts a world of dichotomous opposites grappling for control:

> It's the ways of the flesh to war against the spirit
> Twenty-four hours a day you can feel it and you can hear it
> Using all the devices under the sun
> And He never give up 'til the battle's lost or won.[108]

The apocalypse is certainly not invisible in gospel.[109] But Dylan's songs are unusual in implying that the outcome in the war between good and evil is very much in doubt. His tunes leave more room for uncertainty than most traditional religious songs. These are songs of struggle as much as songs of faith.

This sense of flux surfaces not just in Dylan's musings about the world as a whole but in highly personalized reflections about his own faith. For all the stridency about his beliefs on the born-again albums, Dylan is more open than most gospel singers about the tortuous path he has taken to reach religion, and, in a highly unusual move, he implies that he is struggling to solidify his faith even as he preaches his newfound creed. Generally, gospel songs depict singers' personal faith as unimpeachably solid. The singers imply that their devoutness is a given that they have never questioned or doubted. Their songs focus instead on the rewards that devotion brings them. If a tune does allow that one's faith possibly could be questioned, it locates the spiritual weakness securely in the past. The classic "How I Got Over," for instance, suggests a period of spiritual weakness in a time so long ago that the narrator can scarcely comprehend it: "How I got over / How I got over / My soul look back in wonder / How I got over." The rest of the song moves on to glorify Jesus for all that he has given the narrator in the intervening years. "The Old Ship of Zion," likewise, admits that once the singer "was lost in sin and sorrow," but it assures that the period of dissolution passed when he found the "ship of Zion": "I got aboard early one morning / I got on board / Ain't no danger in the water / I got on board early one morning."[110]

Dylan expresses his religiosity firmly in his gospel work, but he also chronicles an ongoing tug of war within himself between faith and doubt. Often expressions of righteousness and fallibility appear in the same song. "When He Returns," for instance, asserts boldly that "The strongest wall will crumble and fall to a mighty God." But it continues in the first person to express a series of self-rebuking rhetorical questions: "How long can I stay drunk on fear out in the wilderness? / Can I cast it aside, all this loyalty and this pride?" Similarly, "Are You Ready?" is dominated by repeated chants of the challenge posed in the title song's title: "Are you ready, hope you're ready . . . for the judgment?" But midway through the tune, the narrator seems to feel a wave of uncertainty over whether *he* is up to the test: "Have I surrendered to the will of God / Or am I still acting like the boss? / Am I ready, hope I'm ready."[111] To Dylan, gospel was more than a way to do penance to his newfound God. He used it as a medium in which he could explore his beliefs and grapple with the process of becoming a person of faith. As with his embrace of ballads, blues, and country, Dylan did not just parrot the original practitioners of the style but adapted it to fit his needs.

As a folk stylist, then, Dylan strove both to absorb the essence of individual roots traditions and to stretch the boundaries of each genre. The ultimate expression of this goal came when Dylan tried to break down generic boundaries altogether. Many of Dylan's most striking and enduring songs represent the cross-fertilization of several roots-music genres.[112] "Highway 61 Revisited" (1965), for instance, is a thoroughly hybridized blend of religious, ballad, and blues traditions that twists each genre.[113] The song begins with the biblical story of Abraham, but here God and Abraham talk like urban hipsters:

Oh God said to Abraham, "Kill me a son"
Abe say, "Man, you must be puttin' me on."

From here, each verse shifts to the story of another set of characters, each of whom could have been the basis for a narrative ballad: Georgia Sam and poor Howard (a standard folk character), Mack the Finger and Louie the King, "the rovin' gambler" (another character from folk song).[114] But this is a Dylan-styled ballad, and nothing connects these characters from verse to verse. Instead they have a series of absurdist conversations with each other:

> Well Georgia Sam he had a bloody nose
> Welfare Department they wouldn't give him no clothes
> He asked poor Howard where can I go
> Howard said there's only one place I know
> Sam said tell me quick man I got to run
> Ol' Howard just pointed with his gun
> And said that way down on Highway 61.

This chaos unfolds over a blues accompaniment. The song follows the standard chord progression of downhome blues and features a ringing slide guitar played by Chicago bluesman Michael Bloomfield (the Muddy Waters disciple who had played with Dylan at the Newport festival).[115] Throughout, Dylan employs the vocal gymnastics he picked up from blues stylists, compressing "And I said yes I think it can be easily done" in the third verse but stretching the next line ("Just take everything down to Highway 61") across the beat.

The real-life Highway 61 runs between Minnesota and the blues-soaked Mississippi Delta, a route rich in symbolic significance for Dylan.[116] Appropriately, even as "Highway 61 Revisited" shows a strong debt to the blues, it looks at the genre with new eyes. The song does follow the blues form, for example, but it adds a mocking train whistle to the instrumentation. Dylan uses the blues vocal techniques, but he does not follow the A-A-B lyrical pattern and, in fact, seems to poke fun at the form's penchant for superstitious numerical references:

> Now the fifth daughter on the twelfth night
> Told the first father that things weren't right
> My complexion she said is much too white
> He said come here and step into the light he says hmm you're right
> Let me tell the second mother this has been done
> But the second mother was with the seventh son
> And they were both out on Highway 61.

The song, therefore, takes an irreverent attitude toward its source materials. But it is not an empty send-up. By building the song out of deconstructed genres, Dylan fleshes out the portrayal of a modern, even postapocalyptic world of mindless violence, blocked communication, and empty spectacle.

"Tangled Up in Blue" (1975) also blends roots genres. One could easily imagine it as a simple country love song. It is about a rambling man who became infatuated with a woman who "never escaped [his] mind" and whom he pursues coast to coast. That the song is so much richer than this thin synopsis stems from the fact that Dylan laces country's brand of yearning love with other genres. The blues, for instance, are central to the song's power. Despite what the title suggests, the song has little formal connection to the blues genre. It follows neither the twelve-bar form, nor the harmonic progression, nor the A-A-B lyrical pattern characteristic of the blues. Instead, it evokes the mood of the blues, a more ambivalent and nuanced set of emotions than tends to surface in country music. The song's narrator longs to be with the woman yet feels entrapped by her, seeks yet resists her, can't find her yet can't escape her. "Tangled Up in Blue" is an apt metaphor for these ambiguous feelings. Blues songs rarely convey sentimental joy or melodramatic remorse; they generally deal in a more bittersweet realm, where one feels both joy and sorrow, an emotional charge and edgy melancholy. For better *and* worse, the lives of the narrator and his lover are intertwined.

Dylan draws on the ballad form in "Tangled" to delineate the characters' complex relationship. Initially, the song seems to promise a straightforward story. Its opening lines have a once-upon-a-time feel:

Early one mornin' the sun was shinin',
I was layin' in bed
Wond'rin' if she'd changed at all
If her hair was still red.

Almost immediately, though, Dylan disrupts the narrative's chronology. The rest of the first verse shifts to describe a time when he and his lover were together ("Her folks they said our lives together / Sure was gonna be rough") and then depicts a moment that may represent the narrator leaving the woman behind ("And I was standin' on the side of the road ... Heading out for the East Coast"). The second stanza touches on the time when the couple first encountered each other ("She was married when we first met") but soon shifts to a breakup ("Split up on a dark sad night"). Verse three describes a period of loneliness and longing for the woman, but the fourth verse apparently backtracks to the evening they first met ("She was workin' in a topless place / An' I stopped in for a beer"). Strikingly, the sixth verse seems to transport the story back to the nineteenth century, when an unidentified "he" began "dealing in slaves."[117]

"Tangled," therefore, retains the traditional ballad's focus on character and event but fractures its sense of causation and cohesion. Doing so produces not gibberish but rather a different sense of time, one appropriate to the song's theme. Traditional plot development and resolution would have threatened to overly simplify this uneasy tale of attraction and dissolution. This love affair has no purely good or evil players, takes place in fantasy as much as in reality, and is all-consuming in a way that seems to cut across time.[118] It resists climactic denouement.

If on "Tangled Up in Blue" Dylan juxtaposes and adapts roots genres to preserve ambiguity, on "Idiot Wind" (1975) he evokes traditional musical styles to drum home a single message. The song is a compendium of rage against a former lover, with every verse evoking a straightforward theme: you wronged me and you will pay. To accentuate the inevitability of revenge, Dylan draws on imagery of doom from a wide variety of genres. In one verse, for instance, he uses a threatening religious image: "There's a lone soldier on the cross, smoke pourin' out of a boxcar door." But in the next stanza, he turns to country-western elements, snarling, "Visions of your chestnut mare shoot through my head and are makin' me see stars. / One day you'll be in the ditch, flies buzzin' around your eyes, / Blood on your saddle."[119] At another point, he includes an occult reference reminiscent of the blues, warning that he met a fortune-teller who foretold a lightning strike. Far from suggesting multiple viewpoints, these diverse references sharpen the point of the attack. Ranging across genres, Dylan piles poison upon poison.

Even Dylan's most original and idiosyncratic work, therefore, depended on American roots music. Most directly, he turned to traditional genres for lyrical and musical ideas. More subtly, he played with the stylistic conventions of these genres for expressive purposes. Long after his "folk" phase had supposedly passed, Dylan's output remained firmly embedded in the folk process.

As if to emphasize these continuities, in the early 1990s Dylan issued two albums that directly hearkened back to his debut release of roots music thirty years before. Like *Bob Dylan* (1962), *Good as I Been to You* (1992) and *World Gone Wrong* (1993) feature Dylan performing covers of old ballads and blues, accompanied only by his acoustic guitar and harmonica.[120] Dylan followed these albums with *Time Out of Mind*, an alternately anguished, wistful, and bemused meditation on mortality. The album was hailed as Dylan's most creative and deeply personal work in decades. For all its stark originality, though, *Time Out of Mind* shows Dylan reaching back as artfully as ever for American roots traditions. The album blends dirt-road blues, labyrinthian ballads, transcendent spirituals, and heartsick country love songs. Critic Alex Ross finds that "Tryin' to Get to

Heaven" alone borrows "a dozen or more" phrases from the "Spirituals" chapters of Alan Lomax's *Folk Songs of North America*. More than specific references, though, it is the mood of the album that suggests an iron link to roots traditions. These songs have a blurred quality, as if recorded at a tumbledown roadhouse in 1937, not in a studio in 1997. The album unfolds at a dreamlike pace that beckons back to a past that has receded but never departed from memory.

Time Out of Mind won Dylan a Grammy and signaled definitively that he remains a creative force in his own right at the turn of the century. In an ironic twist, though, Dylan has become something of a roots figure himself over the last several years. Ever since the Byrds scored a smash hit in 1965 with their version of "Mr. Tambourine Man," other pop artists have appropriated Dylan songs as their own. Now, though, younger musicians approach Dylan's material from a distance, in a manner not so different from the way in which Dylan appropriated the songs of Blind Lemon Jefferson or Bukka White. In 1987 the arty, postpunk band Siouxsie and the Banshees recorded "This Wheel's on Fire," which had appeared on Dylan's *Basement Tapes* in 1975. In 1991 the soul group the O'Jays gave a gospel flavor to Dylan's "Emotionally Yours" (from *Empire Burlesque* [1985]). British rocker P. J. Harvey released a pounding version of "Highway 61 Revisited" (in waltz time) in 1993. In 1994 Senegalese pop star Youssou N'Dour recorded Dylan's "Chimes of Freedom" (*Another Side of Bob Dylan* [1963]) in his native Wolof language. In 1996 the blaring heavy metal group Ministry showed its sensitive side by covering Dylan's "Lay Lady Lay" (from *Nashville Skyline*).[121]

Other tributes to Dylan have memorialized him more directly. In 1992 Dylan's thirty-year recording career was commemorated with a gala concert at Madison Square Garden, reminiscent of the tributes held in the 1950s and 1960s for Woody Guthrie and Lead Belly. At such occasions, Dylan tends to be painted as a relic from the sixties, the creator of a set of songs that spoke to the baby-boom generation, primarily between 1963 and 1970. When Dylan appeared at Woodstock '94, the press treated him mainly as a link to the era of the original festival twenty-five years before, when Dylan's status as a generational icon was such that his decision to *spurn* the festival was national news.[122] In 1990, likewise, when *Life* magazine honored him as one of the "100 most important Americans of the century," it dubbed him the "Electric Minstrel of Times That Were A' Changin'." Dylan's identity with the past is such that when the critical accolades began pouring in for *Time Out of Mind*, the press seemed almost surprised to hear he was still around: "Dylan Lives," announced a 1997

Newsweek cover story, accompanied by black-and-white photos of the grizzled eminence.[123]

Dylan's legacy, though, transcends generational landmarks such as "The Times They Are A-Changin'" and even extends beyond creative gems like "Highway 61 Revisited" and "Tangled Up in Blue." These individual songs will likely be remembered, just as his contemporaries will probably always recall him fondly as their powerful (if reluctant) generational spokesperson. But Dylan's most enduring product is the example he offered of how to negotiate the relationship between past and present. He demonstrated that dramatic, innovative, even angry change could at the same time be evolutionary and firmly rooted. Some of Dylan's legatees have understood the point. In 1987 the Irish group U2 felt a vague need to reinvigorate their music. Although they were then the most popular rock band in the world, they felt they were drifting. Bono, the band's vocalist, sought out Bob Dylan, fretting, "The music of U2 is in space somewhere. There is no particular musical roots or heritage for us. In Ireland there is a tradition, but we've never plugged into it." "Well, you have to reach back into music," Dylan told him. "You have to reach back." He steered the band to American roots music, spurring them to embark on their own personal exploration of blues, gospel, jazz, and folk traditions. In 1988 this journey, chronicled in the movie *Rattle and Hum*, yielded a triple-platinum album of the same name.[124]

Bruce Springsteen has appreciated Dylan's broader legacy as well. When Dylan was inducted into the Rock and Roll Hall of Fame in 1988, Springsteen gave a speech in honor of his idol. Instead of gushing over specific old songs, he praised Dylan for having shown how to make *new* songs. Dylan, he said, "had the vision and the talent to make a pop song that contained the whole world. He invented a new way a pop singer could sound, broke through the limitations of what a recording artist could achieve and changed the face of rock-'n'-roll forever."[125]

Dylan showed that even in a postindustrial, pop rock culture, a folk stylist could create relevant, contemporary songs rooted in tradition. The folk revival, Dylan's career demonstrated, need not be backward-looking, marginalized, or antimodern—and it could continue long after the gates of the Newport Folk Festival closed.

CODA

At the turn of the twenty-first century, the results of a century of American folk revivalism are all around us. Woody Guthrie's "This Land Is Your Land" is practically an alternative national anthem, sung by schoolchildren from nursery school on. Guthrie's and Lead Belly's albums are reissued by the Smithsonian-owned Folkways label and are sold in the museum's gift shops. Lead Belly and Guthrie are in the Rock and Roll Hall of Fame, as are Willie Dixon, Muddy Waters, Leonard Chess, Pete Seeger, and Bob Dylan. Waters was voted "All-Time Favorite Artist" in *Living Blues* magazine's 1994 Readers' Awards, and the reissue of the 1941 recordings he made for Alan Lomax won "Best Blues Album (historical recording)." With some justification, though, one might say that success in the realm of public memory is measured more in postage stamps than in album sales. In 1994 Waters, along with six other blues and jazz greats, was memorialized by the U.S. Postal Service with a stamp in its Legends of American Music Series. In 1998 Guthrie and Lead Belly received Legends stamps of their own.[1]

At the White House in 1986, Alan Lomax was one of a dozen "titans of the arts" to whom President Reagan presented the National Medal of the Arts. In 1994 Lomax's romantic reminiscences about his collecting days, *Land Where the Blues Began*, won the National Book Critics Circle Award in nonfiction. In 1997 Rounder Records launched a five-year project to issue "The Alan Lomax Collection," more than one hundred compact discs covering Lomax's six decades of field recording.[2]

Pete Seeger continues to write his regular column (now called "Appleseeds") for *Sing Out!* and is the subject of gentle tributes by the likes of Bill Moyers on public television. "Wimoweh" appeared in the 1994 Disney blockbuster *The Lion King* and was featured not only on the film's soundtrack but also in a Burger King commercial promoting *Lion King* products. Twice within two months that fall Seeger set aside his blue jeans for a black tuxedo (one that had been made originally for his father in 1922) and journeyed to Washington. In mid-October, President Clinton honored Seeger with the National Medal of the Arts. Early in December, Clinton presented him with a Kennedy Center Honors award for a lifetime of achievement in the arts. When Seeger won his spot in the Rock and Roll Hall of Fame in 1996, he stood out at the gala induction ceremony with a characteristically flamboyant act of unflamboyance, leaving the stage without uttering a word. In 1998 Appleseed Recordings, an independent record company with activist leanings, issued *Where Have All the Flowers Gone: The Songs of Pete Seeger*, a two-CD tribute. Musicians ranging from Bruce Springsteen to pop-blueswoman Bonnie Raitt to "folk-punk" rocker Ani DiFranco covered songs Seeger had written or adapted.[3]

As the critically acclaimed *Time Out of Mind* returned Bob Dylan to pop preeminence, he continued to receive grand and sometimes startling tributes to his past. In December 1997, he, too, received a Kennedy Center Honors award. That fall, wearing a white cowboy hat for the occasion, Dylan gave a command performance for Pope John Paul II at a religious congress in Bologna. The pope quoted from "Blowin' in the Wind" in his address to a crowd of two hundred thousand and then reportedly listened with eyes closed as Dylan sang "Knockin' on Heaven's Door" and "A Hard Rain's A-Gonna Fall." In the midst of all the accolades, Dylan invoked a predictably eclectic mix of musical forefathers. In the summer of 1997, he suffered a brush with death from a viral infection in the sac around his heart. Columbia Records issued an update on his condition and quoted Dylan: "I'm just glad to be feeling better. I really thought I'd be seeing Elvis soon." In 1998 when *Time Out of Mind* won a Grammy award for "Album of the Year," Dylan in his acceptance speech paid tribute to another 1950s rock hero, Buddy Holly (who died in 1959), saying that he had felt Holly "with us all the time we were making this record." He wrapped up with a quotation from "the immortal Robert Johnson": "The stuff we got'll blow your brains out."[4]

The folk revival of the twentieth century, though, was about more than canonizing its major players. Its leaders hoped to keep folk music alive and generative. Some recent efforts along these lines would please almost everyone involved in the revival. Hundreds of roots-music festivals, for instance, are held annually across the country, catering to audiences for everything from blues to bluegrass, hammered dulcimer to zydeco. In 1998 British singer-songwriter Billy Bragg and retro-country rockers Wilco issued *Mermaid Avenue*, an album of new tunes written to accompany recently rediscovered Woody Guthrie lyrics from the 1940s and 1950s, a period of professional and, increasingly, physical decline for Guthrie. The album, in effect, gave voice to a silent period in a folk hero's career.[5]

Contemporary revivalists were more uncertain about the spectacular success enjoyed by another effort to bring the past to life—the House of Blues, a chain of blues-themed clubs/restaurants/gift shops launched in 1992 by the founder of the Hard Rock Cafe. House of Blues outlets are decorated to evoke the stark rural settings where the blues were born. For the Los Angeles site, workers methodically disassembled the cotton gin house in Clarksdale, Mississippi, where Muddy Waters had worked and trucked it (along with Mississippi dirt) to Sunset Strip, where it was rebuilt inside the new club. Supporters of the House of Blues concept see it as a chance to spread the word about the genre (and employ its practitioners) like never before. Detractors see a Disneyesque caricature of blues culture that cares more about selling T-shirts than preserving a folk tradition.[6]

If revivalists are ambivalent about House of Blues, they might be simply befuddled by the revival efforts of the bands Red Hot Chili Peppers and Soul Asylum. In the late 1980s, the Chili Peppers began to be known for an explosive mix of funk and rock that—coupled with their penchant for performing with their muscular bodies covered in little but tattoos—propelled them to the top of the charts. In 1993 their rapid-fire single "Give It Away" won a Grammy award for "best hard rock performance." But the band's bassist, Flea, insisted that the tune was not hard rock: " 'Give It Away,' " he said backstage at the ceremony, "without a doubt is a folk song." That same week, the postpunk band Soul Asylum expressed its allegiance to roots traditions. Describing the band's music, with its grinding guitars and shouted lyrics, lead singer Dave Pirner says, "It's Woody Guthrie and it's punk rock. . . . I started out with punk rock, and I discovered Woody Guthrie, and I realized it was all the same thing."[7]

Flea's and Pirner's statements may have been cynical publicity gestures, designed to get critics to take their bands seriously. Or perhaps they were genuine moments of self-reflection in which the performers recognized that their free-ranging eclecticism had roots in the folk-revival process of appropriating and renewing old music. The specific meaning of Flea's and Pirner's tributes are debatable, but the ease with which they invoked traditions and the expectation that their allusions would have resonance for their fans suggest the extent of the folk revival's reach in this century.

Looking back on twentieth-century folk revivalism, most accounts tend to focus on two moments—the period of strong institutional support for folk music in the 1930s and the time of pop commercial success in the 1960s. But the effort to preserve and popularize roots music constitutes one of the powerful underlying currents that runs through the century's culture and continues to flow today. In using roots music to undergird their pop sound, Flea and Pirner drew on a tradition that went back to Francis James Child pondering ballad texts in Harvard's library, John and Alan Lomax recording Lead Belly in a Louisiana prison, Willie Dixon tutoring the Rolling Stones in the Chess studios, Pete Seeger studying banjo technique in the Archive of American Folk-Song, and Bob Dylan playing by Woody Guthrie's side in Greystone Hospital. Most directly, these moments (and the revival efforts that emerged from them) shaped how Americans remember the country's musical past. More broadly, they established that the backward glance can be more than nostalgic—that memory can create American culture anew.

NOTES

INTRODUCTION

1. Other historians have filled some of these gaps. Readers thirsting for a fuller account of Guthrie's career should turn to Joe Klein's wonderfully rich *Woody Guthrie* and to the section on Guthrie in Charles J. Shindo's insightful *Dust Bowl Migrants in the American Imagination*. Robert Cantwell has published several provocative pieces on the sixties folk revival, and his book *When We Were Good* is the most wide ranging and intellectually adventurous exploration of the subject to date.
2. Hitchcock, *Music in the United States*, 43–44; Rockwell, *All American Music*, 3.
3. Scheurer, *American Popular Music*, 87–88; Wilder, *American Popular Song*; Hamm, *Yesterdays*.
4. It might be argued that even as men and women pursue the same basic strategies of folk music collecting, they bring different perspectives to the task. This hypothesis would be worth exploring in a future study.

CHAPTER ONE

1. "Discovery" in Burke, *Popular Culture*, 6; "learned culture" in ibid., 8; "Unless our literature" in Bluestein, *Poplore*, 35; for Herder on folk forms and the Enlightenment, see Burke, *Popular Culture*, 9–11, and Bluestein, *Poplore*, 38.
2. Bendix, *In Search of Authenticity*, 41; Burke, *Popular Culture*, 3, 10.
3. Friedman, *Ballad Revival*, 83, 123; Harker, *Fakesong*, 9–13.
4. Dugaw, "Popular Marketing of 'Old Ballads,'" 72–80. Harker (*Fakesong*, 5–6) and Stewart (*Crimes of Writing*, 110) attribute authorship to Ambrose Phillips, an assertion rejected by Dugaw and Friedman (*Ballad Revival*, 147). The punctuation and capitalization given here appears in the original book titles.
5. Harker, *Fakesong*, 27–28.

6. Dugaw, "Popular Marketing of 'Old Ballads,'" 83; Friedman, *Ballad Revival*, 220–11, 226–27.

7. Herder himself had a complicated stance on the idea of a national culture. On the one hand, he took a strong interest in international folk expression (Burke, *Popular Culture*, 11) and called national pride "absurd, ridiculous, and harmful" (in Bendix, *In Search of Authenticity*, 41). On the other hand, he opposed the universalism of the Enlightenment and, through his concept of the *Volk*, sought to identify what was distinctive and unique in the German experience (Bluestein, *Poplore*, 30–31). Bluestein feels Herder encouraged national cultural identity as a step toward a wider internationalism (*Poplore*, 37–40). Increasingly, though, Herder's followers applied his ideas toward more narrowly nationalistic ends (Burke, *Popular Culture*, 11).

8. Bluestein, *Poplore*, 32; Burke, *Popular Culture*, 4–7; Friedman, *Ballad Revival*, 232, 248.

9. In Bendix, *In Search of Authenticity*, 40, 38; in Burke, *Popular Culture*, 12, 8, 3.

10. Burke, *Popular Culture*, 16, 4, 18.

11. Stewart, *Crimes of Writing*, 103–5. Stewart traces the "artifactualization" of the ballad—the process by which ballads became defined as fixed entities created in the distant past, whose worth was measured by their purity of form or "authenticity."

12. Bradford, *As God Made Them*, 202, 212–13, 232–35; McMurtry, *English Language, English Literature*, 89; Gummere, "Day with Professor Child," 422.

13. Zumwalt, *American Folklore Scholarship*, 45. Michael Bell notes that in Child's entry on ballads for *Johnson's Universal Encyclopdia* (1874) Child used the terms "popular" and "people" instead of "folk," even though the last term had already been coined. Bell speculates that Child was uncomfortable with German romanticism's tendency to use "folk" to suggest an all-encompassing historical community stretching back to the dawn of time. Child's treatment of the ballad, Bell feels, was more historically precise. He used "popular" to describe a type of classless unity that he believed had existed in the period before print culture emerged. At the same time, Bell notes that Child's students had no qualms about the term "folk" and that when in 1888 they founded the American Folklore Society, they named Child its first president (Bell, "'No Borders to the Ballad Maker's Art,'" 290–92, 305).

14. "Narrative song" and "common treasure" in Child, "Ballad Poetry," 365–66; "sealed or dried up" in Harker, *Fakesong*, 114.

15. Child, "Ballad Poetry," 366–67; McMurtry, *English Language, English Literature*, 104.

16. In Zumwalt, *American Folklore Scholarship*, 48. Zumwalt notes that Child did spend eight weeks in England and Scotland in 1873, collecting ballads from both manuscript and oral sources.

17. "Indifferent quality" in Child, *The English and Scottish Popular Ballads*, 1:vii; "not at hand" in Harker, *Fakesong*, 113; McMurtry, *English Language, English Literature*, 104.

18. In Gummere, "Day with Professor Child," 422.

19. Harker, *Fakesong*, 116; McMurtry, *English Language, English Literature*, 105–8; Bendix, *In Search of Authenticity*, 84.

20. In 1860 Child published a second edition of the eight-volume set he had produced in 1857–58. Child, *English and Scottish Ballads*, 1:vii; Zumwalt, *American Folklore Scholarship*, 46.

21. Child, *The English and Scottish Popular Ballads*, 1:vii; Zumwalt, *American Folklore Scholarship*, 47. Zumwalt notes that Child issued the work in ten parts, which in 1898 were

combined into five volumes. George Lyman Kittredge, Child's disciple at Harvard, published the last volume two years after Child's death.

22. Kittredge, "Francis James Child," xxv, xxix; Stewart, *Crimes of Writing*, 102.

23. In Harker, *Fakesong*, 113. Harker estimates that for *English and Scottish Ballads* (1857–58) Child drew 25 percent of his texts from the published works of Thomas Percy and Walter Scott and that 70 percent of the texts came from a group of seven predecessors.

24. Child, *English and Scottish Popular Ballads*, 1:x.

25. "Improved" in Child, *English and Scottish Popular Ballads*, 1:x; "tasteless" in Harker, *Fakesong*, 118; Gummere, "Day with Professor Child," 423–24.

26. Shapiro, *Appalachia on Our Mind*, 244. Linn (*That Half-Barbaric Twang*, 155 n. 32) indicates that by the early 1900s these stories made use of ballads. Julian Ralph's story "The Transformation of Em Durham" (1903) uses the Child ballad "Lady Margaret"; Lucy Furman draws on the Child ballad "Barbary Allen" and other ballads in "Hard-Hearted Barbary Allen" (1912) and "Mothering on Perilous" (1911).

27. Edmonds, "Songs from the Mountains of North Carolina." Examples of work that appeared following Edmonds's article include Newell, "Early American Ballads" (1899); Raymond, "British Ballads in Our Southern Highlands" (1899); Belden, "Study of Folk-Song in America" (1905); Kittredge, "Ballads and Rhymes from Kentucky" (1907); Beatty, "Some Ballad Variants and Songs" (1909); Bascam, "Ballads of Western North Carolina" (1909); Coombs, "Traditional Ballad from the Kentucky Mountains" (1910); Kittredge, "Various Ballads" (1913); Perrow, "Songs and Rhymes from the South" (March 1912, June 1913, June 1915); Kittredge, "Ballads and Songs" (1917).

28. Kittredge, "Ballads and Rhymes from Kentucky," 254.

29. Kittredge to Arthur Palmer Hudson, in Wilgus, *Anglo-American Folksong Scholarship*, 145.

30. Whisnant, *All That Is Native and Fine*, 7. Whisnant gives a detailed analysis of the cultural work of the settlement schools. Berea was actually founded in 1855 as a one-room district school, but it did not accept its first freshmen until 1869–70 (*Berea College Catalogue*, 6–7).

31. Whisnant, *All That Is Native and Fine*, 110–11.

32. Shearin, "British Ballads in the Cumberland Mountains," 313, 327.

33. E.g., Perrow, "Songs and Rhymes from the South" (March 1912, June 1913, June 1915); Josiah Combs, a student of Shearin's, published with him "A Syllabus of Kentucky Folk-Songs" (1911) (Whisnant, *All That Is Native and Fine*, 91). Frank Brown began amassing what became a huge collection in the Carolinas in 1912 (Wilgus, *Anglo-American Folksong Scholarship*, 196).

34. Wilgus, *Anglo-American Folksong Scholarship*, 145; Shapiro, *Appalachia on Our Mind*, 250.

35. In Whisnant, *All That Is Native and Fine*, 54; Shapiro, *Appalachia on Our Mind*, 251.

36. Whisnant, *All That Is Native and Fine*, 56; D. K. Wilgus reports that thirteen of the twenty songs in McGill's *Folk Songs of the Kentucky Mountains* (1917) were Child ballads (Wilgus, *Anglo-American Folksong Scholarship*, 169).

As early as 1904 Emma Bell Miles had argued that folk song need not disappear but rather could still be a vibrant part of contemporary culture. She, too, stressed the British roots of the mountain ballads, but she was among the first to recognize that the mountaineers' music, in its current form, was "peculiarly American." Her hope, however, was that outsiders could transform this music into high art, that it would "one day give birth to a music that shall take a high place among the world's great schools of expression" (Miles, "Some Real American Music," 118, 123).

37. E.g., Furman's *Mothering on Perilous* was serialized in *Century Magazine* in 1910–11. See Whisnant, *All That Is Native and Fine*, 85–89, for a discussion of Furman's work; Wilgus, *Anglo-American Folksong Scholarship*, 167; Whisnant, *All That Is Native and Fine*, 54–56.

38. McGill's *Folk Songs* and Wyman and Brockway's *Lonesome Tunes* were paperback.

39. Of the mountain people whom Wyman, Brockway, and McGill cited for contributing songs, ten out of fifteen were women in Wyman and Brockway's *Lonesome Tunes*, seven out of nine in McGill's *Folk Songs* and four out of eight in Wyman and Brockway's *Twenty Kentucky Mountain Songs*; Campbell and Sharp, *English Folk Songs from the Southern Appalachians*.

40. Ives, *Joe Scott*, 393–96. Anne and Norm Cohen contrast domestic music with what they call the "assembly tradition"—music played at public gatherings such as "local dances, parties, cornhuskings, land sales, weddings, medicine shows, fiddle conventions and contests, political rallies, street singing, church music, and even professional concerts." The two traditions, they note, had substantially different repertoires (Cohen and Cohen, "Folk and Hillbilly Music," 52, 53).

41. Karpeles, *Cecil Sharp*, 141, 154–55; Whisnant, *All That Is Native and Fine*, 116; Shapiro, *Appalachia on Our Mind*, 317–55.

42. Karpeles, *Cecil Sharp*, 141, 168; Cohen and Cohen, "Folk and Hillbilly Music," 52.

43. Campbell and Sharp, *English Folk Songs from the Southern Appalachians*, xii; Wilgus, *Anglo-American Folksong Scholarship*, 149.

Olive Dame Campbell is listed as a coauthor of *English Folk Songs from the Southern Appalachians* because she contributed the songs she had collected before Sharp's arrival in the mountains, but she did not travel with Sharp on his expeditions, and she had little to do with writing or arranging the actual book (Karpeles, *Cecil Sharp*, 141–42). Her husband, John C. Campbell, who headed the Southern Highlands Division of the Russell Sage Foundation, did travel with Sharp on his first trip, and he helped direct Sharp to promising locations on future expeditions (Campbell and Sharp, *English Folk Songs from the Southern Appalachians*, iv).

44. Campbell and Sharp, *English Folk Songs from the Southern Appalachians*, 156.

45. Ibid., xxii.

46. Karpeles, *Cecil Sharp*, 54, 46. In 1919, Sharp published *English Folk Songs*, in which he harmonized twelve songs from *English Folk Songs from the Southern Appalachians* for piano accompaniment.

47. Harker, *Fakesong*, 185. Sharp consistently uses the male pronouns in his writings.

48. In ibid., 186.

49. "The value of such songs" in Campbell and Sharp, *English Folk Songs from the Southern Appalachians*, xx. As early as 1906 Sharp had published *English Folk Songs for Schools* (with Sabine Baring Gould). In 1919 Britain's Board of Education appointed Sharp "Occasional Inspector Training Colleges in Folk Song and Dancing" (Karpeles,

Cecil Sharp, 58, 174); "ideal musical food" and "every English child" in Boyes, *Imagined Village*, 67, 45.

50. Campbell and Sharp, *English Folk Songs from the Southern Appalachians*, xx.

51. "Flood the streets" in Harker, *Fakesong*, 185; Boyes, *Imagined Village*, 65.

52. In Karpeles, *Cecil Sharp*, 145–46 (my emphasis).

53. Ibid., 140.

54. Campbell and Sharp, *English Folk Songs from the Southern Appalachians*, iv–v.

55. Ibid., v–vii.

56. In Karpeles, *Cecil Sharp*, 146.

57. Campbell and Sharp, *English Folk Songs from the Southern Appalachians*, vii; diary cited in Harker, *Fakesong*, 202.

58. Campbell and Sharp, *English Folk Songs from the Southern Appalachians*, xx. Whisnant (*All That Is Native and Fine*, 92) discusses racism among settlement school teachers.

59. Ogren, *Jazz Revolution*, 11.

60. Whisnant, *All That Is Native and Fine*, 125; Campbell and Sharp, *English Folk Songs from the Southern Appalachians*, ix; Wilgus, *Anglo-American Folksong Scholarship*, 171.

61. Whisnant, *All That Is Native and Fine*, e.g., 119–24; *Thirteenth Census of the United States*, 588.

62. In Karpeles, *Cecil Sharp*, 158; 1910 census data in Turner, "Demography of Black Appalachia," 238.

63. Toll, *Blacking Up*, 34, 40, 60 n. 29, 30, 27; Lott, *Love and Theft*, 103.

64. Pike, *Jubilee Singers*, 42–46, 73; Marsh, *Story of the Jubilee Singers*, 29, 40–41, 50.

65. Pike, *Jubilee Singers*, 134.

66. E.g., ibid.; Pike, *Singing Campaign for Ten Thousand Pounds*; Marsh, *Story of the Jubilee Singers*.

67. Lovell, *Black Song*, 408; preface to 1909 edition, in Dett, *Religious Folk-Songs of the Negro*, ix; Barton, *Old Plantation Hymns*, 3.

68. Lawrence Levine quotes one former slave as complaining after a concert, "Dose are de same ole tunes, but some way dey do'n sound right" and another as protesting, "I do not like the way they have messed up our songs with classical music" (in Levine, *Black Culture and Black Consciousness*, 166); Cincinnati advertisement cited in Pike, *Jubilee Singers*, 77; Toll, *Blacking Up*, 236.

69. Levine, *Black Culture and Black Consciousness*, 155; Higginson, "Negro Spirituals," 694.

70. Green, "P.L. 94-201," 277; Allen, Ware, and Garrison, eds., *Slave Songs*, iii; Hoyt, introduction to Taylor, *Collection of Revival Hymns*, iv, v; preface to 1891 edition of *Cabin and Plantation Songs* cited in Dett, *Religious Folk-Songs of the Negro*, vii.

Taylor may have been the first African American to publish a book of African American song. He, too, wrote self-consciously of the importance of preserving spirituals as a folk song heritage. He particularly focused on trying to prevent the songs from disappearing from blacks' collective memory: "While these songs remain[,] the colored people, like the Jews of old, will remember that 'they were once bondsmen in Egypt'; and then they will go their way with memory on the alert, lest a worse thing come unto them" (Taylor, *Collection of Revival Hymns*, 4).

71. Fenner, *Cabin and Plantation Songs*, v–vi. See also Levine, *Black Culture and Black Consciousness*, 162.

72. Lovell, *Black Songs*, 403.

73. Allen, Ware, and Garrison, *Slave Songs*, 14. The actual meaning inherent in spirituals is a matter of scholarly debate (see chap. 5, n. 232). Perhaps to blacks' ears, songs that seemed to advocate patience and acceptance actually contained oppositional messages; whites, though, do not seem to have been aware of this possibility.

74. Hoyt, in Taylor, *Collection of Revival Hymns*, iii; Barton, *Old Plantation Hymns*, 3; Moton, preface to the 1909 edition of *Religious Folk Songs of the Negro* cited in Dett, *Religious Folk-Songs of the Negro*, ix; Higginson, "Negro Spirituals," 685.

75. In Sosna, *In Search of the Silent South*, 44–45. As Sosna points out, in the years after World War I, Odum became far more moderate on racial issues.
      In addition to Odum, other academics who collected black songs include Frank C. Brown, E. C. Perrow, C. Alphonso Smith, Newman Ivey White, and Henry C. Davis (Wilgus, *Anglo-American Folksong Scholarship*, 153).

76. Interestingly, most recent scholars seem to have accepted the black-white dichotomy in their own work. Black and white folk music are almost always treated in separate books. Exceptions include Russell's *Blacks, Whites, and Blues* (1970), Green's *Only a Miner* (1971); and Wilgus's *Anglo-American Folksong Scholarship since 1898* (1959), which in an appendix (345–64) traces the historiographical debate about the Anglo versus African roots of spirituals.

77. Lomax, *Adventures of a Ballad Hunter*, 19–20, 33–39; Porterfield, *Last Cavalier*, 17–18, 59, 114–15, 119, 139–40, 161, 490 n. 30, 499 n. 7. Porterfield notes that Lomax also encountered the cowboys' music through so-called cowboy tournaments, the forerunners of rodeos. In his 1947 autobiography, Lomax claims that he began writing down cowboy songs as a young boy and that by the time he went to the University of Texas he carried with him in his trunk a tight roll of cowboy song manuscripts; he showed the collection to an English professor, he writes, who ridiculed the songs. Porterfield questions the veracity of this story. He offers evidence that Lomax may have been the anonymous author of a nostalgic piece about cowboy songs ("The Minstrelsy of the Mexican Border") that appeared in the January 1898 issue of the *University of Texas Magazine*. Aside from this article, though, Porterfield finds no concrete evidence of Lomax's active engagement with cowboy music before 1906.

78. Porterfield, *Last Cavalier*, 153, 233, 147. Porterfield challenges the legend that Lomax traveled by horseback gathering songs for the book, noting that the manuscript was essentially complete before Lomax began the collecting expeditions that the Sheldon Fellowship funded. Although Lomax's book helped popularize "Home on the Range," which soon became a nationwide hit, Porterfield notes that a half-million-dollar lawsuit established that the song had actually been composed by a Kansas doctor in 1873.

79. Lomax, *Cowboy Songs*, xxii.

80. The extent of Lomax's collecting expeditions may have been exaggerated in subsequent accounts (see note 78, above), but in his use of a recording machine they were pioneering nonetheless (see Porterfield, *Last Cavalier*, 147–49).

81. Wilgus, *Anglo-American Folksong Scholarship*, 161; Lomax, *Cowboy Songs*, xxiii.

82. Lomax, *Cowboy Songs*, xvii–xviii, xxi.

83. Ibid., xvii, xxiv.

84. McNutt, "Beyond Regionalism," 146; Porterfield, *Last Cavalier*, 181–269.

85. Malone, *Singing Cowboys*, 90–91; Malone, *Country Music, U.S.A.*, 138.

86. Shapiro, *Appalachia on Our Mind*, 302 n. 2.

87. Malone, *Country Music, U.S.A.*, 34–36; Foreman, "Jazz and Race Records," 273.

88. Porterfield, *Jimmie Rodgers*, 92; Oliver, *Songsters and Saints*, 1, 9.

89. Dixon and Godrich, *Recording the Blues*, 67, 41; Oster, *Living Country Blues*, 21; Titon, *Early Downhome Blues*, 206; Malone, *Country Music, U.S.A.*, 37.

90. Malone, *Country Music, U.S.A.*, 37–38. Richard A. Peterson (citing personal correspondence from Robert Pinson) questions whether an unlabeled custom pressing was actually made, noting that no copies have surfaced despite decades of hunting by record collectors (*Creating Country Music*, 1997, 241 n. 15).

91. Malone, *Country Music, U.S.A.*, 36, 38; Wolfe, "Ralph Peer at Work," 10–11, 68; Porterfield, *Jimmie Rodgers*, 105; Wolfe, "Columbia Records and Old-Time Music," 120.

92. Cohen and Cohen, "Folk and Hillbilly Music," 53; Linn (*That Half-Barbaric Twang*, 138–39) suggests that the market for hillbilly music became more nationwide in the late twenties and thirties, as migration from the rural South increased and powerful clear-channel radio stations broadcast the music across the country. See Peterson's *Creating Country Music* (67–80, 89–94) for a discussion of how early promoters worked to construct a hillbilly image that would have national appeal.

93. Wolfe, "Columbia Records and Old-Time Music," 119, 150. Wolfe notes that Columbia had a "no-returns" policy with its dealers, so these figures more accurately reflect sales to dealers than retail sales.

94. Cohen and Cohen, "Folk and Hillbilly Music," 52–54. After analyzing the body of recordings made by the folklorists and the commercial collectors, the Cohens conclude that "the academic collectors and the A & R men were collecting at opposite ends of the total spectrum of southern mountain folk music."

95. Linn, *That Half-Barbaric Twang*, 138–39; Whisnant, *All That Is Native and Fine*, 183; Malone, *Country Music, U.S.A.*, 37. Anne and Norm Cohen find that Sharp recorded very few instrumentals and only one piece of singing with instrumental accompaniment ("Folk and Hillbilly Music," 52).

96. In Wolfe, "Ralph Peer at Work," 10.

97. Porterfield, *Jimmie Rodgers*, 99.

98. In Kahn, "Carter Family," 108; in Wolfe, "Toward a Contextual Approach to Old-Time Music," 74; Malone, *Country Music, U.S.A.*, 80.

99. Malone, *Country Music, U.S.A.*, 67. "I always insisted" in oral history interview of Peer by Lillian Borgeson, undated session (between January and May) 1959, in Porterfield, *Jimmie Rodgers*, 96; "We ran into a snag" in Peer, "Discovery of the First Hillbilly Great," 20. Rodgers did not meet his deadline and in fact struggled throughout his career to produce original material (Porterfield, *Jimmie Rodgers*, 118–19); Malone, *Country Music, U.S.A.*, 81. "T for Texas" and "My Lovin' Gal, Lucille" are also known as "Blue Yodel" and "Blue Yodel—No. II," respectively (Porterfield, *Jimmie Rodgers*, 119, 138).

Copyrighting folk song arrangements is a controversial practice, but countless folklorists have done it since Peer's time.

100. Porterfield, *Jimmie Rodgers*, 180, 186, 197 n. 15. Porterfield finds that very little material actually was transferred to Peer, who bought Southern back in 1932 (197 n. 15).

101. Oliver, *Songsters and Saints*, 8; Porterfield, *Last Cavalier*, 149; Karpeles, *Cecil Sharp*, 154.

102. Malone, *Country Music, U.S.A.*, 38.

103. Howard W. Odum and Guy B. Johnson do discuss the folk roots of commercial blues in *Negro Workaday Songs*, 23–34.

104. The Hill Billies also appeared in a fifteen-minute short for Warner Brothers (Malone, *Country Music, U.S.A.*, 40); Porterfield, *Jimmie Rodgers*, 216.

105. Niven, *Carl Sandburg*, 447, 444, 33–37.

106. Sandburg, *American Songbag*, ix.

107. Kodish, *Good Friends and Bad Enemies*, 16, 21–23, 29, 31, 88. Kodish quotes Ron Goulart's characterization (in his *Popular History of the Pulp Magazine* [1975]) of *Adventure* as "the *Atlantic Monthly* of the pulps."

108. Ibid., 59, 57, 189, 159; Wilgus, *Anglo-American Folksong Scholarship*, 180. In the 1950s, the archive became simply the Archive of Folk Song. In 1978, the archive was transferred from the library's Music Division to its American Folklife Center, which had been founded in 1976. Reflecting a broadened scope, the archive was renamed the Archive of Folk Culture in 1979. Jabbour, "American Folklife Center: A Twenty-Year Retrospective (Part 1)," 8–9.

109. Sandburg, *American Songbag*, viii (emphasis in original).

110. Alfred Harcourt to Sandburg (June 1, 1926), in Niven, *Carl Sandburg*, 44.

111. Gordon to Carl Engel (April 27, 1928), in Kodish, *Good Friends and Bad Enemies*, 136. After *American Songbag* came out, Gordon was less sanguine about Sandburg, feeling Sandburg had altered his contributions to the book to the point that they were unrecognizable (Kodish, *Good Friends and Bad Enemies*, 135).

112. Quote from Kodish, *Good Friends and Bad Enemies*, 136.

113. The *New York Times* articles appear in Gordon, *Folk-Songs of America*, 64, 70, 110; Gordon to Nevil Henshaw (1926), in Kodish, *Good Friends and Bad Enemies*, 163.

114. Sandburg, *American Songbag*, vii, ix–xx.

115. In D'Alessio, *Old Troubadour*, 38.

116. "Human procession" appears in Sandburg, *American Songbag*, viii.

117. Gordon, *Folk-Songs of America*, 20, 2.

118. "Marvelous assimilator" in Gordon, *Folk-Songs of America*, 2; "white roots" in Kodish, *Good Friends and Bad Enemies*, 66; "basic structure" in Gordon, *Folk-Songs of America*, 34. In 1932 Gordon wrote that he had found "further confirmation" that "the negro . . . built his stanzaic spirituals almost entirely on white models" (Gordon, "Archive of American Folk-Song," 255).

119. Gordon, *Folk-Songs of America*, 4.

120. Kodish, *Good Friends and Bad Enemies*, 174.

121. Ibid., 33, 58. Kodish also notes that in 1925 Gordon appeared on a radio broadcast on New York's WEAF, providing songs for a broadcast. Subsequently he tried, unsuccessfully, to convince the station to fund a field trip in exchange for exclusive rights to any materials he collected.

122. Ibid., 159.

123. Green, "Archive's Shores," 64.

124. Kodish, *Good Friends and Bad Enemies*, 187. A grant from the American Council of Learned Societies extended Gordon's salary through the end of 1932. He continued working at the archive for free until September 1933, when John A. Lomax was appointed the archive's "Honorary Consultant" (soon "Honorary Curator") (Porterfield, *Last Cavalier*, 292–94, 305; Kodish, *Good Friends and Bad Enemies*, 193).

125. Sandburg, *American Songbag*, vii, 325, 94.

126. West's comment, from her preface to Sandburg's *Selected Poems* (1926), is cited in Niven, *Carl Sandburg*, 449; Niven, *Carl Sandburg*, 432, 446, 448. Will Rogers can be seen as a precursor to Sandburg with his folksy persona and attention to image building.

CHAPTER TWO

1. Porterfield, *Last Cavalier*, 264–68.

2. Lomax (John A.) Family Papers, Center for American History, University of Texas at Austin, box 3D213, folder 2: "John A. Lomax, Jr.: Personal: Log of Automobile Tour, 1932"; John Jr. turned twenty-five in June 1932 (*Cotton Patch Rag*, February 10, 1975, n.p.), in John Lomax [Jr.] correspondence file, Folkways Collection, Center for Folklife Programs and Cultural Studies, Smithsonian Institution, Washington, D.C.

3. Lomax (John A.) Family Papers, box 3D213, folder 2: "John A. Lomax, Jr.: Personal: Log of Automobile Tour, 1932," August 16, 1932, 144; August 1, 1932, 130; May 24, 1932, 62.

4. Lomax (John A.) Family Papers, box 3D213, folder 2: "John A. Lomax, Jr.: Personal: Log of Automobile Tour, 1932," August 30, 1932, 148–49.

5. Lomax, "'Sinful Songs' of the Southern Negro," 181; Oliver, *Story of the Blues*, 122. John Jr. continued to dabble in folk song (he helped found the Houston Folklore Society), but he primarily pursued a career as a builder and land developer (*Cotton Patch Rag*, February 10, 1975, n.p.).

6. Porterfield, *Last Cavalier*, 278.

7. Wilgus, *Anglo-American Folksong Scholarship*, 185–86; Wolfe and Lornell, *Life and Legend of Leadbelly*, 110.

8. "Two army cots" in Lomax, *Adventures of a Ballad Hunter*, 111; Lomax, "Field Experiences with Recording Machines," 57, 58. The 350-pound figure comes from Lomax's estimate (in "Field Experiences with Recording Machines"), including the weight of the batteries. Wolfe and Lornell (*Life and Legend of Leadbelly*, 113) say the machine weighed 315 pounds. In 1993, Alan Lomax (*Land Where the Blues Began*, xi) placed the figure at 500 pounds. Porterfield (*Last Cavalier*, 297, 522 n. 22) establishes that the machine was made by the Dictaphone Corporation, even though John Lomax persistently called it an "Edison" in subsequent accounts.

9. Untitled document, in Archive of Folk Culture, American Folklife Center, Library of Congress, Washington, D.C., box: "John A. Lomax Collection, General Correspondence, 1933–1940," folder: "John A. Lomax, 1936."

10. Klein, *Woody Guthrie*, 149; "dammed up" in Lomax and Lomax, *Negro Folk Songs as Sung by Leadbelly*, 35; Porterfield, *Last Cavalier*, 523 n. 29; "the least contact" in Lomax and Lomax, *American Ballads and Folk Songs*, xxx.

11. Lomax (John A.) Family Papers, box 3D171, folders 1 and 2.

12. Lomax (John A.) Family Papers, Lomax to Ruby Terrill, in Parchman Convict Farm, Mississippi (August 10, 1933), box 3D149, folder 3: "John A. Lomax, Sr.: Personal; Family Correspondence: Ruby R. Terrill Lomax, June–October, 1933."

13. E.g., Lomax (John A.) Family Papers, Lomax to Ruby Terrill, in Parchman Convict Farm, Mississippi (August 7, 1933), box 3D149, folder 3: "John A. Lomax, Sr.: Personal; Family Correspondence: Ruby R. Terrill Lomax, June–October 1933"; Lomax (John A.) Family Papers, Lomax to Ruby Terrill, in Cotulla, Texas (February 8, 1934), box 3D149, folder 5: "John A. Lomax, Sr.: Personal: Family Correspondence: Ruby R. Terrill Lomax, January–February 20, 1934."

14. Lomax (John A.) Family Papers, Lomax to Ruby Terrill, in Parchman Convict Farm, Mississippi (August 10, 1933), box 3D149, folder 3: "John A. Lomax, Sr: Personal: Family Correspondence: Ruby R. Terrill Lomax, June–October, 1933"; Lomax, *Adventures of a Ballad Hunter*, 111–12.

15. Although many people are accustomed to the spelling "Leadbelly," recent research indicates that originally (and until around World War II) the name appeared as two words (Killeen, "Lead Belly: More Than a Name," 5).

16. Lomax and Lomax, *Negro Folk Songs as Sung by Lead Belly*, xiii.

17. See Chapter 1 regarding Sandburg and Gordon.

18. Lomax and Lomax, *Our Singing Country*, xi.

19. Lomax (John A.) Family Papers, Lomax to Ruby Terrill, "Twenty miles from Houston," August 1, 1933, box 3D149, folder 3: "John A. Lomax, Sr.: Personal: Family Correspondence: Ruby R. Terrill Lomax, June–October, 1933."

20. Lomax and Lomax, *American Ballads and Folk Songs*, xxxiv.

21. "The tendency" in Alan Lomax, "Folk Lore Collecting" [handwritten draft of lecture], Archive of Folk Culture, box: "Alan Lomax: Mostly Personal, Letters, Diaries, etc.," folder: "Lomax, Alan—Personal (Continued)"; "to convince you" in Alan Lomax, "Adress [*sic*] to the Progressive Education Association of the District of Columbia, Friday, March 8, 1940, on the subject of American Resources in American Folk Music," Archive of Folk Culture, box: "Allen [*sic*] Lomax Papers, Miscellaneous correspondence and photographs ca. 1935," folder: "Lomax, Alan—Personal."

22. Alan Lomax, "Afro-American Folklore, Smithsonian Folklife Festival" [tape], AFS Centennial Stage, Smithsonian Folklife Festival, Washington, D.C., July 3, 1988, SI-FP-1988-RR-151, reel 3/9, Folkways Collection.

23. John A. Lomax, " 'Sinful Songs' of the Southern Negro," 181.

24. Stott, *Documentary Expression and Thirties America*, 67; Marcus and Fischer, *Anthropology as Cultural Critique*, 125.

25. Alan Lomax, "Folk Music in the Roosevelt Era," 14. Lomax told a similar story at the AFS Centennial Stage in 1988 ("Afro-American Folklore, Smithsonian Folklife Festival," July 3, 1988, reel 3/9). Although the appeal of the Lomaxes' Washington links was considerable, folk performers were drawn to sing for them, in many cases, simply by the novelty of the recording machine. Shortly after the 1933 trip, Alan

Lomax wrote, "It was often quite difficult to persuade the first man to record his song, but after he and his fellows had heard his voice, his mistakes, perhaps, coming back to him out of the loudspeaker, there was no longer any difficulty in getting what we wanted. At times our work was even held up by the eagerness of the men to 'git on dat machine'" (Alan Lomax, "'Sinful' Songs of the Southern Negro," 121).

26. Wolfe and Lornell, *Life and Legend of Leadbelly*, 118–19; "Louisiana State Penitentiary Files; Summarized by Rebecca B. Schroeder, Missouri State Sch.; Jefferson City, MO," in Archive of Folk Culture.

27. In the months before arriving in New York, Lead Belly traveled with John Lomax on a field-recording expedition in the South. Lead Belly drove the car and played songs for would-be informants to demonstrate the kinds of material Lomax sought (Porterfield, *Last Cavalier*, 332–34).

28. "Lead Belly Makes His New York Debut before Texans," *New York Herald Tribune*, January 3, 1935, n.p., in Archive of Folk Culture, John Reynolds's clipping collection; March 1935 clipping, unlabeled, in Lomax (John A.) Family Papers; "King of the Twelve-String Guitar," *New York Post*, January 7, 1935, in Lomax (John A.) Family Papers.

29. Harry Hansen, "The First Reader," *World Telegram*, November 25, 1936, n.p., in Lomax (John A.) Family Papers; "King of the Twelve-String Guitar," *New York Post*, January 7, 1935, n.p.; "Leadbelly," *March of Time* 2 (March 2, 1935), transcribed in Herman Gebhard, "'March of Time' 1935," 26.

30. Lomax and Lomax, *Negro Folk Songs as Sung by Lead Belly*, 36.

31. Lomax, *Adventures of a Ballad Hunter*, ix; Lomax and Lomax, *Negro Folk Songs as Sung by Lead Belly*, 45.

32. "Book Marks for Today," n.p., in Lomax (John A.) Family Papers. A handwritten notation dates this article from fall 1936, but internal evidence (the article notes that the Lomaxes' book *American Ballads and Folk Songs* was "just published") places it from fall 1934.

33. Lomax and Lomax, *Negro Folk Songs as Sung by Lead Belly*, x; "Lomax Arrives with Lead Belly, Negro Minstrel," 21.

34. Seeger, "Leadbelly," 7.

35. Asch, foreword to Lomax and Lomax, *Leadbelly*, 5; See also Lee, "Some Notes on Lead Belly," 135–36.

36. Porterfield, *Last Cavalier*, 360–61, 365–66; Lomax and Lomax, *Negro Folk Songs as Sung by Lead Belly*, 41, 59–64. Lead Belly soon returned to New York, this time with his wife, Martha, serving as his manager. He continued to have musical dealings with the Lomaxes, especially Alan, who arranged occasional performance dates and recording sessions for him. See, for example, the 1942 chronology in *Lead Belly Letter* 5 (Winter/Spring 1995): 13, which shows Lomax transferring his royalties on a 1939 album to Lead Belly and arranging for Lead Belly to play a stag party at the home of the U.S. attorney general. See also Wright, "Huddie Ledbetter," 7.

37. "Lomax Arrives with Lead Belly, Negro Minstrel," 21; Lomax and Lomax, *Negro Folk Songs as Sung by Lead Belly*, x, 49; "'Ain't It a Pity?' But Lead Belly Jingles into City," *New York Herald Tribune*, March 2, 1936, n.p., in Lomax (John A.) Family Papers; Kenton Jackson, "Two Time Dixie Murderer Sings Way to Freedom," *Philadelphia Independent* (January 6, 1935), 4, in Lomax (John A.) Family Papers; caption

for photo of Lomax and Lead Belly [1935?], unlabeled clipping, in Lomax (John A.) Family Papers; "Songs Win Cash and Stage Bids for Lead Belly," *New York Herald Tribune*, January 3, 1935, n.p., in Archive of Folk Culture; "Lead Belly Sings the Blues When Bride-to-Be Misses Cue," *Brooklyn Eagle*, January 14, 1935, n.p., in Lomax (John A.) Family Papers; Wolfe and Lornell, *Life and Legend of Leadbelly*, 167; Benét, "Ballad of a Ballad-Singer," 36; J. Frank Dobie, "John Lomax Interprets Character of Lead Belly" [1936?], unlabeled clipping, in Lomax (John A.) Family Papers.

Lead Belly did cause a stir in the press, but the Lomaxes were prone to exaggerate its extent. The *New York Times*, for example, did not mention Lead Belly at all between 1933 and 1941, his prime years.

38. Torgovnick (*Gone Primitive*) analyzes primitivism in modernist painters, Freud, Conrad, and Burroughs.

39. Kuklick, *Savage Within*, 91, 139, 198. Some artists, too, took extended "field trips" among non-Western peoples, notably Paul Gauguin, who left France for Tahiti in the 1890s.

40. Handler, "Boasian Anthropology," 252–55; Simon Bronner notes that the *Journal of American Folklore* was edited either by Boas or by one of his followers from 1908 to 1940 (Bronner, *American Folklore Studies*, 68); Stocking, *Ethnographer's Magic*, 124.

41. In Handler, "Boasian Anthropology," 259.

42. Yurchenco, "Beginning of an Urban Folk-Song Movement in New York," 141.

43. The phrase "I've-seen-America" is Joe Klein's (Klein, *Woody Guthrie*, 146).

44. Lomax, "Leadbelly's Songs," 5.

45. Minton, " 'Our Goodman' in Blackface," 36.

46. Bascomb, "Discography," 4.

47. Library of Congress recording LC-121-A, in Archive of Folk Culture. It is impossible to date early Library of Congress recordings with certainty, but Robert M. W. Dixon and John Godrich believe that this recording was made on July 1, 1934 (Dixon and Godrich, *Blues and Gospel Records*, 432). In the fourth edition of *Blues and Gospel Records*, Dixon and Godrich list LC-121-A as having been reissued on Rounder CD 1097 (*The Titanic*, 1994). Actually, though, the Rounder CD features LC-236-B-3, which was recorded September 27, 1934. As far as I know, the original 121-A recording has not been commercially reissued.

After his release from prison, Lead Belly recorded "Tom Hughes" twice for John Lomax as they traveled the South in the fall of 1934 and again at Lomax's Connecticut home in January 1935. In February of that year, Lead Belly played the song during his first commercial recording date, a session with the American Record Company (ARC) that was supervised by producer Art Satherley with Alan Lomax in attendance. In 1939, Lead Belly recorded "Tom Hughes" again at a session in New York for the Musicraft label. The 1948 sessions, recorded by Frederic Ramsey, featured the song under the titles "Fannin Street" and "Cry for Me" (Bascomb, "Discography," 4).

48. Lomax and Lomax, *Negro Folk Songs as Sung by Lead Belly*, 168–69.

49. "Mr. Tom Hughes' Town," Library of Congress recording 236-B-3 (September 27, 1934), reissued on *Leadbelly: The Remaining ARC and Library of Congress Recordings, Vol. 1, 1934–1935*.

50. "Mister Tom Hughes's Town," American Record Company (February 5, 1935), reissued on *Leadbelly* (Columbia Records).

51. "Fannin Street," *Lead Belly's Last Sessions.*

52. E.g., "Mr. Tom Hughes' Town," Library of Congress recording 137-A (January 21, 1935), reissued on *Leadbelly: The Remaining ARC and Library of Congress Recordings, Vol. 1, 1934–1935.*

53. Because of poor sound quality, some of the words on this recording are difficult to transcribe with certainty. Lead Belly's 1939 Musicraft recording of the song, though, also includes versions of the suggestive verses, and the basic accuracy of my transcription is confirmed by Steve Thomes's transcription of that rendition: "Got a woman living on the backside of the jail, making an honest living by the workin' of her tail" (in Thomes, "Lead Belly's Peak Performance," 7).

54. Some versions, particularly the 1948 renditions on *Last Sessions*, pick up considerable speed as the song progresses.

55. June 17, 1940, reissued on *Leadbelly: Alabama Bound.* "Follow me down I'm on my last go-round" replaces "Follow me down to Mr. Tom Hughes' Town."

56. Billy Altman, *Leadbelly: Alabama Bound*, 7; "Artists Letter Agreement" between Alan Lomax and RCA (June 11, 1940), in Archive of Folk Culture, box: "Allen [*sic*] Lomax Papers, Miscellaneous Correspondence and Photographs ca. 1935," folder: "RCA Manufacturing Company, Inc."; R. P. Wetherald, RCA Manufacturing Co., Camden, N.J., to Alan Lomax, Library of Congress (May 7, 1940), in Archive of Folk Culture, box: "Alan Lomax: General Correspondence, 1939–1941 (Primarily CBS/American School of the Air-Related)," folder: Unlabeled; *Victor Record Review* 3 (March 1941), in Archive of Folk Culture.

57. Reuss, "Roots of American Left-Wing Interest," 261; Reuss, "American Folklore and Left-Wing Politics," 15.

58. Denisoff, *Great Day Coming*, 12, 41; Reuss, "Roots of American Left-Wing Interest," 267; Denning, *Cultural Front*, 293.

59. Denisoff, *Great Day Coming*, 42.

60. Carl Sands, "The Concert of the Pierre Degeyter Club Orchestra," *Daily Worker*, January 2, 1934, in Reuss, "Roots of American Left-Wing Interest," 269. While with the collective, Seeger often wrote under the pseudonym "Carl Sands."

   Michael Denning (*Cultural Front*, 293) feels that the collective was trying to reach not so much "ordinary" workers as "the self-selected workers" who sang in workers choruses. At this the members of collective achieved some success (several members became conductors of the choruses), but their composed music had nothing like the influence suggested by the collective's radical rhetoric.

61. Dunaway, "Unsung Songs of Protest," 7; "Everything we composed" in Dunaway, "Charles Seeger and Carl Sands," 167, 165.

62. See Chapter 4 regarding Seeger's efforts to carve out a niche for folk music within the federal government.

63. Carl Sands, "A Program for Proletarian Composers," *Daily Worker*, January 15, 1934, in Reuss, "Folk Music and Social Conscience," 229.

64. Reuss, "Roots of American Left-Wing Interest," 271; Gold, "Change the World," *Daily Worker*, June 11, 1934, in Dunaway, "Unsung Songs of Protest," 12.

65. "To collect, study, and popularize" in Wolfe and Lornell, *Life and Legend of Leadbelly*, 192; Lieberman, *"My Song Is My Weapon,"* 49.

66. The popularity of folk singers may have been more solid among the party organizers than among the rank and file. Michael Denning finds that "the soundtrack of the Popular Front," the music that captivated the "young factory and office workers who made up the social movement," was not folk music but jazz (Denning, *Cultural Front*, 329). Even so, folk revivalists drew their most reliable and influential audiences from the Left and enjoyed considerable celebrity within the movement.

67. Yurchenco, "Beginning of an Urban Folk-Song Movement," 39–40. In 1940 Lead Belly appeared on Yurchenco's radio program, *Adventures in Music*, on New York's WNYC, and he later secured his own fifteen-minute show on the station, *Folksongs in America*, which Yurchenco produced (Wolfe and Lornell, *Life and Legend of Leadbelly*, 219).

68. Wolfe and Lornell, *Life and Legend of Leadbelly*, 159, 250, 254–55; letter from City of New York Department of Welfare to Alan Lomax (February 1, 1940), in Archive of Folk Culture, Correspondence Folder. The letter says that the department had been supporting the Ledbetters since "the latter part of 1936"; Wolfe and Lornell report that Lead Belly's 1945 income tax return placed his total income for the year at $1,183.

69. In *Negro Folk Songs as Sung by Lead Belly* (xiii), the Lomaxes wrote, "We present this singer [Lead Belly] not as a folk singer handing on a tradition faithfully, but as a folk artist who contributes to the tradition."

70. Lee, "Some Notes on Lead Belly," 138.

71. "I learned by listening," in Don DeMichael, *Leadbelly*, 1; Wolfe and Lornell, *Life and Legend of Leadbelly*, 208.

72. Lead Belly recounts Autry's visit on *Leadbelly's Last Sessions*, disc 4, track 2; Wolfe and Lornell, *Life and Legend of Leadbelly*, 228, 145.

73. Evans, *Big Road Blues*, 109; Minton, "Reverend Lamar Roberts," 12–13; Hoffman quoted in Levine, *Black Culture and Black Consciousness*, 202; Lomax and Lomax, *Negro Folk Songs as Sung by Lead Belly*, 52.

74. E.g., Titon, *Early Downhome Blues*, 191; Ramsey, "Leadbelly," 21; Ahmet Ertegun in *A Vision Shared: A Tribute to Woody Guthrie and Leadbelly*, video produced by the Ginger Group for CBS Music Video Enterprises, CBS Records Inc., 1988.

75. Asch and Lomax, *Leadbelly Songbook*, 38, 91; Barlow, *"Looking Up at Down,"* 75.

76. Naison, *Communists in Harlem during the Depression*, 212–13; Klein, *Woody Guthrie*, 148.

77. Haywood, "Reply," 70. Haywood's reaction to Lead Belly's guitar gymnastics may also reflect a distaste for (or unfamiliarity with) an African American tradition (likely African-derived) of instrument manipulation; Molin, "Lead Belly, Burl Ives, and Sam Hinton," 58–79, 62.

78. Lomax (John A.) Family Papers, John Lomax to Ruby Terrill, January 14, 1935, box 2e391.

79. Lomax, *Folk Songs of North America*, 580; *Victor Record Review* 3 (March 1941), in Archive of Folk Culture.

80. Letter from Huddie Ledbetter to Alan Lomax (October 13, 1940), in Huddie Ledbetter correspondence folder, Archive of Folk Culture. Lead Belly's handwriting

makes parts of this letter difficult to transcribe with certainty; Klein, *Woody Guthrie*, 149.

81. The Weavers' version appeared as "Goodnight Irene," although Lead Belly himself usually referred to the song simply as "Irene" (Wolfe and Lornell, *Life and Legend of Leadbelly*, 52, 257). In the summer of 1950, Frank Sinatra launched a comeback with his own version of "Irene" (Dunaway, *How Can I Keep from Singing*, 142, 144, 151).

82. For tribute concert, see Wolfe and Lornell, *Life and Legend of Leadbelly*, 258; for record albums, see liner notes to *Leadbelly's Last Sessions*, 21, 2, and Wolfe and Lornell, *Life and Legend of Leadbelly*, 252. (Asch was known for keeping *all* of his Folkways catalog in print); for books, see Lomax and Lomax, *Leadbelly*, and Asch and Lomax, *Leadbelly Songbook*; Seeger and Lester, *Twelve-String Guitar as Played by Leadbelly*.

See Chapter 3 for a discussion of Lomax's work abroad and the "skiffle" phenomenon, of which Donegan was a part. See Chapter 5 for further discussion of Seeger and his relationship to Lead Belly.

83. Levenson, "Rock and Roll Hall of Fame Dinner," 11; Moss, "Cray Named Year's Top Blues Wailer," 136; "Nashville Songsters Hold Hall of Fame Fete," 91; the album *Folkways: A Vision Shared* was a joint tribute to Lead Belly and Woody Guthrie; Fine, "Screaming Trees," 56. The song "Where Did You Sleep Last Night" appeared on the Nirvana album *Unplugged in New York* (1994).

84. Seeger, among many others, has frequently expressed this sentiment—e.g., "If Huddie had lived just a few more years, he would have literally seen all his dreams as a musician come true" (in Wolfe and Lornell, *Life and Legend of Leadbelly*, 257).

CHAPTER THREE

1. Lomax, *Land Where the Blues Began*, 17.

2. Palmer, *Deep Blues*, 3; Lomax, *Land Where the Blues Began*, 415.

3. Aldin, *Chess Blues*, 11.

4. African Americans used "downhome" to suggest simple, old-time music made in the country. Consistent with my use of "folk music" (see introduction) and following Titon (*Early Downhome Blues*, xiii–xiv), I use "downhome" to identify music and musicians who audiences thought evoked the spirit of the simple, old-time style. As for the term "bluesman," I have tried where possible to use it only when referring to male performers. There were women who played downhome blues, although they were always a decided minority.

5. Aldin, *Muddy Waters: The Complete Plantation Recordings*, 7.

6. Palmer, *Deep Blues*, 4. Lomax connects "Country Blues" to House's "Gypsy Blues" (Lomax, *Land Where the Blues Began*, 410). John Cowley offers an involved discussion to show that House's tune, not Johnson's, was the predominant influence on Waters's version (Cowley, "Really the 'Walking Blues,'" 57–71); Lomax, *Land Where the Blues Began*, 415.

7. Palmer, *Deep Blues*, 6; Lomax, *Land Where the Blues Began*, 417. Waters eventually received the records, but it is not clear exactly when. Waters wrote inquiring about them in September 1941, and Lomax wrote on January 27, 1942, saying he was

sending them under separate cover. In April, though, when responding to Lomax's request for permission to include his songs on a Library of Congress album (see below), Waters may still have been waiting for his copies. He wrote, "Be sure to send me one of the records down here. I want one of them. I want Country Blues and Trouble Blues" (McKinley Morganfield to Alan Lomax, September 21, 1941, Lomax to Morganfield, January 27, 1942, and Morganfield to Lomax, April 6, 1942, in Archive of Folk Culture, American Folklife Center, Library of Congress, Washington, D.C., McKinley Morganfield correspondence file).

8. Carruthers, "Interview with Alan Lomax," 13; "keep in practice" in Lomax to Morganfield, January 27, 1942, in Cowley, "Really the 'Walking Blues,'" 61; Lomax, *Land Where the Blues Began*, 418.

9. "I was playing the old blues and it wouldn't go in St. Louis," Waters told Pete Welding (in Welding, "Interview with Muddy Waters," 5).

10. Palmer, *Deep Blues* 7; Rooney, *Bossmen*, 109; Obrecht, "Muddy Waters: The Life and Times," 32.

11. Grossman, *Land of Hope*, 1989, 19; Palmer, *Deep Blues*, 12; Obrecht, "Muddy Waters," in Obrecht, *Blues Guitar*, 60; Palmer (*Deep Blues*, 14) quotes Waters as saying he spent his first week with "my sister and her husband Dan"; but Rooney quotes Waters as saying that he first stayed "with some school kids. We'd grown up together" (Rooney, *Bossmen*, 109–10).

12. "I wanted to be nationally known" and "They don't listen" in Palmer, *Deep Blues*, 156, 135; "Are there many of these" in Cowley, "Really the 'Walking Blues,'" 59.

13. Russell, "Clarksdale Piccolo Blues," 30; Palmer, *Deep Blues*, 134–35, 155.

14. Barlow, *"Looking Up at Down,"* 134, 257, 259, 209; Palmer, *Deep Blues*, 135; Rowe, *Chicago Breakdown*, 17.

15. Melrose, "My Life in Recording," 59; Koester, "Lester Melrose," 58; Barlow, *"Looking Up at Down,"* 134–35.

16. Dixon and Snowden, *I Am the Blues*, 62.

17. Evans, *Big Road Blues*, 72–75.

18. Rowe, *Chicago Breakdown*, 17, 25; Charters, *Country Blues*, 183; Palmer, *Deep Blues*, 135; Guralnick, *Listener's Guide to the Blues*, 65.

19. Rooney, *Bossmen*, 111. In a 1983 interview Waters recalled that "back in Mississippi it was usually just me, or maybe two of us" (Tom Wheeler, "Muddy Waters and Johnny Winter," in Obrecht, *Blues Guitar*, 76).

20. Rowe, *Chicago Breakdown*, 67; Rooney, *Bossmen*, 117.

21. Palmer, *Deep Blues*, 155; Wheeler, "Muddy Waters and Johnny Winter," in Obrecht, *Blues Guitar*, 75. The Delta style does feature single-string bottleneck playing, but a delicate, finger-fretted single-string approach is more characteristic of rural Texas blues than of Delta blues. The Texas style (which also features a lighter vocal touch) was an important influence on urban blues (Middleton, *Pop Music and the Blues*, 66–67).

22. "When I went into the clubs," in Rooney, *Bossmen*, 112; uncle's gift of guitar in Obrecht, "Muddy Waters: The Life and Times," 32.

23. Dixon and Snowden, *I Am the Blues*, 62.

24. Palmer reports that the other two performers "rapidly dropped from sight" after the session (*Deep Blues*, 156). The Melrose session was actually Waters's second in

Chicago. In 1982, collectors discovered that a 1945 or 1946 recording of "Mean Red Spider," issued under the name "James 'Sweet Lucy' Carter and His Orchestra," featured Waters as singer and guitarist. Featuring saxophone, guitar, piano, and bass accompaniment, the cut has been described by Jas Obrecht as a "hopping horn version" of the song (Obrecht, "Muddy Waters: The Life and Times," 34). Waters recorded it for race-record producer J. Mayo Williams, and eventually it was released by 20th Century Records (O'Neal, "Muddy's First Record," 4). In 1948, Leonard Chess and Aristocrat Records recorded a more downhome version of "Mean Red Spider," featuring just Waters and bassist Ernest "Big" Crawford; "Hard Day Blues" appears on *Legends of the Blues*, vol. 1.

25. I.e., from B to C to C# to D.

26. In his pioneering study *Urban Blues* (1966), Charles Keil distinguishes between "city blues" (which include post-1940 Chicago blues) and "urban blues" (which originated in Kansas City, post–World War II Texas, and Memphis) (Keil, *Urban Blues*, 218–19). I am treating the term "urban blues" more broadly, using it to refer generally to blues styles indigenous to urban areas.

27. He plays three B-flats in a triplet figure over the second and third beats.

28. Among the thirteen songs, I am including two that featured Waters on guitar but different vocalists. I am not counting separately the multiple versions of five songs that Waters recorded. All subsequent LC songs that I discuss appear on *Muddy Waters: The Complete Plantation Recordings*. The five songs that break from A-A-B form are "Country Blues" (A-B-A-B), "I Be's Troubled" and "I Be Bound to Write to You" (A-B-C-D), "Why Don't You Live So God Can Use You" (A-A-B-B), and "You're Gonna Miss Me When I'm Gone" (A-B-C-C). Moreover, "Why Don't You Live So God Can Use You" follows an eight- instead of twelve-bar structure, while "You Got to Take Sick and Die Some of These Days" consistently uses an uneven eight-and-a-half-bar form.

29. All metronome markings given in this discussion are approximate.

30. Historian Robert Palmer speculates that despite Waters's adjustments, his sound was still "too down-home" for Columbia (*Deep Blues*, 156). Waters, too, interpreted the rejection as a sign that he remained too identifiably a Mississippi bluesman. "That country stuff might sound funny to 'em," he reasoned. "I'd imagine, you know, they'd say, 'This stuff isn't going to sell'" (in O'Neal, "Muddy Waters," 32).

31. To take but one example, the phrase "Father of the Chicago Blues" headlined an article by Peter Guralnick in 1992 when Waters was awarded a Lifetime Achievement Award by the organizers of the Grammy Awards (Guralnick, "Muddy Waters: Father of the Chicago Blues," in Archive of Folk Culture, "Morganfield, McKinley" corporate subject file).

32. Golkin, "Blacks, Whites, and Blues [Part One]," 22–24; Brack and Paige, "Chess and the Blues," 20.

33. Grendysa, "Black Music—An Introduction," 11. Grendysa says "rhythm and blues" came into general use around 1945. *Billboard* changed the name of its black pop chart from "race" to "rhythm & blues" in 1949.

34. Aldin, *Chess Blues*, 9; Palmer credits Chess's talent scout Sammy Goldstein with suggesting Aristocrat's expansion into the blues field (*Deep Blues*, 157). Waters told Pete Welding that it was Goldstein (whom he calls "Goldberg") who brought him

to Chess's attention: "He heard me sing and he said, 'This is it'" (in Welding, "Interview with Muddy Waters," 6).

35. Palmer, *Deep Blues*, 158. As an indication, perhaps, of Waters's uneasiness in the new style, he uses the same guitar line on both "Anna Mae" and "Gypsy Woman," a simple triplet figure that appears over the song's turnaround (the eleventh and twelfth bars of the blues form). "Anna Mae" appears on the box set *Chess Blues*. "Gypsy Woman" appears on *Muddy Waters: The Chess Box*. Unless otherwise specified, all subsequent Chess recordings by Waters that I discuss can be found on the *Muddy Waters* compilation.

36. Dixon and Snowden, *I Am the Blues*, 79; Palmer, *Deep Blues*, 159. The third song that Waters recorded that day, "Mean Disposition," was not released until 1982; "All of a sudden" in O'Neal, "Muddy Waters," 35.

37. Unless otherwise specified, my analysis refers to the first version of "Country Blues" that Waters recorded for Lomax in August 1941.

38. Crawford plays an even more central role on "Can't Be Satisfied," giving the song a springy, danceable beat.

39. In Cowley, "Really the 'Walking Blues,'" 66–67.

40. "I Can't Be Satisfied" features a similar alteration. When Waters recorded the tune as "I Be's Troubled," the opening verse was: "Well, [if] I feel tomorrow / Like I feel today / I'm [gonna] pack my suitcase / And make my getaway." On "Can't Be Satisfied," Waters shifts the geographic direction of the narrator's longing, changing the verse to: "Well I'm goin' away to live / Won't be back no more / Goin' back down South, child / Don't you wanna go?"

41. E.g., "Minutes seem like hours" and "Brooks run into the ocean, the ocean run in, into the sea / If I don't find my baby somebody goin' sure bury me."

42. "If shit is gold": Ron Malo, in Dixon and Snowden, *I Am the Blues*, 195, 144–45; "What's he singing" in Palmer, *Deep Blues*, 159; "Chess didn't like my style" in Welding, "Interview with Muddy Waters," 6; "Leonard Chess never did dig" in O'Neal, "Muddy Waters," 34.

43. Rowe, *Chicago Breakdown*, 79; Marshall Chess recalls a fourth partner, Art Sheridan, whom Chess also bought out at this time (in Golkin, "Blacks, Whites, and Blues [Part One]," 25); "Chess Records: History," in publicity packet of the Blues Heaven Foundation.

44. Brack and Paige, "Chess and the Blues," 21; Guralnick, *Feel Like Going Home*, 185–86, 198.

45. In Petersen, "Chicago Sound," 56; "I always paid" in Brack and Paige, "Chess and the Blues," 22.

46. Aldin, *Chess Blues*, 15. At one point, a cash-strapped Sam Phillips, head of Sun Records, offered to sell a young Memphis singer named Elvis Presley, but Chess turned him down: "We didn't consider ourselves a hillbilly label at the time," Phil Chess recalled (Guralnick, *Feel Like Going Home*, 198).

47. Wolfe and Lornell, *Life and Legend of Leadbelly*, 190; Lomax, *Land Where the Blues Began*, 33, 459.

48. Guralnick, *Feel Like Going Home*, 196; Golkin, "Black, Whites, and Blues [Part One]," 28. Muddy Waters, at least, seems to have shared Phil Chess's sentiment,

recalling, "I didn't even sign no contract with [Leonard Chess], no nothing. It was just 'I belong to the Chess family'" (in Palmer, *Deep Blues*, 162).

49. "Chess would sit there" in Golkin, "Black, Whites, and Blues [Part One]," 27; the story about Chess drumming appears, for example, in Palmer, "Muddy Waters . . . the Man . . . His Music," 14; Golkin, "Blacks, Whites, and Blues [Part One]," 27; Palmer, *Deep Blues*, 164–65; Obrecht, "Muddy Waters," in Obrecht, *Blues Guitar*, 63.

50. "Leonard Chess would get in the booth" in Shaw, *Honkers and Shouters*, 293–94; "Leonard didn't know" in Corritore, Ferris, and O'Neal, "Willie Dixon, Part I," 25.

51. In Dixon and Snowden, *I Am the Blues*, 190.

52. Palmer, "Muddy Waters . . . the Man . . . His Music," 14.

53. E.g., "Rollin' and Tumblin'" was a Delta tune, and Waters's "Rolling Stone" was a variation of the old-time "Catfish Blues" (Vander Woude, "Recorded Music of Muddy Waters: A Repertory Analysis," 153n; Vander Woude, "Recorded Music of Muddy Waters, 1941–1956," 78; Palmer, *Deep Blues*, 163).

54. "Where's My Woman Been" in Vander Woude, "Recorded Music of Muddy Waters, 1941–1956," 69; "They were trying" in Rooney, *Bossmen*, 120.

55. Palmer, "Muddy Waters . . . the Man . . . His Music," 14.

56. Dixon and Snowden, *I Am the Blues*, 7, 24, 43–55.

57. Ibid., 59–75.

58. "My right arm" in Brack and Paige, "Chess and the Blues," 20; Dixon and Snowden, *I Am the Blues*, 81–86, 89.

59. Palmer, *Deep Blues*, 164. "Louisiana Blues" and "She Moves Me" each peaked at number ten on the *Billboard* R & B charts, while Waters's "Long Distance Call" (also recorded in 1951) hit number eight (Whitburn, *Joel Whitburn's Top R & B Singles*, 435). The extent and duration of Waters's breakthrough in the North is difficult to ascertain, but it is safe to assume that he enjoyed relatively small sales there until 1954, when he released "Hoochie Coochie Man," "I'm Ready," and "I Just Want to Make Love to You" (see below). Mike Rowe finds that, overall, Chess blues had little impact on northern markets outside the termini for the southern migration (Chicago, Gary, St. Louis, Detroit), but he does note that at the peak of their popularity Waters and Little Walter each had one record that cracked New York's and Philadelphia's Hot Ten and that several of their records enjoyed heavy play in Newark, New Jersey (*Chicago Breakdown*, 149–50). Rowe does not identify exactly which songs had the success he describes (nor does he identify his sources for the information), but it seems certain that he had Waters's three 1954 chart hits in mind. Even so, until the 1960s, Waters's popularity in the North remained relatively insignificant outside the sites of the African American migration.

60. Waters recorded with this instrumentation on three sessions before the January 1954 "Hoochie Coochie Man" date: September 17, 1952, May 4, 1953, and September 24, 1953 (Ruppli, *Chess Labels*, 22, 23, 25).

61. Dixon and Snowden, *I Am the Blues*, 6.

62. Middleton, *Pop Music and the Blues*, 66, 81, 91.

63. Bridges are eight-bar segments that lyrically and harmonically contrast with surrounding verses.

64. Guralnick, "Willie Dixon," 22.

65. In Dixon and Snowden, *I Am the Blues*, 6.

66. Palmer, *Deep Blues*, 95–96.

67. Sales figures in Whitburn, *Joel Whitburn's Top R & B Singles*, 435; "I'm Ready" uses a twelve-bar blues form but intersperses an eight-bar break and eight-bar choruses. "I Just Want to Make Love to You" is based on an eight-bar form and uses an eight-bar bridge; "Make Love to You" in Vander Woude, "Recorded Music of Muddy Waters: A Repertory Analysis," 203.

68. "I'm Ready" in Dixon and Snowden, *I Am the Blues*, 41; Whitburn, *Joel Whitburn's Top R & B Singles*, 435.

69. In Petersen, "Chicago Sound," 55–56.

70. Kleppner, *Chicago Divided*, 34. Nicholas Lemann uses figures that differ very slightly, finding a rise from 278,000 to 492,000 and then to 813,000 (Lemann, *Promised Land*, 70).

71. Lemann, *Promised Land*, 70; Rowe, *Chicago Breakdown*, 151.

72. Lemann, *Promised Land*, 81–82. In a sociological study conducted around 1960 in Lansing, Michigan, Rose Toomer Brunson found that the degree of retention of traditional practices often correlated more strongly with the socioeconomic status of the migrants in the North than simply with the length of time they had lived there (Brunson, "Socialization Experiences," 123–24). In a familiar pattern, though, in Chicago the most recent immigrants were decidedly the poorest and therefore (under Brunson's formulation) the most likely to retain traditional customs.

73. Lemann, *Promised Land*, 81, 83–84.

74. In Corritore, Ferris, and O'Neal, "Willie Dixon, Part I," 21, 24.

75. In Palmer, *Deep Blues*, 96–97.

76. In one difference, the riff is played by a saxophone on "Evil." Several writers have attributed "Mannish Boy" to Dixon, but neither Dixon's autobiography nor the recent CD box set of Dixon's work (*Willie Dixon: The Chess Box*) credits the song to him. The Muddy Waters box set lists Waters as the songwriter (*Muddy Waters: The Chess Box*).

77. "Mannish Boy" and "Evil" in Vander Woude, "Recorded Music of Muddy Waters: A Repertory Analysis," 213.

78. "Stamping, hollering" in Shaw, *Honkers and Shouters*, 299; "the effect was stunning" in Palmer, *Deep Blues*, 255; Obrecht, "Muddy Waters," in Obrecht, *Blues Guitar*, 65.

79. Dixon and Snowden, *I Am the Blues*, 82, 101, 103; "I Can't Quit You Baby" peaked at number six (Whitburn, *Joel Whitburn's Top R & B Singles*, 360).

80. O'Neal, "I Once Was Lost," 370.

81. Whitburn, *Joel Whitburn's Top R & B Singles*, 435.

82. Hendler, *Year by Year in the Rock Era*, 3–4; Ennis, *Seventh Stream*, 224.

83. "The kids" in Golkin, "Blacks, Whites, and Blues [Part One]," 30–31; Ennis, *Seventh Stream*, 18, 224; Dixon and Snowden, *I Am the Blues*, 185; "Bo Diddley" was number one on the R & B chart in 1955, but Diddley's songs did not start appearing on the pop charts until 1959 (Whitburn, *Joel Whitburn's Top R & B Singles*, 118).

84. Berry, *Chuck Berry*, 98. In its original incarnation, "Maybellene" was called "Ida Red." Dixon takes credit for producing the song in his autobiography, noting that he and Phil Chess cut the record at Chicago's Universal Studios while Leonard Chess was out of town. "When he came back," Dixon writes, " 'Maybellene' was playing on the air because we made a dub of it that quick. Leonard came in and said, 'Man,

somebody's got a record on the air that's burning up.' He didn't know it was our record, his own organization" (*I Am the Blues*, 90–91). Predictably, Chess gives a different account: "I didn't like it as C&W [country and western] so we recut it in our little studio behind the office with two side men. Phil and I were the engineers. We called it 'Mabelline' [*sic*]" (in Brack and Paige, "Chess and the Blues," 20); Berry echoes Chess's account in his autobiography, writing that Dixon "seemed to have little confidence" in the song (*Chuck Berry*, 103).

85. Dixon and Snowden, *I Am the Blues*, 149, 168–69, 243–44, 247.

86. Hendler, *Year by Year in the Rock Era*, 20, 28; Guralnick, *Feel Like Going Home*, 198.

87. Keil quoted in O'Neal, "I Once Was Lost," 369. In the sixties, especially, younger blacks gravitated to soul music, a style associated with black pride.

88. Palmer, *Deep Blues*, 255–56; "when we started" and "when we took the record" in Dixon and Snowden, *I Am the Blues*, 197, 115; Groom, *Blues Revival*, 20; O'Neal, "I Once Was Lost," 356–57.

89. Rowe, *Chicago Breakdown*, 165; Dixon and Snowden, *I Am the Blues*, 143–44, 172. The Chess company did enjoy some soul hits in the 1960s, but it never matched the successes it had enjoyed with Berry and Diddley (Pruter, *Chicago Soul*, 97–99; George, *Death of Rhythm and Blues*, 83).

90. Chatman information in Barlow, *"Looking Up at Down,"* 315; "Slim and I" in Dixon and Snowden, *I Am the Blues*, 115.

91. See Chapter 4.

92. Tirro, *Jazz*, 291.

93. Lornell, *Introducing American Folk Music*, 209; Cohn, *Nothing but the Blues*, 431; Titon, "Reconstructing the Blues," 223.

94. Groom, *Blues Revival*, 26–28. Many of Ramsey's recordings were later issued by Moses Asch's Folkways Records. Another important collector in this period was Harold Courlander, who did extensive fieldwork in the early 1950s that became the basis for his *Negro Folk Music U.S.A.* (1963) (Groom, *Blues Revival*, 27; Cowley, "Don't Leave Me Here," 290).

95. Cowley, "Don't Leave Me Here," 299–301, 306; Lomax, *Land Where the Blues Began*, 518.

96. See Marcus's *Invisible Republic* for a discussion of the *Anthology*'s profound influence on folk revivalists; the Origin Jazz Library and RBF, a subsidiary of Folkways, were particularly important in reissuing blues (Groom, *Blues Revival*, 40); O'Neal, "I Once Was Lost," 360.

97. Groom, *Blues Revival*, 29–30; Titon, "Reconstructing the Blues," 230–31. Titon shows that John Lee Hooker, too, shifted from electric to acoustic guitar after folk-revival impresarios found him. In the later sixties, when electric blues became acceptable in the revival, both Hopkins and Hooker returned to their electric instruments.

98. Titon, "Reconstructing the Blues," 223, 225.

99. Charters, *Country Blues*, 266. After the countercultural surge of the 1960s, Charters claimed that he had relied on such stereotypes knowingly and for highly politicized reasons. In his preface to the 1975 reprint of *The Country Blues*, he wrote, "I was trying to effect a change in the American consciousness by presenting an alternative consciousness. If my books from this time seem romantic it's because I tried to

make them romantic. I was trying to describe black music and black culture in a way that would immediately involve a certain kind of younger, middle-class white American. . . . [The book] was a romanticization of certain aspects of black life in an effort to force the white society to reconsider some of its racial attitudes, and on the other hand it was a cry for help. I wanted hundreds of people to go out and interview the surviving blues artists" (ix–xii). As Jeff Todd Titon points out, this self-serving assessment fails to acknowledge the extent to which Charters was caught up in romanticism as much as strategically employing it ("Reconstructing the Blues," 235–36).

100. McCormick, "Lightnin' Hopkins: Blues," 313.

101. On Pete Seeger, see Chapter 5.

102. Rowe, *Chicago Breakdown*, 172; Newport Folk Festival program (1959), in Archive of Folk Culture; Dixon and Snowden, *I Am the Blues*, 104, 115–16. Dixon's co-author, Don Snowden, writes that Dixon and Slim appeared at the Newport folk festivals in 1957 and 1958, but the festival had not yet been founded then.

 When Slim and Dixon's European trips actually occurred is somewhat in dispute, because of their conflicting memories. Slim recalls his first European gig as occurring during three months in 1960 (in Cook, *Listen to the Blues*, 152); Dixon and Snowden say that the duo went for three months in 1959 (*I Am the Blues*, 105, 123, 125). In the absence of a definitive account, I have chosen 1959 as the year of their first tour because Dixon says that he had been to Europe before the 1960 tour of Israel.

103. Dixon and Snowden, *I Am the Blues*, 104–5, 125, 118; Groom, *Blues Revival*, 69; Hammond, *John Hammond on Record*, 335. No album by Dixon and Slim appears in the selective discography in Hammond's autobiography, but the session was most likely for Vanguard Records, for which Hammond worked in the late fifties. Dixon and Slim also made several recordings for the jazz-oriented Verve label in this period.

104. "Folk Music on Records," 46.

105. Cook, *Listen to the Blues*, 147–52; Tirro, *Jazz*, 58, 160, 184; Killeen, "Lead Belly in Europe," 1, 4; Groom, *Blues Revival*, 11; Barlow, *"Looking Up at Down,"* 100.

106. Dixon and Snowden, *I Am the Blues*, 126; Groom, *Blues Revival*, 12, 14; Rooney, *Bossmen*, 137; Palmer, *Deep Blues*; Obrecht, "Muddy Waters," in Obrecht, *Blues Guitar*, 65.

107. "I didn't have no idea" in Rooney, *Bossmen*, 137; Lifton, *Listener's Guide to Folk Music*, 8–10.

108. Kozinn, "John Lennon's First Known Recording," C13; Groom, *Blues Revival*, 17; Hasted, "Don't Scoff at Skiffle!," 29; Lifton, *Listener's Guide to Folk Music*, 10; Whitburn, *Billboard Book of Top 40 Hits*, 97.

109. "Screaming Guitar" in Rooney, *Bossmen*, 137; "Now I know" in Palmer, *Deep Blues*, 258; Obrecht, "Muddy Waters," in Obrecht, *Blues Guitar*, 65.

110. Studs Terkel, liner notes to *Muddy Waters Sings Big Bill Broonzy*.

111. In Rooney, *Bossmen*, 137.

112. See, e.g., Palmer, "Play the Blues, Man!," 25 (regarding John Allison bringing performers from the "juke joints of the backwoods" of Mississippi to perform in New

York City); "Amity Grad, Blues Legend to Perform at Carnegie Hall," D1, D3 (regarding the Music Maker Foundation having "discovered" thirty artists).

113. Reviewers seem largely to have ignored *Muddy Waters Sings*. The folk-revival journal *Sing Out!* had published an elegiac tribute to Broonzy after his death, in which it had remarked, "Most of all, he will live on in the songs which he composed" ("Big Bill Is Gone," 31). But it paid little attention to Waters's effort to reinterpret these songs. Even in Pete Welding's "Country Blues Round-Up," the recording received only an informational listing in a long list of "other recent discs of interest to blues collectors" (Welding, "Country Blues Round-up," 45).

114. Lippman quoted in Dixon and Snowden, *I Am the Blues*, 121, 129; Groom, *Blues Revival*, 79.

115. Dixon and Snowden, *I Am the Blues*, 122, 127–28, 131–32, 139–40. In one instance Dixon's role was reminiscent of a folklorist's. Groom (*Blues Revival*, 84) relates that in 1963 Dixon "discovered" in Chicago a Tennessee-born singer and guitarist, John Henry Barbee, who had not recorded since 1938. Dixon included him in the 1964 Folk Blues Festival tour, during which Barbee performed in concerts and made a recording in Denmark. Shortly after returning to America, Barbee used his money from the festival to buy a car. A few days later he killed a man in a traffic accident and was sent to jail, where he died of cancer. His story prompted complaints that the American Folk Blues Festival should offer more guidance and support to its older bluesmen.

116. Groom, *Blues Revival*, 78–83, 86. Old-time rural performers continued to be a strong presence at the AFBF as well, particularly on the 1967 program, which featured Son House, Skip James, and Bukka White.

117. Obrecht, "Muddy Waters," in Obrecht, *Blues Guitar*, 65; Norman, *Symphony for the Devil*, 45, 68; Greenfield, "Keith Richard," 25.

118. "I hope they don't think" in Norman, *Symphony for the Devil*, 68; "We were blues purists" in "Rolling Stone Interview: Mick Jagger," 16; "for all the young musicians" in Dixon and Snowden, *I Am the Blues*, 122, 133–34.

119. Dalton, *Rolling Stones*, 348; Norman, *Symphony for the Devil*, 96–97, 120, 140.

120. Dixon had eight children as of around 1960 (Dixon and Snowden, *I Am the Blues*, 66, 113); Baldry sang for Alexis Korner's Blues Incorporated, a group for which Jagger briefly sang as well (Norman, *Symphony for the Devil*, 59–60); Baldry is quoted in Dixon and Snowden, *I Am the Blues*, 123, 136.

121. In Cook, *Listen to the Blues*, 181. As with many telling anecdotes about the blues, I have been unable to find the original source for this story.

122. Norman, *Symphony for the Devil*, 125–26; Dixon and Snowden, *I Am the Blues*, 144. In 1964, with Eric Clapton on lead guitar, the Yardbirds had recorded an album in England with Sonny Boy Williamson (Palmer, *Deep Blues*, 261).

123. Jack Tracy, *Muddy Waters at Newport* [liner notes]; Palmer, *Deep Blues*, 258.

124. Palmer, *Deep Blues*, 259.

125. Even the British audiences of 1958 that had been shocked by the volume of Waters's electric guitar had cheered madly for "I've Got My Mojo," with which Waters had closed most of his shows abroad (ibid., 258); Wheeler, "Muddy Waters and Johnny Winter," in Obrecht, *Blues Guitar*, 76.

126. O'Neal, "I Once Was Lost," 357; Hendler, *Year by Year in the Rock Era*, 40, 48. Four of the tunes on *Folksinger* feature just Waters and Buddy Guy (also acoustic), while another four add a drummer and Dixon on string bass.

127. Ralph Bass, *Muddy Waters, Folk Singer* [liner notes]; "They tried to put me over" in O'Neal, "I Once Was Lost," 358.

128. Obrecht, "Muddy Waters: The Life and Times," 46; Marshall Chess quoted in Petersen, "Chicago Sound," 62. In the early 1970s, Chess left the Chess company to run the Rolling Stones' new record company (Golkin, "Blacks, Whites, and Blues [Part Two]," 28.

129. Rooney, *Bossmen*, 151; Petersen, "Chicago Sound," 60, 62. At around this same time, Marshall Chess produced a pyschedelic album for Howlin' Wolf, entitled *This Is the New Howlin' Wolf Album. He Didn't Like It. But He Didn't Like His Electric Guitar at First Either*, and B. B. King suffered through *Turn On with B. B. King* (O'Neal, "I Once Was Lost," 357); "now what the hell" in Rooney, *Bossmen*, 151.

130. Whitburn, *Billboard Book of Top 40 Hits*. In this period Chess also released two compilation albums of Waters's older material: *The Real Folk Blues* (1966) and *More Real Folk Blues* (1967).

131. O'Neal, "I Once Was Lost," 367, 376; Groom, *Blues Revival*, 76. In the 1960s, annual blues festivals were founded in Ann Arbor, Berkeley, and Memphis. Blues scholarship by Oliver and Guralnick includes the following: Oliver: *Blues Fell This Morning* (1960), *Conversations with the Blues* (1965), *Screening the Blues* (1968), *Songsters and Saints: Vocal Traditions on Race Records* (1984); Guralnick: *Feel Like Going Home* (1971), *Lost Highway: Journeys and Arrivals of American Musicians* (1979), *The Listener's Guide to the Blues* (1982), *Sweet Soul Music* (1986). Strachwitz and Welding also released new blues recordings. A tiny sampling of the rock musicians who expressed their allegiances to urban blues ranges from late 1960s icons such as Eric Clapton, Jeff Beck, Led Zeppelin, Jimi Hendrix, and Fleetwood Mac to more recent figures like George Thorogood, Bonnie Raitt, the Allman Brothers, Stevie Ray Vaughan, ZZ Top, John Mellencamp, Steve Miller, the J. Geils band, U2, Slash, and Richie Sambora.

132. Dixon and Snowden, *I Am the Blues*, 171, 206–12.

133. Aldin, "Blues Heaven," 17; Barlow, *"Looking Up at Down,"* 86, 134; Aldin, "Muddy Waters Scholarship Winner," 4.

134. Dixon and Snowden, *I Am the Blues*, 225, 4.

135. Ibid., 226–27.

136. "They'll always be around" in Sidney Fields, "Mister Blues," *New York Daily News*, December 26, 1972, in Archive of Folk Culture, "Morganfield, McKinley" corporate subject file, n.p.; "the blues have to change" in Welding, "Muddy Waters: Last King of the South Side?," 35.

137. In Welding, "Muddy Waters: Last King of the South Side?," 7; in Guralnick, *Feel . Like Going Home*, 62–63; in Palmer, *Deep Blues*, 260.

138. Rooney, *Bossmen*, 139–46; Palmer, *Deep Blues*, 259; Obrecht, "Muddy Waters," in Obrecht, *Blues Guitar*, 67; Fields, "Mister Blues," n.p.

139. Golkin, "Blacks, Whites, and Blues [Part Two]," 28.

140. Obrecht, "Muddy Waters," in Obrecht, *Blues Guitar*, 67.

141. Obrecht, "Muddy Waters: The Life and Times," 72; Obrecht, "Muddy Waters," in Obrecht, *Blues Guitar*, 68. Albums that Waters recorded in this period include *Hard Again* (1976), *I'm Ready* (1977), *Muddy "Mississippi" Waters Live* (1979), and *King Bee* (1981).

142. Palmer, *Deep Blues*, 260; Leonard Chess was inducted into the Hall of Fame the same year as Waters (Golkin, "Blacks, Whites, and Blues [Part One]," 22), and Willie Dixon followed in 1994 (Rule, "Pop Life," C16).

CHAPTER FOUR

1. Whisnant, *All That Is Native and Fine*, 191–93; "a lovely dignity": John Powell, in ibid., 193.

2. "Folk Music in the Roosevelt White House," cover photo; Malone, *Singing Cowboys*, 89, 91; Roosevelt, "Folk Music in the White House," 8; Kirk, *Musical Highlights from the White House*, 110; "Visit of Their Britannic Majesties to the White House: A Program of American Music," in "Folk Music in the Roosevelt White House," 22.

3. Letter from Alan Lomax to President Estenio Vincent, Port-au-Prince, Haiti (February 13, 1937), in Archive of Folk Culture, American Folklife Center, Library of Congress, Washington, D.C., box: "Allen [*sic*] Lomax Papers, Miscellaneous correspondence, ca. 1935"; Bartis, "History of the Archive," 57–8, 65, 61, 63.

4. Bartis, "History of the Archive," 79, 76, 93–94, 86–89, 98.

5. McDonald, *Federal Relief Administration and the Arts*, 638–39, 579–80; Botkin, "WPA and Folklore Research," 8; Pescatello, *Charles Seeger*, 141, 154.

6. Herbert Halpert of the Federal Theater Project also did some folk song work.

7. Bronner, *American Folklore Studies*, 81–86, 74–76, 60–65. Radcliffe-Brown's more sociological approach was generally known as "structuralism" rather than "functionalism," and he and Malinowski were often seen as at odds by their partisans within the field. Nonetheless, both men and their successors focused broadly on function and can be seen as together having moved American thought in a functionalist direction (Kuper, *Anthropology and Anthropologists*, 36, 68, 72, 86).

8. See Chapter 2 for a discussion of Boas. Malinowski, *Scientific Theory of Culture and Other Essays*, 32, 27; Bronner, *American Folklore Scholarship*, 71–73.

9. Botkin, "Folkness of the Folk," 464.

10. Botkin, in Stewart, *Fighting Words*, 11.

11. Botkin, "WPA and Folklore Research," 14; Seeger, "Folkness of the Non-Folk," 1, 2, 6. Writing in the 1960s, Seeger here identifies the functionalists' opponents as "structuralists," identifying them as more "purist," and backward-looking collectors. This term, though, would have had somewhat different connotations in the 1930s, when "structuralism" referred to A. R. Radcliffe-Brown's brand of functionalism (Bronner, *American Folklore Studies*, 79; see also note 7, above); Botkin, "Folkness of the Folk," 465.

12. Hirsch, "Modernity, Nostalgia, and Southern Folklore Studies," 203.

13. Lomax and Lomax, *American Ballads and Folk Songs*, xxvi, xxvii.

14. Lomax and Lomax, *Our Singing Country*, xiv, xii.

15. Ibid., 149.

16. Seeger, "Grass Roots for American Composers," 149; Lomax in "Conference on the Character and State of Studies in Folklore," 508; Botkin, *Treasury of American Folklore*, xxii.

17. Robertson in Pescatello, *Charles Seeger*, 141; Botkin in "Conference on the Character and State of Studies in Folklore," 512; Botkin, *Treasury of American Folklore*, 819.

18. Botkin, "WPA and Folklore Research," 8; Botkin, *Treasury of American Folklore*, xxii, 9–10.

19. Botkin, "We Called It 'Living Lore,'" 198, 193. Novelist Nelson Algren directed the Chicago unit (Penkower, *Federal Writers' Project*, 148).

20. Botkin, "We Called It 'Living Lore,'" 187, 193; "Negro street cries" in Botkin, *Treasury of American Folklore*, 8.

21. Seeger, "General Considerations for Music Directors in Leading Community Programs," 1937, in Pescatello, *Charles Seeger*, 142; Botkin, "WPA and Folklore Research," 7, 10. Alan Lomax directly cited Malinowski in urging a political role for folklorists. Noting that Malinowski had said that the anthropologist "has the duty to speak as the native's advocate," Lomax echoed, "Just so, the folklorist has the duty to speak as the advocate of the common man" (Lomax and Lomax, *Folk Song U.S.A.*, ix).

22. Warren-Findley, "Passports to Change," 199–200.

23. Pescatello, *Charles Seeger*, 139.

24. Warren-Findley, "Passports to Change," 203, 207.

25. Seeger in ibid., 235.

26. Warren-Findley, "Passports to Change," 231–32; Pescatello, *Charles Seeger*, 149–50.

27. Bartis, "History of the Archive," 69, 66. Bartis says the funding came for fiscal year 1937, which began in June 1936, but he says that Alan Lomax was hired as assistant-in-charge in June 1937.

28. Philip H. Cohen, Chief, Radio Research Project, to Archibald MacLeish, Librarian of Congress (February 24, 1942), in Cohen et al., *Report of the Radio Research Project*, bk. 1, n.p.; Bartis, "History of the Archive," 102–3.

29. Alan Lomax, "Documentary Activities," in Cohen et al., *Report of the Radio Research Project*, bk. 1, pt. 3, 10.

30. "'Sugarland,' Rec. #2, Side #2, p. 1, 'Ballad Hunter' [radio] Transcript," and "Rock Island Line," record #3, side #2, pp. 4–5, in Cohen et al., *Report of the Radio Research Project*, vol. 5, n.p.

31. Lomax, "Documentary Activities," 11.

32. Bannerman, *Norman Corwin and Radio*, 75.

33. Lomax, "Documentary Activities," 3–9.

34. Alan Lomax, Script for "Report to the Nation" [TVA episode], in Cohen et al., *Report of the Radio Research Project*, vol. 5, n.p.

35. See Chapter 2.

36. Cohen et al., *Report of the Radio Research Project*, bk. 1, pt. 1, n.p.

37. Bartis, "History of the Archive," 110–11; Seeger, "Wartime and Peacetime Programs in Music Education" (January 1943), in Pescatello, *Charles Seeger*, 192.

38. Cohen to Archibald MacLeish (February 24, 1942); Lomax, "Documentary Activities," 10.

39. In a parenthetical note, handwritten on the draft, Lomax offered that "these sugges-tions may be applied with appropriate changes to Negro camps."

40. Alan Lomax to Archibald MacLeish, February 22, 1941, in Archive of Folk Culture, box: "Alan Lomax: Mostly Personal, Letters, Diaries, etc."; not in a folder.

41. This recommendation is crossed out on this draft of the proposal.

42. In Graham, "Folk Songs May Inspire America's Soldiers," B8. The previous fall MacLeish had written two letters to Eleanor Roosevelt, asking her about the pos-sibility of bringing folk music to army camps (October 14, 1940, and November 29, 1940, in Records of the Library of Congress, Central File, box 900, folder: "MUS 8-2-1, 1940–1").

43. Lomax, "Documentary Activities," 11.

44. At times, Lomax was explicit about his goals for the documentary programs. He noted that documentary radio "is one of the ways in which the British Broadcasting Corporation has helped to keep the attention of the British people focused sharply and passionately on the war effort. We might well follow their example" (ibid., 11).

45. "Report to the Nation—Library of Congress—Radio Research [script]," October 7, 1941, in Cohen et al., *Report of the Radio Research Project*, vol. 5, n.p. [emphasis in the original]. The script for the October 7, 1941, show says that "Report to the Nation" was broadcast every Tuesday, but I have only been able to find evidence of these two episodes.

46. Cohen to Archibald MacLeish (February 24, 1942).

47. Bannerman, *Norman Corwin and Radio*, 71–75, 13, 254 n. 30; Cohen to Archibald MacLeish (February 24, 1942). The OFF had been founded on October 7, 1941. On June 13, 1942, it was absorbed by the Office of War Information.

48. Corwin, *We Hold These Truths*, 35, 37.

49. Bannerman, *Norman Corwin and Radio*, 80–81, 85, 180. For his 1944 "Word from the People" Corwin used an alternative casting strategy, choosing a twenty-year-old marine sergeant as the play's narrator and personification of the Common Man.

50. [Introduction], Cohen et al., *Report of the Radio Research Project*, n.p.; Corwin, *This Is War!*, 20–21; Bannerman, *Norman Corwin and Radio*, 100, 153; Corwin, *On a Note of Triumph*, 11–12; Reuss, "American Folklore and Left-Wing Politics," 254, 256; "The Martins and the Coys," 3. Reuss suggests that "several of the old Almanac singers" performed the song for "On a Note of Triumph," but Bannerman makes no men-tion of this fact and cites Bond instead.

51. Alan Lomax to the Librarian of Congress [Archibald MacLeish], October 9, 1942, in Archive of Folk Culture, box: "Alan Lomax: Mostly Personal, Letters, Diaries, etc."; not in a folder. In this letter Lomax requests that he be allowed to return to the archive "at the end of the emergency period." He did not do so. In a 1960 article, Lomax suggested he left the archive because a "grass-roots Congressman" led an attack against it, stripping it of government funds and leaving it unable to mount field trips (Lomax, "Saga of a Folksong Hunter," 46–48). I have found no record of a congressional attack or funding interruption.

52. The Voice of America was headed by John Houseman, the theater and radio direc-tor famous for his "War of the Worlds" collaboration with Orson Welles, and its music division was run by Nicholas Ray, with whom Lomax had produced a folk

music radio program before the war (Houseman, *Front and Center*, 67). After the war, Ray went on to direct *Rebel without a Cause*.

53. Reuss, "American Folklore and Left-Wing Politics," 254.

54. Seeger, *Army Song Book*; Roosevelt quoted in Graham, "Folk Songs May Inspire America's Soldiers," B8.

55. Lomax, "Folk Music in the Roosevelt Era," 17; Cohen to Archibald MacLeish (February 24, 1942); Bartis, "History of the Archive," 103.

    Alan Lomax did work for the OWI, but it is difficult to ascertain the extent of his influence within it. "Freedom Songs of the United Nations," for example, was mimeographed, not formally published, and it is unclear how much circulation the OWI gave it. Similarly, I have no information about how widely heard were the OWI's hundred hours of folk music programming. The vast majority of these recordings, Richard Reuss found, were never released as records (Reuss, "American Folklore and Left-Wing Politics," 254, 303 n. 11).

56. Flanagan, *Arena*, 335, 338, 336; Mangione, *Dream and the Deal*, 304–5, 308, 290.

57. Mangione, *Dream and the Deal*, 5, 329.

58. Ibid., 330, 346–48; Penkower, *Federal Writers' Project*, 234.

59. In Tischler, *American Music*, 156.

60. Service Letter No. 3, WPA, April 18, 1942, in McDonald, *Federal Relief Administration*, 319.

61. Penkower, *Federal Writers' Project*, 237.

62. Kirk, *Musical Highlights from the White House*, 124.

63. Jackson, "Benjamin A. Botkin (1901–1975)," 3. Botkin's anthologies include *A Treasury of American Folklore* (1944), *A Treasury of New England Folklore* (1947), *A Treasury of Southern Folklore* (1949), *A Treasury of Western Folklore* (1951), *A Treasury of Mississippi River Folklore* (1955), *New York City Folklore* (1956).

64. Lieberman, *"My Song Is My Weapon,"* 67–69, 126–29; Reuss, "American Folklore and Left-Wing Politics," 259.

65. "First singing campaign" in Klein, *Woody Guthrie*, 347; "I've Got a Ballot" lyrics in Lieberman, *"My Song Is My Weapon,"* 135. Lieberman notes that the Progressive Party backed People's Songs' efforts by giving it some funds, "half of which paid the salary of [Mario] 'Boots' Casetta, who maintained the music desk at party headquarters" (Lieberman, *"My Song Is My Weapon,"* 131).

66. Klein, *Woody Guthrie*, 346; Lieberman, *"My Song Is My Weapon,"* 134, 136.

67. "Why did our songs" in Lieberman, *"My Song Is My Weapon,"* 134; "How a man" in Klein, *Woody Guthrie*, 347.

68. Dunaway, *How Can I Keep from Singing*, 130; *Red Channels*, 103; liner notes to *The Alan Lomax Sampler*, 22.

69. Pescatello, *Charles Seeger*, 174–80, 184. In 1945 the Pan-American Union was recognized by the United Nations, and in 1948 the PAU established and became integrated into the Organization of American States, a regional organization under UN charter.

70. Pescatello, *Charles Seeger*, 180, 184.

71. Seeger, "Arts in International Relations," 42. See also Seeger, "UNESCO," 168; Pescatello, *Charles Seeger*, 207–11.

72. On Dobie: Porterfield, *Last Cavalier*, 274, 465; James Weldon Johnson, "Racial Contributions to American Culture" [typescript of lectures], "Revised 1935," in the James Weldon Johnson Papers, Beinecke Library, Yale University, folder 480A-3; on Barnicle: Wolfe and Lornell, *Life and Legend of Leadbelly*, 189–90; and Killeen, "NYU Fans," 2; survey of folklore course offerings in Alan Lomax and Benjamin A. Botkin, "Folklore, American," 366, reprinted from *Ten Eventful Years* (Encyclopedia Britannica, Inc., 1947), in Folkways Collection, Smithsonian Institution, box: "Disc—1940s—Early FW, unmarked"; folder: "Folk & Other Thing [*sic*]."

Barnicle is a partial exception to the idea that academic teaching was just a sidelight for folklorists. She was a prolific collector (she is said to have recorded more of Lead Belly's songs than the Lomaxes), but she also taught courses on folklore at New York University for more than a decade.

73. Dorson, "Stith Thompson," 3–4; Martin, *Stith Thompson*, 33. In 1939 Thompson's title became professor of English and folklore, and in 1953 it changed to Distinguished Service Professor (Richmond, *Studies in Folklore*, xiii–xiv).

74. Thompson once described the New Deal's folklore projects as "rather worthless" (in Williams, "Radicalism and Professionalism in Folklore Studies," 222); Martin, *Stith Thompson*, 33; Dundes, "Ways of Studying Folklore," 43; Zumwalt, *American Folklore Scholarship*, 56–60; Bronner, *American Folklore Studies*, 72–73.

75. Martin, *Stith Thompson*, 26, 9; Dorson, "Stith Thompson," 4.

76. Mechling, "Richard M. Dorson and the Emergence of the New Class," 13. Dorson received the fifth doctorate the program awarded, after Henry Nash Smith, Daniel Aaron, Frederick B. Tolles, and Edmund S. Morgan.

77. Harrah-Conforth, "Dorson and the Indiana University Folklore Program," 341; Dorson, "Theory for American Folklore," 16.

78. Abrahams, "Representative Man," 33; Dorson, "Theory for American Folklore," 28, 47–48; MacGregor-Villarreal, "Brazilian Parallels," 359; Dorson, "Theory for American Folklore," 52.

79. Stern ("Dorson's Use and Adaptation," 47–50) and Ben-Amos ("Historical Folklore of Richard M. Dorson," 60, 55–57) feel that at the very end of his career Dorson was moving toward a more nuanced vision of American history; Dorson, "Theory for American Folklore Reviewed," 51.

80. "Monolithic peasant class" in Dorson, "Theory for American Folklore Reviewed," 59–60; "romantic nationalsim" in Dorson, *American Folklore*, 3; "Folklore has served" in Dorson, "Introduction by the Editor," 287; Stern, "Dorson's Use and Adaptation," 43.

81. Although describing debates that occurred after World War II, I continue to use "New Deal folklorists" here to identify the people (Botkin, Alan Lomax, Charles Seeger, and their colleagues) who had worked in government during the New Deal era and whose views on popularizing folklore were shaped during these years.

82. Dorson, "Theory for American Folklore," 26–27; Dorson, "Replies to Questions," 330. As the "banjo-pickers" epithet suggests, Dorson had a well-known dislike of folk music. See, e.g., Reuss and Lund, *Roads into Folklore*, 51, and Harrah-Conforth, "Dorson and the Indiana University Folklore Program," 343.

83. Dorson, "Fakelore," 6, 14. Regina Bendix notes that, ironically, Dorson drew heavily on printed sources in his own research (Bendix, *In Search of Authenticity*, 91).

NOTES TO PAGES 165–69

84. Dorson, *"Treasury of Southern Folklore* [review]," 480–82.

85. "The hope for scholarly attitudes" in Georges, "Richard M. Dorson's Conceptual and Methodological Concerns," 4; Jackson, "Benjamin A. Botkin (1901–1975)," 3.

86. Jackson, "Ben Botkin," 23; "there is an art" in Botkin, "We Called It 'Living Lore,'" 199; "Whereas a pure folklorist" in Botkin, "Applied Folklore," 199.

87. Harrah-Conforth, "Dorson and the Indiana University Folklore Program," 342; Montenyohl, "Richard M. Dorson and the Internationalization of American Folkloristics," 350–51. The library had been established by Stith Thompson, but Dorson worked to expand it and keep it separate from the rest of the university's collections (Dorson, "Stith Thompson," 4; Harrah-Conforth, "Dorson and the Indiana University Folklore Program," 346).

88. In Harrah-Conforth, "Dorson and the Indiana University Folklore Program," 344–46. W. Edson Richmond makes the same point somewhat differently, estimating that if not for Dorson, "fully half of the folklorists now in the United States would be in other disciplines if they were involved in academics at all" (Richmond, "Richard Mercer Dorson," 96). Other universities, of course, had influential folklore programs in the fifties and sixties, too, particularly the University of Pennsylvania, headed by MacEdward Leach, and, to a somewhat lesser degree, the University of California at Los Angeles, headed by Wayland Hand (Williams, "Radicalism and Professionalism in Folklore Studies," 224; Dorson, "Comment on Williams," 236).

89. Widner, "Lore for the Folk," 10–11, 13, 16. Widner cites unconvincing examples to suggest that by the mid-1970s Dorson had moderated his views on Botkin's work. She also uses obituaries to show, again not very effectively, that Botkin's standing among folklorists had improved by the end of his life; Jackson, "Ben Botkin," 32.

90. Williams, "Radicalism and Professionalism in Folklore Studies," 227. David Dunaway shows that Emrich also established a cooperative relationship with the FBI, giving the bureau information on Pete Seeger's People's Songs organization and relaying his concern about "the efforts of Communists and Communist sympathizers to infiltrate and gain control of Folksinging" (in Dunaway, *How Can I Keep from Singing*, 134).

91. Pescatello, *Charles Seeger*, 202, 217. Seeger had been a visiting lecturer at the University of California at Los Angeles in 1957.

92. Pescatello, *Charles Seeger*, 254, 219.

93. Lomax, "Adventure of Learning, 1960," 10–13. Simultaneously with cantometrics, Lomax advanced choreometrics, a classification system for world dance styles.
   Although this phase in Lomax's career represented a turn toward academia, it received significant government funding. In 1970, Elli Köngäs Maranda noted that Lomax ran the cantometrics project on an eight-year grant from the National Institute of Mental Health (Maranda, "Deep Significance and Surface Significance," 174). In the early 1990s Lomax moved the project to Hunter College.

94. Lomax, "Song Structure and Social Structure," 427, 430; Lomax, "Cantometrics," n.p.; "open-style singing" and "infant stress" in Lomax, *Folk Song Style and Culture*, 195–96, 213. Although Lomax feels his data strongly support the link between infant stress and vocal range, he is careful to add that the correlation between these two variables may be due to a third variable, and he suggests one possibility, tallness: "Tall individuals may have wider range and more forceful accent either because they

are physically larger and stronger or because physical size increases their psychological feeling of boldness" (*Folk Song Style and Culture*, 219).

95. Lomax, "Song Structure and Social Structure," 434. Although cantometrics garnered some popular interest, academic respect was generally not forthcoming (Maranda, "Deep Significance and Surface Significance," 174).

96. Charles Seeger to Richard Reuss, May 20 and June 18, 1971, in Pescatello *Charles Seeger*, 284.

97. Lomax, "Appeal for Cultural Equity," 129, 133; Sawyers, "Lomax's Global Jukebox," 1; Rule, "Folklorist Offers Insight," 11.

98. Publicity packet, 1967 festival, Center for Folklife Programs and Cultural Studies, file of festival programs. (There was no published program for the 1967 festival; but shortly after the fact, it seems, the Smithsonian put together this packet of clippings and promotional materials.)

99. Cantwell, *Ethnomimesis*, 52–53; Kurin, *Reflections of a Culture Broker*, 120, 126; Kurin, *Smithsonian Folklife Festival*, 104.

100. Kurin, *Reflections of a Culture Broker*, 118–19; Cantwell, *Ethnomimesis*, 52; Kurin, *Smithsonian Folklife Festival*, 104.

101. Cantwell, *Ethnomimesis*, 128; Rinzler in Gross Bressler, "Culture and Politics," 27.

102. Richard, "Folk Art Show Opens," D1; *Washington Evening Star* quoted in Kurin, *Smithsonian Folklife Festival*, 99; *The Congressional Record*, July 20, 1967, p. H9160, in publicity packet, 1967 festival; *Festival of American Folklife 1968*, 18–19; Kurin, *Smithsonian Folklife Festival*, 131, 9.

Tensions between Rinzler and Morris also contributed to the split between the Division of Performing Arts and Office of Folklife Programs. Subsequently, the Office of Folklife Programs acquired other duties, including (in 1987) the ownership and operation of Folkways Records. In 1992 it renamed itself the Center for Folklife Programs and Cultural Studies (Kurin, *Smithsonian Folklife Festival*, 136, 145, 140).

103. On the festival as a showpiece: Green, "Public Folklore's Name," 51; on bringing Yarborough to the Mall: conversation with Richard Kurin, director, Center for Folklife Programs and Cultural Studies, May 12, 1998; on Yarborough and Lomax's book: *American Folklife Foundation Act*, 22; Gross Bressler, "Culture and Politics," 38–44.

104. Green, "Public Folklore's Name," 51; *American Folklife Foundation Act*, 36. In 1975, after the legislation had been changed to place the Folklife Center at the Library of Congress instead of the Smithsonian, Lomax turned against the legislation (Gross Bressler, "Culture and Politics," 211).

105. Gross Bressler, "Culture and Politics," 25, 156, 167; *American Folklife Foundation Act*, 25.

106. *American Folklife Foundation Act*, 85. Dorson expressed support for the more narrowly research-oriented aspects of the proposed foundation; Dorson, "Comment on Williams," 39.

107. Gross Bressler discusses a range of possible explanations for the Smithsonian board's reluctance to take on the Folklife Center, including a hesitation about becoming a grant-giving agency (although this provision was later dropped from the bill); elitist discomfort with giving folklore a larger role beyond the folklife

festival; a fear of appearing too ambitious in the eyes of Congress ("empire building"); and, finally, personality clashes and indecision within the institution (Gross
Bressler, "Culture and Politics," 62–72).

108. "Public Law 94-201, 94th Congress, H.R. 6673," January 2, 1976, in Archive of
Folk Culture, corporate subject file: "American Folklife Preservation Act.corp."

109. Gross Bressler, "Culture and Politics," 121–28; "Folk Arts Program History—May
1993," internal document, National Endowment for the Arts, 3–4; Loomis, *Cultural Conservation*, 105–6.

110. Kurin, *Reflections of a Culture Broker*, 204–11. The Center for Folklife Programs had
previously helped the inaugural committees for Presidents Carter and Reagan plan
programs with the Smithsonian museums.

111. In ibid., 210. Kurin himself wrote the message for the White House.

112. Molotsky, "Folk Center's Funds Eliminated by the House," 11; conversation with
Alan Jabbour, director of the American Folklife Center, May 8, 1998; conversation
with Judith Gray, American Folklife Center, May 29, 1999; Brenson, "Washington's
Stake in the Arts," 29; conversation with Dan Sheehy, director, Folk and Traditional Arts, National Endowment for the Arts, May 8, 1998.

In the spring of 1999, President Clinton's budget for fiscal year 2000 requested
an increase in the NEA's budget from $98 million to $150 million. At the time of
this writing, it is unclear how Congress will respond ("Presidential Budget Request
Includes Big Increases," 1). In what could be an encouraging sign about vernacular
music's standing in Washington, Bill Ferris, blues scholar and former director of
the Center for the Study of Southern Culture, was confirmed in November 1997 as
chair of the National Endowment for the Humanities; in May 1998, Bill Ivey, formerly director of the Country Music Foundation, was confirmed to lead the NEA.

113. Conversation with Kurin, May 12, 1998.

CHAPTER FIVE

1. Attendance estimate in Shelton, "Newport Folk-Music Festival Opens," 9.

2. "Everyone sing to the baby" in Nelson, "Newport Folk Festival, 1965," 74; Shelton, *No Direction Home*, 302–3; Dunaway (*How Can I Keep from Singing*, 246) says
Dylan's shirt was yellow. Joe Boyd, the festival's production manager, recalls a
"puffed polka-dotted dueling shirt" (in Goodman, *Mansion on the Hill*, 8).

3. Paul Rothchild in Von Schmidt and Rooney, *Baby, Let Me Follow You Down*, 261. In a
1995 interview, Seeger suggests that he had expressed only a hypothetical desire
for the ax, recalling his words as "Goddamit, it's terrible! You can't understand the
words! If I had an ax, I'd cut the cable right now!" (in Goodman, *Mansion on the
Hill*, 9); Heylin, *Bob Dylan: Behind the Shades*, 142–44; Von Schmidt and Rooney,
Baby, Let Me Follow You Down, 261–62; Scaduto, *Bob Dylan*, 212–13; Shelton, *No
Direction Home*, 302; Dunaway, *How Can I Keep from Singing*, 246–47; Klein, *Woody
Guthrie*, 432–33; Marcus, *Invisible Republic*, 13. Alex Ross questions the intensity of
audience response, finding that on a tape of the performance "it's difficult to hear
boos amid the applause" ("The Wanderer," 61).

4. Dunaway, *How Can I Keep from Singing*, 247–48; Silber, "What's Happening," 5; Nelson, "What's Happening," 7–8; Bikel in Brauner, "Study of the Newport Folk Festival," 116; Yarrow in Goodman, *Mansion on the Hill*, 9.

5. See Chapters 2 and 3 regarding "folk promoters" and Chapter 4 regarding "folk bureaucrats."

6. Dunaway, *How Can I Keep from Singing*, 37, 43.

7. Ibid., 36, 53, 48; Pescatello, *Charles Seeger*, 162; "Pete had the four-string" in Dunaway, *How Can I Keep from Singing*, 48.

8. Dunaway, *How Can I Keep from Singing*, 49–50.

9. Ibid., 55–61; Alan Lomax, lecture at D.C. Librarians Meeting, 1938, in Archive of Folk Culture, American Folklife Center, Library of Congress, Washington, D.C., box: "Allen [*sic*] Lomax Papers, Miscellaneous correspondence and photographs ca. 1935"; folder: "Lomax, Alan—Personal"; "Alan Lomax Will Journey on 'Own': Folklorist Leaves on Expedition," *Austin Statesman*, December 1, 1936, in Archive of Folk Culture, box: "Allen [*sic*] Lomax Papers, Miscellaneous correspondence and photographs ca. 1935"; not in a folder; "It was an ear-opening" in *Sing Out!*, October 1962, in Seeger and Schwartz, *Incompleat Folksinger*, 230.

10. "Almost continuously" in Dunaway, *How Can I Keep from Singing*, 61; Toll, *Blacking Up*, 27; Tex Allen (actually Irving E. Theodore Baehr) came from Mount Vernon; Fred Scott was from Fresno; and Roy Rogers (then known as Leonard Slye) grew up in Cincinnati (Green, "Singing Cowboy," 21–24, 29, 36).

11. "Folk Music in the Roosevelt White House," 14; Klein, *Woody Guthrie*, 152–53. See Chapter 1 regarding Sandburg; see Chapter 4 regarding Lomax and folk music's federal presence.

12. One can certainly chart different stages in Seeger's career—from the agitprop ensemble the Almanac Singers, to the pop-oriented arrangements the Weavers, to his most influential role as a solo performer at summer camps, college campuses, and concert halls. David Dunaway (*How Can I Keep from Singing*) and Robert Cantwell (*When We Were Good*) do so convincingly, but I see Seeger's various guises as, fundamentally, variations on the same project and have chosen to assess his career as a whole.

13. Lomax was not the first on the folk revival scene to recognize Guthrie's potential. Actor Will Geer had met him in Los Angeles, where Guthrie hosted a radio show, had invited him to New York, and had arranged his 1940 debut in the city (Klein, *Woody Guthrie*, 125–27, 142–43). After Lomax heard this performance, though, he became a driving force in promoting Guthrie's career, securing concert dates, recording sessions, and book contracts for him.

14. Dunaway, *How Can I Keep from Singing*, 67; Seeger and Schwartz, *Incompleat Folksinger*, 28; Seeger, "Woody Guthrie—Some Reminiscences," 25–26; Seeger et al., *Woody Guthrie*, 26; Seeger and Schwartz, *Incompleat Folksinger*, 43; Dunaway, *How Can I Keep from Singing*, 65–70.

15. Wolfe and Lornell, *Life and Legend of Leadbelly*, 255; Klein, *Woody Guthrie*, 370–93; Seeger and Schwartz, *Incompleat Folksinger*, 49; Seeger's songbooks include *American Favorite Ballads* (1961), *The Bells of Rhymney* (1964), *Henscratches and Flyspecks* (1973), *Where Have All the Flowers Gone* (1993); Dunaway, *How Can I Keep from Singing*, 151,

156. "Kisses" was an old Irish tune to which Lead Belly added a chorus and Seeger added verses (Ed Badeaux, liner notes to *American Favorite Ballads*, 3:1).

16. Dunaway, *How Can I Keep from Singing*, 6, 304. Dunaway does not give an exact date for the letter to Senator Harris (whom he inaccurately calls "Frank Harris"), but Harris served from 1964 to 1972 (*Biographical Directory*, 1138). In addition to the *Woody Guthrie*, Seeger's other sloop was named the *Sojourner Truth*.

17. Seeger, May 1965, in Seeger and Schwartz, *Incompleat Folksinger*, 271.

18. Seeger, *American Favorite Ballads* [book]. The amount of overlap between Seeger's book and the Lomaxes' is likely actually higher, since different artists often give different titles to the same folk tune.

19. Seeger, *American Favorite Ballads* [book], 77. Seeger writes that Cecil Sharp collected "The Water Is Wide" (which he titled "Waillie Waillie") in the Appalachians.

20. "All Mixed Up" (1965), in Seeger and Schwartz, *Incompleat Folksinger*, 541–42. Later in his career, Seeger partially reconsidered his vision of global culture. In 1972 he wrote of his fear that "the tremendous power of mass-produced culture from the United States is liable to swamp the rest of the world," and he considered the "need for barriers" to protect indigenous cultures (Seeger and Schwartz, *Incompleat Folksinger*, 545–46). Seeger's repertoire, though, remained decidedly multinational.

21. "A few songs" in Seeger, *Sing Out!*, 1964, in Seeger and Schwartz, *Incompleat Folksinger*, 260. Seeger's internationlism is illustrated on the live album *Precious Friend*; Seeger and Schwartz, *Incompleat Folksinger*, 392.

22. Seeger recorded *Songs of the Lincoln Brigade* with Tom Glazer, Baldwin Hawes, and Bess Hawes. Folkways later reissued the album as *Songs of the Civil War—Vol. I* (Dunaway, *How Can I Keep from Singing*, 340–41); Seeger, *Bells of Rhymney*, 62–69; Dunaway, *How Can I Keep from Singing*, 339–81.

23. "Folk Song As It Is," 80; Moses Asch letter of introduction "To Whom It May Concern" (August 14, 1963), Danny Seeger personal correspondence folder, Folkways Collection, Center for Folklife Programs and Cultural Studies, Smithsonian Institution, Washington, D.C.

24. Jasen, *Tin Pan Alley*, 67–69; Tirro, *Jazz*, 133; Porterfield, *Jimmie Rodgers*, 409; Kinkle, *Complete Encyclopedia*, 2:278, 785.

25. *Folk Song: U.S.A.* included two minstrel tunes (94–97) and *American Ballads and Folk Songs* (249–63) featured five. "Taken over by the people" in Lomax and Lomax, *Folk Song: U.S.A.*, 78.

26. "O Susannah" and "Camptown Races." Seeger's *American Favorite Ballads* included these two, as well as Foster's "Swanee River."

27. In what may have been Seeger's only American field-recording trip, in 1951 he, his wife (Toshi), John Lomax Jr., and some others recorded in a black prison south of Houston (Seeger and Schwartz, *Incompleat Folksinger*, 67).

28. "I try not to get in the argument" in Seeger, "Why Folk Music?," 48; "All definitions change" and "Is a Greek-revival" in Seeger, "Johnny Appleseed, Jr.," 41; "Face it" in Seeger and Schwartz, *Incompleat Folksinger*, 62.

29. Seeger and Schwartz, *Incompleat Folksinger*, 145.

30. Smith's version featured accompaniment by a reed organ and a cornet played by Louis Armstrong (Williams, *Smithsonian Collection of Classic Jazz*, 37).

31. Seeger never claimed to be a superior technician. In a 1965 self-assessment, he wrote, "His brother Mike can play rings around him, not only on the banjo, of course, but on guitar and half a dozen other instruments which Pete does not attempt" ([Toshi] Seeger, "Pete Seeger," 85; Seeger used his wife's name as a pseudonym for this article).

32. Seeger, *Darling Corey and Goofing-Off Suite*; Seeger, "How I Composed (Swiped) the *Goofing-Off Suite*."

33. "Bill Moyers' Journal" [television interview with Seeger], PBS, May 20, 1994); Marine, "Guerrilla Minstrel," 41.

34. Seeger and Schwartz, *Incompleat Folksinger*, 331; Dunaway, *How Can I Keep from Singing*, 307; Arlo Guthrie jokes that Seeger "sings the song twice at the same time" (on *Precious Friend*).

35. In Dunaway, *How Can I Keep from Singing*, 222.

36. Seeger and Schwartz, *Incompleat Folksinger*, 260, 216, 294; Seeger, *How to Play the Five-String Banjo*, 5–8, 68, 64, 2.

37. Seeger, "How to Make a Chalil" (self-published, May 1955), (Dunaway, *How Can I Keep from Singing*, 333); Seeger, *Henscratches and Flyspecks*. Many of Seeger's short instructional pieces were reprinted in Seeger and Schwartz, *Incompleat Folksinger*, 325–421. This volume does not date the articles but notes that most of them were written in the 1950s (325).

38. Seeger, in Seeger and Schwartz, *Incompleat Folksinger*, 328, 345–47.

39. Seeger, *Sing Out!* (1954), in Seeger and Schwartz, *Incompleat Folksinger*, 155; Dunaway, *How Can I Keep from Singing*, 148; Friesen, "Songs of Our Time," 131–33; Seeger and Schwartz, *Incompleat Folksinger*, 399.

40. In "Bill Moyers' Journal."

41. Dunaway, *How Can I Keep from Singing*, 236–41; Seeger and Schwartz, *Incompleat Folksinger*, 104–11. Dunaway (241) writes that "for two glorious days, [Seeger] had found the singing movement he had hoped for since he was twenty-one. He seemed as excited about the singing as at the movement's more concrete achievements." Within a year, Seeger's excitement was dampened as the militancy of Black Power overtook the civil rights movement. Dunaway (243) quotes a SNCC worker in the late sixties as saying, "Man, the workers are too busy getting ready to fight to bother with singing anymore."

42. Dunaway, *How Can I Keep from Singing*, 239–41.

43. Ibid., 74; Cantwell, "He Shall Overcome," 63.

44. Cantwell, *When We Were Good*, 145; Klein, *Woody Guthrie*, 194; Dunaway, *How Can I Keep from Singing*, 135–37.

45. Seeger and Schwartz, *Incompleat Folksinger*, 13–15.

46. Dunaway, *How Can I Keep from Singing*, 13–21, 80–82, 208; "A person shouldn't have" in Cantwell, "He Shall Overcome," 70.

47. Hays quoted in Dunaway, *How Can I Keep from Singing*, 122; ibid., 236, 254, 296, 7; Seeger eventually agreed to pose for the photo (Chaffin, "Keeping the Faith," 43).

48. E.g., Seeger and Blood, *Where Have All the Flowers Gone*, 11–12; Dunaway, *How Can I Keep from Singing*, 36–53.

49. Seeger and Schwartz, *Incompleat Folksinger*, 460, 564, 13.

50. Dunaway, *How Can I Keep from Singing*, 236; [Toshi] Seeger, "Pete Seeger," 85, 87; Seeger and Schwartz, *Incompleat Folksinger*, 553.

51. In Dunaway, *How Can I Keep from Singing*, 310.

52. Cantwell, "He Shall Overcome," 62. See Chapter 4 for a discussion of Rinzler and the Festival of American Folklife.

53. Seeger, *Sing Out!* (1956), in Seeger and Schwartz, *Incompleat Folksinger*, 108; on folk-song clubs, see Green, "Campus Folksong Club," 61–72; Seeger and Schwartz, *Incompleat Folksinger*, 347; Dunaway, *How Can I Keep from Singing*, 189.

54. To take just one example, in the mid-1960s folklorist John Greenway was doing fieldwork with Australian aborigines who, he decided, did not realize that the hard lives they faced constituted unjust suffering. "I tried," Greenway writes, "to bring the beginning of understanding to these people by singing a few of Woody's songs to them" (Greenway, "Woody Guthrie," 186).

55. The other great musical influence on the 1960s revival was Harry Smith's *Anthology of American Folk Music*, an eccentric compendium of recordings from the 1920s and 1930s that ranged across genres (from hillbilly to blues to gospel to cowboy). The collection inspired countless revivalists to re-create the old-time styles and, in some cases, track down the musicians who had recorded the songs decades before (see Chapter 3). For a close reading of the *Anthology*, see Cantwell's "Smith's Memory Theater." For fascinating riffs on the *Anthology*'s connections to Bob Dylan, see Marcus's *Invisible Republic*.

56. See, e.g., Friesen, "Something New Has Been Added," 12–23.

57. Scaduto, *Bob Dylan*, 3, 27; Shelton, *No Direction Home*, 87, 90.

58. Shelton, *No Direction Home*, 68–69; Scaduto, *Bob Dylan*, 66; Dylan to Izzy Young, in Scaduto, *Bob Dylan*, 67; "Cowboy styles" in Shelton, *No Direction Home*, 128; "I was born in Duluth" in Shelton, *No Direction Home*, 110; "Hey, man" in Scaduto, *Bob Dylan*, 69; "I Am My Words," 94–95; Shelton, *No Direction Home*, 131.

59. "I Am My Words," 94; Welles, "Angry Young Folk Singer," 109; Shelton, *No Direction Home*, 92.

60. Pankake and Nelson, "Bob Dylan," 260; Welles, "Angry Young Folk Singer," 109; Dylan in "Worth Quoting," 92; Shelton, *No Direction Home*, 164.

61. Shelton, *No Direction Home*, 73–74, 134, 120, 53.

62. Scaduto, *Bob Dylan*, 39, 52–53, 56, 62, 74–75; Klein, *Woody Guthrie*, 427.

63. Riley, *Hard Rain*, 38–39, 41; Mellers, *Darker Shade of Pale*, 122–23; Shelton, *No Direction Home*, 118–23; Heylin, *Bob Dylan: The Recording Sessions*, 8.

64. *The Freewheelin' Bob Dylan* [liner notes]. Ross ("The Wanderer," 61) says that "Hard Rain" was actually written at least a month before the missile crisis; Shelton, *No Direction Home*, 155–56; Scalet, "Song Was There before Me," 13, 15.

65. Dylan, *Lyrics*, 53. Greil Marcus says the melody to "Blowin' in the Wind" comes from an antebellum song sung by runaway slaves, "No More Auction Block" (or "Many Thousands Gone") (Marcus, *Invisible Republic*, 20); "was influenced of course" in Crowe, *Biograph*, 2 [among unnumbered sheets of song descriptions]; Shelton, *No Direction Home*, 156, 214.

66. "I don't have to bs" in Turner, "Bob Dylan," 6; "the times call for truth" in Shelton, *No Direction Home*, 191; Shelton, *No Direction Home*, 170, 240–41; Scaduto, *Bob Dylan*, 151; Cott, *Dylan*, 68.

67. Turner, "Bob Dylan," 6; Silber, "Bob Dylan," 53; Jackson in Turner, "Bob Dylan," 6.

68. "Most creative troubadour" in De Turk and Poulin, "I Will Show You Fear in a Handful of Songs," 271; Shelton, *No Direction Home*, 140. Seeger included Dylan's "Hard Rain" and "Who Killed Davey Moore" at his landmark "We Shall Overcome" concert at Carnegie Hall, which was issued as an album (Dunaway, *How Can I Keep from Singing*, 228); Pankake, "Pete's Children," 285; Dylan, "Letter from Bob Dylan." Shelton (*No Direction Home*, 208) says this letter was written in the fall of 1963 and published the next January; Dylan, *Lyrics*, 115.

69. "Hey, that's our music," boast about Presley recordings, and "John Hammond" in Scaduto, *Bob Dylan*, 6, 68, 108; senior yearbook and "when nobody was around" in Shelton, *No Direction Home*, 43, 39, 131.

70. Scaduto, *Bob Dylan*, 227, 222, 155–56.

71. The three electric albums Dylan released are *Bringing It All Back Home* (released March 1965), *Highway 61 Revisited* (September 1965), and *Blonde on Blonde* (June 1966). Dylan was not the only young folk enthusiast to shift toward pop. In the mid-1960s, erstwhile revivalists founded the Byrds, the Grateful Dead, and the Lovin' Spoonful, among others. None of their founders, though, had had nearly Dylan's stature within the folk revival before their transformations. The Byrds gained their fame initially for their pop cover of Dylan's "Mr. Tambourine Man" (1965), which they followed the next year with a hit version of Pete Seeger's "Turn, Turn, Turn."

72. "Who knows" in Seeger and Schwartz, *Incompleat Folksinger*, 460; "I like the 1966" in *Sing Out!*, in Seeger and Schwartz, *Incompleat Folksinger*, 288. Seeger's *Rainbow Race* uses an electric bass, and *Precious Friend* (1980) features Arlo Guthrie's rock band, complete with electric guitar solos.

73. Shelton, *No Direction Home*, 295, 154. Dylan also recorded other electrified tunes at the 1962 session, but they (like "Mixed-Up Confusion") were left off this album (*The Freewheelin' Bob Dylan*).

74. In Dunaway, *How Can I Keep from Singing*, 247. Dylan later claimed that people hostile to his electric sound intentionally distorted it: "They twisted the sound. They didn't like what I was going to play and they twisted the sound on me before I began" (in Ephron and Edmiston, "Bob Dylan Interview," 87). Many writers, though, say that the sound controls were manned by Dylan associates (e.g., Heylin, *Bob Dylan: Behind the Shades*, 142; Dunaway, *How Can I Keep from Singing*, 247; Goodman, *Mansion on the Hill*, 9). In *Where Have All the Flowers Gone* (172–3), Seeger again asserts that he was not upset with Dylan going electric but with the distorted sound system: "Bob was singing 'Maggie's Farm,' one of his best songs, but you couldn't understand a word."

I use "performance" here in the most literal sense of the vocalizing of songs. I do not mean to imply that loud concerts produce completely passive audience members. At even the most deafening rock shows, audience members may take part more indirectly in a variety of other "performances," from screaming and waving their arms to slamming into each other in mosh pits, to solemnly flicking cigarette lighters.

75. In Shelton, *No Direction Home*, 293; "Folk and the Rock," 88.

76. "Blowin'" appears on *The Freewheelin' Bob Dylan* and in Dylan, *Lyrics*, 53; "Highway 61" on *Highway 61 Revisited* and in Dylan, *Lyrics*, 202; "Ballad of a Thin Man" on

Highway 61 Revisited and in Dylan, *Lyrics*, 198. One can make a convincing case that Pete Seeger is the out-of-touch thin man whom Dylan savages in this song.

77. Dylan, *Lyrics*, 182. The lowercase "i" appears in the original. In 1965, Dylan told Nora Ephron and Susan Edmiston, "Truth is chaos. Maybe beauty is chaos" (in Ephron and Edmiston, "Bob Dylan Interview," 86).

78. In Shelton, *No Direction Home*, 284, 291, 305. Dylan echoes the "glad I'm not me" statement in the liner notes to his *Biograph* box set, telling Cameron Crowe, "I don't think of myself as Bob Dylan. It's like Rimbaud said, 'I is another'" (in Crowe, "Biograph," 7 [among unnumbered sheets of song descriptions]).

79. In Dunaway, *How Can I Keep from Singing*, 249, 247.

80. I am using "pre-1965" and "post-1965" as shorthand for pre- and post-March 1965, when Dylan released *Bringing It All Back Home*.

81. In Cohen, "Conversations with Bob Dylan," 9; Dylan, *Writings and Drawings by Bob Dylan*; in Crowe, "Biograph," 4 [among unnumbered sheets of song descriptions].

82. Shelton, *No Direction Home*, 271; "You gotta listen" in Ephron and Edmiston, "Bob Dylan Interview," 89; "I consider Hank Williams" in Shelton, *No Direction Home*, 196; "Rasputin" in "Austin Interview," 163.

83. In Cohen, "Conversations with Bob Dylan," 11; in Saal, "Dylan's Country Pie," 297; in Shelton, *No Direction Home*, 480; in Worrell, "'It's All Right in Front,'" 123; in Crowe, "Biograph," 31 [in bound booklet].

84. In Shelton, *No Direction Home*, 488.

85. Both of these tunes are Child ballads that appear on Seeger's *American Favorite Ballads* anthology.

86. Dylan recorded "Donald White" for a radio show in 1962 (under the pseudonym Blind Boy Grunt). The recording was issued on a compilation album, *Broadside Reunion, Volume Six*, in 1972 (Heylin, *Bob Dylan: The Recording Sessions*; Riley, *Hard Rain*, 211). Subsequent dates for songs in the text refer to when a recording was released; *The Times They Are A-Changin'*; Dylan, *Lyrics*, 31, 102.

87. E.g., "Joey" (*Desire*) or "Tweeter and the Monkey Man" (*Traveling Wilburys, Volume 1*).

88. *John Wesley Harding*; Dylan, *Lyrics*, 253–55.

89. *Highway 61 Revisited*; Dylan, *Lyrics*, 204–6.

90. See Chapter 2 for a more detailed discussion of the blues form.

91. *Sing Out!* (1965), in Seeger and Schwartz, *Incompleat Folksinger*, 280.

92. E.g., "She Belongs to Me" (*Bringing It All Back Home*; Dylan, *Lyrics*, 163); "Meet Me in the Morning" (*Blood on the Tracks*; Dylan, *Lyrics*, 363); "10,000 Men" (*Under the Red Sky*); "Dirt Road Blues" (*Time Out of Mind*).

93. *Bringing It All Back Home*; Dylan, *Lyrics*, 168.

94. See Chapter 2 regarding Muddy Waters's vocal styling. "Sitting on a Barbed-Wire Fence" was recorded for *Highway 61 Revisited* but did not actually appear on the album. It appears on Bob Dylan, *The Bootleg Series*, vol. 2. The lyrics given here are as heard on the recording. Those in Dylan's anthology (*Lyrics*, 213) differ somewhat.

95. The stanzas begin with eight bars on the I (or tonic) chord (instead of the traditional four), followed by two on the IV, then four (instead of the customary two) on the I chord, two on the V, and two on the I. (The third stanza displaces one bar of the tonic to later in the pattern. The fourth stanza has one extra measure.)

96. *Bringing It All Back Home*; Dylan, *Lyrics*, 164; Riley, *Hard Rain*, 98–101.

97. Malone, *Country Music, U.S.A.*, 1–22, 423, 184, 200; Malone, "Country Music," 517; *The Very Best of Hank Williams*.

98. Spitz, *Bob Dylan*, 392–93. Dylan had also recorded his previous two albums in Nashville, *Blonde on Blonde* and *John Wesley Harding* (Heylin, *Bob Dylan: The Recording Sessions*, 46, 69).

99. In a 1969 interview, Dylan disingenuously attributed the change in his singing to having quit smoking, proclaiming, "Stop smoking those cigarettes (Laughter) . . . and you'll be able to sing like Caruso" (in Wenner, "Rolling Stone Interview," 323).

100. *Nashville Skyline*; Dylan, *Lyrics*, 276, 270.

101. "John Wesley Harding" on *John Wesley Harding* and in Dylan, *Lyrics*, 249; "Isis" on *Desire* and in Dylan, *Lyrics*, 378.

102. The fuller voice does surface on some of the tracks of *Self-Portrait*; "If Not for You" on *New Morning* and in Dylan, *Lyrics*, 285; "You Angel You" on *Planet Waves* and in Dylan, *Lyrics*, 348.

103. Levine, *Black Culture and Black Consciousness*, 174–76. The precise nature of the difference between gospel and spirituals is a matter of some debate among scholars. Levine sees spirituals as encouraging a search for salvation on earth. He characterizes gospel songs, by contrast, as having a more "otherworldly" focus, with heaven clearly distinct from and unreachable during one's present lifetime. Paul Oliver, though ("Gospel Music," 557), suggests the opposite—that spirituals tell followers simply to endure the tribulations of contemporary life, while gospel holds out the possibility of redemption in this lifetime. Oliver also says that many gospel songs are "musically little more than spirituals with a modern beat." Since I am primarily interested in the presence of religious imagery in Dylan's work, I have not dwelled on the spiritual-gospel distinction. I also have not considered white gospel in this discussion, since Dylan was most directly influenced by the African American tradition.

104. Hillsman, *Gospel Music*, 36–37.

105. A partial exception came in 1959 when Seeger put words from the Book of Ecclesiastes (plus one line of his own) to music and scored a hit with "Turn, Turn, Turn" (Seeger, *Where Have All the Flowers Gone*, 173).

106. On "Father of Night," Dylan respectfully invokes "Father of air and Father of trees / Who dwells in our hearts and our memories, / Father of minutes, Father of days, / Father of whom we most solemnly praise" (*Desire*; Dylan, *Lyrics*, 297; Shelton, *No Direction Home*, 419). "Forever Young" echoes the Golden Rule: "May God bless and keep you always, / May your wishes all come true, / May you always do for others / And let others do for you" (*Planet Waves*; Dylan, *Lyrics*, 346). *Empire Burlesque* and *Knocked Out Loaded* do not include explicitly religious songs but use gospel-styled choruses of background singers. "Knockin'" on *Pat Garrett and Billy the Kid* and in Dylan, *Lyrics*, 337. "God Knows" on *Under the Red Sky*.

107. The Davis Sisters (1952), on *Jubilation!*, vol. 2; The Caravans (ca. 1964), on *Jubilation!*, vol. 2.

108. "When You Gonna" on *Slow Train Coming* and in Dylan, *Lyrics*, 432; "Solid Rock" on *Saved* and in Dylan, *Lyrics*, 446.

109. E.g., on "By and By," the Davis Sisters sing "I'll soon be through fire on this battlefield / That's when I'll lay down my sword and shield."

110. "How I Got Over," as sung by Clara Ward (1950, *Jubilation!*, vol. 1) and by Mahalia Jackson (1951, *Jubilation!*, vol. 2); "The Old Ship of Zion," as sung by the Roberta Martin Singers (1950, *Jubilation!*, vol. 1).

111. "When He Returns" on *Slow Train Coming* and in Dylan, *Lyrics*, 437; "Are You Ready?" on *Saved* and in Dylan, *Lyrics*, 450.

112. To some extent at least, the converse of this formulation seems to be true as well. Dylan's most critically reviled album, *Self-Portrait*, suffered because it consisted mostly of covers of other writers' songs that Dylan had not personalized or seeded with other influences.

113. "Highway 61 Revisited" on *Highway 61 Revisited* and in Dylan, *Lyrics*, 202.

114. Lead Belly recorded "Po' Howard" for John and Alan Lomax in 1935 (reissued on *Gwine Dig a Hole to Put the Devil In*). "The Roving Gambler" appears in the Lomaxes' *American Ballads and Folk Songs*, 150–51.

115. The song deviates slightly from the twelve-bar form by having the first set of tonic chords last for eight measures instead of four.

116. Patton, "Who Owns the Blues?," 35. Dylan also covered an old blues tune called "Highway 51" on his first album (*Bob Dylan*).

117. "Tangled Up in Blue" on *Blood on the Tracks* and in Dylan, *Lyrics*, 357–59; Riley, *Hard Rain*, 234.

118. In 1985 Dylan described "Tangled" as "another one of those things where I was trying to do something that I didn't think had ever been done before. In terms of trying to tell a story . . . without being some kind of fake, sappy attempted tearjerker. . . . I wanted to defy time" (Heylin, *Bob Dylan: Behind the Shades*, 240).

119. Riley (*Hard Rain*, 241) says that this line comes from a song by country singer Tex Ritter; "Idiot Wind" on *Blood on the Tracks* and in Dylan, *Lyrics*, 367–68.

120. *Good as I Been to You*, 1992; *World Gone Wrong*, 1993.

121. On Siouxsie and the Banshees: Riley, *Hard Rain*, 293; Harvey, *Rid of Me*; on N'Dour: Strauss, "Two Styles," C19; Strauss, "New Releases," 34.

122. E.g., "Banner-Strangled Stars": "[Dylan] did what everyone was hoping he would, taking a reflective tack on 'Don't Think Twice It's All Right' and rocking out with powerful arrangements of 'All Along the Watchtower,' 'Highway 61 Revisited' and 'Rain Day Women'"; Jon Pareles, "Minor Discord amid the Nostalgia-Trip Harmony," B4: "Bob Dylan played Woodstock '94 tonight, 25 years after he avoided the first Woodstock festival. Except for only two recent songs, Mr. Dylan and his four-man band played a set they could have performed at the original festival: one masterpiece after another from the 1960's." Pareles also referred to Dylan as "the chief icon" of the baby-boomer generation at the festival (Jon Pareles, "Woodstock's Children," sec. 2, 25).

123. "Bob Dylan: Electric Minstrel of Times That Were A' Changin'," 14; Gates, "Dylan Revisited" (the front cover of this *Newsweek* issue did not use the title of the article itself).

124. Cocks, "U2 Explores America," 146; U2, *Rattle and Hum* (1988).

125. Springsteen, "Speech at the Rock-and-Roll Hall of Fame," 287.

CODA

1. Pareles, "Rock Hall of Fame Inductees Honored," C17; "The 1994 *Living Blues* Readers' Awards," 10; "Stamp of Approval," 19. In addition to Guthrie and Lead Belly, the "folk musician" stamp set also featured Josh White and Sonny Terry.

2. "A Dozen Arts Figures Honored," 119; "Book Award Winners Focus on Black Life and the Blues," C18; Jennings, "Gathering in a Reaper's Harvest," 1; *The Alan Lomax Sampler*, 7.

3. Pareles, "Kennedy Honors," C11; "Clinton Presents National Arts and Humanities Awards," 1; Dunn, "Hall of Fame '96," 18; *Where Have All the Flowers Gone: The Songs of Pete Seeger*.

4. Gates, "Dylan Revisited," 64; "Pope's Speech Plays off of Dylan Performance," 2A; "Dylan Released," 10A; Grammy speech (February 25, 1998) transcribed from television broadcast by author.

5. "Festival and Camp Guide," 158–69; Bragg and Wilco, *Mermaid Avenue*.

6. Patton, "Who Owns the Blues?," 1, 35.

7. Flea quoted in "Clapton Gathers Top Grammy Honors," 2; Pirner quoted in Schoemer, "Can Winner Be a Loser?," C15.

BIBLIOGRAPHY

MANUSCRIPT COLLECTIONS

Austin, Texas
The University of Texas at Austin, The Center for American History
    Lomax (John A.) Family Papers
New Haven, Connecticut
Yale University, Beinecke Library
    James Weldon Johnson Papers
Washington, D.C.
Library of Congress
    American Folklife Center, Archive of Folk Culture
Smithsonian Institution
    Center for Folklife Programs and Cultural Studies
        The Folkways Collection

BOOKS, ARTICLES, AND UNPUBLISHED WORKS

Aarons, Leroy. "Woody Guthrie Gets Award Here." *Washington Post*, April 7, 1966, D28.
Abrahams, Roger D. "The Foundations of American Public Folklore." In *Public Folklore*, edited by Robert Baron and Nicholas R. Spitzer, 245–62. Washington, D.C.: Smithsonian Institution Press, 1992.
——. "Representative Man: Richard Dorson, Americanist." *Journal of Folklore Research* 26 (January–April 1989): 27–34.
Agee, James. "Pseudo-Folk." *Partisan Review*, Spring 1944, 219–23.
Alan Lomax Sampler, The [liner notes]. CD1700. Cambridge, Mass.: Rounder Records Corp., 1997.
Aldin, Mary Katherine. "Blues Heaven." *Living Blues*, July/August 1988, 17.

——. *Chess Blues* [liner notes]. CHD4-9340. Universal City, Calif.: MCA Records, 1992.

——. *Muddy Waters: The Complete Plantation Recordings* [liner notes]. CHD-9344. Universal City, Calif.: MCA Records, 1993.

——. "Muddy Waters Scholarship Winner." *Living Blues*, July/August 1989, 4.

Allen, William, Charles Pickard Ware, and Lucy McKim Garrison. *Slave Songs of the United States*. New York: A. Simpson and Co., 1867.

Altman, Billy. "A Village Folk Scene Rooted in Rock." *New York Times*, June 13, 1999, sec. 2, 30.

——. *Leadbelly: Alabama Bound* [liner notes]. 9600-2-R. New York: RCA, 1989.

American Folklife Foundation Act: Hearing before the Subcommittee on Education of the Committee on Labor and Public Welfare, United States Senate, Ninety-first Congress, Second Session on S. 1591 to Establish an American Folklife Foundation and for Other Purposes, May 18, 1970. Washington, D.C.: U.S. Government Printing Office, 1970.

"Amity Grad, Blues Legend to Perform at Carnegie Hall." *New Haven Register*, April 21, 1994, D1, D3.

"The Archive of Folk Song: A Fiftieth Anniversary Celebration" [program booklet]. Washington, D.C.: Library of Congress, 1978.

Armstrong, Dan. " 'Commercial' Folksongs—'Product of Instant Culture.' " *Sing Out!*, February–March 1963, 20–22.

Asch, Moses. Foreword to *Leadbelly: A Collection of World-Famous Songs by Huddie Ledbetter*, edited by John A. and Alan Lomax. New York: Folkways Music Publishers, 1959.

Asch, Moses, and Alan Lomax, eds. *The Leadbelly Songbook: The Ballads, Blues, and Folksongs of Huddie Ledbetter*. New York: Oak Publications, 1962.

"Austin Interview, The" [1965]. In *Bob Dylan: The Early Years: A Retrospective*, edited by Craig McGregor, 161–63. 1972. New York: Da Capo Press, 1990.

Autry, Gene, and Mickey Herskowitz. *Back in the Saddle Again*. Garden City, N.Y.: Doubleday and Co., 1978.

Badeaux, Ed. "Pete Seeger . . . His Songs and His Work" [liner notes to *American Favorite Ballads* (vol. 3)]. FA2322. New York: Folkways, 1959.

Bannerman, R. LeRoy. *Norman Corwin and Radio: The Golden Years*. University: University of Alabama Press, 1986.

"Banner-Strangled Stars, The." *Times Newspapers Limited*, August 16, 1994.

Barlow, William. *"Looking Up at Down": The Emergence of a Blues Culture*. Philadelphia: Temple University Press, 1989.

Baron, Robert. "The Professionalization of Folklore Studies." In *Public Folklore*, edited by Robert Baron and Nicholas R. Spitzer, 308–37. Washington, D.C.: Smithsonian Institution Press, 1992.

Baron, Robert, and Nicholas R. Spitzer, eds. *Public Folklore*. Washington, D.C.: Smithsonian Institution Press, 1992.

Bartis, Peter. "A History of the Archive of Folk Song at the Library of Congress: The First Fifty Years." Ph.D. diss., University of Pennsylvania, 1982.

Barton, William E. *Old Plantation Hymns*. New York: AMS Press, 1972 [1899].

Bascam, Louise Rand. "Ballads of Western North Carolina." *Journal of American Folklore* 22 (June 1909): 238–50.

Bascomb, David. "Discography." In Sean Killeen, "Fannin Street: The Setting and the Song." *Lead Belly Letter* 2 (Winter 1992): 4.

Bass, Ralph. *Muddy Waters, Folk Singer* [liner notes]. 5907. Universal City, Calif.: MCA Records, 1986 [1964].

Bauman, Richard. "Proposal for a Center of Applied Folklore." In *Papers on Applied Folklore*, edited by Dick Sweterlitsch, 1–5. *Folklore Forum*, Bibliographic and Special Studies, no. 8, 1971.

Bauman, Richard, Roger D. Abrahams, and Susan Kalcik. "American Folklore and American Studies." *American Quarterly* 28 (Bibliography Issue, 1976): 360–77.

Beatty, Arthur. "Some Ballad Variants and Songs." *Journal of American Folklore* 22 (March 1909): 63–71.

Becker, Jane S., and Barbara Franco, eds. *Folk Roots, New Roots: Folklore in American Life*. Lexington, Mass.: Museum of Our National Heritage, 1988.

Belden, Henry Marvin. "The Study of Folk-Song in America." *Modern Philology* 2 (June 1904): 573–79.

Bell, Michael J. " 'No Borders to the Ballad Maker's Art': Francis James Child and the Politics of the People." *Western Folklore* 47 (October 1988): 285–307.

Ben-Amos, Dan. "The Historical Folklore of Richard M. Dorson." *Journal of Folklore Research* 26 (January–April 1989): 51–60.

Bendix, Regina. *In Search of Authenticity: The Formation of Folklore Studies*. Madison: University of Wisconsin Press, 1997.

Benét, William Rose. "Ballad of a Ballad-Singer." *New Yorker*, January 19, 1935, 36.

Berea College Catalogue, 1991–1993. Berea, Ky.: Berea College, 1991.

Berry, Chuck. *Chuck Berry: The Autobiography*. New York: Harmony Books, 1987.

"Big Bill Is Gone." *Sing Out!*, Winter 1959, 31.

Bindas, Kenneth J. "All of This Music Belongs to the Nation: The Federal Music Project of the WPA and American Cultural Nationalism, 1935–1939." Ph.D. diss., University of Toledo, 1988.

Biographical Directory of the United States Congress. Washington, D.C.: U.S. Government Printing Office, 1989, 1138.

Blacking, John. "Making Artistic Popular Music: The Goal of True Folk." *Popular Music* 1 (1981): 9–14.

Bluestein, Gene. *Poplore: Folk and Pop in American Culture*. Amherst: University of Massachusetts Press, 1994.

——. *The Voice of the Folk: Folklore and American Literary Theory*. Amherst: University of Massachusetts, 1972.

Blum, John Morton. *V Was for Victory*. New York: Harcourt Brace Jovanovich, 1976.

"Bob Dylan: Electric Minstrel of Times That Were A'Changin'." *Life*, Fall 1990, 14.

"Book Award Winners Focus on Black Life and the Blues." *New York Times*, February 14, 1994, C18.

Botkin, B. A. "Applied Folklore: Creating Understanding through Folklore." *Southern Folklore Quarterly* 17 (September 1953): 199–206.

——. "The Folkness of the Folk." *English Journal* (College Edition) 26 (June 1937): 461–69.

——. *A Treasury of American Folklore: Stories, Ballads, and Traditions of the People*. New York: Crown Publishers, 1944.

———. "We Called It 'Living Lore.'" *New York Folklore Quarterly* 14 (Fall 1958): 189–201.

———. "WPA and Folklore Research: 'Bread and Song.'" *Southern Folklore Quarterly* 3 (March 1939): 7–14.

Boyes, Georgina. *The Imagined Village: Culture, Ideology, and the English Folk Revival*. New York: Manchester University Press, 1993.

Brack, Ray, and Earl Paige. "Chess and the Blues: From the Streets to the Studio." *Billboard*, June 24, 1967, sec. 2, 20–22.

Bradford, Gamaliel. *As God Made Them: Portraits of Some Nineteenth-Century Americans*. Cambridge, Mass.: Riverside Press, 1929.

Brauner, Cheryl Anne. "A Study of the Newport Folk Festival and the Newport Folk Foundation." M.A. thesis, Memorial University of Newfoundland, 1983.

Brenson, Michael. "Washington's Stake in the Arts." *New York Times*, April 12, 1998, sec. 2, 1, 29.

Bronner, Simon J. *American Folklore Studies: An Intellectual History*. Lawrence: University Press of Kansas, 1986.

Brunson, Rose Toomer. "Socialization Experiences and Socio-Economic Characteristics of Urban Negroes as Related to Use of Selected Southern Foods and Medical Remedies." Ph.D. diss., Michigan State University, 1962.

Budin, David. "Spreading like a Prairie Fire." *CWRU: The Magazine of Case Western Reserve University*, February 1997, 10–15.

Burke, Peter. *Popular Culture in Early Modern Europe*. New York: New York University Press, 1978.

Burlin, Natalie Curtis. *Hampton Series Negro Folk-Songs Recorded by Natalie Curtis Burlin*. 4 vols. New York: G. Schirmer, 1918–19.

Callahan, North. *Carl Sandburg: His Life and Works*. University Park: Pennsylvania State University Press, 1987.

Campbell, Olive Dame, and Cecil J. Sharp. *English Folk Songs from the Southern Appalachians*. New York: G. P. Putnam and Sons, 1917.

Canon, Neal. "Art for Whose Sake: The Federal Music Project of the WPA." In *Challenges in American Culture*, edited by Ray B. Browne, Larry N. Landrum, and William K. Bottorff, 85–100. Bowling Green, Ohio: Bowling Green University Popular Press, 1970.

Cantwell, Robert. *Ethnomimesis: Folklife and the Representation of Culture*. Chapel Hill: University of North Carolina Press, 1993.

———. "He Shall Overcome: Pete Seeger." *New England Review* 13 (Fall 1990): 61–75.

———. "Smith's Memory Theater: *The Folkways Anthology of American Folk Music*." *New England Review* 13 (Spring–Summer 1991): 362–97.

———. *When We Were Good: The Folk Revival*. Cambridge, Mass.: Harvard University Press, 1996.

Capaldi, Jim. "Conversation with Mr. Folkways." *Folkscene*, May 1978 and June 1978, 16–22 and 2–4.

Carby, Hazel V. *Race Men*. Cambridge, Mass.: Harvard University Press, 1998.

Carruthers, Sleepy Geoff. "An Interview with Alan Lomax." *WKCR Program Guide* 4 (June 1988): 7–14.

Chaffin, Tom. "Keeping the Faith." *Horizon*, October 1981, 42–47.

Charlton, Katherine. *Rock Music Styles: A History*. Dubuque, Iowa: William C. Brown Publishers, 1990.

Charters, Samuel B. *The Country Blues*. 1959. New York: Da Capo Press, 1975.

Child, Francis James. "Ballad Poetry." In *Johnson's New Universal Cyclopedia*, edited by F. A. P. Barnard, 365–68. New York: A. J. Johnson and Sons, 1874.

——, ed. *English and Scottish Ballads*. 1857–58. Boston: Little, Brown, and Co., 1860.

——. *The English and Scottish Popular Ballads*. Boston: Houghton, Mifflin and Co., 1898.

"Clapton Gathers Top Grammy Honors." *New Haven Register*, February 25, 1993, 2.

"Clinton Presents National Arts and Humanities Awards." *AVISO*, November 1994, 1, 5.

Cocks, Jay. "U2 Explores America." *Time*, November 21, 1988, 146.

Coffin, Tristram Potter, ed. *Our Living Tradition: An Introduction to American Folklore*. New York: Basic Books, 1968.

Cohen, John. "Conversations with Bob Dylan." *Sing Out!*, October–November 1968, 6–23, 67.

——. "The Folk Music Interchange." *Sing Out!*, January 1964, 42–49.

——. "In Defense of City Folksingers: A Reply to Alan Lomax." *Sing Out!*, Summer 1959, 32–34.

——. "Roscoe Holcomb at Zabriskie Point." *Sing Out!*, September–October 1970, 20–21.

Cohen, Norm. " 'I'm a Record Man'—Uncle Art Satherley Reminisces." *JEMF Quarterly* 8 (Spring 1972): 18–21.

Cohen, Norm, and Anne Cohen. "Folk and Hillbilly Music: Further Thoughts on Their Relation." *JEMF Quarterly* 13 (Summer 1977): 50–57.

Cohen, Philip H., Joseph Liss, Alan Lomax, and Dorothy Allen, eds. "Report of the Radio Research Project." Library of Congress, 1942.

Cohn, Lawrence, ed. *Nothing but the Blues: The Music and the Musicians*. New York: Abbeville Press, 1993.

Collier, James Lincoln. "The Faking of Jazz: How Politics Distorted the History of the Hip." *New Republic*, November 18, 1985, 33–40.

"Conference on the Character and State of Studies in Folklore [Proceedings of April 11–12, 1942, conference]." *Journal of American Folklore* 100 (October–December 1946): 495–527.

Cook, Bruce. *Listen to the Blues*. New York: Charles Scribner's Sons, 1973.

Coombs, Josiah H. "A Traditional Ballad from the Kentucky Mountains." *Journal of American Folklore* 23 (September 1910): 381–82.

Corritore, Bob, Bill Ferris, and Jim O'Neal. "Willie Dixon, Part I [interview]." *Living Blues*, July/August 1988, 16–25.

——. "Willie Dixon, Part II [interview]." *Living Blues*, September/October 1988, 20–31.

Corwin, Norman. *On a Note of Triumph*. New York: Simon and Schuster, 1945.

——. *This Is War! A Collection of Plays about America on the March*. New York: Dodd, Mead and Co., 1942.

——. *We Hold These Truths*. New York: Howell, Soskin, 1942.

Cott, Jonathan. *Dylan*. Garden City, N.Y.: Doubleday and Co., 1984.

Cowley, John H. "Don't Leave Me Here: Non-Commercial Blues: The Field Trips,

1924–1960." In *Nothing but the Blues: The Music and the Musicians*, edited by Lawrence Cohn, 265–311. New York: Abbeville Press, 1993.

——. "Really the 'Walking Blues': Son House, Muddy Waters, Robert Johnson, and the Development of a Traditional Blues." *Popular Music* 1 (1981): 57–72.

Crowe, Cameron. *Biograph* [liner notes]. 38830. New York: Columbia, 1985.

Current, Gloster B. "The Gospel Sound." *Black Perspective in Music* 1 (Spring 1973): 231. Reprinted from the *Crisis*, October 1972.

Curtis, Jim. *Rock Eras: Interpretations of Music and Society*. Bowling Green, Ohio: Bowling Green State University Popular Press, 1987.

D'Alessio, Gregory. *Old Troubadour: Carl Sandburg with His Guitar Friends*. New York: Walker and Co., 1987.

Dalton, David, ed. *Rolling Stones*. New York: Amsco Music Publishing, 1972.

——. *Rolling Stones in Their Own Words*. New York: Putnam Publishing Group, 1980.

Davis, Francis. "Napoleon in Rags." *Atlantic Monthly*, May 1999, 108–17.

Davis, Natalie Zemon. "*AHR Forum*: Toward Mixtures and Margins." *American Historical Review* 97 (December 1992): 1409–16.

Davis, R. G. "Music from the Left." *Rethinking Marxism* 1 (Winter 1988): 7–25.

DeCurtis, Anthony. "Willie Dixon and the Wisdom of the Blues." *Rolling Stone*, March 23, 1989, 109–14.

DeMichael, Don. "Father and Son: An Interview with Muddy Waters and Paul Butterfield." *Down Beat*, September 1989, 68–71.

——. *Leadbelly* [liner notes]. 30335. New York: Columbia Recores, 1989.

Denisoff, R. Serge. *Great Day Coming: Folk Music and the American Left*. Urbana: University of Illinois Press: 1971.

Denning, Michael. *The Cultural Front: The Laboring of American Culture in the Twentieth Century*. New York: Verso, 1996.

Dett, R. Nathaniel. *Religious Folk-Songs of the Negro As Sung at the Hampton Institute*. Hampton, Va.: Hampton Institute Press, 1927.

De Turk, David A., and A. Poulin Jr., eds. *The American Folk Scene: Dimensions of the Folksong Revival*. New York: Dell Publishing, 1967.

——. "I Will Show You Fear in a Handful of Songs." In *The American Folk Scene: Dimensions of the Folksong Revival*, edited by David A. De Turk and A. Poulin Jr., 271–79. New York: Dell Publishing, 1967.

Dixon, Robert M. W., and John Godrich, *Recording the Blues*. New York: Stein and Day, 1970.

——, eds. *Blues and Gospel Records, 1902–1943*. 3d ed. Chigwell, Essex: Storyville Publications, 1982.

Dixon, Willie, and Don Snowden. *I Am the Blues: The Willie Dixon Story*. New York: Quartet Books, 1989.

Dobrin, Arnold. *Voices of Joy, Voices of Freedom*. New York: Coward, McCann and Geoghegan, 1972.

Dorson, Richard M. *American Folklore*. Chicago: University of Chicago Press, 1959.

——. *American Folklore and the Historian*. 1969. Chicago: University of Chicago Press, 1971.

——. "Applied Folklore." In *Papers on Applied Folklore*, edited by Dick Sweterlitsch, 40–42. *Folklore Forum*, Bibliographic and Special Studies, no. 8, 1971.

———. "Comment on Williams." *Journal of the Folklore Institute* (Indiana University) 11 (March 1975): 235–39.

———. "Fakelore." In *American Folklore and the Historian*, edited by Richard M. Dorson, 3–14. 1969. Chicago: University of Chicago Press, 1971.

———. "Introduction by the Editor [to special issue "Folklore Research around the World"]." *Journal of American Folklore* 74 (October–December 1961): 287–92.

———. "Replies to Questions on 'A Theory for American Folklore.'" *Journal of American Folklore* 73 (October–December 1960): 327–30.

———. "Stith Thompson (1885–1976)." *Journal of American Folklore* 90 (October–December, 1977): 3–7.

———. "A Theory for American Folklore." In *American Folklore and the Historian*, edited by Richard Dorson, 15–48. 1969. Chicago: University of Chicago Press, 1971.

———. "A Theory for American Folklore Reviewed." In *American Folklore and the Historian*, edited by Richard M. Dorson, 49–77. 1969. Chicago: University of Chicago Press, 1971.

———. "*A Treasury of Southern Folklore* [review]." *Journal of American Folklore* 63 (October–December 1950): 480–82.

"Dozen Arts Figures Honored by President, A." *Variety*, July 16, 1986, 119.

Duberman, Martin Bauml. *Paul Robeson*. New York: Alfred A. Knopf, 1988.

Dugan, James, and John Hammond. "In Retrospect . . . an Early Black-Music Concert from Spirituals to Swing." *Black Perspective in Music* 2 (Fall 1974): 191–208.

Dugaw, Dianne. "The Popular Marketing of 'Old Ballads': The Ballad Revival and Eighteenth-Century Antiquarianism Reconsidered." *Eighteenth-Century Studies* 21 (Fall 1987): 71–90.

Dunaway, David K. "Charles Seeger and Carl Sands: The Composers' Collective Years." *Ethnomusicology* 24 (May 1980): 159–68.

———. *How Can I Keep from Singing: Pete Seeger*. 1981. New York: Da Capo Press, 1985.

———. "Unsung Songs of Protest: The Composers Collective of New York." *New York Folklore* 5 (Summer 1979): 1–19.

Dundes, Alan. "Ways of Studying Folklore." In *Our Living Tradition: An Introduction to American Folklore*, edited by Tristram Potter Coffin, 37–46. New York: Basic Books, 1968.

Dunn, Jancee, and Nilou Panahpour. "Hall of Fame '96." *Rolling Stone*, February 22, 1996, 18.

Dunson, Josh. "Folk Rock: Thunder without Rain." *Sing Out!*, January 1966, 12–17.

———. *Freedom in the Air: Song Movements of the Sixties*. New York: International Publishers, 1965.

———. "The Grassroots Folk Revival." *Sing Out!*, Winter 1969–70, 14–16.

Dyer-Bennet, Richard. "Some Thoughts on the Folk Song Revival." *Sing Out!*, April–May 1962, 17–22.

Dylan, Bob. "A Letter from Bob Dylan." *Broadside*, January 20, 1964.

———. *Lyrics, 1962–1985*. New York: Alfred A. Knopf, 1985.

———. *Writings and Drawings by Bob Dylan*. New York: Alfred A. Knopf, 1973.

"Dylan Released: Won't 'See Elvis Soon' after All." *St. Paul Pioneer Press*, June 3, 1997, 10A.

Edmonds, Lila W. "Songs from the Mountains of North Carolina." *Journal of American Folklore* 6 (June 1893): 131–34.

Engel, Carl. "Views and Reviews." *Musical Quarterly* 21 (January 1935): 107–12.

Ennis, Philip H. *The Seventh Stream: The Emergence of Rocknroll in American Popular Music.* Hanover, N.H.: Wesleyan University Press, 1992.

Ephron, Nora, and Susan Edmiston, "Bob Dylan Interview" [1970]. In *Bob Dylan: The Early Years: A Retrospective*, edited by Craig McGregor, 82–90. 1972. New York: Da Capo Press, 1990.

Ervin, Mike. "Pete Seeger's Homemade Music." *Progressive*, April 1986, 35–37.

Evans, David. *Big Road Blues: Tradition and Creativity in the Folk Blues.* New York: Da Capo Press, 1982.

Feintuch, Burt, ed. *The Conservation of Culture.* Lexington: University Press of Kentucky, 1988.

Fenner, Thomas P. *Cabin and Plantation Songs as Sung by the Hampton Students.* New York: G. P. Putnam's Sons, 1876.

"Festival and Camp Guide." *Sing Out!*, August/September/October 1994, 158–69.

Festival of American Folklife 1968. Washington, D.C.: Smithsonian Institution, 1968.

Fielding, Raymond. *The March of Time, 1935–1951.* New York: Oxford University Press, 1978.

Finé, Jason. "Screaming Trees." *Rolling Stone*, August 22, 1996, 56.

Fiott, Stephen. "Commercial Folksingers." *Sing Out!*, December–January 1962–63, 43–45.

Flanagan, Hallie. *Arena.* New York: Duell, Sloan, and Pearce, 1940.

Fleischhauer, Carl, and Beverly W. Brannan, ed. *Documenting America, 1935–1943.* Berkeley: University of California Press, 1988.

"Folk and the Rock, The." *Newsweek*, September 20, 1965, 88–90.

Folk Music in the Roosevelt White House: A Commemorative Program. Washington, D.C.: Office of Folklife Programs, Smithsonian Institution, 1982.

"Folk Music on Records." *Sing Out!*, December 1960–January 1961, 46.

"Folk Song As It Is." *Newsweek*, April 14, 1958, 80.

Freedomways, ed. *Paul Robeson: The Great Forerunner.* 1965. New York: Dodd, Mead and Co., 1978.

Friedman, Albert B. *The Ballad Revival: Studies in the Influence of Popular on Sophisticated Poetry.* Chicago: University of Chicago Press, 1961.

Friesen, Gordon. "Something New Has Been Added." *Sing Out!*, October–November 1963, 12–23.

——. "Songs of Our Time from the Pages of *Broadside* Magazine." In *The American Folk Scene: Dimensions of the Folksong Revival*, edited by David A. De Turk and A. Poulin Jr., 130–39. New York: Dell Publishing, 1967.

Furman, Lucy. "Hard-Hearted Barbary Allen." *Century Magazine*, March 1912, 739–44.

——. "Mothering on Perilous." *Century Magazine*, February 1911, 561–65.

Gates, David. "Dylan Revisited." *Newsweek*, October 6, 1997, 62–67.

Gebhard, Herman. "'March of Time' 1935: Leadbelly." *Living Blues*, November–December 1976, 26.

George, Nelson. *The Death of Rhythm and Blues.* New York: Pantheon Books, 1988.

Georges, Robert A. "Richard M. Dorson's Conceptual and Methodological Concerns." *Journal of Folklore Research* 26 (January–April 1989): 1–10.

Goldman, Lawrence. "Bobby Dylan: Folk-Rock Hero." In *The Age of Rock: Sounds of the American Cultural Revolution*, edited by Jonathan Eisen, 208–13. New York: Random House, 1969.

Golkin, Pete. "Blacks, Whites, and Blues: The Story of Chess Records, Part One." *Living Blues*, September/October 1989, 22–32.

———. "Blacks, Whites, and Blues: The Story of Chess Records, Part Two." *Living Blues*, November/December 1989, 25–29.

Goodman, Fred. *The Mansion on the Hill: Dylan, Young, Geffen, Springsteen, and the Head-On Collision of Rock and Commerce*. New York: Random House, 1997.

Gordon, Robert Winslow. "Archive of American Folk-Song." 1932. In *The Conservation of Culture*, edited by Burt Feintuch, 253–57. Lexington: University Press of Kentucky, 1988.

———. *Folk-Songs of America*. New York: National Service Bureau, Works Progress Administration, 1938.

Graham, Katharine. "Folk Songs May Inspire America's Soldiers." *Washington Post*, February 23, 1941, B8.

Graves, Michael. *Song and Dance Man: The Art of Bob Dylan*. New York: E. P. Dutton and Co., 1972.

Green, Archie. "The Archive's Shores." In *Folklife Annual, 1985*, edited by Alan Jabbour and James Hardin, 61–73. Washington, D.C.: American Folklife Center, Library of Congress, 1985.

———. "The Campus Folksong Club: A Glimpse at the Past." In *Folk Music Revivals Examined*, edited by Neil V. Rosenberg, 61–72. Urbana: University of Illinois Press, 1993.

———. "Dobie's Cowboy Friends [Commercial Music Graphics, #36]." *JEMF Quarterly* 12 (Spring 1976): 21–29.

———. "Hillbilly Music: Source and Symbol." *Journal of American Folklore* 78 (July–September 1965): 204–28.

———. *Only a Miner: Studies in Recorded Coal-Mining Songs*. Urbana: University of Illinois Press, 1971.

———. "P.L. 94-201—A View from the Lobby: A Report to the American Folklore Society." 1976. In *The Conservation of Culture*, edited by Burt Feintuch, 269–79. Lexington: University Press of Kentucky, 1988.

———. "Public Folklore's Name: A Partisan's Notes." In *Public Folklore*, edited by Robert Baron and Nicholas R. Spitzer, 49–63. Washington, D.C.: Smithsonian Institution Press, 1992.

Green, Douglas B. "The Singing Cowboy: An American Dream." *Journal of Country Music* 7 (May 1978): 4–61.

———. "Tex Ritter." *Frets* 1 (July 1979): 10–12.

Greenfield, Robert. "Keith Richard: The Rolling Stone Interview." *Rolling Stone*, August 19, 1971, 24–36.

Greenway, John. "Woody Guthrie: The Man, the Land, the Understanding." In *The American Folk Scene: Dimensions of the Folksong Revival*, edited by David A. De Turk and A. Poulin Jr., 184–202. New York: Dell Publishing, 1967.

Grendysa, Peter. "Black Music—An Introduction." In *Joel Whitburn's Top R & B Singles, 1942–1988*, edited by Joel Whitburn, 9–11. Menomonee Falls, Wis.: Record Research, 1988.

Groom, Bob. *The Blues Revival*. London: Studio Vista, 1971.

Gross Bressler, Sandra. "Culture and Politics: A Legislative Chronicle of the American Folklife Preservation Act." Ph.D. diss., University of Pennsylvania, 1995.

Grossman, James R. *Land of Hope: Chicago, Black Southerners, and the Great Migration*. Chicago: University of Chicago Press, 1989.

Gruen, John. "'As a People Live, So Do They Sing.'" *New York Times*, March 26, 1978, sec. 2, 20.

Gummere, Francis B. "A Day with Professor Child." *Atlantic Monthly*, March 1909, 421–25.

Guralnick, Peter. *Feel Like Going Home: Portraits in Blues and Rock 'n' Roll*. New York: E. P. Dutton and Co., 1971.

——. *The Listener's Guide to the Blues*. New York: Quarto Marketing, 1982.

——. "Muddy Waters (1915–1983)." *Living Blues*, Autumn 1983, 22, 53–54.

——. "Willie Dixon: Producing a Legend." *Musician*, September 1988, 20–26, 115.

——. *Searching for Robert Johnson*. New York: E. P. Dutton, 1989.

Hagan, Chet. *Grand Ole Opry*. New York: Henry Holt and Co., 1989.

Hamm, Charles. *Yesterdays: Popular Song in America*. New York: W. W. Norton and Co., 1979.

Hammond, John, and Irving Townsend. *John Hammond on Record*. New York: Ridge Press, 1977.

Handler, Richard. "Boasian Anthropology and the Critique of American Culture." *American Quarterly* 42 (June 1990): 252–73.

Harker, Dave. *Fakesong: The Manufacture of British "Folksong," 1700 to the Present Day*. Philadelphia: Open University Press, 1985.

Harrah-Conforth, Jeanne. "Dorson and the Indiana University Folklore Program: Oral Histories." *Western Folklore* 48 (October 1989): 339–48.

Harrington, Richard. "The Halls That Willie Dixon Built." *Washington Post*, January 19, 1994, C7.

Hasted, John. "Don't Scoff at Skiffle!" *Sing Out!*, Spring 1957, 28–30.

Hatch, David, and Stephen Millward. *From Blues to Rock: An Analytical History of Pop Music*. Manchester, England: Manchester University Press, 1987.

Hatch, Elvin. *Culture and Morality: The Relativity of Values in Anthropology*. New York: Columbia University Press, 1983.

Hawes, Bess Lomax. "Preserving Folk Arts: The National Endowment for the Arts, Folk Arts Program." In *Festival of American Folklife 1981*, edited by Jack Santino, 29–31. Washington, D.C.: Smithsonian Institution, 1981.

Haywood, Charles. "Reply." *Journal of American Folklore* 71 (January 1958): 58–79.

Hendler, Herb. *Year by Year in the Rock Era: Events and Conditions Shaping the Rock Generations That Reshaped America*. Westport, Conn.: Greenwood Press, 1983.

Hentoff, Nat. "The Future of the Folk Renascence." *Sing Out!*, February–March 1967, 10–13.

Heylin, Clinton. *Bob Dylan: Behind the Shades*. New York: Summit Books, 1991.

——. *Bob Dylan: The Recording Sessions, 1960–1994*. New York: St. Martin's Press, 1995.

Higginson, T. W. "Negro Spirituals." *Atlantic Monthly*, June 1867, 685–94.

Hillsman, Joan R. *Gospel Music: An African American Art Form*. Washington, D.C.: Middle Atlantic Regional Press, 1990.

Hirsch, Jerrold. "Folklore in the Making: B. A. Botkin." *Journal of American Folklore* 100 (January–March 1987): 3–38.

——. "Modernity, Nostalgia, and Southern Folklore Studies: The Case of John Lomax." *Journal of American Folklore* 105 (Spring 1992): 183–207.

Hitchcock, H. Wiley. *Music in the United States: A Historical Introduction*. 1969. Englewood Cliffs, N.J.: Prentice-Hall, 1974.

Holden, Stephen. "As the Sun Sets Slowly in the West . . ." *New York Times*, January 14, 1990, 29.

Holston, Noel. "At 75, Singer Pete Seeger Is Still Swinging That Hammer." *Star Tribune*, 27, May 1994, 11E.

Houseman, John. *Front and Center*. New York: Simon and Schuster, 1979.

"I Am My Words." *Newsweek*, November 4, 1963, 94–95.

Ives, Burl. *Wayfaring Stranger*. New York: McGraw-Hill, 1948.

——. *The Wayfaring Stranger's Notebook*. Indianapolis: Bobbs-Merrill Co., 1962.

Ives, Edward D. *Joe Scott: The Woodsman-Songmaker*. Urbana: University of Illinois Press, 1978.

Jabbour, Alan. "The American Folklife Center: A Twenty-Year Retrospective (Part 1)." *Folklife Center News* 18 (Winter–Spring 1996): 3–19.

——. "The American Folklife Center: A Twenty-Year Retrospective (Part 2)." *Folklife Center News* 18 (Summer–Fall 1996): 3–21.

Jackson, Bruce. "Ben Botkin." *New York Folklore* 12 (Summer–Fall 1986): 23–32.

——. "Benjamin A. Botkin (1901–1975)." *Journal of American Folklore* 89 (January–March 1976): 1–6.

James, Thelma G. "The English and Scottish Popular Ballads of Francis J. Child." In *The Critics and the Ballad*, edited by MacEdward Leach and Tristram P. Coffin, 12–19. Carbondale: Southern Illinois Press, 1961.

Jasen, David A. *Tin Pan Alley: The Composers, the Songs, the Performers, and Their Times*. New York: Donald I. Fine, 1988.

Jennings, Dana Andrew. "Gathering In a Reaper's Harvest of Song." *New York Times*, April 13, 1997, sec. 2, 1, 36.

Kahn, Edward A. "The Carter Family: A Reflection of Changes in Society." Ph.D. diss., University of California, Los Angeles, 1970.

——. "Hillbilly Music: Source and Resource." *Journal of American Folklore* 78 (July–September 1965): 257–66.

Karpeles, Maud. *Cecil Sharp: His Life and Work*. Chicago: University of Chicago Press, 1967.

Keil, Charles. *Urban Blues*. 1966. Chicago: University of Chicago Press, 1969.

Kelley, Robin D. G. "*AHR Forum*: Notes on Deconstructing 'The Folk.'" *American Historical Review* 97 (December 1992): 1400–1408.

Kening, Dan. "Landmark in Honor of Landmark Musician." *Crain's Chicago Business*, March 14, 1994, 35.

Killeen, Sean. "Fannin Street: The Setting and the Song." *Lead Belly Letter* 2 (Winter 1992): 1, 4, 6.

——. "Lead Belly: More Than a Name." *Lead Belly Letter* 2 (Winter 1992): 5–6.

——. "Lead Belly in Europe." *Lead Belly Letter* 3 (Fall 1993): 1, 4.

——. "NYU Fans." *Lead Belly Letter* 3 (Winter/Spring 1993): 2.

——. "Out on the Western Plain." *Lead Belly Letter* 1 (Spring 1991): 1, 4.

"King of the Twelve-String Guitar." *New York Post*, January 7, 1935.

Kinkle, Roger D. *The Complete Encyclopedia of Popular Music and Jazz, 1900–1950*. New Rochelle, N.Y.: Arlington House Publishers, 1974.

Kirk, Elise K. *Musical Highlights from the White House*. Malabar, Fla.: Krieger Publishing Co., 1992.

Kittredge, George Lyman. "Ballads and Rhymes from Kentucky." *Journal of American Folklore* 20 (December 1907): 251–77.

——. "Ballads and Songs." *Journal of American Folklore* 30 (September 1917): 283–369.

——. "Francis James Child." In *The English and Scottish Popular Ballads*, edited by Francis James Child, 1:xxiii–xxxi. Boston: Houghton, Mifflin and Co., 1898.

——. "Various Ballads." *Journal of American Folklore* 26 (June 1913): 180–82.

Klein, Joe. *Woody Guthrie: A Life*. New York: Alfred A. Knopf, 1980.

Kleppner, Paul. *Chicago Divided: The Making of a Black Mayor*. DeKalb: Northern Illinois University Press, 1985.

Kodish, Debora. *Good Friends and Bad Enemies: Robert Winslow Gordon and the Study of American Folksong*. Urbana: University of Illinois Press, 1986.

Koester, Bob. "Lester Melrose: An Appreciation." *American Folk Music Occasional* 2 (1970): 58.

Kozinn, Allan. "John Lennon's First Known Recording Is for Sale." *New York Times*, July 21, 1994, C13.

Kuklick, Henrika. *The Savage Within: The Social History of British Anthropology, 1885–1945*. New York: Cambridge University Press, 1991.

Kuper, Adam. *Anthropology and Anthropologists: The Modern British School*. 1983. New York: Routledge and Kegan Paul, 1991.

Kurin, Richard. *Reflections of a Culture Broker*. Washington, D.C.: Smithsonian Institution Press, 1997.

——. *Smithsonian Folklife Festival: Culture of, by, and for the People*. Washington, D.C.: Center for Folklife Programs and Cultural Studies, Smithsonian Institution, 1998.

Lampell, Millard, ed. *California to the New York Island*. 1958. New York: Guthrie Children's Trust Fund, 1960.

Landau, Jon. "John Wesley Harding." In *The Age of Rock: Sounds of the American Cultural Revolution*, edited by Johnathan Eisen, 214–29. New York: Random House, 1969.

Lawrenson, Helen. "Black and White and Red All Over." *New York*, August 21, 1978, 36–43.

Lears, T. J. Jackson. "*AHR Forum*: Making Fun of Popular Culture." *American Historical Review* 97 (December 1992): 1417–26.

Lee, Hector. "Some Notes on Lead Belly." *Journal of American Folklore* 76 (April 1963): 135–36.

Legman, G. "Folksong, Fakelore, and Cash." *Sing Out!*, October–November 1960, 29–35.

Lemann, Nicholas. *The Promised Land: The Great Migration and How It Changed America*. New York: Alfred A. Knopf, 1991.

Levenson, Jay. "Rock and Roll Hall of Fame Dinner." *Down Beat*, April 1988, 11.

Levine, Lawrence, W. *"AHR Forum*: The Folklore of Industrial Society: Popular Culture and Its Audiences." *American Historical Review* 97 (December 1992): 1369–99.

———. *"AHR Forum*: Levine Responds." *American Historical Review* 97 (December 1992): 1427–30.

———. "American Culture and the Great Depression." *Yale Review* 74 (Winter 1985): 196–223.

———. *Black Culture and Black Consciousness: Afro-American Folk Thought from Slavery to Freedom.* New York: Oxford University Press, 1977.

Levy, Alan Howard. *Musical Nationalism: American Composers' Search for Identity.* Westport, Conn.: Greenwood Press, 1983.

Lieberman, Robbie. *"My Song Is My Weapon": People's Songs, American Communism, and the Politics of Culture, 1930–1950.* Urbana: University of Illinois Press, 1989.

Lifton, Sarah. *The Listener's Guide to Folk Music.* New York: Facts on File, 1983.

Linn, Karen. *That Half-Barbaric Twang: The Banjo in American Popular Culture.* Urbana: University of Illinois Press, 1991.

Lisle, Andria. "Bob Dylan's Mississippi." *Oxford American*, Summer 1999, 117.

Lomax, Alan. "The Adventure of Learning, 1960." *ACLS Newsletter* 13 (February 1962).

———. "Appeal for Cultural Equity." *Journal of Communication* 27 (Spring 1977): 125–38.

———. "Cantometrics: An Approach to the Anthropology of Music." *Lifelong Learning* 46 (April 11, 1977): n.p.

———. "Folk Music in the Roosevelt Era." In *Folk Music in the Roosevelt White House: A Commemorative Program*," 14–17. Washington, D.C.: Office of Folklife Programs, Smithsonian Institution, 1982.

———. "The 'Folkniks'—and the Songs They Sing." *Sing Out!*, Summer 1959, 30–31.

———. *Folk Song Style and Culture.* Washington, D.C.: American Association for the Advancement of Science, 1968.

———. "Folk Song Traditions Are All around Us." *Sing Out!*, February–March 1961, 17–18.

———. *The Folk Songs of North America.* Garden City, N.Y.: Doubleday, 1960.

———. *The Land Where the Blues Began.* New York: Pantheon Books, 1993.

———. "Leadbelly's Songs." In *Leadbelly: A Collection of World-Famous Songs by Huddie Ledbetter*, edited by John A. Lomax and Alan Lomax, 5. New York: Folkways Music Publishers, 1959.

———. "Saga of a Folksong Hunter." *HiFi/Stereo Review*, May 1960. In *The Alan Lomax Sampler.* CD1700. Cambridge, Mass.: Rounder Records Corp., 1997: 43–57.

———. " 'Sinful' Songs of the Southern Negro: Experiences Collecting Secular Folk-Music." *Southwest Review* 19 (January 1934): 105–31.

———. "Song Structure and Social Structure." *Ethnology* 1 (January 1962): 425–52.

Lomax, John A. *Adventures of a Ballad Hunter.* New York: Macmillan, 1947.

———. *Cowboy Songs and Other Frontier Ballads.* New York: Macmillan, 1910.

———. "Field Experiences with Recording Machines." *Southern Folklore Quarterly* 1 (June 1937): 57–60.

———. "'Sinful Songs' of the Southern Negro." *Musical Quarterly* 20 (April 1934): 177–87.

Lomax, John A., and Alan Lomax, eds. *American Ballads and Folk Songs*. New York: Macmillan, 1934.

———. *Folk Song: U.S.A.* New York: Duell, Sloan and Pearce, 1947.

———. *Leadbelly: A Collection of World-Famous Songs by Huddie Ledbetter*. New York: Folkways Music Publishers, 1959.

———. *Negro Folk Songs as Sung by Lead Belly*. New York: Macmillan, 1936.

———. *Our Singing Country: A Second Volume of American Ballads and Folk Songs*. New York: Macmillan, 1941.

"Lomax Arrives with Lead Belly, Negro Minstrel." *New York Herald Tribune*, January 3, 1935.

Loomis, Ormond H., ed. *Cultural Conservation: The Protection of Cultural Heritage in the United States*. Washington, D.C.: Library of Congress, 1983.

Lornell, Kip. *Introducing American Folk Music*. Madison, Wis.: Brown and Benchmark Publishers, 1993.

Lott, Eric. *Love and Theft: Blackface Minstrelsy and the American Working Class*. New York: Oxford University Press, 1993.

Lovell, John. *Black Song, the Forge, and the Flame: The Story of How the Afro-American Spiritual Was Hammered Out*. New York: Macmillan, 1972.

Lumer, Robert. "Pete Seeger and the Attempt to Revive the Folk Music Process." *Popular Music and Society* 15 (Spring 1991): 45–58.

McCormick, Mack. "Lightnin' Hopkins: Blues." In *Jazz Panorama: From the Pages of Jazz Review*, edited by Martin Williams, 311–18. New York: Crowell-Collier Press, 1962.

———. "Sam 'Lightnin'' Hopkins—A Description." *Sing Out!*, October–November 1960, 4–8.

McDonald, William F. *Federal Relief Administration and the Arts: The Origins and Administrative History of the Arts Projects of the Works Progress Administration*. Columbus: Ohio State University Press, 1969.

McDonough, John. "The Multiple Lives of John Hammond." *High Fidelity*, June 1976, 59–72.

MacDougall, Curtis D. *Gideon's Army*. New York: Marzani and Munsell, 1965.

McGill, Josephine. *Folk Songs of the Kentucky Mountains: Twenty Traditional Ballads and Other English Folk-Songs*. New York: Boosey and Co., 1917.

McGregor, Craig, ed. *Bob Dylan: The Early Years: A Retrospective*. 1972. New York: Da Capo Press, 1990.

MacGregor-Villarreal, Mary. "Brazilian Parallels to Dorson's 'Theory for American Folklore.'" *Western Folklore* 48 (October 1989): 359–69.

McGuire, Phillip. "Black Music Critics and the Classic Blues Singers." *Black Perspective in Music* 14 (Spring 1986): 103–25.

McMurtry, Jo. *English Language, English Literature: The Creation of an Academic Discipline*. Hamden, Conn.: Archon Books, 1985.

McNutt, James. "Beyond Regionalism: Texas Folklorists and the Emergence of a Post-Regional Consciousness." Ph.D. diss., University of Texas, 1982.

Malinowski, Bronislaw. *A Scientific Theory of Culture and Other Essays*. Chapel Hill: University of North Carolina Press, 1944.

Malone, Bill C. "Country Music." In *The New Grove Dictionary of American Music*, edited by H. Wiley Hitchcock and Stanley Sadie, 516–17. New York: Macmillan, 1986.

———. *Country Music, U.S.A.* 1968. Austin: University of Texas Press, 1985.

———. *Singing Cowboys and Musical Mountaineers: Southern Culture and the Roots of Country Music*. Athens: University of Georgia Press, 1993.

Malone, Bill C., and Judith McCulloh, eds. *Stars of Country Music: Uncle Dave Macon to Johnny Rodriguez*. Urbana: University of Illinois, 1975.

Mangione, Jerre. *The Dream and the Deal: The Federal Writers' Project, 1935– 1943*. Boston: Little, Brown and Co., 1972.

Maranda, Elli Köngäs. "Deep Significance and Surface Significance: Is Cantometrics Possible?" *Semiotica* 2, no. 2 (1970): 173–84.

Marcus, George E., and Michael M. J. Fischer. *Anthropology as Cultural Critique: An Experimental Moment in the Human Sciences*. 2d ed. Chicago: University of Chicago Press, 1999.

Marcus, Greil. *Invisible Republic: Bob Dylan's Basement Tapes*. New York: Henry Holt and Co., 1997.

Marine, Gene. "Guerrilla Minstrel." *Rolling Stone*, April 13, 1972, 40–48.

Marsh, J. B. T. *The Story of the Jubilee Singers, with Their Songs*. Cambridge, Mass.: Riverside Press, 1880.

Martin, Peggy. *Stith Thompson: His Life and His Role in Folklore Scholarship*. Folklore Monograph Series. Vol. 2. Bloomington: Folklore Publications Group, Indiana University, 1978.

"Martins and the Coys, The." *Radio Times*, June 23, 1944, 3.

Mechling, Jay. "Richard M. Dorson and the Emergence of the New Class in American Folk Studies." *Journal of Folklore Research* 26 (January–April 1989): 11–26.

Mellers, Wilfrid. *A Darker Shade of Pale: A Backdrop to Bob Dylan*. New York: Oxford University Press, 1985.

Melrose, Lester. "My Life in Recording." *American Folk Music Occasional* 2 (1970): 59–61.

Merriam, Alan P. "*Folk Song Style and Culture* [review]." *Journal of American Folklore* 82 (October–December 1969): 385–87.

Middleton, Richard. "Editor's Introduction to Volume 1." *Popular Music* 1 (1981): 3–7.

———. *Pop Music and the Blues: A Study of the Relationship and Its Significance*. London: Victor Gollancz, 1972.

———. *Studying Popular Music*. Philadelphia: Open University Press, 1990.

Miles, Barry. *Mick Jagger in His Own Words*. New York: Omnibus Press, 1982.

Miles, Emma Bell. "Some Real American Music." *Harper's Monthly Magazine*, June 1904, 118–23.

Minton, John. " 'Our Goodman' in Blackface and 'The Maid' at the Sookey Jump: Two Afro-American Variants of Child Ballads on Commercial Disc." *JEMF Quarterly* 18 (Spring/Summer 1982): 31–40.

———. "The Reverend Lamar Roberts and the Mediation of Oral Tradition." *Journal of American Folklore* 108 (Winter 1995): 3–37.

Molin, Sven Eric. "Lead Belly, Burl Ives, and Sam Hinton." *Journal of American Folklore* 71 (January 1958): 58–79.

Molotsky, Irvin. "Folk Center's Funds Eliminated by the House." *New York Times*, June 24, 1995, 11.

Montenyohl, Eric L. "Richard M. Dorson and the Internationalization of American Folkloristics." *Western Folklore* 48 (October 1989): 349–57.

Moss, Phil. "Cray Named Year's Top Blues Wailer." *Variety*, November 26, 1986, 136.

Murray, Charles Shaar. *Crosstown Traffic: Jimi Hendrix and the Post-War Rock 'n' Roll Revolution*. New York: St. Martin's Press, 1989.

Naison, Mark. *Communists in Harlem during the Depression*. Urbana: University of Illinois Press, 1983.

"Nashville Songsters Hold Hall of Fame Fete, Induct Four." *Variety*, October 22, 1980, 91.

Nelson, Paul. "Bob Dylan: Another View." *Sing Out!*, February/March 1966, 69.

———. "Newport Folk Festival, 1965." In *Bob Dylan: The Early Years: A Retrospective*, edited by Craig McGregor, 73–76. 1972. New York: Da Capo Press, 1990.

———. "What's Happening (Folk Music News from All Over)." *Sing Out!*, November 1965, 6–8.

Newell, William Wells. "Early American Ballads." *Journal of American Folklore* 12 (October –December 1899): 241–54.

"1994 *Living Blues* Readers' Awards, The." *Living Blues*, July/August 1994, 10.

Niven, Penelope. *Carl Sandburg: A Biography*. New York: Charles Scribner's Sons, 1991.

Norman, Philip. *Symphony for the Devil: The Rolling Stones Story*. New York: Simon and Schuster, 1984.

Obrecht, Jas. "Muddy Waters." In *Blues Guitar: The Men Who Made the Music*, edited by Jas Obrecht, 78–97. San Francisco: Miller Freeman Publications, 1990.

———. "Muddy Waters: The Life and Times of the Hoochie Coochie Man." *Guitar Player*, March 1994, 30–48, 72.

———, ed. *Blues Guitar: The Men Who Made the Music*. San Francisco: Miller Freeman Publications, 1990.

O'Brien, Geoffrey. "Recapturing the American Sound [book review]." *New York Review*, April 9, 1988, 45–51.

Odum, Howard W., and Guy B. Johnson. *Negro Workaday Songs*. 1925. New York: Negro Universities Press, 1969.

Ogren, Kathy J. *The Jazz Revolution: Twenties America and the Meaning of Jazz*. New York: Oxford University Press, 1989.

Oliver, Paul. *Songsters and Saints*. New York: Cambridge University Press, 1984.

———. *The Story of the Blues*. Philadelphia: Chilton Book Co., 1969.

———, ed. *The Blackwell Guide to Blues Records*. Cambridge, Mass.: Basil Blackwell, 1989.

Oliver, Paul, and Harry Eskew. "Gospel Music." In *The New Grove Dictionary of Music and Musicians*, edited by Stanley Sadie, 544–59. Washington, D.C.: Macmillan, 1980.

O'Neal, Jim. "I Once Was Lost, but Now I'm Found: The Blues Revival of the 1960s." In *Nothing but the Blues: The Music and the Musicians*, edited by Lawrence Cohn, 347–87. New York: Abbeville Press, 1993.

———. "Muddy's First Record." *Living Blues*, Spring 1982, 4.

———. "Muddy Waters." *Living Blues*, March–April 1985, 15–40.

Oster, Harry. *Living Country Blues*. Detroit: Folklore Associates, 1969.

Palmer, Robert. *Deep Blues*. New York: Penguin Books, 1982.

———. "Muddy Waters . . . the Man . . . His Music." *Muddy Waters: The Chess Box* [liner notes]. CHD3-8002. Universal City Plaza, Calif.: MCA Records, 1989.

——. "Play the Blues, Man! And They're Still Doing It." *New York Times*, May 7, 1989, sec. 2, 25.

Pankake, Jon. "Pete's Children." In *The American Folk Scene: Dimensions of the Folksong Revival*, edited by David A. De Turk and A. Poulin Jr., 280–86. New York: Dell Publishing, 1967.

Pankake, Jon, and Paul Nelson, "Bob Dylan." In *The American Folk Scene: Dimensions of the Folksong Revival*, edited by David A. De Turk and A. Poulin Jr., 259–62. New York: Dell Publishing, 1967.

Pareles, Jon. "Kennedy Honors: Art Bests Politics." *New York Times*, December 5, 1994, C11, C20.

——. "A Life of Giving Voice to Those Rarely Heard." *New York Times*, March 7, 1989, C15.

——. "Minor Discord amid the Nostalgia-Trip Harmony." *New York Times*, August 14, 1994, B4.

——. Rock Hall of Fame Inductees Honored. *New York Times*, January 21, 1988, C17.

——. "Woodstock's Children." *New York Times*, August 28, 1994, sec. 2, 1, 25.

Patton, Phil. "Who Owns the Blues?" *New York Times*, November 26, 1995, sec. 2, 1, 35.

Peer, Ralph, "Discovery of the First Hillbilly Great." *Billboard*, May 16, 1953, 20–21, 35.

Penkower, Monty Noam. *The Federal Writers' Project: A Study in Government Patronage of the Arts*. Urbana: University of Illinois Press, 1977.

Perrow, E. C. "Songs and Rhymes from the South." *Journal of American Folklore* 25 (March 1912): 36–55; 26 (June 1913): 23–27; 28 (June 1915): 120–90.

Pescatello, Ann M. *Charles Seeger: A Life in American Music*. Pittsburgh: University of Pittsburgh Press, 1992.

Petersen, Clarence. "The Chicago Sound." *Chicago Tribune Magazine*, May 11, 1969, 48–66.

Peterson, Richard A. *Creating Country Music: Fabricating Authenticity*. Chicago: University of Chicago Press, 1997.

Pike, G. D. *The Jubilee Singers and Their Campaign for Twenty Thousand Dollars*. Boston: Lee and Shepard, 1873.

——. *The Singing Campaign for Ten Thousand Pounds*. Boston: Lee and Shepard, 1874.

Pomerance, Alan. *Repeal of the Blues: How Black Entertainers Influenced Civil Rights*. New York: Citadel Press, 1988.

"Pope's Speech Plays off of Dylan Performance." *Raleigh News and Observer*, September 28, 1997, 2A.

Porterfield, Nolan. *Jimmie Rodgers: The Life and Times of America's Blue Yodeler*. Urbana: University of Illinois Press, 1979.

——. *Last Cavalier: The Life and Times of John A. Lomax, 1867–1948*. Urbana: University of Illinois Press, 1996.

"Presidential Budget Request Includes Big Increases for Cultural Agencies." *Aviso*, March 1999, 1–2.

Pruter, Robert. *Chicago Soul*. Urbana: University of Illinois Press, 1991.

Radosh, Ron. "Commercialism and the Folk Song Revival." *Sing Out!*, Spring 1959, 27–29.

Ralph, Julian. "The Transformation of Em Durham." *Harper's Monthly Magazine*, June 1903, 269–76.

Ramsey, Frederic, Jr. "Leadbelly: A Great Long Time." *Sing Out!*, March 1965, 21.

Raymond, C. Rexford. "British Ballads in Our Southern Highlands." *Berea Quarterly* 4 (November 1899): 12–14.

Red Channels: The Report of Communist Influence in Radio and Television. New York: American Business Consultants, 1950.

Reuss, Richard A. "American Folklore and Left-Wing Politics, 1927–57." Ph.D. diss., Indiana University, 1971.

———. "Folk Music and Social Conscience: The Musical Odyssey of Charles Seeger." *Western Folklore* 38 (October 1979): 221–38.

———. "The Roots of American Left-Wing Interest in Folksong." *Labor History* 12 (Spring 1971): 259–79.

Reuss, Richard A., and Jens Lund, eds. *Roads into Folklore: Festschrift in Honor of Richard M. Dorson*. Bloomington, Ind.: Folklore Forum Society, 1975.

Richard, Paul. "Folk Art Show Opens at Mall." *Washington Post*, July 2, 1967, D1.

Richmond, W. Edson. "Richard Mercer Dorson, March 12, 1916–September 11, 1981." *Journal of the Folklore Institute* (Indiana University) 18 (May–December 1981): 95–96.

———, ed. *Studies in Folklore in Honor of Distinguished Service Professor Stith Thompson*. Bloomington: Indiana University Press, 1957.

Riley, Tim. *Hard Rain: A Dylan Commentary*. 1992. New York: Vintage Books, 1993.

"Rock and Read: Will Percy Interviews Bruce Springsteen." *Doubletake*, Spring 1998, 36–43.

Rockwell, John. *All American Music: Composition in the Late Twentieth Century*. New York: Alfred A. Knopf, 1983.

"Rolling Stone Interview: Mick Jagger." *Rolling Stone*, October 12, 1968, 16–18.

Rooney, James. *Bossmen: Muddy Waters and Bill Monroe*. New York: Dial Press, 1971.

Roosevelt, Eleanor. "Folk Music in the White House." In *Folk Music in the Roosevelt White House: A Commemorative Program*, 8–9. Washington, D.C.: Office of Folklife Programs, Smithsonian Institution, 1982.

Rosenberg, Neil V., ed. *Folk Music Revivals Examined*. Urbana: University of Illinois Press, 1993.

Ross, Alex. "The Wanderer." *New Yorker*, May 10, 1999, 56–67.

Rourke, Constance. "Work Songs and Hollers." *New Republic*, December 30, 1936, 280.

Rowe, Mike. *Chicago Breakdown*. New York: Drake Publishers, 1975.

Rule, Sheila. "Folklorist Offers Insight into Cultural Connections." *New York Times*, July 4, 1992, 11.

———. "The Pop Life." *New York Times*, January 19, 1994, C16.

Ruppli, Michel, ed. *The Chess Labels: A Discography*. Westport, Conn.: Greenwood Press, 1983.

Russell, Ross. "Illuminating the Leadbelly Legend." *Down Beat*, August 6, 1970, 12–14, 33.

Russell, Tony. *Blacks, Whites, and Blues*. New York: Stein and Day, 1970.

———. "Clarksdale Piccolo Blues." *Jazz and Blues*, November 1971, 30.

Saal, Hubert. "Dylan's Country Pie" [1969]. In *Bob Dylan: The Early Years: A Retrospective*, edited by Craig McGregor, 295–97. 1972. New York: Da Capo Press, 1990.

Sandburg, Carl. *American Songbag*. New York: Harcourt, Brace, 1927.

Sawyers, June. "Lomax's Global Jukebox Lets World's Voices Speak." *Tribune*, October 26, 1994, sec. 2, 1.

Scaduto, Anthony. *Bob Dylan*. New York: Grosset and Dunlap, 1971.

Scalet, Elizabeth Butler. "The Song Was There before Me: The Influence of Traditional Music on the Songs of Bob Dylan." *Heritage of the Great Plains* 8, no. 2 (1975): 11–16.

Scheurer, Timothy E., ed. *American Popular Music: Readings from the Popular Press*. Vol. 1, *The Nineteenth Century and Tin Pan Alley*. Bowling Green, Ohio: Bowling Green State University Popular Press, 1989.

Schoemer, Karen. "Can Winner Be a Loser? Riddle for a Rebel." *New York Times*, February 23, 1993, C11, C15.

Schone, Mark. "Critics Unfairly Dismiss Folk Scholar Alan Lomax." *New York Observer*, May 4, 1998, 1, 26, 39.

Schultz, Fred L. "Profile: Pete Seeger." *American History Illustrated*, October 1982, 16–19.

Seeger, Charles. "The Arts in International Relations." *Journal of the American Musicological Society* 2 (Spring 1949): 36–43.

———. "The Folkness of the Non-Folk vs. the Non-Folkness of the Folk." In *Folklore and Society: Essays in Honor of Benjamin A. Botkin*, edited by Bruce Jackson, 1–9. Hatboro, Pa.: Folklore Associates, 1966.

———. "Grass Roots for American Composers." *Modern Music* 16 (March–April 1939): 143–49.

———. "On Proletarian Music." *Modern Music* 11 (March–April 1934): 121–27.

———. "UNESCO, February 1948." *Music Library Association Notes* 5, ser. 2 (March 1948): 165–68.

———, ed. *Army Song Book*. Washington, D.C.: Adjutant General's Office, in collaboration with the Library of Congress, 1941.

Seeger, Pete. *American Favorite Ballads*. New York: Oak Publications, 1961.

———. *The Bells of Rhymney*. New York: Oak Publications, 1964.

———. *Henscratches and Flyspecks*. New York: Berkley Medallion Books, 1973.

———. "How I Composed (Swiped) the *Goofing-Off Suite*" [liner notes]. *Darling Corey and Goofing-Off Suite*. SF40018. 1954. Washington, D.C.: Smithsonian/Folkways Recordings, 1993.

———. *How to Play the Five-String Banjo*. 1948. Beacon, N.Y.: By the author, 1961.

———. "Johnny Appleseed, Jr." Column in *Sing Out!* beginning 1954.

———. "Leadbelly." In *Leadbelly: A Collection of World-Famous Songs by Huddie Ledbetter*, edited by John A. Lomax and Alan Lomax, 7. New York: Folkways Music Publishers, 1959.

———. "Welcome Back, Alan." *Sing Out!*, Winter 1959, 7.

———. "Why Folk Music?" In *The American Folk Scene: Dimensions of the Folksong Revival*, edited by David A. De Turk and A. Poulin Jr., 44–49. New York: Dell Publishing, 1967.

——. "Woody Guthrie—Some Reminiscences." *Sing Out!*, July 1964, 25–29.

Seeger, Pete, and Peter Blood. *Where Have All the Flowers Gone*. Bethlehem, Pa.: Sing Out Corporation, 1993.

Seeger, Pete, and Julius Lester. *The Twelve-String Guitar as Played by Leadbelly*. New York: Oak Publications, 1965.

Seeger, Pete, Phil Ochs, Gordon Friesen, and Josh Dunson. *Woody Guthrie: A Tribute*. New York: Guthrie Children's Trust Fund, [ca. 1963]. Reprinted from *Mainstream* magazine, August 1963.

Seeger, Pete, and Jo Metcalf Schwartz. *The Incompleat Folksinger*. 1972. Lincoln: University of Nebraska Press, 1992.

Seeger, [Toshi]. "Pete Seeger." *Sing Out!*, March 1965, 85–87.

Shapiro, Henry D. *Appalachia on Our Mind: The Southern Mountains in the American Consciousness, 1870–1920*. Chapel Hill: University of North Carolina Press, 1978.

Shaw, Arnold. *Honkers and Shouters: The Golden Years of Rhythm and Blues*. New York: Macmillan, 1978.

Shearin, Hubert. "British Ballads in the Cumberland Mountains." *Sewanee Review* 19 (July 1911): 313–27.

Sheller, Kate Van Winkle, and Genevieve Shimer. *The Playford Ball: 103 Early Country Dances, 1651–1820, as Interpreted by Cecil Sharp and His Followers*. Chicago: A Cappella Books and the Country Dance and Song Society, 1990.

Shelton, Robert. "Folkways in Sound . . . or the Remarkable Enterprises of Mr. Moe Asch." *High Fidelity*, June 1960.

——. "Newport Folk-Music Festival Opens 3-Day Run before 13,000." *New York Times*, July 27, 1963, 9.

——. *No Direction Home: The Life and Music of Bob Dylan*. New York: Beech Tree Books, 1986.

Sherman, Robert. "This Land Is Our Land." *Stages* [Carnegie Hall program], April 1994, 8–12.

Shindo, Charles J. *Dust Bowl Migrants in the American Imagination*. Lawrence: University Press of Kansas, 1997.

——. "Voices of the Migrant: Democracy and Culture in the Dust Bowl Works of John Steinbeck, John Ford, and Woody Guthrie." Ph.D. diss., University of Rochester, 1991.

Silber, Irwin. "Bob Dylan." *Sing Out!*, February–March 1964, 53.

——. "Folk Music—1963." *Sing Out!*, October–November 1963, 2–4.

——. "Folk Music and the Success Syndrome." *Sing Out!*, September 1964, 2–4.

——. "An Open Letter to Bob Dylan." *Sing Out!*, November 1964, 22–23.

——. "The 'Pop-Folk' Music Scene." *Sing Out!*, February–March 1964, 63–65.

——. "The Singing Weavers." *Sing Out!*, April–May 1963, 13–14.

——. "Topical Song: Polarization Sets In." *Sing Out!*, February/March 1966, 67–68.

——. "Traditional Folk Artists Capture the Campus." *Sing Out!*, April–May 1964, 8–15.

——. "What's Happening (Folk Music News from All Over)." *Sing Out!*, November 1965, 3–6.

Silliman, Ron. "Pete Seeger and the Avant-Garde." *Socialist Review* 17 (March–April 1987): 120–28.

Siporin, Steve. "Public Folklore: A Bibliographic Introduction." In *Public Folklore*, edited by Robert Baron and Nicholas R. Spitzer, 340–70. Washington, D.C.: Smithsonian Institution Press, 1992.

Sosna, Morton. *In Search of the Silent South: Southern Liberals and the Race Issue*. New York: Columbia University Press, 1977.

Spitz, Bob. *Bob Dylan: A Biography*. New York: McGraw-Hill, 1989.

Spivacke, Harold. "The Archive of American Folk-Song in the Library of Congress." *Southern Folklore Quarterly* 2 (March 1938): 31–5.

Springsteen, Bruce. "Speech at the Rock-and-Roll Hall of Fame." In *The Dylan Companion*, edited by David Gutman, 286–88. New York: Dell, 1990.

"Stamp of Approval." *Guitar World*, December 1994, 19.

Stein, Johanna. "Musicology for Music Therapists: The Lomax Study." *Journal of Music Therapy* 10 (Spring 1973): 46–51.

Stekert, Ellen. "Cents and Nonsense in the Urban Folksong Movement: 1930–1966." In *Folklore and Society: Essays in Honor of Benjamin Botkin*, edited by Bruce Jackson, 153–68. Hatboro, Pa.: Folklore Associates, 1966.

Stern, Stephen. "Dorson's Use and Adaptation of Prevailing Historical Models of American Folklore." *Journal of Folklore Research* 26 (January–April 1989): 43–51.

Stewart, Donald Ogden, ed. *Fighting Words*. New York: Harcourt, Brace and Co., 1940.

Stewart, Susan. *Crimes of Writing*. New York: Oxford University Press, 1991.

Stocking, George W., Jr. *The Ethnographer's Magic and Other Essays in the History of Anthropology*. Madison: University of Wisconsin Press, 1992.

Stott, William. *Documentary Expression and Thirties America*. New York: Oxford University Press, 1973.

Strauss, Neil. "New Releases: Ministry: 'Filth Pig.'" *New York Times*, February 25, 1996, 34.

———. "Two Styles, One Concert, Much Audience Bewilderment." *New York Times*, June 28, 1994, C19.

Susman, Warren. *Culture as History: The Transformation of American Society in the Twentieth Century*. New York: Pantheon Books, 1984.

Sweterlitsch, Dick, ed. *Papers on Applied Folklore*. Folklore Forum, Bibliographic and Special Series, no. 8, 1971.

Taruskin, Richard. "'Nationalism': Colonialism in Disguise?" *New York Times*, August 22, 1993, sec. 2, 24.

Tawa, Nicholas E. *Serenading the Reluctant Eagle: American Musical Life, 1925–1945*. New York: Schirmer Books, 1984.

Taylor, Marshall W. *A Collection of Revival Hymns and Plantation Melodies*. 1882. Cincinnati: Marshall W. Taylor and W. C. Echols, 1883.

Thirteenth Census of the United States, Taken in the Year 1910: Statistics for North Carolina. Washington, D.C.: U.S. Government Printing Office, 1913.

Thomes, Steve. "Lead Belly's Peak Performance." *Lead Belly Letter* 3 (Winter/Spring 1993): 7.

Thomson, Elizabeth, and David Gutman, eds. *The Dylan Companion*. New York: Dell Publishing, 1990.

Tichi, Cecelia. *High Lonesome: The American Culture of Country Music*. Chapel Hill: University of North Carolina Press, 1994.

Tirro, Frank. *Jazz: A History*. New York: W. W. Norton and Co., 1977.

Tischler, Barbara E. *An American Music: The Search for an American Musical Identity*. New York: Oxford University Press, 1986.

Titon, Jeff Todd. *Early Downhome Blues: A Musical and Cultural Analysis*. Urbana: University of Illinois Press, 1977.

———. "Reconstructing the Blues: Reflections on the 1960s Blues Revival." In *Transforming Tradition: Folk Music Revivals Examined*, edited by Neil V. Rosenberg, 220–40. Urbana: University of Illinois Press, 1993.

Toll, Robert. *Blacking Up: The Minstrel Show in Nineteenth-Century America*. New York: Oxford University Press, 1974.

Torgovnick, Marianna. *Gone Primitive: Savage Intellects, Modern Lives*. Chicago: University of Chicago Press, 1990.

Tracy, Jack. *Muddy Waters at Newport* [liner notes]. 31269. Universal City, Calif.: MCA Records, 1986 [1960].

Turner, Gil. "Bob Dylan—a New Voice Singing New Songs." *Sing Out!*, October–November 1962, 5–10.

Turner, William H. "The Demography of Black Appalachia, Past and Present." In *Blacks in Appalachia*, edited by William H. Turner and Edward J. Cabbell, 237–61. Lexington: University Press of Kentucky, 1985.

Vander Woude, Matthew. "The Recorded Music of Muddy Waters: A Repertory Analysis and Anthology of Song Texts." M.A. thesis, York University, 1986.

———. "The Recorded Music of Muddy Waters, 1941–1956." *Jazz Research* 20 (1988): 65–87.

Von Schmidt, Eric, and Jim Rooney. *Baby, Let Me Follow You Down*. Garden City, N.Y.: Anchor Press, 1979.

Walls, Richard C. "Once and Future Hero." *High Fidelity*, November 1987, 71.

Warren-Findley, Jannelle. "Journal of a Field Representative: Charles Seeger and Margaret Valiant." *Ethnomusicology* 24 (May 1980): 197–210.

———. "Passports to Change: The Resettlement Administration's Folk Song Sheet Program, 1936–1937." *Prospects* 10 (1985): 197–241.

Watrous, Peter. "He Made the Blues Worth Listening to Again [Willie Dixon]." *New York Times*, February 9, 1992, sec. 2, 27.

———. "Robert Johnson: Once Largely Myth, Now a Hit." *New York Times*, February 26, 1991, C11.

Welburn, Ronald G. "American Jazz Criticism, 1914–1940." Ph.D. diss., New York University, 1983.

Welding, Pete. "Country Blues Round-up." *Sing Out!*, April–May 1961, 41, 43, 45.

———. "An Interview with Muddy Waters." *American Folk Music Occasional* 2 (1970): 2–7.

———. "Muddy Waters: Last King of the South Side?" October 8, 1964, interview. *Down Beat*, February 1994, 32–35.

Welles, Chris. "The Angry Young Folk Singer." *Life*, April 9, 1964, 109–14.

Wells, Evelyn. *The Ballad Tree*. New York: Ronald Press Co., 1950.

Wenner, Jann. "The Rolling Stone Interview: Dylan." In *Bob Dylan: The Early Years: A Retrospective*, edited by Craig McGregor, 317–56. 1972. New York: Da Capo Press, 1990.

Wheeler, Tom. "Muddy Waters and Johnny Winter." In *Blues Guitar: The Men Who Made the Music*, edited by Jas Obrecht, 98–105. San Francisco: Miller Freeman Publications, 1990.

Whisnant, David. *All That Is Native and Fine: The Politics of Culture in an American Region*. Chapel Hill: University of North Carolina Press, 1983.

Whitburn, Joel. *The Billboard Book of Top 40 Hits*. New York: Billboard Publications, 1987.

———. *Joel Whitburn's Top R & B Singles, 1942–1988*. Menomonee Falls, Wis.: Record Research, 1988.

Widner, Ronna Lee. "Lore for the Folk: Benjamin A. Botkin and the Development of Folklore Scholarship in America." *New York Folklore* 12 (Summer–Fall 1986): 1–22.

Wilder, Alec. *American Popular Song*. New York: Oxford University Press, 1972.

Wilgus, D. K. *Anglo-American Folksong Scholarship since 1898*. New Brunswick, N.J.: Rutgers University Press, 1959.

———. "An Introduction to the Story of Hillbilly Music." *Journal of American Folklore* 78 (July–September 1965): 195–203.

Williams, John Alexander. "Radicalism and Professionalism in Folklore Studies: A Comparative Perspective." *Journal of the Folklore Institute* (Indiana University) 11 (March 1975): 211–34.

Williams, Martin. *The Smithsonian Collection of Classic Jazz* [liner notes]. Washington, D.C.: Smithsonian Collection of Recordings, 1987.

———, ed. *Jazz Panorama: From the Pages of Jazz Review*. New York: Crowell-Collier Press, 1962.

Wilson, William A. "Richard M. Dorson as Romantic-Nationalist." *Journal of Folklore Research* 26 (January–April 1989): 35–42.

Wissolik, Richard David, ed. *Bob Dylan: American Poet and Singer: An Annotated Bibliography and Study Guide of Source and Background Materials, 1961–1991*. Greensburg, Pa.: Eadmer Press, 1991.

Wolfe, Charles. "Columbia Records and Old-Time Music." *JEMF Quarterly* 14 (Autumn 1978): 118–25, 144, 150.

———. "Ralph Peer at Work: The Victor 1927 Bristol Sessions." *Old-Time Music* (Summer 1972): 10–15.

———. "Toward a Contextual Approach to Old-Time Music." *Journal of Country Music* 5 (Summer 1974): 65–75.

Wolfe, Charles, and Kip Lornell. *The Life and Legend of Leadbelly*. New York: HarperCollins, 1992.

Wolff, Daniel. "Tomorrow, When It Will Be Too Late." *DoubleTake*, Spring 1998, 44–49.

Worrell, Denise. " 'It's All Right in Front': Dylan on Life and Rock." *Time*, November 25, 1985, 123.

"Worth Quoting." *Sing Out!*, December 1963–January 1964, 92.

Wright, Richard. "Huddie Ledbetter, Famous Negro Folk Artist Sings the Songs of Scottsboro and His People." *Daily Worker*, New York City ed., August 12, 1937, 7.

Wyman, Loraine, and Howard Brockway. *Lonesome Tunes: Folk Songs from the Kentucky Mountains*. New York: H. W. Gray Co., 1916.

———. *Twenty Kentucky Mountain Songs*. Boston: Oliver Ditson Co., 1920.

Yurchenco, Henrietta. "The Beginning of an Urban Folk-Song Movement in New York: A Memoir." *Sonneck Society Bulletin* 13 (Summer 1987): 39–43.

Zumwalt, Rosemary Lévy. *American Folklore Scholarship: A Dialogue of Dissent*. Bloomington: Indiana University Press, 1988.

DISCOGRAPHY

Anthology of American Folk Music. Folkways F-2591, F-2592, F-2593, 1952.
Bragg, Billy, and Wilco. *Mermaid Avenue*. Elektra 62204-2, 1998.
Broadside Reunion. Broadside-Folkways BR-5315, 1972.
Chess Blues. MCA Records 9340, 1992.
Dixon, Willie. *Willie Dixon: The Chess Box*. MCA Records 16500, 1990.
Dylan, Bob, and the Band. *The Basement Tapes*. Columbia 33682, 1975.
Dylan, Bob. *Biograph*. Columbia 38830, 1985.
———. *Blonde on Blonde*. Columbia 841, 1966.
———. *Blood on the Tracks*. Columbia 33235, 1975.
———. *Bob Dylan*. Columbia 38221, 1962.
———. *The Bootleg Series*. Columbia 47382, 1991.
———. *Bringing It All Back Home*. Columbia 9128, 1965.
———. *Desire*. Columbia 33893, 1976.
———. *Empire Burlesque*. Columbia 40110, 1985.
———. *The Freewheelin' Bob Dylan*. Columbia 8786, 1963.
———. *Good as I Been to You*. Columbia 53200, 1992.
———. *Highway 61 Revisited*. Columbia 9189, 1965.
———. *John Wesley Harding*. Columbia 9604, 1967.
———. *Knocked Out Loaded*. Columbia 40439, 1986.
———. *Nashville Skyline*. Columbia 9825, 1969.
———. *New Morning*. Columbia 30290, 1970.
———. *Pat Garrett and Billy the Kid*. Columbia 32460, 1973.
———. *Planet Waves*. Columbia 37637, 1974.
———. *Saved*. Columbia 36553, 1980.
———. *Self-Portrait*. Columbia 30050, 1970.
———. *Slow Train Coming*. Columbia 36120, 1979.
———. *Time Out of Mind*. Columbia 68556, 1997.
———. *The Times They Are A-Changin'*. Columbia 8905, 1964.
———. *Traveling Wilburys, Volume 1*. Wilbury Records/Warner Bros. 9 25796-2, 1988.

——. *Under the Red Sky*. Columbia 46794, 1990.

——. *World Gone Wrong*. Columbia 57590, 1993.

Folkways: A Vision Shared. Columbia 44034, 1988.

Harvey, P. J. *Rid of Me*. Island 314-514-696-2, 1993.

Jubilation! Great Gospel Performances. Vols. 1 and 2. Rhino Records 70288 and 70289, 1992.

Ledbetter, Huddie. *Gwine Dig a Hole to Put the Devil In*. Rounder 1045, 1991.

——. *Leadbelly*. Columbia 30035, 1989.

——. *Leadbelly: Alabama Bound*. RCA 9600-2-R, 1989.

——. *Leadbelly: The Remaining ARC and Library of Congress Recordings*. *Vol. 1* (1934–35) and *Vol. 2* (1935). Document Records 5591 and 5592, 1997.

——. *Lead Belly's Last Sessions*. 1953. Smithsonian/Folkways Recordings SF 40068/71, 1994.

——. *The Titanic*. Rounder 1097, 1994.

Legends of the Blues. Vol. 1. Columbia 46215, 1990.

Nirvana. *Unplugged in New York*. Geffen 24727, 1994.

Seeger, Pete. *American Favorite Ballads*. Folkways FA2321, 1957; FA2322, 1959; FA2323, 1960; FA2324, 1961; FA2445, 1962.

——. *Darling Corey and Goofing-Off Suite*. 1954. Smithsonian/Folkways Recordings SF40018, 1993.

——. *Precious Friend* (with Arlo Guthrie). Warner Bros. 3644, 1982.

——. *Rainbow Race*. Columbia 30739, 1973.

U2. *Rattle and Hum*. Island 7 91003-2, 1988.

Waters, Muddy. *Muddy Waters: The Chess Box*. MCA Records 8002, 1989.

——. *Muddy Waters: The Complete Plantation Recordings*. MCA Records 9344, 1993.

——*Muddy Waters, Folk Singer*. 1964. MCA Records 5907, 1986.

——. *Muddy Waters at Newport*. 1960. MCA Records 31269, 1986.

——. *Muddy Waters Sings Big Bill Broonzy*. 1960. MCA Records 5907, 1986.

Where Have All the Flowers Gone: The Songs of Pete Seeger. Appleseed Recordings 1024, 1998.

Williams, Hank. *The Very Best of Hank Williams*. Polygram Records 823-292-4 Y-1, 1963.

PERMISSIONS

INDEX

Abrahams, Roger, 204

Acuff, Roy: "Freight Train Blues," 208

Adventure, 40, 43, 244 (n. 107)

African Americans: in Appalachia, 27; appeal of Chicago blues for, 89–90, 95–96, 103, 105–8, 131, 255 (n. 59); and Army Music Program, 263 (n. 39); British musicians' assimilation of music of, 121–23; Chess as promoter of music of, 90–95, 108, 110, 112–13, 125–26, 255 (n. 59); and civil rights movement, 112, 200–201, 271 (n. 41); Dylan and religious music of, 218–19, 224, 225–27, 230, 275 (n. 196); early collections of folk songs of, 31–32, 38, 241 (n. 70), 242 (n. 75); European reception of music of, 116–18, 120–21; and folk-blues revival, 115–16, 257–58 (n. 99); Gordon and songs of, 41–43; Lead Belly as exemplar of song tradition of, 52–55, 58–59, 72, 250 (n. 77); Lomaxes and music of, 50–51, 52–54, 56, 76, 113, 114, 263 (n. 39); marginalization vs. centrality of in American folk song heritage, 25–26, 27, 31–32, 36, 41–43, 52–54, 242 (n. 76), 244 (n. 118); and negative associations of blues, 112; nineteenth-century interest in folk music of, 27–31; and rock and roll, 110–13; Sandburg and songs of, 41–42; and second great migration, 78, 105, 255 (n. 59). *See also* Blues; Boogie-woogie; Chicago; Gospel music; Minstrelsy; Race; Race records; Rhythm and blues; Soul music; Spirituals; Swing

Allen, William Francis, 29, 35; *Slave Songs of the United States* (with Ware and Garrison), 29

Almanac Singers, 158, 162, 190, 199, 209, 269 (n. 12); "Round and Round Hitler's Grave," 158, 263 (n. 49)

American Council of Learned Societies, 44, 49, 174, 245 (n. 124)

American Folk Blues Festival (AFBF), 120–21, 122, 127, 259 (nn. 115, 116)

American Folk Festival, 177

American Folklife Center (Library of Congress), 179–80, 181, 244 (n. 108), 267 (nn. 104, 107)

American Folklife Foundation. *See* American Folklife Center

American Folklore Society, 16, 167, 173, 238 (n. 13)

American Music League, 70

American People's Chorus, 68

American Record Company, 35, 248 (n. 47)

Angola prison (Louisiana State Penitentiary), 51, 66, 114

Appalachia: alleged "purity" of culture of, 23–27; British ballads/culture in, 16–26 passim, 138, 207–8, 239–40 (n. 36); collecting of folk songs of, 15–21, 40, 136, 243 (nn. 94, 95), 270 (n. 19); music of as vernacular music, 4

Appleseed Recordings, 234

Archive of American Folk-Song (Library of Congress): Army Music Program of, 152–53, 159, 263 (n. 39); Botkin and, 161, 173; credibility lent to collectors by, 56–57, 59; funding for, 40, 44, 135–36, 145, 151, 159, 161, 262 (n. 27), 263 (n. 51); Gordon and, 40, 44, 46, 56; Lead Belly songs recorded for, 58, 59; Alan Lomax and, 1, 56–57, 58, 136, 145, 151, 158, 159, 161, 173, 189, 262 (n. 27), 263 (n. 51); John Lomax and, 1, 49, 56–57, 136, 145, 151, 159, 189, 245 (n. 124); Pete Seeger and, 189, 207, 236; and sponsorship of collecting trips, 135–36, 173; takes on more academic orientation under Emrich, 173; and war effort, 145–59 passim, 263 (n. 44)

Archive of Folk Culture (Library of Congress), 244 (n. 108)

Archive of Folk Song (Library of Congress), 180, 244 (n. 108)

Aristocrat Records, 87, 88, 91, 253 (nn. 24, 34)

Armstrong, Louis, 117, 270 (n. 30); "Gut Bucket Blues," 114

Aron, Evelyn, 91

Asch, Moses, 61–62, 74, 117, 193

Asheville, N.C., 40, 177, 188

Atlanta, Ga., 35

Atlantic Monthly, 29

Atlantic Records, 114, 124

Authenticity, cult of: constraint vs. flexibility within, 131–32; creation of, 49; Dixon and, 126–28, 132; Dylan and, 206–7, 210; Lead Belly and, 58–63, 64, 71, 72–74, 75, 90, 120, 131; Lomaxes and, 7, 49, 55, 57–63, 64, 65, 72, 73,

131, 139–40; Pete Seeger and, 202–4; Waters and, 3, 77, 90, 119, 120, 124–25, 128, 129–32

Autry, Gene, 71–72; "That Silver-Haired Daddy of Mine," 72

Baez, Joan, 183

Baker, La Vern, 112

Baldry, Long John, 123, 259 (n. 120)

Ballads: academic study of by literary folklorists, 10–12, 16, 21, 164–65, 238 (n. 15); and contemporary music, 139–41, 148–49; defined, 12; early European collections of, 10–12; popularization of, 17–21

—British: in Appalachia, 16–21, 23–26, 138, 207–8, 239 (n. 26), 239–40 (n. 36); canon of (*see* Child canon); Child as collector of, 12–15, 238 (n. 16); commercial companies' disinterest in, 36, 38; and country music, 222; Dylan and, 208–9, 218–19, 227–28, 229–30; early collections of, 10–11; Gordon and, 41; Sandburg and, 41; Pete Seeger and, 190–91, 218; as source of America's folk song tradition, 16, 23, 25–27, 31, 33, 34 (*see also* Child canon)

Band, the, 129

Barbee, John Henry, 259 (n. 115)

Barber, Chris, 117, 118

Barnicle, Mary Elizabeth, 165, 265 (n. 72)

Barton, William E., 28, 31

Bascam, Louise Rand, 20

Basie, Count, 79, 114; "Good Morning Blues," 114

Bass, Ralph, 125

Bauman, Richard, 179

BBC, 118, 263 (n. 44)

Beatles, 123, 212

Beat poets, 115, 211–12

Bechet, Sidney, 117

Beecher, Henry Ward, 28

Belafonte, Harry, 200–201

Benedict, Ruth, 64

Benét, William Rose, 62

Bennett, Richard Dyer, 189

Berea College, 16, 239 (n. 30)

Berry, Chuck, 110, 111, 112, 122, 257 (n. 89); "Carol," 122; "Come On," 122; "Maybellene," 110, 111, 256–57 (n. 84); "You Can't Catch Me," 122

Big Three Trio, 96, 97

Bikel, Theodore, 183, 184, 210

Bill Haley and the Comets: "Rock around the Clock," 110, 112, 211

Blackwell, Scrapper, 217

Bloomfield, Michael, 129, 228

Bluebird Records, 80–81, 113

Blues, 136, 233, 235, 277 (n. 1); and AFBF, 120–22, 127; audience for, 34, 105–8, 113, 116–17, 119, 121, 128–29, 255 (n. 59); Chess as promoter of, 87–99 passim, 104, 108–9, 112–13, 119, 125–26, 129, 131; content and style of, 80, 103, 222; and country music, 222; decline in popularity of, 111–12; Dixon and, 96–113 passim, 120, 122–23, 126–28; Dylan and, 207, 216, 217, 218, 220–22, 227–28, 229, 230, 276 (n. 116); early commercial recordings of, 34; electric, 81, 82–84, 89, 99, 118, 121, 257 (n. 97); festivals devoted to, 126, 234–35, 260 (n. 131); and jazz, 79, 80, 81, 83, 100, 101, 114, 117, 120, 124; Lead Belly and, 72; Alan Lomax's recordings of, 76–77; Melrose as promoter of, 79–81; negative associations of, 112; 1950s/1960s revival of, 113–23, 126; performed at White House, 134; and pop music, 79, 80, 99, 100, 101–5, 113, 126; popularity and appeal of, 88–90, 99, 103–8; race recordings of, 34, 36, 80; reception and influence of in Britain, 117–18, 121–23, 259 (n. 125); reception of in Europe, 116–17, 120–21, 258 (n. 102); and rock and roll, 4, 111, 113, 125–26; as roots music, 4, 127; Sandburg and, 42; Pete Seeger and, 220; Texas, 100, 252 (n. 21); Waters's downhome-urban hybrid of, 88–90, 95–96, 97–110, 118, 124, 128–30, 256 (n. 67)

—Chicago: and AFBF, 121; and "city blues," 253 (n. 26); commercial decline of, 110; as roots music, 121–23; Waters and, 78, 118; before Waters, 79. *See also* Blues: Waters's downhome-urban hybrid of

—downhome (country, rural, Delta): and AFBF, 259 (n. 116); content and style of, 80, 82, 83, 84–86, 88–89, 96, 99–101, 103, 220–22, 252 (n. 21); defined, 251 (n. 4); Dylan and, 208, 220–22; and folk-blues revival, 114, 118–19, 124; popularity and appeal of, 79, 88–90, 99, 128–29; and urban blues, 80–86, 87, 253 (nn. 28, 30), 254 (nn. 35, 40); Waters and, 77–88 passim, 99, 103, 119–20, 124, 125

—urban: and AFBF, 121, 122; and boogie-woogie, 100; content and style of, 80–86, 87, 100; defined, 253 (n. 26); Dixon and, 96, 99, 113, 121, 124, 126; and downhome blues, 80–86, 87, 253 (nn. 28, 30), 254 (nn. 35, 40); influences on, 100, 252 (n. 21); Lead Belly and, 90; and jazz, 100; popularity and appeal of, 79, 121; as roots music, 113, 123, 124, 126, 128–29; Waters and, 78–79, 81–86, 87

Blues Heaven Foundation, 127

Blues Unlimited, 126

Bluesville Records, 117

Boas, Franz, 64, 137, 248 (n. 40)

Bolden, Buddy, 217

Bond, Johnny, 158, 263 (n. 49)

Bono, 232

Boogie-woogie, 79, 83, 84, 87, 100

Botkin, B. A.: at Archive of American Folk-Song, 161, 173; Dorson and, 168–73, 180, 266 (n. 89); and functionalism, 137–38, 143, 179; at FWP, 137, 142–43, 161, 172; methods and standards of, 169–72, 173, 266 (n. 89); and popularization of folklore, 137, 138–39, 142–43, 265 (n. 81); *Treasury of American Folklore*, 142, 169, 173; *Treasury of Southern Folklore*, 169

Bragg, Billy: *Mermaid Avenue*, 235

Bristol, Tenn., 37

Britain: folk song tradition of, 10–12 (*see also* Child canon); influence of American blues in, 121–23; Alan Lomax in, 74, 113, 118, 163, 174; reception of Lead Belly's music in, 74, 118; Waters performs in, 117–18, 259 (n. 125)

Broadside, 199, 211

Brockman, Polk, 34

Brockway, Howard, 18, 20, 35; *Lonesome Tunes* (with Wyman), 18, 240 (nn. 38, 39); *Twenty Kentucky Mountain Songs* (with Wyman), 18, 19, 20, 240 (n. 39)

Brooklyn Eagle, 62

Broonzy, Big Bill, 79, 114, 117–18, 119–20, 259 (n. 113)

Butterfield, Paul, 129

Byrds, 273 (n. 71); "Mr. Tambourine Man," 231, 273 (n. 71); "Turn, Turn, Turn," 273 (n. 71)

Campbell, John C., 240 (n. 43)

Campbell, Olive Dame, 6, 16, 17, 20–21, 36, 240 (n. 43); *English Folk Songs from the Southern Appalachians*, 240 (n. 43)

Cantometrics, 174–76, 193, 266–67 (nn. 93–95)

Caravans: "Walk around Heaven All Day," 225

Carr, Leroy, 217

Carroll, Hattie, 209

Carson, Fiddlin' John, 34

Carter, Jimmy, 130, 268 (n. 110)

Carter Family, 37

Cash, Johnny, 224

CBS, 154, 156, 158

CBS Records, 129

Chandler, Len, 205

Charters, Samuel, 80, 114, 115, 116, 117, 131, 257–58 (n. 99); *The Country Blues*, 114, 116

Chatman, Peter. *See* Memphis Slim

Checker, Chubby, 111; "Let's Twist Again," 125; "The Twist," 125

Chess, Leonard (Lazer Shmuel Chez), 233, 254 (n. 46), 261 (n. 52); and Aristocrat Records, 87, 91; and Marshall Chess, 91–92; and Phil Chess, 87, 91, 256–57 (n. 84); death of, 129; and Dixon, 93, 95, 97, 103, 109; family and background of, 86–87; and folk-blues revival, 119; launches Chess Records, 91, 254 (n. 43); as promoter of African American blues, 90–95, 108; and rock and roll, 110, 112, 125–26, 129, 256–57 (n. 84); and soul music, 112–13, 257 (n. 89); and Waters, 87, 90–91, 95–96, 100, 109, 112, 119, 124–26, 129, 131, 253–54 (n. 34). *See also* Chess Records

Chess, Marshall, 91–92, 112, 125, 254 (n. 43), 260 (nn. 128, 129)

Chess, Phil, 87, 91, 92–93, 254 (nn. 46, 48), 256–57 (n. 84)

Chess Records, 91, 104, 109, 112–13, 121–22, 123, 124, 129, 257 (n. 89), 260 (nn. 128, 130). *See also* Chess, Leonard

Chez, Lazer Shmuel. *See* Chess, Leonard

Chicago, Ill., 3, 46, 127, 143; AFBF and, 120, 121; African American music scene in, 78–79, 81, 88, 91; African American population of, 105, 256 (n. 70); British bands visit, 123; Chess's family emigrates to, 87; development of urban blues in, 79; Dixon emigrates to, 96; socioeconomic distinctions among African Americans in, 105–8, 256 (n. 72); southern blacks in, 78, 79, 89–90, 91, 105–6; South Side, 88, 91, 105, 106, 108; Waters and Dixon as part of African American community in, 106, 107–8; Waters as part of music scene in, 78–79, 81, 88, 106, 128; Waters emigrates to, 78, 252 (n. 11); West Side, 78, 105, 106

Chicago Blues All-Stars, 126

Child, Francis James, 29, 43, 207, 236, 238 (n. 13); and British ballads, 12–14; *English and Scottish Ballads*, 14, 15, 238 (n. 20), 239 (n. 23); *The English and Scottish Popular Ballads*, 14, 15, 18, 238–39 (n. 21); as folk song collector, 12–14,

164–65, 238 (n. 16); and idea of "pure" folk music, 3, 12–13, 138; as literary folklorist, 12, 13, 164–65; John Lomax and, 32–33, 138; methods and standards of, 12–15; Sharp and, 23. *See also* Child canon

Child canon, 20, 191, 239 (nn. 26, 36); acceptance and documentation of, 15, 16, 17–18, 21, 36, 239 (n. 36); criteria for and development of, 12–15; expansion of and challenges to, 32–34, 36, 38, 39, 41–42, 52–55, 58, 141

Clancy Brothers, 217

Clarksdale, Miss., 76, 78, 79, 235

Classical (fine-art, high-art) music: Dylan and, 216; and early agitprop music, 68–70; folk sources as inspiration for composers of, 22; and New Deal music programs, 136, 144; performed at White House, 134, 161; Pete Seeger and, 196, 203; vs. vernacular music, 4, 13

Clear Rock, 149

Clinton, Bill, 181, 234

Coahoma County, Miss., 76

Cobra Records, 109

Cohen, Philip H., 145–47, 155, 156, 159

Cole, Nat "King," 79, 84

Collection of Old Ballads, A, 10

Collective memory: and appeal of blues, 108, 113. *See also* Public memory

Collier, Jimmy, 201

Columbia Records, 34, 35, 36, 74, 80, 82, 234, 243 (n. 93), 253 (n. 30); World Library of Primitive and Folk Music of, 193

Columbia University, 64, 136, 174

Commercialism: and country music, 222–23; Dylan and, 183, 215; and memory, 131, 233; and roots music, 4, 7, 63, 233, 236; "pure" folk music as untainted by, 3, 24, 73, 115, 119, 144; Pete Seeger and, 198, 203, 215. *See also* Commercial music

Commercial music: folk music seen as superior to, 144; producers of as middlemen/folk promoters, 5, 7, 34–39

(*see also* Chess, Leonard; Dixon, Willie; Melrose, Lester); roots music as source of, 4. *See also* Commercialism

Communists/Communist Party (U.S.), 48, 68–70, 72, 159–60, 162–63, 202, 266 (n. 90)

Composer's Collective, 69–70, 249 (n. 60)

Congress, U.S., 104, 160. *See also* House of Representatives, U.S.; Senate, U.S.

Coolidge, Calvin, 39

Copland, Aaron, 69, 163

Copyrighting of songs, 37–38, 80, 243 (n. 99)

Corwin, Norman, 156, 158, 263 (n. 49)

Cotton, James, 119

Country music: content and style of, 222–24; Dylan and, 208, 217, 218, 222–24, 229, 230; origins of, 222–23; as pop music, 193, 223; and rock and roll, 112; as roots music, 223; Pete Seeger and, 223

Courlander, Harold, 193, 257 (n. 94); *Negro Folk Music U.S.A.*, 257 (n. 94)

Cousin Emmy, 184

Cowboy songs: and Army Music Program, 152–53; and British folk tradition, 33; character of, 33–34; Lead Belly and, 71, 72, 90; John Lomax as collector of, 32–34, 38, 178, 242 (nn. 77, 78, 80); performed at White House, 134; Pete Seeger and, 191, 223; and singing cowboys, 34, 71, 189, 269 (n. 10)

Cowell, Henry, 163

Crawford, Ernest "Big," 89, 95, 253 (n. 24), 254 (n. 38)

Cream, 122

Daily Worker, 69, 70

Daily Worker Chorus, 68

Davis, Jimmie: "You Are My Sunshine," 193

Davis, Miles, 117

Davis, Roquel "Billy," 112

Davis Sisters: "By and By," 225

Decca Records, 80, 161

Desanto, Sugar Pie, 121

Detroit, Mich., 91, 255 (n. 59)

Diddley, Bo, 111, 112, 123, 257 (n. 59); "Bo Diddley," 110, 256 (n. 83); "I'm a Man," 110, 111; "I Need You Baby (Mona)," 122; "Pretty Thing," 111; "You Can't Judge the Book by Its Cover," 111

Dies, Martin, 159–60

Diffusionism, 137–38

Di Franco, Ani, 234

Dixon, Willie, 233, 236, 256 (n. 76), 261 (n. 142); and AFBF, 120–21, 127, 259 (n. 115); appearance and personality of, 122–23; "Back Door Man," 109; and Berry and Diddley, 111; and Chess, 93, 95, 96, 97, 103, 108–9, 127; and Cobra Records, 109; and cult of authenticity, 126–28, 132; family and background of, 96; and folk-blues revival, 113, 116–17, 119, 122–23, 126–28, 258 (n. 102); "I Can't Quit You Baby," 109; "I Got My Brand on You," 124; "I Just Want to Make Love to You," 103, 104, 107, 108, 122; "I'm Ready," 103–4, 107, 108; "I'm Your Hoochie Coochie Man," 97–109 passim, 121, 124; "I Want to Be Loved," 122; "Little Red Rooster," 109, 122; and Melrose, 81, 96–97; as middleman/folk promoter, 7, 96, 97, 99, 113, 120, 126–28, 131; as performer, 96–97, 111, 113, 116–17, 258 (nn. 102, 103); "Pretty Thing," 111; as record producer, 97, 108, 111, 127; and rock and roll, 110–11, 112; as songwriter, 97, 99–100, 101–8, 109–10, 111; "Spoonful," 109; "Tiger in Your Tank," 124; and Waters, 96, 97, 99, 103, 104–6, 108–9, 110, 120, 131, 132; "You Can't Judge the Book by Its Cover," 111; "You Need Love," 109; "You Shook Me," 109

Dobie, J. Frank, 62–63, 165

Domino, Fats, 84, 112

Donegan, Lonnie, 74, 118; "Rock Island Line," 74, 118

Dorson, Richard M., 265 (nn. 76, 79); and Botkin, 168–73, 180, 266 (n. 89); and folklore as an academic discipline, 7, 166–73, 175, 266 (nn. 87, 88); influence of, 172–73, 175, 176, 266 (n. 88); methods and standards of, 166–73, 179–80, 265 (n. 83), 267 (n. 106); "A Theory for American Folklore," 167–68

Dupree, Jack, 217

Dylan, Bob (Robert Zimmerman); and African American religious music, 218–19, 224, 225–27, 230, 275 (n. 196); *Another Side of Bob Dylan*, 231; apolitical nature of post-1965 music of, 213–14; "Are You Ready?," 227; "Ballad of a Thin Man," 214; "Ballad of Donald White," 218, 274 (n. 86); "The Ballad of Frankie Lee and Judas Priest," 219; "The Ballad of Hollis Brown," 209; and ballads, 218–19, 227, 229–30; *Basement Tapes*, 231; becomes born-again Christian, 225; *Biograph*, 216, 274 (n. 78); *Blonde on Blonde*, 127 (n. 71); "Blowin' in the Wind," 184, 209, 213, 234, 272 (n. 65); and blues, 207, 217, 218, 219–22, 227, 228, 229, 230; *Bob Dylan*, 208, 230; "Bob Dylan's Dream," 208–9; Bono and, 232; breaks with Seeger and folk revival, 184–86, 211–15, 218, 220, 273 (n. 74), 274 (n. 76); *Bringing It All Back Home*, 212, 214, 216, 273 (n. 71); "Chimes of Freedom," 231; commitment of to American roots music, 215–18, 230, 232; and connection of folk music to social activism, 205, 208, 209, 211–12, 213, 215; and country music, 217, 218, 222, 223–24, 229, 230; "Country Pie," 223–24; *Desire*, 225; "Desolation Row," 219; electric music of, 184, 212–13, 273 (nn. 71, 73, 74); and Elvis, 211, 217; "Emotionally Yours," 231; *Empire Burlesque*, 231, 275 (n. 196); family and background of, 205, 206; "Father of the Night," 225, 275 (n. 196); as folk stylist, 184–86, 215–18, 227, 232; "For-

Lennon, John, 118
Lenya, Lotte, 216
Levenethal, Harold, 216
Lewis, Jerry Lee, 84
Lewis, William, 156
Library of Congress, 114, 159; as folk song repository, 1, 56, 65–66; joint field study with Fisk University, 76–77, 79; Alan Lomax and, 137; Music Division of, 40, 151; Waters recordings for, 76–77, 82, 84, 85, 86, 88, 251–52 (n. 7), 253 (n. 28). *See also* American Folklife Center; Archive of American Folk-Song; Archive of Folk Culture; Archive of Folk Song; Radio Research Project
Life, 65, 206–7, 231
Lincoln, Abraham, 157
Lion King, The, 234
Lippman, Horst, 120, 126, 131
Little Richard, 4, 74, 112, 211; "Tutti Frutti," 111
Living Blues, 126, 233
Lloyd, A. L., 118
Log Cabin Settlement, 16
Lomax, Alan: and African American folk music, 50–51, 52–54, 76, 113, 114, 263 (n. 39); *American Ballads and Folk Songs* (with John Lomax), 54, 139–40, 191, 193, 270 (n. 25); and American folk music revival, 48, 205; and American vs. British (Child canon) folk song tradition, 52–55, 141, 191; and cantometrics, 174–76, 193, 266–67 (n. 94); and connection of folklore to social activism, 150, 154, 161–63, 205, 262 (n. 21); and connection of folklore to war effort, 151, 152–53, 154, 155, 158, 159, 263 (nn. 39, 44); and cult of authenticity, 7, 49, 55, 57–63, 64, 65, 72, 73, 131, 139–40; and Decca Records, 161; in England, 74, 113, 118, 163, 174; and federal government as folk promoter, 7, 133, 179, 181, 265 (n. 81) (*see also* Archive of American Folk-Song: Alan Lomax and); and Festival of American Folklife, 177, 178; field recording by,

1–2, 49–51, 55–57, 76–77, 136, 145, 193, 245 (n. 8), 246–47 (n. 25); as folk song collector, 49–51, 55–57, 76–77, 136, 190; *The Folk Songs of North America*, 191, 231; *Folk Song: U.S.A.* (with John Lomax), 191, 193, 270 (n. 25); as folk stylist, 189; "Freedom Songs of the United Nations" (with Jakobson), 158, 264 (n. 55); and functionalism, 139–41, 142, 149, 175, 262 (n. 21); "Global Jukebox" of, 176; and Guthrie, 162–63, 189, 190, 269 (n. 13); and idea of folklorist as scholar, 175–76; and idea of "pure" folk music, 58–59, 63, 65, 71, 72, 73, 139–40; "I've Got a Ballot," 162, 163; *Land Where the Blues Began*, 233; and Lead Belly, 51–68 passim, 72, 73, 74, 76, 115, 131, 190, 236, 247 (n. 36), 248 (nn. 37, 47), 250 (n. 69); leftist sympathies of, 48, 72, 113, 115, 161–62, 163; and John Lomax, 1, 47–72 passim, 139, 145, 151, 152, 178; "The Martins and the Coys," 158; methods and standards of, 50–51, 55, 115; as middleman/folk promoter, 7, 47–49, 55, 57–60, 62–63, 64, 65–66, 131, 133, 145, 152–53, 190; *Negro Folk Songs as Sung by Leadbelly* (with John Lomax), 59–60, 62; 1980s and 1990s accolades for, 233; *Our Singing Country* (with John Lomax), 52, 139, 140–41, 188, 191; and OWI, 158, 264 (n. 55); and People's Songs, 161–63; and pop music, 193–94; and proposed American Folklife Foundation, 179; and Radio Research Project, 145–47, 148, 149, 150, 154, 155, 158, 263 (n. 44); and Charles Seeger, 188; and Pete Seeger, 183, 188, 189, 190, 191–94, 205, 207; at Taos Pueblo, 48; and Waters, 76–89 passim, 92, 99, 100, 118, 233, 251–52 (n. 7)
Lomax, Elizabeth, 158
Lomax, John, 48; and African American folk music, 50–51, 52–54, 56, 113, 114; *American Ballads and Folk Songs* (with

Alan Lomax), 54, 139–40, 191, 193, 270 (n. 25); and American vs. British (Child canon) folk song tradition, 32–34, 52–55, 141; "The Ballad Hunter," 148–49; and connection of folklore to war effort, 151, 152; and cowboy songs, 32–34, 38, 242 (nn. 77, 78); *Cowboy Songs and Other Frontier Ballads*, 32, 33, 47, 178, 242 (n. 78); and cult of authenticity, 7, 49, 55, 57–63, 64, 65, 72, 73, 131, 139–40; Dorson and, 168; and federal government as folk promoter, 133 (*see also* Archive of American Folk-Song: John Lomax and); and Festival of American Folklife, 178; field recording by, 1–2, 38–39, 49–51, 55–57, 136, 242 (n. 80), 245 (n. 8), 246–47 (n. 25), 247 (n. 27); as folk song collector, 32–33, 47, 49–51, 55–57, 136, 138, 148–49, 242 (nn. 78, 80); *Folk Song: U.S.A.* (with Alan Lomax), 191, 193, 270 (n. 25); hiatus in collecting activities of, 34, 47; and idea of "pure" folk music, 33–34, 58–59, 63, 65, 71, 72, 73, 139–40, 148–49; and Lead Belly, 51–68 passim, 72, 73, 76, 115, 131, 236, 247 (nn. 27, 36), 248 (nn. 37, 47), 250 (n. 69); and Alan Lomax, 1, 47–72 passim, 139, 145, 151, 152, 178; methods and standards of, 33, 50–51, 55, 115; as middleman/folk promoter, 7, 33, 47–49, 55, 57–60, 62–63, 64, 65–66, 131, 133; "The Minstrelsy of the Mexican Border," 242 (n. 77); *Negro Folk Songs as Sung by Leadbelly* (with Alan Lomax), 59–60, 62; *Our Singing Country* (with Alan Lomax), 52, 139, 140–41, 188, 191; and pop music, 193–94; Charles Seeger and, 188; Pete Seeger and, 191–94; as student of Wendell and Kittredge at Harvard, 32, 33, 39, 165; Thompson and, 165

Lomax, John, Jr., 47–48, 245 (n. 5), 270 (n. 27)

Lönnrot, Elias, 12; *Kalevala*, 12

Los Angeles, Calif., 48–49, 235

Lowell, James Russell, 14

Luce, Henry, 162

Lummis, Charles F., 38

Lunsford, Bascom Lamar, 134, 188

McCarthyism. *See* Red Scare

McCartney, Paul, 123

MacColl, Ewan, 118

McCormick, Mack, 114, 116

McGhee, Brownie, 117

McGill, Josephine, 6, 18, 20, 35; *Folk Songs of the Kentucky Mountains*, 18, 19, 239 (n. 36), 240 (nn. 38, 39)

MacLeish, Archibald, 152, 153, 155, 156, 159, 263 (n. 42)

McTell, Blind Willie, 217

Makem, Tommy, 217

Malinowski, Bronislaw, 137–38, 261 (n. 7), 262 (n. 21)

Mall (Washington, D.C.), 176–78, 181

March on Washington (1963), 210

Martha and the Vandellas, 216

Matthiessen, F. O., 167

Mead, Margaret, 6, 64

Mellencamp, John, 127, 260 (n. 131)

Melrose, Lester, 79–81, 86, 87, 97, 113, 118, 127, 131

Memphis Minnie, 79

Memphis Slim (Peter Chatman), 113, 116–17, 119, 120, 258 (nn. 102. 103)

Meredith, James, 209

Messinger, Bob, 128–29, 131

Miller, Norman, 176

Miller, Perry, 167

Ministry: "Lay Lady Lay," 231

Minstrelsy, 27, 28–29, 189, 222, 270 (n. 25)

Miracle, Homer, 176

Mississippi: blues style in, 79, 82–85, 87–89, 108, 252 (n. 21); Dixon from, 97; migrants from in Chicago, 78, 88, 106; song collecting in, 38, 76–77, 136; Waters's early life and music in, 76–78, 79

Modern Jazz Quartet, 120

Monroe, Bill, 216

Montgomery, Little Brother, 127

Morganfield, McKinley. *See* Waters, Muddy

Morris, James, 177, 267 (n. 102)

Morton, Jelly Roll, 217

Mutual Broadcasting System, 152

Nashville, Tenn., 28, 223

National Endowment for the Arts, 180, 181, 182, 268 (n. 112); Folk Arts Program of, 180, 181–82

National Endowment for the Humanities, 268 (n. 112)

NBC, 151, 157

N'Dour, Youssou: "Chimes of Freedom," 231

Nelson, Willie, 74

New Deal, 162, 265 (n. 74); agencies and programs of, 134–61 passim; opponents of, 159–61

New Deal folklorists: and folk song as tool for social betterment, 133–51, 262 (n. 21); and war effort, 151–61; work of in postwar period, 161–64, 265 (n. 81)

New Orleans, La., 114

Newport Folk Festival, 116, 177, 183–84, 212–13, 215, 232

Newport Jazz Festival, 116, 124

Newsweek, 206, 213, 217, 231–32

New York, N.Y., 18, 28, 35, 38, 110, 157, 160, 244 (n. 121), 250 (n. 67); Dylan in, 205–6, 207–8, 211; FWP Living Lore Unit in, 143; folk performers and the Left in, 69, 70, 190; Guthrie in, 190, 269 (n. 13); Lead Belly in, 58, 59–60, 66, 70, 71, 74, 188, 247 (n. 36); Pete Seeger in, 188–89, 190, 202

New York Daily News, 210

New Yorker, 62

New York Herald-Tribune, 62

New York Post, 59

New York Times, 40, 71, 206, 248 (n. 37)

New York Times Magazine, 41, 42

New York University, 165, 265 (n. 72)

Niles, John Jacob, 189

Nirvana, 74, 251 (n. 83)

Ochs, Phil, 205

Odum, Howard, 31, 38, 242 (n. 75); "Folk Songs of the Southern Negroes," 31

Office of Emergency Management, 152

Office of Facts and Figures, 155–56, 263 (n. 47)

Office of War Information (OWI), 158, 159, 263 (n. 47), 264 (n. 55)

Ogan, Sarah, 70

O'Jays: "Emotionally Yours," 231

Okeh Records, 34, 35, 80

Oliver, Paul, 109, 126, 275 (n. 103)

Organization of American States, 163, 264 (n. 69)

Original Dixieland Jazz Band: "Livery Stable Blues," 114

Oster, Harry, 114

Pan-American Union (PAU), 163, 164, 193; Inter-American Music Council of, 163, 264 (n. 69)

Pankake, John, 207, 210

Paramount Records, 34, 35

Paris Jazz Festival, 117

Parker, Charlie, 117

Paul Butterfield Blues Band, 123, 184

Paxton, Tom, 205

Payne, Odie, 93

Pearl Harbor attack, 155, 156, 160

Peckinpah, Sam: *Pat Garrett and Billy the Kid*, 224

Peer, Ralph, 34–46 passim, 57, 244 (n. 100)

People's Songs, 162–63, 264 (n. 65), 266 (n. 90)

Percy, Thomas, 10–11, 12, 14, 239 (n. 23); *Reliques of English Poetry*, 10–11

Peter, Paul, and Mary, 183

Peterson, Clarence, 126

Pettit, Katherine, 20

Pierre Degeyter music club, 69

Pine Mountain Settlement, 16, 18

Pirner, Dave, 235–36

Pollock, Charles, 145

Pop music: and Army Music Program, 152–53; black, 80, 87; and blues, 79,

80, 99; 100, 101–5, 113, 121, 126, 193;
and commercialism, 38, 193; content
and style of, 99; country music as, 193,
223; defined, 4; Dixon and, 96, 99, 100,
101–5, 116, 121; Dylan and, 184, 215,
217; folklorists' distaste for, 38, 72, 73,
193–94; vs. folk music, 145, 184, 188,
195–96, 211, 273 (n. 71); folk music as,
207, 236; hillbilly music as, 38, 142,
193; Lead Belly and, 51, 71, 72, 90;
Lomaxes and, 193–94; and rock and
roll, 110; roots music as source of, 4,
235–36; Pete Seeger and, 188, 190–91,
193–96, 211, 217, 223; Waters and, 77,
99, 101–5. See also Tin Pan Alley
Popular Front, 217, 218; promotion of
folk music by, 70, 183, 205, 250 (n. 66);
and social/political purpose of folk
music, 72, 213, 215
Populism: of New Deal folklorists, 147–
48, 151, 153, 156–57, 158; outsider,
64–65, 71; and Sharp's view of national
culture, 22–23
Pound, Louise, 20
Presley, Elvis, 211, 217, 254 (n. 46)
Prestige Records, 117
Pride, Charley, 217
Primitivism, 3, 63–65
Progressive Party, 162, 264 (n. 65)
Promise, Martha, 62, 247 (n. 36)
Public memory: and commercialism, 131,
233; continual rather than incremental
crafting of, 6–7; creative power of,
236; defined, 5; Lead Belly's appeal in,
75, 131; Lomaxes' cult of authenticity
as tool for shaping, 131; role of middlemen in shaping of, 8, 131; Waters's
movement into, 130–32

Race: black musicians and white ideas
about, 131; Lomaxes and, 48–49; role
of in early efforts to define America's
folk song heritage, 25–26, 31–32, 42–
43
Race records, 115; as black pop music,
80–81, 253 (n. 33); Melrose and, 80–

81; origins and early marketing of, 34–
35, 36, 38, 41; R & B as successor to,
253 (n. 33)
Radcliffe-Brown, A. R., 137, 261 (nn. 7,
11)
Radio Research Project (Library of Con-
gress), 145–51, 152, 154–58, 159, 161,
263 (n. 49)
Raitt, Bonnie, 234, 260 (n. 131)
Ramsey, Frederic, Jr., 74, 114, 257 (n. 94)
Rau, Fritz, 120
RCA Victor, 46, 80
Reagan, Ronald, 233, 268 (n. 110)
Reagon, Bernice Johnson, 201
Red Hot Chili Peppers, 235; "Give It
Away," 235
Red Scare, 113, 164. See also Commu-
nists/Communist Party
Reed, Jimmy, 112, 121, 127, 207; "Honest
I Do," 122
Rees, Thomas M., 178
Resettlement Administration (RA): docu-
mentary photography of, 65; and folk
song preservation and promotion, 135,
136, 142, 143, 144–45, 161; Charles
Seeger's work with, 136, 137, 142, 143,
144–45, 188; Special Skills Division of,
144, 145
Rhythm and blues (R & B): Chess and,
87; Dixon and, 103, 104; as name for
black pop music, 87, 253 (n. 33); and
rock and roll, 110, 112; Waters and,
97–99, 103, 104, 110, 255 (n. 59)
Richards, Keith, 122
Riddle, Almeda, 176
Rinzler, Ralph, 177, 179, 204, 267 (n. 102)
Ripley, S. Dillon, 176–77, 178
Ritchie, Jean, 118, 208
Robertson, Sidney, 142
Robeson, Paul, 202
Robinson, Earl, 72, 189
Rock and roll: beginning of, 110; and
blues, 4, 111, 113, 116, 125–26; Chess
and, 110–11, 124, 125–26; content and
style of, 111; and country music, 112;
Dylan and, 184, 211–12, 218, 232; vs.